A Legacy of Innovation

Commemorating the Centennial of the
National Governors Association

Governors at the White House, May 13–15, 1908

A Legacy of Innovation

Governors and Public Policy

EDITED BY ETHAN G. SRIBNICK

PENN

University of Pennsylvania Press

Philadelphia

Published by
University of Pennsylvania Press
Philadelphia, Pennsylvania 19104-4112

The views expressed here are those of the authors and do not necessarily represent those of the National Governors Association or the Woodrow Wilson Presidential Library.

Printed in the United States of America on acid-free paper
10 9 8 7 6 5 4 3 2 1

Library of Congress Cataloging-in-Publication Data

A legacy of innovation : governors and public policy / edited by Ethan G. Sribnick.
    p.   cm.
  Includes bibliographical references and index.
  ISBN 978-0-8122-4095-5 (hardcover : alk. paper)
    1. Governors—United States—History—20th century.   2. United States—Politics and government—20th century.   I. Sribnick, Ethan G.
JK2447.L44   2008
320.60973—dc22

2008000036

Frontispiece: Governors at the White House, May 13–15, 1908. Invited by President (and former governor) Theodore Roosevelt to discuss conservation issues, governors assembled for this group photograph outside the White House. Roosevelt is seated near the middle of the first row. The president and governors are joined by cabinet members, Supreme Court justices, and other dignitaries, including Andrew Carnegie and William Jennings Bryan (seated fourth and fifth from left in first row). Reprinted with permission of the National Governors Association.

Contents

Illustrations follow page 148

Foreword

We live, to a great extent, in a country that governors helped create. It is interesting to note that seventeen state governors in our nation's history have become president—seven of them over the course of the twentieth century. Perhaps more significantly, four out of the past five presidents were former governors, a testament to the importance citizens ascribe to the states' highest office.

In May 1908, President Theodore Roosevelt convened the nation's governors at the White House to discuss conserving the country's resources. Both the president and vice president attended, as did cabinet members, Supreme Court justices, and thirty-nine state and territorial governors. They were joined by a cadre of guests known for their innovative thinking and influential actions, including populist William Jennings Bryan and industrialist Andrew Carnegie.

The meeting achieved its goal, yielding a policy declaration concerning conservation, but it also was notable for another idea—the creation of a national organization for governors. As Louisiana Governor Newton Blanchard noted, "Personally, I have long thought that, if the governors of the states could themselves from time to time get together, exchanging ideas and views touching the governmental and other affairs of their states, much good would come out of it." The idea found favor among his colleagues, and in 1910 New Jersey Governor-elect Woodrow Wilson proposed its formation. The organization was formally constituted in 1912.

A century after the 1908 meeting, governors representing all of the states, territories, and commonwealths convene today as the National Governors Association. The bipartisan association assists governors on domestic policy and state management issues and provides a forum for governors to speak with one voice to the President and Congress.

The 2008 meeting in Philadelphia marks the centennial for the organization, and this book and a companion volume have been published as part of that commemoration. *A Legacy of Innovation* highlights the role of governors in developing new policy responses to emerging challenges. From welfare to Medicaid to race relations, governors played a major role in shaping the economic and social climate of today. Readers will finish this book with a new and deeper understanding of American political development and policymaking in the gubernatorial office.

Early in the planning of this book, the National Governors Association partnered with the Woodrow Wilson Presidential Library because of both the library's unique scholarly approach to the life and contributions of one of our most admired governors and Wilson's role in the development of the National Governors Association. We are fortunate that some of the finest scholars in the nation wrote individual chapters, and we owe them a debt of gratitude for their contributions.

Raymond C. Scheppach   Eric J. Vettel
Executive Director   Executive Director
National Governors Association Woodrow Wilson Presidential Library

Introduction
Directing Democracy

Brian Balogh

If the states are the "laboratories of democracy," to quote Supreme Court Justice Louis Brandeis, governors have been the lab directors. And like scientific lab directors over the course of the twentieth century, governors developed a new set of skills to deal with the constantly changing environment in which they worked. Governors have become "skilled negotiators," as Larry Sabato put it, "and crucial coordinators." Governors have ranged well beyond their political parties, electoral base, and executive span of control. They have been publicists, lobbyists, enthusiasts for business development, and even nationalists, arguing for federally funded services delivered by units of government that citizens could trust.[1]

In an adaptation of the laboratory metaphor, Jon C. Teaford has suggested that states have been "factories of government" as well as laboratories of democracy. This would make governors their CEOs. Like contemporary CEOs, who as Lee Iacocca recounts, initially only went to Washington "to try to get the government off our backs" but soon returned asking for a subsidy because "it's the only game in town," governors adapted to the opportunities presented by an enlarged federal government. Iacocca and many other CEOs also grappled with a rapidly changing economic environment where they faced unprecedented global competition. Governors also reacted to these economic changes, scouring the country, and eventually the world, to attract good jobs for their states.[2]

Factories and laboratories are rarely democratic. Yet bridging the gap between lab-like innovation, factory-like production, and democratic participation has been the governors' most distinctive contribution to public policy. Though many initially resisted, governors ultimately capitalized upon the dramatic changes that radically altered the way citizens access state government (and lowered barriers to access). Citizens today are far more likely to exercise influence through the interest groups they belong to than through loyal allegiance to a political party (as was the case in the late nineteenth century). The participation of women, especially after the Nineteenth Amendment, and African Americans, after World War II, altered the constituencies that governors served.

These were changes that reshaped the entire political system, not just the states. Responding to interest group demands required expertise and considerable administrative capacity—which the executive branch of government excels at. Catering to a far broader and more diverse electorate, in turn, required a different set of skills—a leader who embodied the will of the people. It was governors, more than any other set of elected officials, who personally reconciled the tension between access and action.[3]

The chapters that follow chart how governors have adapted to a changing political, social, and technological landscape to shape public policy over the past one hundred years. By way of introduction, it is useful to summarize some of the fundamental challenges governors have addressed. Governors have adapted both the nature of their offices and the role of the states in a federal system to mitigate four tensions in the twentieth century American political system: (1) democratization versus expert control; (2) the political tug of war between powerful interest groups and political parties; (3) the enduring allure of regional ties threatened by progressive racial attitudes, a nationalizing (and eventually globalizing) economy, and Cold War–induced nationalism; and (4) the rising demand for services offset by long-standing fears of distant, centralized government.

Some of these same tendencies—especially the rise of interest groups, the turn to expert control, the powerful counter-force of social movements, the enduring Cold War, and the relentless demand for services— produced an administratively and fiscally muscular federal government. This national "proministrative state," which merged professional agendas with enhanced administrative capacity, was a powerful force that threatened to dwarf state government. Governors, however, shaped innovative solutions to this challenge, honing their skills as lobbyists on behalf of their states, and crafting creative outlets for the delivery of federally funded services.[4]

Thus governors have molded a contemporary form of federalism around a central government that is far more visible than the one their nineteenth-century predecessors engaged during the era of "dual federalism." Recent governors have used the national government to their advantage, often lobbying for increased federal spending. The states, governors have insisted, are the ideal vehicles for delivering those federally funded services. Extensive enough to claim comprehensive coverage and economies of scale for policies ranging from transportation to social services, yet sufficiently accountable to assuage fears of big government, if states did not exist today, a shrewd politician would have to invent them. She might even consider running for governor.[5]

Laboratory or Democracy?

At the dawn of the twentieth century, Americans displayed two, often contradictory, political impulses. They clamored for a direct say in the political decisions that influenced their lives. Referenda on matters of public policy and direct primaries to choose candidates for office replaced backroom partisan negotiations. Direct elections of senators replaced state legislative horse trading. Direct democracy trumped representative democracy in many instances, as intermediary institutions were castigated for distorting the will of the people.[6]

Simultaneously, and often at the behest of the very same democratizers, Americans deferred to "experts" and administrators. Whether their supposed objectivity was derived from professionalized knowledge, as was the case with public health officials, or their stance outside partisan politics, as with the administrators who presided over newly consolidated school systems, experts were granted greater discretion in the belief that they would solve problems more efficiently than their lay predecessors.

That the vast majority of this activity took place at the state and local level surprised few observers. Americans craved the benefits that experts promised, but wanted to keep these public servants close to home—where they seemed more accountable. As Teaford has noted, "twentieth-century state government balanced a rising devotion to expertise and managerial efficiency and persistent fears of concentrated national authority, fears that were endemic to American thought. These twin forces in large part determined the direction and growth of state rule."[7]

Demands that the people be heard and calls for more expertise often swept through the polity sequentially. During the first decade of the twentieth century, the discovery by millions that big business corrupted the political process animated reformers in cities and states across the nation. Usually sparked by a scandal, such as the 1905 New York investigation of the life insurance industry, and fanned by a muckraking press, public outrage burst through politics as usual. This passion quickly translated into waves of legislation, ranging from restrictions on lobbyists to regulating corporate campaign contributions. Fears about corporate corruption catapulted primaries to the top of reformers' agendas. Two powerful Progressive Era governors, Robert M. La Follette and Charles Evans Hughes, for instance, advocated direct primaries. Hughes, who had spearheaded the investigation into corrupt insurance practices, was determined to root out the special interests, "stealthily and persistently endeavoring to pervert the government to the service of their own ends. All that is worst in our public life," Hughes insisted, "finds its readiest means of access to power through the control of the nominating machinery of parties."[8]

Yet intense passions, often aroused on the local level, were mediated and mollified through regulatory mechanisms enacted at the state level. There, reliance on "impartial experts" predominated. Typically, reformers set up a commission. Getting party bosses and politicians out of the process and injecting "objective" specialists into the process was a solution that reformers and a good number of the implicated industries ultimately supported. Between 1905 and 1907 states created fifteen new railroad commissions. In addition, at least fifteen existing commissions were strengthened. Commissions soon regulated a wide range of utilities, from electricity to telephones. They extended their reach to insurance and banking.[9]

During this period in American history governors emerged as the single individual in their states who both embodied the democratic will and directed a burgeoning administrative apparatus. The warring democratic and technocratic impulses literally occupied the same ground in governors' mansions across the land. Gubernatorial leadership, from Governor Woodrow Wilson's perspective, was the predictable response to the overwhelming democratic demands that he and his colleagues were subjected to in the early twentieth century. "The whole country," Wilson proclaimed, "is clamoring for leadership, and a new role, which to many persons seems little less than unconstitutional, is thrust upon our executives." Although these were tumultuous times, Progressive era governors were not dragged kicking and screaming to this task. They were both eager to publicize the people's concerns and ultimately instrumental in guiding raw sentiment toward public policy solutions.[10]

The essays in this volume contain dozens of examples of governors who served as conduits of the democratic will. Brooke Masters cites an excellent instance in her chapter on balancing economic development with consumer protection. Fiery redhead Walter Stubbs was elected governor of Kansas in 1908. The first Kansas governor nominated by primary election, Stubbs had amassed a fortune in the railroad business. Stubbs was an advocate of "blue sky laws" that would protect small investors from stock fraud by licensing and regulating securities dealers. Stubbs barnstormed the state, firing up the populace and lining up votes for his reform agenda. From the perspective of the Speaker of the House of Representatives Joe Cannon, Stubbs was a rabble-rouser. As Stubbs supporters saw it, he was merely articulating demands bubbling up from citizens freed from the political machine's oppressive practices.[11]

Sarah Phillips notes that governors publicized the need for conservation even though this field was largely preempted by the federal government during the Progressive era. Michigan Governor Fred Warner addressed conservation in his State of the State message in 1909. Fiscal reform also addressed democratic demands. In Wisconsin, Governor Robert La Follette took his fight for a progressive income tax directly to the people.[12]

While the crusading style was muted during the 1920s, several highly visible governors soon bucked that trend. As Phillips reports, Pennsylvania Governor Gifford Pinchot championed farmers denied the benefit of electrification. New York's dynamic Governor Franklin D. Roosevelt pressed for state-developed hydroelectric plants. Though neither proposal gained legislative approval, Roosevelt would return to both as part of his New Deal program. As governor, Roosevelt also embraced the crusade for progressive taxation. Roosevelt proposed a steep increase in New York's income tax, endorsing the principle of ability to pay, Ajay Mehrotra and David Shreve report. After the stock market crash and in the face of a deepening depression, the legislature approved Roosevelt's tax package. Even Governor Frank Merriam, who some viewed as an unreconstructed reactionary, was driven by the times to campaign for California's first personal income tax. He got what he campaigned for and signed the bill into law in 1935.[13]

The tradition of governors articulating agendas based upon powerful democratic impulses continued after World War II and persists today. They did not always advocate progressive causes. Jason Sokol chronicles the history of civil rights in Virginia and Massachusetts—narratives with a surprising number of parallels. Yet simply listing the names of several Southern governors—Barnett, Faubus, Maddox, and Wallace—reminds us that governors sometimes traded upon regional customs and mass publicity with tragic results. In California, Proposition 13, a voter-initiated referendum passed in 1978, slashed property taxes by 57 percent. Approved by a two-to-one margin, this populist measure demonstrated just what could happen if governors failed accurately to address broad social impulses. Certainly Governor Jerry Brown had adequate warning. His office had received more than 200,000 letters from angry taxpayers in the previous year. "I'm tired of paying for politicians' dinners and lunches when my family can't afford to go out to dinner even once a month," one irate constituent wrote Brown in 1978.[14]

For the most part, however, governors continued to read populist signals correctly. Ron Haskins points out that the "Gingrich Revolution" of 1994 was not the only revolution that year. Republicans captured ten new governorships and played an important role in the reforms that replaced Aid to Families with Dependent Children with Temporary Assistance for Needy Families (TANF).[15] A consensus position developed by the nation's governors was crucial to breaking the logjam on welfare reform in Washington in the winter of 1996.[16] As Haskins's essay illustrates, few issues in the twentieth century better represented the ability of governors to tap populist sentiment, craft complicated policy solutions, lobby the federal government, and work cooperatively. Rarely did all of these skills come together. It was equally unusual for governors to work together so effectively. But when they did, their efforts could lead to national reform.

In education, however, governors, especially Southern governors, beat competing jurisdictions to the punch, Maris A. Vinovskis reports. Another list of Southern governors—Baliles, Clinton, Graham, Hunt, Riley, to name just a few—embarked upon a program of school reform designed to address broad concerns about economic competitiveness. By appealing to voters' concerns about jobs, these governors were able to redirect resources to education, which had been underfunded in their states for years. Many of the policies that governors put in place influenced subsequent national educational reform.[17]

Heightened responsiveness has come at a price. Populist furor and the policies it produced often have not stood the test of time. The states' recent intervention into the highly contested realm of universal health care coverage is a good example. Colleen Grogan points out that in Massachusetts, despite solid Democratic majorities in 1994 and 1995, the legislature failed to implement the state's path-breaking Health Security Act. Similarly, Oregon balked at actually applying employer-mandated health insurance in 1995, even though legislation required such coverage.[18]

Governors have weathered three dramatic shifts in the electorate across the twentieth century. The first, the expansion of suffrage to women, which in western states preceded the 1920s, was galvanized by the Nineteenth Amendment. While previously engaged in politics through voluntary organizations and partisan persuasion, the preferences of women now carried the weight of their votes. Even in southern states, where participation for men had been low and the women's vote fiercely resisted, after women obtained the vote they were invited to join campaign staffs and male politicians scrambled to procure invitations to address women's organizations. Women's participation shifted the substance of political debate toward social issues like prohibition enforcement and health.[19]

The civil rights revolution, which gained momentum after World War II, also reshaped statewide constituencies, first in northern states, and eventually, in the South. Although the millions of African Americans who migrated north during the world wars faced massive employment and housing discrimination, they were able to vote. By 1948, they had become a force within the northern wing of the Democratic Party. The civil rights movement realized one of its most impressive victories in the Voting Rights Act of 1965. The impact on African American voting in the South was stunning. Within a year of the act's passage, African American voter registration in the six deep South states covered by the original act increased from 30 to 46 percent. Alabama witnessed the most dramatic transformation. African American voter registration skyrocketed from 23 percent in 1964 to 61 percent by 1969.[20]

The landmark Supreme Court decisions *Baker v. Carr* (1962) and *Reynolds v. Sims* (1964) altered the balance of power among rural, suburban, and urban counties. Proclaiming the principle of "one man, one vote," *Reynolds v. Sims* took aim at the disproportionate political power that rural districts had enjoyed through malapportionment. Over the following decade legislative districts were redrawn to give far greater weight to urban areas and the rapidly growing suburbs. As a result, legislative constituencies began to look more like the statewide majorities to which governors often owed their office. Dealing with legislators who looked more like themselves and who shared an interest in the same issues made life easier for governors. More important, legislatures followed their gubernatorial counterparts in modernizing and professionalizing states' administration, reducing the strain between governors and legislatures over the mechanics of governance.[21]

After stirring these democratic fires, or at least adapting to the new electoral landscape, governors put on their lab coats. They were too close to the electorate—especially the demands expressed through powerful interest groups—to hide, even if they wanted to. Constituents preferred state to federal government precisely because they felt that they could hold state officials accountable. Governors were the most visible state officials and the elected officials with the most resources at their disposal. Because governors were uniquely positioned to represent all the citizens of their state, they often articulated and shaped popular demands in ways that led to state-administered or -regulated policies. If they did not personally care to dive into the details, their growing staffs were happy to do so. La Follette, for instance, had little patience with the administrative details of tax policy, but he sensed that public opinion supported a tax that disproportionately targeted wealthy individuals.[22]

To return to the prairie fires ignited by Stubbs, Kansas enacted the first "blue sky" law in the nation and began enforcing it in 1911. It regulated the sales of corporate stock within the state in order to protect citizens against fraud. It subjected securities salesmen to registration and oversight, driving many out of the state entirely. The legislation granted extensive discretion to bank commissioner Joseph N. Dolley, who could reject any application for a license if he found that the company did not promise "a fair return" on the stocks it sold, or if any provision of the proposal was "unfair, unjust, inequitable or oppressive to any class of contributors." In simpler terms, Dolley promised to do something about the "swindlers" and "hucksters" who were robbing the "widows" and "orphans" of Kansas. The Kansas approach soon spread to surrounding states.[23]

Back in Michigan, Governor Warner pushed through legislation that set up a conservation commission to oversee the state's public land and forest reserves, another practice that was imitated by many states. Governor La Follette had already moved on to the U.S. Senate by the time Wisconsin passed the nation's first effective state income tax in 1911. It too was emulated by several states within the next five years.[24]

Governors assiduously pursued administrative consolidation in the early twentieth century. Legislatures had responded to growth after the Civil War by establishing a blizzard of boards, commissions, and state agencies. Few of these were coordinated or controlled by a chief executive. As late as 1925, Georgia's governor griped that "We are board-ridden, commission-ridden and trustee-ridden in this state." Consolidation offered greater control over the administrative apparatus and promised to narrow the gap between populist promises and effective solutions. Gubernatorial appointment of agency heads made administration more accountable and strengthened the governors' claim to speak for all of the people. Charles Evans Hughes put the New York legislature on notice in his 1910 annual message: "It would be an improvement . . . in state administration if the executive responsibility were centered in the governor who should appoint a cabinet of administrative heads, accountable to him." Once consolidated, the kind of power that best achieved this objective was budgetary authority. States rationalized and centralized the budget process during the second decade of the twentieth century. Led by California and Wisconsin, this "scientific budgeting" initiative sought transparency, coordination, and greater discretion by trained, "objective" specialists. Here too, the trajectory was toward executive control.[25]

States increasingly turned to experts to handle new responsibilities. The federal government served as both a model and a threat in this regard. When Teddy Roosevelt and Gifford Pinchot first called the governors together in 1908 to consider collective action promoting conservation measures, Pinchot's reputation as the leading American forestry expert was on full display. This was precisely the kind of expertise that might allow governors to claim the administrative discretion required to wrestle with difficult problems like water use or deforestation. The governors left their first national meeting with another federally inspired mechanism in hand—uniform administrative structures that would be replicated across the states. As Sarah Phillips records, each state was to establish a commission on natural resources following the meeting, and many did. Western states protested vigorously, however. As Phillips reports, Wyoming Governor Bryant Brooks wanted conservation but did not care for the economic stagnation he feared it might bring. Where hydrologists and geologists failed to convince, federal aid often did. Most western governors eagerly embraced federal irrigation projects, in spite of the administrative requirements that accompanied them.[26]

A similar pattern dominated transportation. Robert Dilger argues that the Federal Road Act of 1916 began a century-long process that consolidated and professionalized highway administration in the states. Because federal aid was funneled through the states (which also matched funding), the federal government was able to impose upon states standards that had been developed by professional engineers. States, in turn, were encouraged to develop their own professional staffs housed in a consolidated administrative organization. Federal and state professionals worked in tandem to raise the bar for local and county officials. They used both their professional and their fiscal leverage to achieve results.[27]

Another policy area for which localities traditionally shouldered the burden followed this pattern—welfare. The Depression overwhelmed the capacity of local and state government to cope with the nation's needs. Although the 1935 Social Security Act injected the federal government into this field in dramatic fashion, with the exception of Title II (the contributory old-age insurance program that today, we generally call Social Security), this vast expansion was administered at the state and local level. The federal government, worried that charges of corruption would torpedo political support for welfare programs, pressured states to hire professional social workers and consolidate local administration.[28]

A new wave of reorganization and consolidation swept through state houses in the 1960s and 1970s. Twenty-one states embarked upon comprehensive reorganization between 1965 and 1979. The objectives remained the same. "The basic reason for reorganization has not changed over the years," the director of research for the Council of State Governments noted in 1972. It is "the improvement of administration through grouping agencies having related functions, and the need of pinpointing responsibility through giving the Governor authority and a manageable span of control." Perhaps the passion for functional grouping went too far when Idaho created the Department of Self Governing Agencies, which predictably, had no head. Unlike the Progressive era, however, the reforms were not driven by populist impulses.

Rather, they were the product of lengthened gubernatorial terms. This, in turn, enhanced opportunities for governors to effect reform. The number of states with two-year terms dropped from fifteen in 1964 to four by 1980. At the same time, voters returned incumbent governors to office at higher rates than in the past. The combined impact of these changes allowed governors to spend more time in the lab and less time with both ears to the ground.[29]

As federal influence grew, it increased the pressure for consolidating and professionalizing state administration. Maris Vinovskis chronicles the significance of the Elementary and Secondary Education Act, passed during the Great Society. Beyond the federal dollars that flowed through state coffers, Title V of the act doubled the size of state education agencies' professional staffs. Federal funding also enhanced state data collection capacity. Federal grant-in-aid spending for crime soared in the late 1960s, funded by the Omnibus Crime Control and Safe Streets Act. To collect the new data required by the federal government, every state set up a planning agency which was usually housed in the governor's office.[30]

Governors negotiated the pressures of democratization and professionalization in a variety of ways. Over the course of the twentieth century, the balance shifted from populist leader to technocratic fixer. The governor's mansion became the site where these two impulses frequently competed. Governors did not always come up with elegant solutions. But they were better positioned than most elected officials to reconcile the revolution in democratic participation and the demands for administrative efficiency.[31]

Interest Group or Partisan Politics?

The late nineteenth century represented a high point for politics organized around a seminal attachment between the voter and his political party. This political bond was literally handed down from father to son. Voting occurred strictly along party lines. Turnout ran high, reaching 84 percent of the eligible electorate in the North for the 1896 and 1900 presidential elections. Politics was a social activity; it was integrated into other aspects of the citizen's life. It penetrated social networks and work. Party affiliation often correlated highly with religion and ethnicity—two other identities that organized life in late nineteenth-century America.[32]

At the same time, the nation underwent a veritable revolution in the number of associations that Americans belonged to. By the early twentieth century, Americans began to express political preferences through these associations—labeled pressure or interest groups. Both voters and elected officials felt more comfortable when their party allegiance lined up with their preferred interest groups. However, things did not always match this neatly. Politicians used both parties and interest groups as vital sources of intelligence about their constituents in an era before public opinion polls. The interest group often proved to be a more reliable source, in part, because it could specify the kinds of voters who supported its policies, could deliver these votes on election day, and was eager to tailor public policies specifically to its constituency. This reduced the likelihood that a politician might satisfy one group of voters, only to discover that he had alienated a larger segment of his constituency. It delivered benefits to the specified group in ways that were not terribly visible to the electorate at large. Parties were rarely able to draw such fine distinctions. They were, however, able to reward supporters with jobs and contracts. They also distributed economic benefits broadly, such as favorable tariff treatment.[33]

As civil service and professional administration replaced partisan hiring, and as experts increasingly determined who would receive public benefits, the advantages of partisanship waned. So too did voter turnout. By the 1920s, turnout for presidential elections plummeted below 60 percent, where it remained for much of the twentieth century.[34] While nineteenth-century political parties thrived on mass mobilization of voters, interest groups often preferred a far less participatory policy environment where legislative and administrative details could be hammered out by specialists. Interest groups had a great stake in convincing elected officials that the group had supporters and that those supporters voted. But pressure groups had little interest in mass mobilization, which might well serve to negate the group's special interest.

Interest group politics did not replace partisan politics. But it did carve out a significant space for this way of expressing voter preferences in a two-party political system. Governors played a key role in this century-long evolution. Some of the Progressive Era reformers we have already observed rose to power on promises to cripple partisan political machines. Robert M. La Follette, for instance, attacked the Republican machine as he pilloried the public service corporations that fueled its electoral reach. Over the course of the twentieth century, governors made their peace with political parties, especially if they had higher political ambitions. But they also mastered the techniques of interest group politics, even when it cut against the partisan grain. By 1974, Oregon's Republican Governor Tom McCall could cross partisan and state boundaries to support the reelection bid of Idaho Democratic Governor Cecil Andrus without raising eyebrows.[35]

Several contributors to this volume illustrate how governors capitalized on interest group support to put together important policy innovations. Reconsidering Kansas through the interest group prism casts new

light on the original blue sky law. To be sure, Governor Stubbs stirred up a flurry of popular support for securities licensing—and his banking commissioner fanned these winds. But as Brooke Masters implies, some unlikely interests backed this legislation, namely small-scale bankers who worried that potential assets were being lost to fraud. A February 1911 issue of *Bankers Magazine* did not pull any punches. "Had this money gone into legitimate investments," by which *Bankers Magazine* meant the kinds of loans made by banks, it would "have added in no small way toward upbuilding the country's wealth." Legitimate business, banking interests argued, was hurt by the money wasted in securities fraud. Historian Dan Holt contends that the problem was larger than a few criminals scamming investors. Banks were concerned that their bread and butter client, the small investor, was being diverted to securities. Banks were keen to encourage "a savings bank habit," and worried that the public would grow impatient with "only the ordinary return." Thus, blue sky laws, which undoubtedly were the product of populist agitation, were also propelled by a powerful interest group. Governors often had to negotiate these two competing styles of political influence in the twentieth century. In the case of blue sky laws, they aligned neatly, which explains their legislative success.[36]

Environmental politics provides another unlikely example of the role that governors have played in forging coalitions of interests. It too is generally associated with ideological appeals, supported by a powerful social movement. Sarah Phillips does not neglect these elements in her survey of the shift from conservation to environmentalism. Yet she argues that governors who succeeded at promoting environmental programs after World War II were able to transcend "local developmental interests" by assembling "alternative growth coalitions" that demanded responsible growth and balanced development.[37]

Gaylord Nelson was Wisconsin's "conservation governor" from 1959 to 1963. As Phillips recounts, Nelson crafted the Outdoor Recreation Action Plan. This program funneled millions of dollars toward natural resources, ranging from fish and game management to restoring lakes and shorelines. The key to Nelson's success, however, was shifting the rationale for conservation. These were investments, Nelson argued. He created the Department of Resource Development, to inventory these "assets" and to plan for their economic development. To prove the economic viability of this plan, Nelson touted tourism—the state's third largest industry. Nelson grounded his argument for the environment in the bedrock of economic development—a policy field, as Teaford shows, that governors embraced after World War II.[38]

To protect the environment in the quest of economic development was precisely the language that Congressman John Blatnik employed when he convinced his gang of "sewer democrats" to fund a massive program of water treatment. Federal matching grants were the mechanism, but jobs were clearly an important objective for the New Deal Democrats. Needless to say, construction unions liked this program, whatever its environmental consequences. As congressional scholar Paul Milazzo has noted, housing interests, growing increasingly concerned about the dwindling supply of clean water during an East Coast drought, liked it too. This was a language that New York Governor Nelson Rockefeller understood as well. Embracing his "edifice complex," Rockefeller embarked upon the Pure Waters Program in 1965. It pleased the beneficiaries of the billions in construction funds it distributed and also appealed to those who one day hoped to swim in newly cleansed waters. Commercial development interests were delighted because it lowered their infrastructure costs. As Phillips suggests, governors were in a unique position to put together such coalitions because they stood squarely at the intersection of local developmental interests and statewide pressure to protect natural resources in a society that had more disposable income, the time to enjoy it, and greater access to natural areas than ever before. Unlike presidents, governors were not insulated by layers of bureaucracy. They performed this delicate balancing act in public. Indeed, it was this very kind of accountability that led many Americans to prefer local and state government to federal government.[39]

The Regional Legacy

That region continued to exercise a powerful influence over Americans in the first half of the twentieth century should not be surprising. Even before Southern statesmen like Thomas Jefferson crafted a constitutional rationale for states rights, British North Americans conceived of the fragile union that they created as a loose alliance. Critics of the newly formed nation were convinced that it would follow the European example, breaking up into several regional confederations. While the Civil War resolved that issue once and for all, it failed, in the long run, to tackle the problem of the twentieth century—as W.E.B. Dubois put it—the color line. Jim Crow segregation in the South and social discrimination in the North turned Dubois into a prophet. Regional economic and political ties also continued to exercise a powerful influence well into the twentieth century.[40]

World War II and the ensuing Cold War certainly looked like they would change this. Racially, World War II created a "rising wind" of expectations among African Americans fueled by symbolic gestures like a combat role for African American soldiers and Truman's integration of the military in 1948. Hitler's blatantly racist ideology changed the very meaning of racism for millions of Americans, making it far more poison-ous. Although the Cold War dampened Americans' appetite for social protest and cast a pall over radical solutions to racial inequality, it also increased pressure upon Cold War liberals to demonstrate racial prog-ress. Winning the hearts and minds of nonaligned nations, many popu-lated by people of color, demanded no less. Economically, the war also appeared to break down regional divisions. The military-industrial com-plex sought cheap land and labor in Sunbelt areas, modernizing the economies of southern and western states.[41]

Yet region still mattered, especially when it came to race relations. Jason Sokol's essay lyrically illustrates the trajectory of these regional ties over the post–World War II period. Polar opposites at the outset, both liberal Massachusetts and reactionary Virginia zigzagged inexorably toward a national mean by the twenty-first century. The turning point in both regions came in the 1970s and 1980s. That is when demograph-ics—middle-class suburban voters—and ideology—what Matt Lassiter has labeled racially "innocent" middle-class consciousness—trumped region. That is also when the national judiciary intervened directly, forc-ing the issue for many voters and their elected leadership.[42]

Impersonal generalizations such as these, however, neglect the crucial role that leadership played in addressing racial issues. Initially, *Brown v. Board of Education* reinforced regional difference. Governor Lindsay Almond's 1958 inaugural address to his fellow Virginians vowed to mar-shal "a massive resistance" to the Court's decision. It was the defiant resistance of Almond and most other southern governors that tarnished the legitimate role of states in a federal system for decades to come. While the two governors who succeeded Almond bobbed and weaved on the desegregation question—and while the courts remained quiet—Republican Governor John Volpe responded to his traditionally liberal constituency in Massachusetts by signing the Racial Imbalance Act. Yet like his southern counterparts, Volpe was hardly eager to desegregate.[43]

Elected in 1969 as a Republican governor of a heavily Democratic state, Linwood Holton broke the stalemate in Virginia. Although Holton spoke a far more enlightened political language than his predecessors, he let the courts do the work when it came to school desegregation. In contrast to a number of other southern governors, Holton refused to defy *Alexander v. Holmes County*, which ordered that fourteen states desegregate schools immediately. In spite of its obvious unpopularity, Holton stood his ground, sending his own children to public schools with majority African American populations.[44]

About the same time that Holton defended an unpopular court order, Massachusetts Governor Francis Sargent struggled to implement the

Racial Imbalance Act, even vetoing legislation in 1973 that would have suspended it for a year. But after facing rising white resistance, Sargent finally caved. He endorsed a weak alternative to the Racial Imbalance Act in 1974. So did the next governor, Michael Dukakis, who defeated Sargent that year. As Sokol notes, despite inheriting unprecedented gubernatorial power, Dukakis used none of it on the issue of forced desegregation. The *Boston Globe* derided the "largely invisible" Dukakis on this issue. As was the case with Holton, Dukakis chose to let the courts do the heavy lifting. The difference was each state's history. Given Virginia's legacy, Holton's position was politically courageous; Dukakis took the politically prudent course and lived to run another day. A Supreme Court that was determined to impose uniform racial standards across the nation and voters who were strongly opposed to court-ordered desegregation, regardless of their regional accent, wrung much of the geographical difference out of this long-standing regional divide.[45]

While racial practice narrowed, albeit slowly, economic competition between the states increased after World War II. A more fully integrated national economy and one that increasingly competed in a global marketplace encouraged the belief that governors could influence corporate decisions about where to locate. As Teaford recounts, governors in the post–World War II period became de facto executive directors of their state's chamber of commerce. Lucrative opportunities simply dropped into the laps of some governors. Such was the case when, in 1980, Citibank relocated to South Dakota in return for legislation that lifted caps on interest rates. This allowed the bank to issue credit cards with interest rates that delivered profits, despite skyrocketing inflation. More often, such moves were courted by a bevy of governors, each hoping to land a source of good jobs for their states.[46]

North Carolina Governor Luther Hodges set the standard for such efforts. Between 1954 and 1961 Hodges made economic development his top priority. He created the North Carolina Business Development Corporation, which supplied long-term capital to new and expanding businesses. He used fiscal policy to attract industry—adapting the state income tax to this end. In his most visionary move, Hodges created the North Carolina Research Triangle aimed at attracting high-wage employers. He forged a link between research and economic growth.[47]

None of this would have mattered if Hodges had not been a tireless promoter. Nor would it have mattered if North Carolina, like most other southern states, had not been a "right to work" state where unions had trouble gaining a foothold. Soon, governors were competing for international business. Teaford chronicles the progression of governors who forged special relationships with foreign trading partners. Lamar Alexander, in Tennessee, was among the first, reaching out to Japan in the hope of building his own version of North Carolina's research triangle. What began as a zero-sum game to move business from another (usually northern) state or, better yet, a foreign country, soon emerged as a broad-based rationale for improving the business climate at home. As already noted, governors justified energetic education initiatives in economic terms. An educated citizenry would attract the kind of high-skill jobs that would boost the state's economy.[48]

That economic development was pursued by so many governors simultaneously ultimately blunted the competitive edge to this trend. For one thing, governors worked collectively, often along regional lines, to attract business. As early as 1948, Teaford reports, the Conference of Western Governors vowed to pursue a collective program to advance industrialization in the West. Three decades later a group of southern governors pressed for educational reforms in order to overcome long-standing economic disadvantages. As Vinovskis recounts, by the turn of the century governors from fifty states—acting collectively through the National Governors Association—pressed for a series of national reforms, beginning with "America 2000" and culminating in the No Child Left Behind Act.[49]

After World War II, governors—whether they liked it or not—were protagonists in one of the most dramatic changes in the nation's history. Regional racial difference narrowed as governors converged toward a more centrist position on race. Whether heroic or cautious, governors played a key role in mediating between court-ordered initiatives that were distasteful to the vast majority of Americans and grudging public acceptance of the law of the land. Seizing upon microeconomic policy, governors initiated a round of competition in the mid-twentieth century that was every bit as fierce as the battles over transportation routes a century earlier. Yet an odd thing happened on the way to the state treasury. Because this role was regularized across all states, what should have been a fiercely competitive process sometimes evolved into broader programmatic initiatives that often entailed cooperation between the states, rather than competition. Governors still battled over which state would land the BMW or Toyota factory, but they also worked cooperatively to increase federal funding to ensure a skilled work force.

Governor Goldilocks and the "Just Right" Solution to Service Delivery

The United States evolved from an industrial economy to a service economy in the second half of the twentieth century. By 1994, expenditures for services accounted for a greater portion of the gross domestic product than spending for goods. What is rarely noted, however, is that the services that Americans most demanded were provided by government. Expenditures at all levels of government grew dramatically between 1890 and 1990. These services were not foisted upon Americans— citizens clamored for them. As economic historian Louis Galambos points out, "Unless you are willing to claim that voters were systematically misled for an entire century, you cannot avoid the conclusion that Americans chose to forgo buying consumer goods so that they could 'buy' more government." Governors delivered more than their fair share of these services, from transportation to stem cell research.[50]

But Americans were far more sensitive to how these services were delivered and what they cost when they were provided by government than when they were offered by the private sector. Because Americans could choose individually whether or not to purchase a service from the private sector, few challenged the premise that the market price for these services reflected demand. Indeed, most periods of organized protest have coincided with government efforts to "fix" prices or limit supply, during wartime or crisis. Nor have Americans been overly sensitive to the way in which these services have been delivered by the private sector. During the twentieth century, Americans grew more comfortable with gigantic corporations, corporate mergers, and even the multinational cast to many of the companies from which they bought goods and services.[51]

Public services, however, were a different matter. In a *National Tax Journal* article written in 1979, Jack Citrin asked about attitudes toward public spending, "Do People Want Something for Nothing?" Yes, he answered. Aggregating data from both national surveys and a survey of Californians during the height of the California "tax revolt," Citrin found that despite their demand for lower taxes, Americans actually advocated *higher* spending for a range of services from health to education and environmental protection. Only space exploration, welfare, and foreign aid failed to garner popular majorities. How did most Americans reconcile this discrepancy? Waste and inefficiency, Citrin hypothesized. Americans consistently preferred services delivered by units of government that were close to home and politically accountable. That meant that they preferred local to state government, and state government to federal government.[52]

Again, governors found themselves at the intersection of two conflicting impulses: the demand for services and the reluctance to pay for such services, especially if the provider was not politically accountable. Governors crafted what might be called the "Goldilocks" approach to this dilemma. They argued that localities were too small and the federal government too big: states were just the right size to achieve efficiencies and economies of scale while remaining politically accountable to citizens consuming their services.

The chapters that follow document the range of services that states offered and the balancing act that many governors performed to convince the public that state government was "just right" for the task. Roads are the best example of this. While local governments were the first to absorb the impact of traffic—especially in urban areas—during the 1920s, governors quickly stepped into the breach. Spurred on by the Federal Highway Act, which shared the costs on a fifty-fifty matching basis, states took the lead in construction. States, governors argued, were large enough to carry out the kind of comprehensive planning required for an orderly program of road building. The federal legislation funneled federal matching funds through state road commissions, which were required by law. States could also spread the costs of their matching share across a larger population. By 1929, every state in the nation had passed a gasoline tax.[53]

If states were more extensive, efficient, and professional than localities, wouldn't the same reasoning apply to direct federal administration? For reasons having largely to do with political accountability, both the governors and Congress kept highway building firmly under the control of the states. Despite resistance from the Governors' Conference, Congress did pass a federal gasoline tax in 1932. Although governors continued to fight what they perceived to be federal intrusion into a valuable source of state revenue, they did like the idea of dedicating the proceeds from an increase in the federal gasoline tax in 1956 to a Highway Trust Fund. This mechanism restricted these funds exclusively to highway construction, which continued to be administered by the states. While federal administration might have been even more professional and efficient than the existing system, the fear of big government meant that state administration was "just right" from a political standpoint.[54]

In the social services, states became the gatekeepers that carried out a long-standing responsibility to distinguish deserving from undeserving poor. Once again, federal policy reinforced the states' role as service delivery intermediaries. As Ron Haskins notes, the trajectory of welfare programs was toward federal fiscal and policy control.[55] But states continued to play a key role as intermediaries. Matching grants under Aid to Families with Dependent Children, for instance, funneled funds through state departments of social services. Unlike highways, upholding Jim Crow in southern states was clearly one reason for this mechanism. But even after such racial distinctions began to fade, state agencies continued to distinguish between the "worthy" and "unworthy" poor.[56] And as Haskins notes, states were partially successful in regaining policy control over several social programs during the 1990s, continuing what he aptly calls the "Kabuki dance" of federalism.[57]

Colleen Grogan and Vernon Smith tell the fascinating story of why this long-standing responsibility began to break down in the case of state-delivered health care. The essence of the problem was the prohibitive cost of medical care. Rising costs pushed middle-class citizens, who in theory were supposed to obtain employer-based health care and social security assisted retirement income, onto publicly assisted Medicaid. The growing number of Americans who could not get employer-based health care added to this problem, and states were pressed to fill this gap. They have done so by stretching Medicaid coverage, and by taking advantage, since the mid-1980s, of federal matching funds to cover a greater number of children and pregnant women. For the past ten years, states have used matching funds from the State Children's Health Insurance Program (SCHIP) to fill gaps in health care coverage left by shrinking employer-based health insurance. Forty-one states covered children with family incomes at or above 200 percent of the poverty line by 2005.[58]

An increasing percentage of these publicly funded clients are either workers or children of workers. In short, the clear lines between needy and middle-class citizens have been blurred, at least when it comes to health care. With states staggering under the expense of the growing health care burden, and with an ever more mobile population, no longer stigmatized by the Jim Crow system in the South, it is not clear how much longer this division of responsibility in today's federal system will endure. States seeking to provide universal coverage have come up with a variety of innovative approaches. As Grogan and Smith point out, the successful ones connect federal-state funding through Medicaid and SCHIP to private health plans that give all citizens access to mainstream health services. Whether the perception of political accountability will make this complicated set of intergovernmental relations worth the effort in the long run remains an open question.[59]

The Other

Cultural historians have made much of the "other" in the past twenty years. Interpretations of American revolutionary nationalism, for instance, define it in opposition to the British empire; Cold War nationalism is framed as a reaction to the Soviet "other." The growing administrative and fiscal clout of the federal government over the course of the twentieth century has created an "other" that has made intergovernmental relations a top priority for governors. This is not to say that the federal government is always perceived to be an enemy, or even a competitor. Often, states have treated it like a partner or even rich uncle.

Partner or pariah, the federal government's reach makes the "Kabuki" dance of federalism every governor's top priority today. Whether Fed-baiting, bashing, or begging, governors develop agendas in reaction to the federal elephant in the room. No contemporary governor can ignore the federal government. Measured as a percentage of GNP, all government has grown since 1890. Public spending accounted for 7 percent of GNP in 1890; it was 40 percent of GNP one hundred years later. The ratio between federal spending per person and state/local spending per person, however, has been reversed. In 1890, states and local governments accounted for 64 percent of all government spending; the federal government consumed 36 percent. By 1990, federal spending accounted for 63 percent of all government spending; state and local government spent 37 percent.[60]

In the meantime the number of federal agencies has proliferated, and the administrative complexity of the requirements imposed upon the states has increased dramatically. During the 1970s, almost one quarter of state revenues flowed from federal categorical grants. This was money essential to state governance, but money with requirements and mandates attached to it. Even more troubling to the states were unfunded mandates. Many of these were attached to the new social regulation, such as the clean air and water acts. As Phillips notes, such acts relied upon "technology-forcing" standards that were set without regard to the cost of achieving their ends. As we have already observed, the federal government claimed for itself two of the states' new sources of revenue in the twentieth century—the income tax and the gasoline tax. While these remain important revenue sources for the states, the federal income and gasoline taxes inevitably limit their growth at the state level.[61]

But the states have contributed to some of this federal growth. Governors often have acted as lobbyists. In the field of transportation, Dilger documents the long history of state pressure on the federal government. The National Governors Association has led the way in this field. In order to bolster its impact on a number of policy areas, NGA created a policy research arm in 1974. Standing committees have helped governors reach a consensus on policy-related issues. All governors could agree that federal funds came with too many strings attached. NGA lobbied successfully for mechanisms like block grants and revenue sharing which have given states more leeway in spending federal dollars.[62]

Despite the reversal in spending ratios over the century and a far more visible federal presence, states continue to play an important role in citizens' lives. States have lobbied for federal funds, secure in their belief that whether for education, health care, highways, or prison-building, Americans will continue to prefer government that is close to home and states will continue to offer extensive coverage and economies of scale that localities and counties cannot match.

Three of the four conflicting impulses we have discussed continue to dominate the polity today. Governors remain well-positioned to negotiate struggles between populist demands and technocratic fixes. The tension between reinvigorated political parties and long-standing interest groups, and the insatiable demand for services, tempered by popular insistence that they be delivered cheaply by accountable units of government, also occupy a great deal of gubernatorial attention.

Region seems to exercise a far less powerful pull on states than it did one hundred years ago. While the occasional battle over which flag should fly above the state capitol still stirs passions, and while the states certainly remain distinctive, governors today are less divided by their economic or racial program than they have been in the past. In place of regional concerns stands the increased importance of the federal relationship. This is a common concern that has unified rather than divided the governors. Fighting for federal dollars while insisting that services delivered through states are "just right" for Americans wary of big government is a task that should further unite governors in the next decade. They will need both good microphones and clean lab coats to succeed.

Part I
Creativity Within the Confines of Federalism

The twentieth century witnessed massive growth in the federal government. In many policy areas, federal expansion preempted action by the governors and the states. The chapters in this section, however, demonstrate that the extension of federal power has not put an end to state innovation and experimentation. Governors have continued to respond to the demands of the citizens of their states and to address the issues of their times regardless of federal initiative. The greatest creativity of governors, in fact, is the ways they have developed public policies within, around, and outside the constraints created by federal intervention. And it is in these instances where the federal government failed to act, deferred to state discretion, or allowed for state experimentation that governors found the opportunity to become national leaders.

The policy areas examined in the following three chapters are realms where the federal government has dominated for much if not all of the twentieth century. Sarah Phillips recounts that the federal government took the lead in environmental policy, bringing the issue to the attention of the states when President Theodore Roosevelt called a conference of the nation's governors in 1908. Ajay K. Mehrotra and David Shreve highlight how the expansion of the federal income tax in the 1930s and 1940s forever changed the parameters of state taxation. And Ron Haskins demonstrates how the Social Security Act of 1935 permanently altered the roles of states and governors in welfare policy.

By closely investigating states and governors, these chapters provide a fuller picture of our national past. Phillips argues, for example, that the history of what we now call environmental policy, of the shift from conservation to environmentalism, cannot be truly understood without an examination of the role of governors. Furthermore, she explains, now, perhaps more then ever before, governors are making decisions that will affect the future of our environment. Mehrotra and Shreve assert that untangling the unique structure of fiscal federalism requires an investigation of state policy and that governors have created, and continue to create, diversity within the federal constraints on taxation. Finally, Haskins reveals how the more recent state role in developing welfare policy is part of a long tradition of state policy innovation in this area; a tradition, he argues, that should be encouraged. All these chapters demonstrate, then, not only that governors were essential to the development of environmental, taxation, and welfare policy over the twentieth century, but also that these policy areas will remain at the top of governors' agendas well into the twenty-first.

Chapter 1

Resourceful Leaders

Governors and the Politics of the American Environment

SARAH PHILLIPS

Over the twentieth century, a commitment to economic growth has generated a powerful political consensus that crosses both partisan and regional boundaries. Most politicians have viewed growth either as a democratic end in itself, or as the source of public resources for reform and the raw material for interventionist economic management. Not without reason was ecology dubbed the "subversive science": notions of environmental limits pose significant challenges to expectations of continued economic expansion.

It remains somewhat surprising, then, that the twentieth century also witnessed a series of shifting yet sustained attempts to manage the nation's natural resources for future generations and to restrict ecologically exploitative activities. Though the term "environmental policy" was largely unknown before the 1960s, strategies of public management over natural resources and urban waste prompted new forms of governance and administration beginning around the turn of the twentieth century. While significant action took place at the state level, the federal government took the lead in this Progressive Era transition, setting aside vast tracts of public land and forests, initiating programs of river management, and sponsoring a network of conservation professionals. Indeed, historians often pinpoint one particular White House gathering called by President Theodore Roosevelt in 1908—the Conference of Governors on the Conservation of Natural Resources—as a crucial moment in ushering in this new sensibility.

The federal government has continued to occupy center stage in most analyses of conservation history, and for good reason: the federal government owns much public land, especially in the West, and it has historically provided the funding and institutional expertise for agricultural expansion and large public works projects. Pressures on the national government only intensified in the period following World War II, which witnessed a key transition from earlier, "conservationist" policy regimes promoting the use and public supervision of income-generating natural resources to a new "preservationist" regulation of environmental quality, which included measures to curb air and water pollution and to protect besieged recreational areas and endangered ecosystems. Because environmental problems never confined themselves within state borders, the formulation of federal policy has usually remained front and center in both activism and scholarship.

This almost exclusive focus on the national government, however, has concealed an important history of policy innovation and negotiation at the state level. "All politics is local," as the saying goes, but nothing strikes the local resident more concretely than sudden shifts in land use or the despoliation of the air, a river, or a favorite natural haunt. Indeed, environmental concerns often percolated from the bottom up, and activists usually called upon statehouses and governors' offices for assistance. Although many natural resource and environmental problems required regional or national solutions, states often took the lead in publicizing threats, passing protective or regulatory legislation, and forcing the national government's hand by crafting standards exceeding federal guidelines.

In fact, a specific focus on state governors offers not only a more complete perspective on the development of twentieth-century environmental policy; it also offers an opportunity to address one of the thorniest scholarly questions about the assumed trajectory of this area of public policy. Historians have most often accepted a picture of discontinuity between the conservation era of the early decades and the environmental era of the postwar and contemporary periods. The salient change appears to have been a profound shift from a regime of resource utilization to one of resource protection, or from a politics of production and development to an affluence-driven politics of consumption fueled by the desire for environmental amenities among the rapidly expanding postwar middle class.[1] It is difficult to argue with this model of discontinuity given environmentalists' remarkable cultural and political success in cultivating ecological sentiment, curbing pollution, preserving open space, and restoring degraded landscapes and waterways.

Yet this picture of an abrupt transition raises the question of how a postwar political economy geared toward unprecedented economic expansion would have opened up any significant maneuvering room for politicians and policymakers to embrace environmental concerns.[2] Rarely do firmly established institutional missions and cultural prerogatives turn on a dime, so how exactly did the environmental policy regime emerge from the earlier conservationist one? A look at state governors reveals a more continuous story in which the seemingly new discourse of environmentalism overlapped and resonated with traditions of economic development and resource utilization. This framework finds support in recent work that highlights political actors, many of them unlikely environmentalists, who helped to usher in the environmental era with arguments that would have been quite familiar to earlier conservationists: that the potential for economic expansion ultimately depended on the availability of abundant and unspoiled natural resources.[3] Here an important distinction must be drawn between environmental*ism* and environmental *policy*—environmental activists often flagged the issues and raised the alarm, but modern environmental policymaking drew the most strength (and achieved the most lasting political success) when it adopted the more longstanding precedent of redirecting economic growth rather than stopping it.

This essay will review the past century of conservation and environmental policy, arguing that governors negotiated both eras by rejecting the apparent dichotomy between economic growth and environmental protection. As chief executives representing states in their entirety, governors have often been able to transcend local developmental interests and to articulate long-term visions and plans, but only if they could promise replacement opportunities in return. Especially after the 1950s and 1960s, a period that witnessed a steady increase in the competence and professional orientation of state executives, governors often seized opportunities to assemble alternative growth coalitions that served environmental ends. Aware of the ever-present race for economic expansion, and constrained by comparatively strict financial options and budgetary requirements, governors attempted to build support for policy that balanced new economic opportunities with long-term sustainability imperatives.[4]

The evidence suggests that governors achieved environmental policy success when they downplayed the language of sacrifice and combined calls for environmental responsibility with calls for "responsible" or "balanced" growth. Indeed, governors have proven particularly nimble at weaving together the seemingly incongruent promises of future economic expansion, equity, sustainability, and protection of the quality of life. They did not invent this political language—that honor belongs to a set of conservation pioneers who sought to nationalize resource policy at the turn of the twentieth century—but governors seized upon its political flexibility to assemble postwar coalitions representing a wide range of interest groups.

Such continuity across the twentieth century suggests a new model for explaining the endurance of certain forms of environmental stewardship, and it offers a usable past ready for the taking. Less triumphantly, however, a model of continuity also helps clarify the reasons for the nation's obvious environmental shortcomings. Today, the concerned observer is struck more often by the limits of environmental policy than by its many accomplishments. Americans have yet to address the challenges posed by residential and commercial sprawl, habitat depletion, soil exhaustion, declining fisheries, profligate garbage generation, oil dependency, persistent toxic contamination, or the inequitable social distribution of environmental hazards and benefits. It is painfully clear that continued reliance on growth coalitions to effect change has obvious drawbacks when environmental degradation is rooted in the very economic and demographic expansion these coalitions require for their political maneuverability. But resourceful governors have nonetheless played an important historical role in managing the American environment for the better. As the twenty-first century begins, in fact, a few state executives have been busy supporting policy to address climate change, the nation's (and arguably the world's) most pressing environmental challenge. These activities, intended to fill the gap left open by federal inaction, are nonetheless firmly anchored in the time-tested strategy of envisioning ways to secure the natural resource base for economic expansion—a story that begins at the start of the previous century.

Executive Appeal: The Conference of Governors

In 1908, President Theodore Roosevelt gathered the nation's state governors together for the first time to discuss the future of the nation's natural endowments—its minerals, forests, watersheds, and soils. "My dear governor," each invitation read, "it seems to me time for the country to take account of its natural resources and to inquire how long they are likely to last. . . . We are prosperous now; we should not forget that it will be just as important to our descendants to be prosperous in their time."[5] The event was to be no simple information session, however; the president and his close associate, conference organizer and Forest Service chief Gifford Pinchot, intended to build support for *federal* conservation leadership among a hitherto untapped political resource: other executives.

The Roosevelt administration's initial experiments with resource management policy had proven daring and controversial. At bottom, it was the ambition of Roosevelt, Pinchot, and their administrative allies to curtail the national government's longstanding practice of disbursing public land, willy-nilly, to private interests. Given the real possibility of future resource shortages, timber famine, and dried-up rivers, such short-sighted largesse threatened the nation's long-term viability. The federal government, these conservationists believed, should supervise a system of public forests and more systematically manage the country's public domain and its waterways. Tentative steps had already been taken: geographic surveys had been commissioned, forest reserves had been expanded and brought under federal management, and mineral and waterpower sites had been demarcated. Yet such activity raised hackles, especially in the West, where ranchers wanted unregulated access to open range, where savvy timber and mining interests benefited from land laws designed for homesteaders, and where any talk of restrictive policy or land set-asides threatened the heart of frontier ideology. Indeed, mounting rage emanating from across the Mississippi had compelled Pinchot to speak in person before a hostile Denver audience in 1907. There he skillfully defused the immediate crisis with arguments even the sunniest frontier booster could understand: that forest cover protected water supply, that ample water allowed for increased irrigation and consistent navigation, and that the carrying capacity of the rangeland determined its potential for use, not the short-term self interest of individuals or corporations.[6]

Pinchot's rhetorical genius was to drive a wedge between traditional resource users and concepts of the public good by arguing that long-term prosperity, democratically distributed, required restraints on short-term private exploitation. "Conservation," he explained, "means the greatest good to the greatest number for the longest time."[7] Exhaustible resources simply required continuous management by an indissoluble guardian—the state. Indeed, the conservationist state that Pinchot and Roosevelt labored to build was premised on administrative action and expert discretion. For too long, they thought, the government had acted legalistically as an umpire adjudicating between competing private parties; it was time for the executive branch to collect its own data, formulate long-range policy, and step boldly into the bewitching legal space where such action was neither specifically authorized nor categorically prohibited.[8] Surely the fellow executives gathered in Washington in the spring of 1908 could share the long view, and surely they could also understand that states were unequipped to handle the enormous burden alone. "The wise use of all our natural resources is the great material question of today," Roosevelt declared before the opening session of the Governors' Conference. "I have asked you to come together now because the enormous consumption of these resources, and the threat of imminent exhaustion . . . calls for common effort, common action."[9]

Many of the governors in attendance agreed. The most glowing endorsement of Roosevelt's policies sprang from the more industrialized East, where a few states had recently established forestry programs to protect stream flow and commercial navigation, and where they had begun to assemble their own forest reserves as a "playground for the

People," in the words of Governor John Fort of New Jersey.[10] New York's commissioner of fish and game proudly boasted that his state was far ahead of the curve in having established the vast Adirondack forest preserve and suggested that other states study its example: "The condition of New York is the condition in all the states," he warned.[11] Several southern and midwestern governors also offered the president support, familiar as they were with the lumber interests that rapidly cleared forested land, moved on to better pickings out West, and left the states wondering how to restore watersheds and vast cutovers. "A condition and not a theory confronts us," remarked Robert Glenn, governor of North Carolina: "There must be an end to this waste. . . . Unless it is stayed, there is no hope for preserving our resources or protecting our soil. Our forests denuded, our trees gone; no longer any decaying matter or leaves as sponges to take up the rains as they fall from heaven. . . . *The States by themselves are helpless. The arm of the Nation must be used to aid the people.* . . . [Should we] wait until all our forests are cut down and denuded; until all the lands along our rivers are destroyed; until the rivers themselves are filled up with mud and gravel, our manufactories discontinued, our harbors made ineffectual, and our commerce paralyzed?"[12]

Not surprisingly, the westerners supplied more mixed reviews. "My people want the conservation of natural resources outlined so splendidly by the President," Wyoming Governor Bryant Brooks remarked, "[but] we want the conservation, not stagnation. . . . Wyoming spends thousands of dollars yearly trying to get new settlers; that is the best conservation, the very best of all."[13] Governor Frank Gooding of Idaho spoke more pointedly to the source of western resentment—the federal government's continued grip over vast stretches of public land. Gooding insisted that special care must be taken to protect the liberties of the people of the states who "have given up so much of their domain to the national forests . . . they have a right to insist on the fullest use."[14]

Still, the West did not speak with one voice—several conference-goers understood that Roosevelt and his band of conservation nationalists held out the juicy plum of federally sponsored irrigation projects. The western reclamation program, begun only a few years' prior to the conference, watered only a small number of acres by 1908 but inspired visions of small family farms multiplying across the arid landscape. On behalf of his state, former California Governor George Pardee expressed unqualified support for national forest reserves and federal land management strategies that preserved headwaters and assured ample water supplies. Such policies, he explained, provided the long-term resource base for a more prosperous future, a future in which nature's bounty was harnessed for the benefit of the many rather than for the few. "The time of the great ranch has passed," Pardee declared: "Let me . . . say what the Reclamation Service has been doing in the West and South-west. Dams are being built to store the waters of the rivers at present unused, so that . . . in the time to come, the great civilization of this land, and therefore of this world, will be congregated . . . And this kind of work is what will give the land to those American families who are now unable to find homes on our disappearing public lands."[15]

The political appeal of conservation policy lay in its promise to pro-vide both abundance and democratic opportunity. Collective restraint was unneeded; prosperity and profits were assured as long as regular Americans and their political representatives took heed of their society's long-range resource requirements and granted independent authority to scientific professionals such as foresters, hydrologists, and agrono-mists. Planning was to replace laissez-faire, but continued economic expansion would be the solemn pledge of any new public stewardship. It was only the short-sighted resource exploiters who would bear the bur-den, or so the argument ran. This language, which offered amelioration without radical change or citizen sacrifice, established the lasting terms for environmental policymaking, for better and for worse.

The governors ended their first joint gathering with a declaration affirming that the nation's resources were indeed threatened, and that the integrity of any one resource—forests, streams, or soil—was linked to all the others. Each state, the declaration continued, should establish a commission of natural resources, and the federal government should continue its forest policy and its program of waterways development. "Let us conserve the foundations of our prosperity," the participants pledged.[16] After wrapping up their visit to Washington, the governors began to plan regular annual meetings independent of the president, gatherings from which emerged what is now the National Governors Association.[17]

The conference also helped to stimulate new state-level programs for forests, fish, and game.[18] In Michigan, for example, the national conser-vation impulse helped to legitimate and strengthen activities already underway. The nation's leading producer of lumber during the late nineteenth century, Michigan entered the twentieth century suffering from the collapse of the timber industry. Its northern lands were a waste—farmers abandoned the infertile cutover in droves; thousands of acres reverted to state ownership due to nonpayment of taxes; frightful forest fires swept through the region; and many observers believed that rapid forest clearing was responsible for precipitous drops in Great Lakes water levels. A consensus emerged that the state had been swin-dled. Prompted by sportsmen, who worried about declining fish and game habitat, and by professional foresters, who insisted that scientific forestry promised good business returns for the state, Michigan set about establishing rudimentary forest reserves. After a particularly ruinous fire season, however, Governor Fred Warner was under pressure to do more. In his 1909 State of the State message, Warner declared his support for measures that would "place our state in line with the progressive policy regarding forestry that prevails throughout the United States."[19] The legislature soon established a new commission with authority over all of Michigan's public lands and reserves. The stage was set for the remarkable rebirth of the forests of the Upper Midwest.

The 1920s and the New Deal Order of Public Works

Conservationists in the Progressive Era had essentially confined their efforts to forests, waterways, and recreational lands, and they had advocated public ownership (mostly in the sparsely settled West) as the primary remedy for individual and corporate misuse. During the 1920s and 1930s, however, conservationists broadened these concerns to focus on the vexing problem of rural poverty. They argued that helping rural citizens achieve standards of living equal to their urban counterparts required attention to *private* lands, to the threatened soils that sustained farmers' incomes, and to the untapped waterways that could generate much-needed electricity for rural areas left ignored by private utilities. These "new conservationist" concerns, which linked farmers' economic welfare to the proper use and equitable distribution of renewable natural resources, prepared the way for the expanded conservation programs of the New Deal.[20]

Before this new rural conservation reached the level of national policy, however, two governors did much to formulate and popularize it— Republican Gifford Pinchot of Pennsylvania and Democrat Franklin D. Roosevelt of New York. Pinchot had not lost his earlier zest for conservationist battle, and in the mid-1920s he decided to open a new front against the inequitable distribution of electricity. Private utilities and electric companies had decided that most farmers simply did not have the income to put them in the customer class; it was far more profitable to serve more densely populated urban areas. American farmers therefore faced two kinds of economic disadvantage in the power market: 90 percent could not get distribution lines strung to their homes, and the lucky 10 percent who did often paid double the urban rate.[21] Governor Pinchot wanted to establish a system of state-level regulation to distribute electricity more cheaply and on an area-wide basis to rural residents, for he believed this revolutionary source of power would decentralize industry and "put the farmer on an equality with the townsman." From the power field, the governor predicted, "we can expect the most sub-stantial aid in raising the standard of living."[22] The Pennsylvania legisla-ture rejected Pinchot's ambitious power proposals, but in any case Pinchot had begun these efforts hoping that they would jumpstart the regulatory powers of the *federal* government. He would not have to wait long.

Franklin Roosevelt sought similar policies to benefit New York's rural inhabitants during his governorship from 1929 to 1932. Faced with unprecedented rates of farm abandonment, Roosevelt asked for state-wide land and soil surveys to determine which lands were suitable for continued farming and which might be more suited to reforestation and watershed protection, and during his tenure voters approved a multimil-lion dollar bond issue to purchase and manage an enlarged system of forests and parks. Roosevelt also promised to provide rural New Yorkers with inexpensive electricity from state-developed hydropower facilities on the St. Lawrence River. While his power proposals faltered in New York State, they helped to launch his lustiest rhetoric during the presi-dential election of 1932. During the campaign he promised federal development of waterpower sites on the Tennessee, Colorado, St. Law-rence, and Columbia rivers. The government would not only build the required hydroelectric infrastructure; it would also distribute the elec-tricity to the surrounding communities at the lowest possible cost. "Each one of these [projects]," Roosevelt declared, "will forever be a national yardstick to prevent extortion against the public and to encourage the wider use of . . . electricity."[23]

As Roosevelt promised, federal conservation activities expanded under the New Deal in the 1930s. The remaining public domain was closed to further private entry; the government added to the national parks and wildlife preserves; and the acreage under U.S. Forest Service management increased, this time east of the Mississippi. Farmers received cash benefits and technical assistance to halt soil erosion and exhaustion—a cause rendered even more urgent after the nation absorbed shocking images of the Dust Bowl—and the federal govern-ment financed construction of massive hydroelectric dams and power distribution systems. Beginning with the Tennessee Valley Authority Act of 1933, every public dam-building agency (such as the TVA, Bureau of Reclamation, and Corps of Engineers) was required to produce and dis-tribute power with the aim of serving surrounding rural areas, a task accomplished with the assistance of other New Deal creations such as the Rural Electrification Administration and Public Works Administra-tion.

During the Great Depression, governors usually found themselves bypassed in the conservation policy arena. On the federal side, national

administrators raced around state governments to establish direct relationships with individual citizens or with the growing number of public
authorities that sprang up to receive federal funds like mushrooms after
a rain. On the local side, a young liberal Democrat like Lyndon Johnson,
for example, found that he had to make an end run around the conservative arena of Texas state government to secure New Deal benefits for
the rural and urban residents of his Congressional district.[24]

New Deal resource policy began with the expectation that income
security for American farmers would catalyze national economic recovery. Mobilization for World War II, however, transformed the political
and economic context dramatically and permanently. The economy
recovered, rural residents streamed toward the cities to work in defense
plants, and industry became less concentrated in the East as factories
relocated to the South and West to use the cheap power so generously
provided by the federal government's gleaming new dams. The hydroelectric and irrigation infrastructure, originally intended to promote
family farming and to sustain agricultural populations, soon subsidized
the opposite: postwar urban expansion, industrial and metropolitan
growth, and agribusiness. Planners and politicians now viewed water
projects on the Tennessee, Colorado, and Columbia rivers as powerful
instruments of regional economic development.[25]

Nowhere was the New Deal order of public works more visible than in
the West, which came of age in the decades after World War II. There,
local growth coalitions locked themselves into "iron triangles" with the
Bureau of Reclamation, Corps of Engineers, and key members of Congress to promote and sustain an enduring regime of multipurpose river
development that lasted through the 1950s and 1960s. Few western
waterways escaped the giant concrete plugs and reservoirs built by the
government's professional river-pushers, and no western state more successfully pushed around its (and other states') rivers than California.[26]
Only the determination to wring every last drop of water from its high-
lands and transport it to its parched valleys and coastal communities
allowed California to surpass New York as the most populous state and
to generate the nation's most prolific agricultural and metropolitan
growth. California's leaders and its voters hoped initially to shoulder the
burden alone, but the Depression prompted the state to request federal
takeover of the massive Central Valley Project. As it neared completion
in the 1950s, the project consisted of a geographically dispersed system
of dams, reservoirs, and canals to control floods, prevent saltwater intrusion, improve navigation, and provide water for irrigated farming and
burgeoning urban and suburban populations.[27]

Californians, however, still thirsted for more. In particular, the state's
large farm interests wanted more water and with it the assurance that

the federal government would not attempt to restrict the amount of sub-sidized water available to agribusiness. Why not put forward a *state* water project consisting of more storage dams in the north and a long, artificial river to bring that water south? Yet such a scheme required an argument with a broad-based appeal, for California voters would have to approve the biggest bond issue ever contemplated by any state. Furthermore, northern Californians had little interest in bottling up their streams to support corporate growers and uncontrolled metropolitan sprawl in the south.

Sensing an unprecedented political opportunity to provide for California's future prosperity and to guarantee the state's continued preeminence, Democratic Governor Pat Brown threw himself into the fight for a state water project. Brown forged legal compromises between the north and south, and he presented the project as benefiting the work-ingmen, the average people, of the state. "What are we do to?" he explained, "Build barriers around California and say nobody else can come in because we don't have enough water to go around?" Brown mixed his own ambitions with the concrete of the State Water Project: "I wanted this to be a monument to *me*," he later reflected.[28] Voters approved the bond, and the project squeaked through the legislature. It indeed provided a boon to agribusiness. However, by supplying water to metropolitan areas far in advance of need, Brown had preserved California's capacity to grow. His Faustian bargain was to ignore corporate growers' wasteful ways and their exploitative labor practices, and to envision the day when California's cities and suburbs claimed the water for themselves.[29]

Another set of claimants to California's water was also on the horizon: those who believed that the hydraulic society had wreaked havoc on the natural environment and that rivers and streams should be left unpushed, their sensitive ecologies unmolested. By the mid-1960s the postwar spirit of buoyant optimism had yielded to a more skeptical set of questions about the value of untrammeled growth and the unforeseen consequences of technological hubris. Just five years after Pat Brown's water project victory, in fact, California biologist Raymond Dasmann criticized the state's ethos of unchecked development in *The Destruction of California*. "California is being hacked and battered by the forces of ignorance and greed," Dasmann declared; the state was losing the qualities that attracted people to it in the first place.[30] In fact, Pat Brown's son, Governor Jerry Brown, found himself in tune with the newer environmental concerns but still propelled by the same calculations as his father. Unsuccessfully, Jerry Brown attempted to please both environmentalists and California's more longstanding water constituencies. In the 1970s and early 1980s, a broadly organized environmental opposition brought down the proposed Peripheral Canal—a final link in the State Water Project—despite Brown's support. California voters had rejected the first major water proposal since the 1920s. An era of limits had arrived, besting even the governor most willing to embrace its rhetoric.[31]

From Conservation to Environment

As the California story has foreshadowed, modern environmentalism emerged from the unprecedented period of growth and economic expansion that followed World War II. Skyrocketing levels of industrial production, mass consumption, and affluence in general produced both the demand for material goods and a desire to enjoy the environmental amenities that the production of these goods put in jeopardy. The realization that development threatened even the nation's most scenic places prompted a reinvigorated Sierra Club to battle the western river-pushers and to save Echo Park and the Grand Canyon from inundation. Such instances of revived preservationist agitation drew strength and national support from an expanding and prosperous middle class, many of them new suburbanites. After the war, the federal government had underwritten a surge to the suburbs, where a majority of the population lived by 1970. Upon relocation, these pioneers of the crabgrass frontier discovered they had purchased front-row seats to watch the bulldozers tear up the meadows, trees, marshes, and orchards that had originally lured them beyond the city limits. Thus primed, many Americans supported more vigorous efforts to protect parks, open space, and wilderness lands nationwide as well as closer to home. At the city and county levels, they squared off against real estate interests and enforced new regulations that restricted development on sensitive lands. At the state level, the governments of California, Michigan, and New York took the lead in authorizing large new appropriations for parks and outdoor recreation.[32]

The environmental consequences of the postwar boom could also be measured in the astounding amount of raw sewage flowing untreated into the nation's rivers and lakes, the clouds of poisonous exhaust fumes gathering over the new roads and expressways, and the industrial waste lurking unmarked beneath vacant and soon-to-be-developed land. Americans began to rely on entirely new categories of environmentally damaging products, such as detergents and plastics. Perhaps most important, the postwar era witnessed an abrupt shift in the composition and use of synthetic chemicals. Companies involved in government-sponsored research on synthetics like DDT during World War II were quick to establish both agricultural and home-and-garden markets for highly toxic pesticides and herbicides. Most Americans falsely believed that the government protected them from these harmful compounds.[33] No wonder, then, that Rachel Carson's *Silent Spring* shot to the bestseller list when it appeared in 1962. Carson gracefully introduced the basic concepts of ecological science to her audience, and argued that humans could not presume to poison parts of the environment without also poisoning themselves. "We have seen that [these chemicals] now contaminate soil, water, and food, that they have the power to make our streams fishless and our gardens and woodlands silent and birdless," she wrote. "Man, however much he may like to pretend the contrary, is part of nature. . . . Can he escape a pollution that is now so thoroughly distributed throughout our world?"[34] Ecological concepts were not new in the 1960s, but more and more Americans found persuasive the idea that the environment was an interconnected system, a seamless web, rather than a set of predictable or easily manipulated components.

The environmental impulse that began to congeal in the 1960s included a wide range of concerns and a diverse set of adherents. Women in particular responded to Rachel Carson's message, and middle-class mothers, housewives, and professionals were often the first to organize. But environmental critiques also emanated from the era's more emblematic ideological battlefields. Radical political critics, often veterans of the New Left, traced environmental despoliation to the interlocked hierarchies of capitalist and political power, and countercultural critics attempted to build anti-materialist alternatives to mainstream American society. Such diversity was on full display across the country during the first Earth Day in April 1970.[35]

At its most radical, environmental sentiment posed a fundamental set of challenges to development in general, and to the postwar economic order in particular. Liberal politicians and policymakers expected economic growth to obviate the need for redistributive policy and to provide the funds for an expanding array of government services. It was not just that a rising tide would lift all boats—a concerted program of assertive fiscal "growthmanship" would also provide additional funds for all sorts of goodies.[36] When environmentalists asked whether the earth could handle any more increases in the "American standard of living," they were not merely demanding a seat at the table for a destabilizing set of new values. They were also raising the specters of enforced scarcity and redistribution, policy options that neither history nor ideology had prepared many Americans to accept.

Much better to have it all—and that was how environmental concerns first made their way into policy at the state and federal levels in the 1960s. While the environment would soon become a cause with bipartisan support, liberal Democrats were the first to envision how environmental amenities were themselves part of Americans' rising materialist expectations. As the historian Arthur M. Schlesinger, Jr., put it, the "quantitative liberalism" of the 1930s had to give way to a "qualitative liberalism" that took into account "the quality of people's lives and opportunities." And a better quality of life was something only an expanded public sphere could provide. The postwar boom may have allowed consumers to pick and choose from an endless array of products, but they could not go out on their own and purchase uncrowded, litter-free parks or unpolluted air and water.[37]

The environmental components of Lyndon Johnson's Great Society embodied the "quality of life" liberalism at the federal level. In 1964 Johnson signed two landmark pieces of legislation: the Wilderness Act, which set aside roadless tracts of the public domain and provided for the future growth of these wilderness areas, and the Land and Water Conservation Fund Bill, which financed a hefty extension of parkland and wildlife work at the state and federal levels. He followed up with additional legislation that protected wild and scenic rivers and created new national seashores, lakeshores, and recreational areas.[38]

At the forefront of these federal efforts was Gaylord Nelson, considered the leading environmentalist in the Senate and the visionary behind the first Earth Day. He had originally launched this reputation, however, as Wisconsin's "conservation governor" from 1959 to 1963. The beneficiary of a revived Democratic Party in Wisconsin, Nelson promoted an assertive program of fiscal management to spur economic growth. From the proceeds he intended to make a variety of public investments in highways, education, welfare, and—above all—resource management and outdoor recreation. His innovations were administrative and legislative. First, finding that uncooperative Republicans controlled the existing conservation commission, Nelson created a new executive planning agency, the Department of Resource Development, to coordinate economic development and inventory the state's resources. Pouncing on studies that showed tourism to be the state's third-largest industry, Nelson then proposed massive appropriations for more recreational land and facilities to serve the growing populations of southeastern Wisconsin and metropolitan Chicago. The suggestion wasn't merely academic: on the Fourth of July weekend of 1960 every state park was packed full, and many families were turned away. The constituency for outdoor recreation had clearly expanded beyond hunters and fishermen. Nelson's legislative coup was the passage of the Outdoor Recreation Act Plan, or ORAP, which provided millions of dollars for parks and forests, lakes and shorelines, fish and game management, and urban recreation. ORAP spent federal funds as generously as state funds, and it also showered benefits across the state, which pleased northern Wisconsin, not typically a Democratic stronghold.[39]

The acquisition and management of recreational and wilderness areas at all levels of government was more in line with traditional conservation activities than with the emerging environmental focus on pollution and its dangers to ecological systems and human health. But the expanded liberalism of the 1960s also provided the context for new programs of investment in clean water and air. In 1960, President Eisenhower had declined to support federal funding for waste treatment plants on the grounds that water pollution was a "uniquely local" issue, but the Kennedy and Johnson administrations backed and expanded such assistance. Money for construction—and for union-approved paychecks—fit easily within the patterns of the existing regime of public works. Along with these subsidies also came a gradual shift toward the nationalization of water and air quality standards. But this too emerged from more long-standing developmental arrangements: the originators of such standards, such as Senator Edmund Muskie, viewed clean air and water as essential to future economic expansion; pollution was simply another form of waste. During the 1960s, however, the federal government did not yet apply uniform national standards; it asked the states to set and enforce their own.[40]

Developing in tandem with the expansion of activism at the federal level was a period of growth and professionalization of state government, catalyzed in large part by the Supreme Court's reapportionment cases giving greater representation to urban and suburban populations and thus greater opportunity for activist governors.[41] This new activism included environmental affairs, especially since those states most willing to jumpstart their own environmental programs stood to gain the most in federal assistance. Michigan Governor George Romney, for example, moved assertively to establish a state air pollution control program because the state was eligible for matching federal grants.[42] At the forefront of 1960s gubernatorial activism, though, was Republican Nelson A. Rockefeller of New York, whose views on pragmatic governance and on the healing potential of economic growth closely matched those of the liberal mainstream.[43]

Like the federal government's clean water programs, Rockefeller's emerged from his first policy preference: construction. Admitting he had an "edifice complex," Rockefeller was well acquainted with the economic and electoral benefits of building more roads, school campuses, and medical facilities. Why not treatment plants? The Pure Waters Program, begun in 1965, provided $1 billion to localities to stop dumping their raw sewage into the state's waterways. The program pleased an array of groups—recreational boaters and swimmers, as well as real

estate and commercial development interests whose costs would be lowered by public sewage systems. The Pure Waters program reflected not
only Rockefeller's distributive approach to politics; it also embodied his
cooperative style. The state offered more carrots than sticks, and authorities believed that persuasion alone would change the waste disposal
practices of public municipalities and private industries. This is not to
argue that Rockefeller remained inflexible; on the contrary, as concerns
about pollution mounted in the late 1960s, he pushed forward with a
major administrative reorganization in 1970—the creation of a single
Department of Environmental Conservation to address pollution problems. However, studies published a few years after the DEC's founding
showed that state authorities, hesitant to impose costly regulations, were
having difficulties making the transition from persuasion to enforcement.[44]

Governors and the Environment Since 1970

Rockefeller had launched New York's DEC just as the environmental
movement reached fever pitch. The Cuyahoga River caught fire (again)
in 1969; a major oil spill blackened miles of pristine California shore-
line; and the Apollo mission would soon return from space with the first
photographs of Earth, vulnerable and finite. Increasingly unsatisfied
with the state-based cooperative approach of the 1960s, environmentalists set their sights on the federal government. By and large, states had
not established the legal and administrative machinery to control pollution. Part of the problem was geographical: water and air pollutants did
not remain within state boundaries. But the larger problems were political: state governments were hesitant to raise taxes or to force cash-
strapped municipalities to institute new reforms. Industrial interests also
wielded tremendous influence in state and local governments. Businesses controlled their own emissions and disposal practices, resisted
regulation, and often kept the environment off the public agenda by
threatening to relocate.[45]

After 1970, U.S. environmental policy entered a different era. A far-
reaching series of legislative and administrative changes required the
federal government to set minimum water and air quality standards and
charged a new Environmental Protection Agency (EPA) with enforcing
them. These would not be the cooperative-style compliance schedules
drawn up in cozy meetings between state agencies and industrial leaders; they would be "technology *forcing*" standards based on the needs of
human health and determined without regard to cost. Environmental
legislation had bipartisan support through the 1970s, including the initial endorsement of President Richard Nixon. Congress not only set

goals for clean air and water; it also passed new regulations covering pesticides, toxic substances, solid and hazardous waste, coastal zones, endangered species, marine mammals, wetlands, and the public lands and forests.[46] The environmental legislation was part of a wave of new social regulation that transformed American federalism in the 1960s and 1970s, granting to the federal government the previously inconceivable authority to regulate the activities of state and local governments as well as the relations between these governments and individual citizens.[47]

The nationalization of environmental protection brought new opportunities and new burdens to state governments. Like New York, many states undertook administrative reorganizations and established "mini-EPAs." New York also followed another important federal precedent. After prompting by Democratic Governor Hugh Carey in 1975, the legislature passed a law that required the state and localities to prepare an "environmental impact statement" (EIS) before beginning any new project. An EIS included a description of the potential environmental impacts of the project, a list of alternatives to the existing proposal, and an explanation of how any damage would be mitigated. Builders and the building trades were on record against such a law; three years earlier, in fact, Nelson Rockefeller had vetoed a similar measure.[48] The fears of the developers were justified—the EIS quickly became one of the most potent weapons in citizens' attempts to halt and delay new construction.

Armed with new weapons like the EIS, public interest groups became the heroes of many environmental showdowns. Governors, however, often had to perform a trickier balancing act between economic and environmental considerations. Making this task even more difficult was the recession of the 1970s. After supporting New York's EIS law, for example, Governor Carey was told by members of his administration to take more "pro-business" positions if he wanted industry to remain in the state. Given that Carey's primary concern during the 1970s was to keep both New York State and New York City out of bankruptcy, it should come as little surprise that he moved a bit too timidly on two major environmental emergencies: polychlorinated biphenyl (PCB) contamination of the Hudson River, and Love Canal. When it became clear that the public was at risk from the carcinogenic PCBs that General Electric was discharging into the river, Carey issued public warnings and entered into negotiations with GE. But he supported a settlement with the company that was more lenient than many environmentalists would have preferred because he was fearful of job losses in a job-scarce area of the state. "It will do little good if we rescue our environment at the cost of our economy," Carey explained in 1976.[49] Similarly, when it emerged that the Love Canal residential neighborhood in Niagara Falls had been built over a leaky toxic waste dump, Carey committed state money to relocate the homeowners closest to the site. But he balked at relocating all the affected residents; the state simply could not afford the expense. Crucially, however, the federal government's presence in both instances allowed Carey to address the problems without overextending the state's meager resources. Compliance deadlines set by the federal EPA helped state officials prod GE into assuming part of the PCB clean-up costs; and at Love Canal the federal government eventually provided the additional funds to relocate the remaining residents, an action that helped bring about the national Superfund law.

The vastly increased federal presence in environmental management did not squelch gubernatorial innovation, however. In particular, a trio of moderate Republican governors—William Milliken of Michigan, Russell Peterson of Delaware, and Tom McCall of Oregon—embodied the environmental decade's bipartisan spirit and revived Theodore Roosevelt's conservationist tradition. They challenged powerful economic and industrial interests in their states and declared environmental commodities—clean air and water, wilderness and open space, leisure and recreational opportunities—the rightful heritage of every American. In so doing, they blazed a trail for future Republican mavericks to follow as the national party became ever more reflexively antiregulatory and antienvironmental. "The preservation of our environment is the critical issue of the Seventies," Milliken announced. "We are already the most affluent nation on earth, but we have paid too high a price." During his fourteen years in office from 1969 to 1983, Milliken boldly faced down polluting industries (some of them large employers and contributors to the Republican Party), supported legislation granting all citizens the legal standing to bring an environmental lawsuit, fought to expand scenic and recreational areas, and pushed successfully for legislation regulating wetlands drainage, even wetlands in private hands. "The truth is that the quality of human life in Michigan depends on nature," Milliken explained.[50]

But there was economic potential, too, in a better quality of life. This was Russell Peterson's political insight in Delaware. Worried about pollution in general and encroaching development near the state's wildlife preserves in particular, Peterson called a moratorium on all new industrial development in the state's coastal areas in 1970. Then, in 1971, he persuaded the legislature to pass the Coastal Zone Act, which established a sweeping new zoning program tilted against heavy industry. With these actions Peterson blocked a plan hatched by the U.S. Commerce Department in concert with several oil companies and shipping concerns to turn Delaware Bay into a refinery complex and supertanker port. "Governors usually embrace whatever new enterprise will produce new taxes and new jobs," Peterson later wrote in his autobiography, "yet here I was, the new governor, questioning whether this was what we wanted." But Peterson understood that he could not simply oppose new industrial facilities; he had to propose something in return. He gathered support for his land-use plans from commercial interests and labor organizations by explaining that development would not come to a standstill. Instead, the state would simply promote "better" kinds of growth: agriculture, transportation, research facilities, assembly plants, industrial parks, and so on. "We favored both business and environmental protection," Peterson explained: "By preventing our coast from being destroyed by short-sighted development we were preserving, instead of foreclosing, future options: by controlling industrial development in the coastal zone, we were helping, not hindering, the state's economy; by encouraging tourism and recreation and compatible development, we were fostering the creation of more, not fewer jobs. . . . Though the phrase had not yet been coined, what we were after was *sustainable development*, the kind that uses our resources without using them up, that meets the needs of the present generation without shortchanging the future."[51]

"Sustainable development" would have been an idea equally appealing to Tom McCall of Oregon had the phrase been available. Behind McCall's environmental leadership was the urgent question of what he called the state's "livability." Governor from 1967 to 1975, McCall had first focused his energy on reducing air and water pollution. Then, in the 1970s, he turned his attention to one of the most politically intractable environmental problems: rampant sprawl. The growth of a prosperous middle class may have provided a new base of support in the struggle against pollution, but it also resulted in the promiscuous expansion of mini-ranches and bedroom communities across the countryside. In McCall's view, this uncontrolled growth not only threatened Oregon's beauty but also jeopardized the state's two most important (and iconic) resource bases: its forests, which provided jobs for a declining but still-vibrant timber industry; and its agricultural land, which produced some of the nation's most flavorful fruit crops. In 1973, McCall threw his support behind a nationally pathbreaking land-use law. It required cities and counties to draw up comprehensive land-use plans in keeping with guidelines set by state planning authorities, and it effectively contained urban growth within certain pre-determined boundaries.[52]

McCall's environmental stewardship was controversial from the start and became even more so as the 1970s recession deepened and Oregon's industries—especially its lumber and milling firms—felt the pinch. Enemies seized on McCall's apparent disregard for the promotion of economic expansion, and the governor only added fuel to their fire when he asked a national television audience to "come visit us again and again. . . . But for heaven's sake, don't come here to live."[53] Still, McCall was no hard-line environmental protectionist (he never spoke out against logging, for example), nor was his administration responsible for the timber industry's decline. McCall's farsighted land-use policies, in fact, attracted a new migration to Oregon of professionals and nature-seekers who sought a taste of the lifestyle the governor promoted. Indeed, McCall had foreseen how prudent growth controls could complement expansion and new job creation. "We have sought to have a balance between the ecology and the economy," he explained in 1974: "If we could hold the line in Oregon we could look outside our state and see a queue of people trying to get businesses in this state, so a little belt-tightening now would give us the ability to pick and choose later on. I inveighed against having a parade of smokestacks running from the Pacific Ocean to the state of Idaho. . . . We don't have a 'no-growth' policy, we have a wise growth policy. . . . I'd like to get, maybe, an electronics industry or two. . . . Nice clean industry that doesn't use much power and pays pretty good money."[54]

The economic uncertainty of the late 1970s made it difficult for moderates to maintain the initial bipartisan emphasis of environmental policy, especially as the modern conservative movement rose to power on an assertively libertarian and anti-regulatory platform.[55] Land-use controls that governed private property were sharply criticized as unconstitutional "takings," and federal management of the public domain came under attack in an era when the states saw more potential in resource extraction than in recreation or ecological protection. Republican Governor Robert List of Nevada embodied the most visible product of this rising anger: the "Sagebrush Rebellion," an attempt on the part of several western states to claim the federal land within their boundaries.[56] While ultimately unsuccessful, the Sagebrush Rebellion demonstrated that recent environmental controls overlapped explosively with more longstanding patterns of federal dominance (in Nevada, for example, the federal government owned almost 90 percent of the land). Short-lived but potent, the rebellion reminded the nation that Westerners depended on federal assistance yet squirmed under its presence.

Opposing the sagebrushers was Democrat Bruce Babbitt, governor of Arizona from 1978 to 1987, who explained that "when federal lands have been given to the states in the past, they wound up being dominated by special interests."[57] But Babbitt's rhetorical populism served an economic expansionist purpose: he needed federal assistance in order to remake Arizona's water policy. Babbitt skillfully put together the political coalition needed to institute a much needed program of water conservation—a coalition made possible only because the federal government's Central Arizona Project would deliver Colorado River water for future metropolitan growth and tourist development.[58] Democratic Governor Bob Graham of Florida pursued a similar water policy, though in a much wetter state. Graham's family wealth was based upon the three activities that had drained and polluted Florida's Everglades: sugar growing, cattle ranching, and developing real estate. Yet Graham assembled an alternative growth coalition in 1983 to support a major Everglades ecological restoration program. Only a bold plan funded in partnership with the federal government, he argued, would provide South Florida's booming population with a stable supply of fresh water. While the restoration program—still ongoing—promises far less than genuine ecological integrity, Graham worked hard to overcome stiff opposition from the business community and the agricultural interests of the state. "The lesson I learned," he explained, "is that you've got to have an inclusive policy that includes all the stakeholders." Accommodating "rapid growth in a fragile environment" was the task Graham set for himself and for Florida's future governors.[59]

From the 1970s to the 1990s, Americans made significant environmental progress in expanding parks and preserves and in controlling the so-called first-generation pollutants, or the pollutants that generally remain in a single medium (the air and water). Less progress was forthcoming on the second-generation environmental problems caused by contaminants that move across different media (such as toxic and hazardous wastes), or, for that matter, on the third-generation problems that threatened environmental destruction on a regional or global scale (such as deforestation, habitat loss and deterioration, and global warming). Indeed, the legislation of the 1970s was not designed to address these issues, nor did the inflexible federal enforcement mechanisms and fragmented administrative setups allow for easy extensions of regulatory capacity. "Top-down regulation works best for large, clearly identifiable sources of pollution, like smokestacks, water treatment plants, and toxic waste dumps," as one political scientist has observed. "The command-and-control model is more difficult to implement when there are large numbers of polluters and when it is difficult to monitor what each polluter contributes to an environmental problem."[60]

Further exacerbating these policy challenges was a movement toward national environmental policy retrenchment, a conservative-led "brownlash" that began with the election of Ronald Reagan in 1980 and remained potent in Congress throughout the 1990s. This retrenchment took the form not only of executive and legislative trimming but also of devolutionary pressures on the states to accept greater financial and administrative responsibility for environmental programs. However, the "new federalism," though rightly perceived as a deliberate effort to cut back on government services, did help catalyze a remarkable expansion of state environmental capacity. Many states established air and water quality standards that exceeded federal regulations. In 1990, for example, California instituted strict new-car emissions standards and clean fuel requirements that served as models for other states. Strong "right-to-know" measures also appeared first at the state level. California again took the lead in 1986 when voters overwhelmingly approved Proposition 65, the Safe Drinking Water and Toxic Enforcement Act, which required mandatory disclosures of known carcinogenic or toxic chemicals. Four years later, the Minnesota legislature passed a measure compelling several hundred firms to submit an annual toxic pollution prevention plan. Finally, neighboring states often entered into stringent cooperative agreements to protect regional water quality and have together sued the federal government to enforce its own regulations. Leading the charge against laggard federal installations, the National Governors Association lobbied strenuously for the Federal Facilities Compliance Act of 1992. The FFCA forced the federal government to comply with all federal, state, and local solid and hazardous waste regulations in the same manner as any private party.[61]

While devolution and state-level innovation alone cannot address the many environmental challenges Americans face, states have continued to play a critical role in recent policymaking, especially as federal activism has receded and a wide gap has opened between the professed environmental values of most citizens and the national leadership. In fact, it is at the state level where the most innovative policies (indeed, the *only* policies) to reduce greenhouse gases have emerged. Climate change is a classic third-generation environmental challenge: because carbon dioxide, methane, and other greenhouse gases are produced by so many sources, they cannot easily be regulated by the same methods that control emissions from a small set of targets. In many state capitals, however, creative policy entrepreneurs have been developing a variety of policy tools to reduce these pollutants, ranging from formal carbon dioxide emission caps to portfolio requirements for the generation of renewable energy. "Alongside the extremist rhetoric and the barriers to serious engagement at the federal level," explains the foremost analyst of this trend, "an almost stealth-like process of policy development has been evolving."[62]

In all these cases—in which New Jersey, Oregon, Wisconsin, and the New England states stand at the forefront—the new policies have been developed, packaged, and sold as economic development opportunities for the state. Republican Governor Christine Todd Whitman of New Jersey certainly saw the green-dollar potential of a growing technological sector geared toward environmental mitigation: "The fact is that climate change associated with greenhouse gases has an effect on every aspect of our daily lives. The environmental and economic benefits that stem from controlling greenhouse gases are enormous."[63] For her environmental positions Whitman has ruffled many Republicans' feathers, especially after she became the federal EPA director under a presidential administration hostile both to regulation and to scientific reason. Yet Whitman's environmental commitments continue to inspire her political philosophy: "As a matter of principle, Republicans have long been the major advocates of less rather than more regulation. . . . In the past, however, the party has been willing to make sensible compromises in order to address the many serious threats to the environment."[64]

George Pataki, Republican governor of New York from 1995 to 2006, would agree with Whitman;[65] so too would Republican Governor Arnold Schwarzenegger of California, who seems, perhaps unknowingly, to have revived Theodore Roosevelt's hypermasculine conservationist swagger. "Biofuel is not like some wimpy feminine car," he explained to the automobile-mad audience of the television show *Pimp My Ride*.[66] While Schwarzenegger came into office in 2003 without the backing of environmentalists, he has since embraced a pro-business "cap and trade" system to reduce air pollutants and has committed the state to a 25 percent reduction in greenhouse gases by 2020. Schwarzenegger is building this environmental record on the state legislature's landmark 2002 decision to regulate the carbon dioxide emissions of motor vehicles, as well as on California's tradition of serving as the nation's pacesetter in air-pollution control.[67] As the leader of one of the world's largest economies, and certainly of one of the world's largest producers of greenhouse gas, Schwarzenegger may well symbolize the future of environmental politics. A generation of "girly men" hesitant to sacrifice their material comforts may indeed find themselves drawn to and reassured by Hollywood's version of the strenuous life.

Chapter 2

"To Lay and Collect"

Governors, Fiscal Federalism, and the Political Economy of Twentieth-Century Tax Policy

AJAY K. MEHROTRA AND DAVID SHREVE

Throughout the twentieth century, state governments and the individuals who have led them have played a vital role in the development of American tax policy. From the Progressive Era search for equitable and effective tax systems to the conservative property tax revolts of the 1970s, governors have been critical participants in a century-long debate over tax reform. As the political leaders of our country's "laboratories" of democracy, state executives have helped forge fiscal policies that have not only spread from state to state but have also been emulated by national lawmakers.

At the same time, governors have been constrained in their ability to shape tax reform. Broad structural forces limited their individual actions, and the American federal system of governance has forced states to compete with each other and the federal government in the making of tax policy. In addition, regional differences and changing historical conditions together have created a tremendous amount of diversity in state-level tax laws and policies. Forced to adapt to both varying economic and social circumstances and emerging fiscal responsibilities, states and their governors produced tax laws and policies that have varied greatly across time and place, with historical sectional differences often determining critical distinctions and patterns of development.[1]

Despite these variations and the restrictions on governors' roles, two broad trends help explain the tax policy choices made by state executives over the course of the twentieth century. First, governors, along with other state policymakers, often had to consider both equity and expediency in choosing tax vehicles. Increasingly, equity came to imply a tax system based on the principle of ability to pay, in which a moderately progressive income tax was often adopted as the ideal tax base.

FIGURE 2.1. STATE TAX REVENUES, 1902–1992

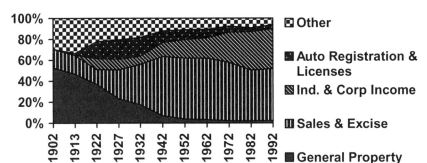

Source: *Historical Studies of the United States: Earliest Times to the Present*, Susan B. Carter et al., eds., Millennial Edition (New York: Cambridge University Press, 2006), Table Ea348-384.

Conversely, expediency reflected the ways in which governors and their states more typically responded to revenue shortfalls and fiscal crises by enacting solutions that proved more convenient than equitable. The relative visibility of the particular taxes they used often emerged as a principal factor in this process.

Indeed, it was the relentless hostility toward property taxes that compelled governors to wrestle with the tension between equity and expediency quite early in the century. The dissatisfaction with the prevailing general property tax was a driving force for state and local tax reform. From the progressives' assault on the antiquated taxation of personal property, to the dire demands during the 1930s and 1940s for alternatives to property taxes, to the post–World War II property tax revolts, the rising social and political antagonism toward property taxes looms large in any history of American taxation. The different ways in which governors engaged this enmity illustrates how they have negotiated between the demands for tax fairness and convenient revenue. One principal result has been that state governments' reliance on property taxes has declined steadily throughout the century (Figure 2.1).

Second, the tax policy decisions of states and governors were also limited and shaped by the institutional constraints of fiscal federalism. Forced to share power, resources, and fiscal responsibilities with localities and the national government, while competing with other states to provide public services and levy reasonable taxes, governors have had to navigate a complex matrix of taxing and spending options.[2] Jealously guarding their political prerogatives, governors have often attempted to wrest power away from local legislators and county tax assessors while simultaneously resisting the national centralization of taxing powers. In the process, state executives have helped facilitate some fiscal reforms while frustrating others. In some cases, they have been able to harness changing historical conditions to further their visions of fiscal progress and consolidate their executive power; at other times they have been overwhelmed and debilitated by the emergence of broad structural forces that have fueled the centralization of national authority or the inflexibility of local governments.[3]

These dynamics in and of themselves, however, do not explain the history of American governors and taxation. To understand the system of taxation that states developed over the twentieth century, it is also necessary to consider these themes in the context of the broad historical forces and critical events that shaped the American past. The new demands placed on state government by urbanization and industrialization, the crisis of the Great Depression, the growth of an expansive federal government, the mobilization of World War II, the prosperity of the 1950s and 1960s, and the economic downturn of the 1970s all affected the calculus of equity and expediency and the dynamics of fiscal federalism. Consequently, the twentieth-century history of state tax policy can be divided into three distinct time periods.

In the first period, during the Progressive Era, state governors attempted to address the inequities and ineffectiveness of the property tax by relegating this levy to the local level and ultimately replacing it with newly created graduated taxes on incomes and inheritances. It was during this period that tax theorists and activists were leading a conceptual revolution in thinking about the meaning of taxation. Eschewing the traditional notion that taxes were simply the price paid for government benefits, political economists and tax reformers argued that in the increasingly interdependent world of industrial capitalism taxes ought to reflect the new bonds of social solidarity; they should be levied, therefore, in accordance with one's faculty or ability to pay. Building on this intellectual foundation, many states across the country began to enact moderately progressive income taxes just as they worked out an intergovernmental system of separating the sources of tax revenue between states and localities.

The second historical period stretched from the onset of the Great Depression to the end of the first post–World War II decade. It was during these years of protracted fiscal crisis—amid skyrocketing property tax delinquency and flagging income tax revenues—that states turned to sales taxes and expanded their reliance on gasoline excise taxes and motor vehicle registration and licensing fees. Economic experts continued to tout the progressive income tax as an equitable and effective replacement for property taxes, and many states in the 1930s followed their advice. But the narrow reach of many of the early state income taxes, the resulting instability of income tax revenues, and the immediate need for revenue during the height of the Depression compelled many governors, led by Mississippi's Martin S. Conner, to turn to more regressive sales taxes. In subsequent decades, as the beginnings of a culture of consumption began to take hold in the United States, sales taxes became a significant source of new revenue.[4] Once World War II compelled the federal government to transform the national income tax into a broader and much more progressive levy, the intergovernmental division of tax sources appeared to be sealed: the income tax and payroll taxes would become the main source of federal funds, the property tax would be relegated to localities, and states would come to rely on a combination of sales and use taxes, excise levies, and income taxes.

During the third period, from roughly the 1950s to the present, states cemented their reliance on sales and income taxes to underwrite both moderately expansive budgets and indirect local property tax relief. They appeared to be embracing, as well, the notion that progressive taxes enhanced both revenues and economic activity. Thus, despite a flurry of new sales taxes in the 1960s related to public school funding and tentative desegregation, many governors began to urge and to pass tax reforms that increased state reliance upon progressive income taxes. Yet this was also the period in which states, having left the property tax in the hands of local government, found that this municipal levy had spawned a local fiscal crisis that few governors could ignore. Municipal responsibilities had grown so markedly and problems with the local property tax had become so profound that property tax reform became a principal state tax issue. The property tax revolts of the 1970s, which culminated with California's Proposition 13, ultimately produced a political environment that forced American governors to heed both heightened demands for revenue and a growing popular aversion to the most transparent (and often the most progressive) tax regimes. Governors such as California's Jerry Brown—an initial opponent of property tax protests—soon learned that they had unleashed, unwittingly perhaps, a conservative anti-tax backlash with far-reaching political consequences. By the turn of the twenty-first century, anti-tax sentiment had become a critical constraint on state tax policymaking.

The Progressive Era and the Search for a Fair and Effective Tax Base

State tax officials faced a dual set of pressures at the turn of the twentieth century. Most noticeable, on the one hand, were the broad social dislocations wrought by the modern forces of industrialization, urbanization, and mass migration.[5] As immigration increased and factories sprung up throughout the country, fostering a vast internal migration from farms to urban industrial centers, states realized that they had to improve their dilapidated infrastructure and social provisions. Although municipalities in the aggregate may have outspent the states during this time, the local dependency on state funds and the growing inequality and instability of the times pressed nearly all governors to raise and expend vast new sums of revenue.[6]

At the same time, states were constrained by their reliance on an archaic property tax. The journalist and public intellectual Herbert Croly lamented in 1909 that, applied to modern conditions, the property tax "has become both unjust and unproductive."[7] Because both states and localities shared the same property tax base, local property owners and assessors had an incentive to undervalue their property for state tax purposes. Doing so would shift the state tax burden, of course, onto other localities. One way to mitigate this incentive, reformers argued, was for states to abandon the use of the property tax as a revenue source.[8]

The local undervaluation of property was further exacerbated by the generally corrupt and incompetent local assessment process. Charged with the responsibility of determining the value of their neighbors' property, local assessors had neither the expertise nor the gumption to measure accurately the value of real estate or personal intangible property such as financial assets. The property tax also suffered from a disjunction between the formal requirements of the law and its actual operation. The formal property tax laws in most states applied equally to real and personal property. Under the letter of the law, owners of tangible and corporeal property such as land, buildings, and machinery were to be taxed at the same rate as those who held their wealth in personal property such as household items, financial assets, and cash salaries. Taxing such intangible wealth had long been a challenge for tax officials. But with the rise of finance capitalism and the institutional convergence of American manufacturing and Wall Street, intangible personal property became increasingly common and even more difficult to assess. Accordingly, most tax experts began to assert that the property tax not only failed to provide adequate public funds, but that it also fell disproportionately on those who held most of their wealth in real rather than personal property.[9]

Governors were especially mindful of the distributional consequences of the property tax. "The lands of the farmer being visible and easily accessible never escape taxation," proclaimed Alabama Governor Emmet O'Neal before the seventh meeting of the governors in 1914. "It can be asserted with confidence that the farmer pays more taxes in proportion to his property holdings than any other class of our citizens."

Although O'Neal sought to improve rather than eliminate the property tax, he recognized that all citizens need to bear their fair share of the tax burden. "Under every system of taxation," he concluded, "the most acute and important question is not how to reach the land of the farmer, but by what method that vast mass of property known as intangible or invisible personal property can be subjected to taxation and made to bear its just proportion of the general burden."[10] O'Neal's concern for farmers was shared by many governors of the era; it also came to spark a growing interest in income taxes as an alternative to the general property tax.[11]

Before governors and other state lawmakers turned to alternative revenue sources such as an income tax, however, they attempted to mitigate the defects of the property tax. Since assessing personal intangible property was one of the principal problems, some states attempted to increase compliance by enacting a "classified" tax system that taxed "invisible" personal property at a lower rate than real property. Minnesota Governor A. O. Eberhart led the charge for such classifications in 1910 with some impressive results. The state's value of assessed intangibles rose from nearly $14 million in 1910 to over $135 million by 1920.[12] Nonetheless, state constitutional restrictions prevented many other states and commonwealths from following suit, and even where states amended their constitutions and introduced lower tax rates for intangibles, the anticipated rise in revenue often failed to materialize.[13]

Tax reformers in the Progressive Era also touted the separation of revenue sources between states and localities. By abandoning the state property tax and leaving it to localities, experts argued that such tax segregation would remove the prevailing incentive for local undervaluation. Subsequently, state governments would be able to tax other sources that extended beyond the confines of local jurisdictions, such as corporate property or income. In time, this same logic would be used by federal officials as they drew corporate income taxation away from many states. In an effort to eliminate its reliance on a property tax, for example, California in 1910 transferred its general property tax to its localities and replaced it with a corporate income tax. Backed by the California Tax Commission and its cadre of experts, the idea soon caught on with other states. The National Tax Association, a newly formed organization of leading tax academics and administrators, began considering as early as 1908 just such a separation of revenue as part of its model system of state and local taxation.[14]

But the separation of sources did not completely solve the property tax problem. What it accomplished was to shift an increasingly outdated and inequitable levy to the municipal level. At the same time, however, it hastened the state-level adoption of a more centrally administered income tax. California realized that after relinquishing the property tax and casting its fate with the corporate income tax, its revenues became much more volatile than expected. Not yet able to see a way beyond these levies, but faced with fiscal crisis, Governor Hiram Johnson recommended raising taxes on public utilities and other state corporations on more than one occasion. In the end, the California experience convinced many governors and tax officials that they needed to consider reforms beyond the separation of sources, including the adoption of a broad-based income tax regime.[15]

Still, the desire for greater equity in state taxation did not automatically encourage the adoption of progressive income taxes. The outpouring of support for Henry George's single-tax at the turn of the century revealed how populist forces could restrain progressive tax reform. In its purest variant, the single-tax was designed as a flat levy imposed solely on the "unearned increment" of land values. Targeted at land speculators, the single-tax was intended to be a solution for all the ills of industrial capitalism. In recommending this panacea and touting its cascading benefits, George sought to limit the powers of government to this one tax. Governors who embraced the single-tax, such as Rhode Island's Lucius Garvin, were never numerous, but George's persuasive indictment of land speculators only made it more difficult to abandon property-based taxation, despite its increasingly obvious weaknesses.[16]

It was not until 1911 that Wisconsin, led by a series of progressive governors, was able to enact the first, effective state-level income tax. Rudimentary forms of income taxes had existed in other states and commonwealths since the colonial era, but most of these laws suffered from a lack of administrative capacity and thus raised little revenue. Interestingly, the emerging state regulation of public utilities, railroads, and other corporations, designed mostly to generate equitable rate schedules, also granted states the kind of corporate accounting data that made a new income tax practical. Building on these administrative developments, Wisconsin was able to centralize the administration of tax laws and enact a crude version of information withholding. These innovations illustrated that state-level income taxes could generate significant revenue in a fair and effective manner.[17]

Wisconsin's experiment was also the logical culmination of a conceptual shift in tax theory that academic political economists had been facilitating at the turn of the century. Columbia University professor Edwin R. A. Seligman and University of Wisconsin political economist Richard T. Ely had been recommending since the late nineteenth century that graduated taxation of income was one way to awaken the civic sensibilities of taxpayers and citizens. For these theorists, direct and progressive taxes also reflected the new meaning of fiscal citizenship that was taking shape at the turn of the century.[18] As early as 1888, Ely had confidently proclaimed that the income tax "is the fairest tax ever devised. It places a heavy burden when and where there is strength to bear it, and lightens the load in case of temporary or permanent weakness. Large property does not always imply ability to pay taxes, as taxes should come from income."[19]

The creation of the Wisconsin income tax had begun with the campaign to rationalize the state's unwieldy tax system. Along with a call for a direct primary, tax reform was one of the two major planks of Robert La Follette's first gubernatorial campaign in 1898. After falling short in that campaign but winning the governor's office in 1900, La Follette and his progressive successors continued to press for changes to the state's tax system. Wisconsin began its march towards the income tax by creating a state tax commission that brought together leading tax experts, including T. S. Adams, a Wisconsin professor of political economy who was one of Ely's first students. The commission also began to draft the outlines of a constitutional amendment and state income tax law.[20]

Enacted in 1911, five years after La Follette left the Wisconsin statehouse, the income tax law was the logical product of the Wisconsin progressive movement and its quest for a more equitable tax structure. When Governor Francis E. McGovern signed the bill, he explained how the newly created administrative reforms and the distribution of the proceeds to municipalities ensured the success of the new levy. The income tax would replace the taxation of personal property and provide valuable local government services. Under the new law, taxes would be "more widely and equitably distributed," announced McGovern. "Practically every penny will go to support local government. It will be spent to pave streets, build roads and bridges, maintain hospitals and jails, provide fire and police protection, and support courts for those who pay the tax."[21]

The Wisconsin reform triggered the adoption of similar income tax laws in eight other states between 1912 and 1919, yet the rationale for adoption varied widely. Mississippi's income tax, adopted in 1912, appeared to spring from little more than Governor Earl Brewer's call for expanded appropriations and more revenue. By contrast, New York, with Seligman's assistance, enacted an income tax that followed Wisconsin's commitment to creating an equitable and effectively administered tax system. Seligman, one of the leading academic proponents of basing taxes on the ability-to-pay principle, had long contended that the interdependency of modern industrial society required a new vision of the relation between citizens and their states—a new vision that entailed the reconfiguration of taxation and civic identity. "To say that he supports the state only because it benefits him," Seligman had argued, "is a narrow and selfish doctrine. We pay taxes not because we get benefits from the state, but because it is our duty to support the state as to support ourselves or our family." Proposed first in 1917, New York's income tax went into effect in 1919.[22]

If governors had come to embrace progressive income taxes for their own purposes, some remained anxious about the potential federal adoption of the same tax vehicle. New York Governor Charles Evans Hughes was concerned that the possible federal taxation of interest on state and municipal bonds would undermine or restrict his own fiscal autonomy. As a result, he nearly derailed New York's ratification of the U.S. constitutional amendment permitting a federal income tax. Ultimately, it was Seligman's public rebuke of Hughes, his former Columbia law school classmate and longtime friend, that helped mollify and stave off Hughes's initial objections. Still, other governors appeared to share Hughes's concern about the potential loss of fiscal sovereignty. At the 1912 Governors' Conference, former Kentucky Governor Augustus E. Willson, one of the founding members of the organization now known as the National Governors Association, warned his fellow executives that with the Sixteenth Amendment awaiting ratification "our consideration of any state income tax will be almost academic, for no party could hold power in any state if it should uphold a state income tax on top of a federal income tax." Few governors, it seems, were willing to embrace tax reform that might threaten their own executive prerogatives or fiscal authority.[23]

During the 1920s, many states continued to move away from the property tax as changes in technology, particularly the advent of the mass-produced automobile, also began to shape tax policy. As cars became more ubiquitous, states came under increasing pressure to build and modernize their roadways. States naturally spied the automobile, then, as a potential source of new revenue, and, by the end of the 1920s, all states had adopted gasoline taxes.[24] This ability to harness new technology for revenue purposes also foreshadowed how governors would be forced to address similar issues in the digital age of the late twentieth century.[25]

Harry Byrd, Sr., of Virginia, elected in 1925 as the youngest Virginia governor since Thomas Jefferson, best exemplified how a gubernatorial tax reformer channeled a variety of reform impulses and the new forces of technology. Imbibing the doctrine of tax segregation from his father, Richard, who had served as speaker of the Virginia General Assembly, Harry Byrd championed the separation of revenues above all other tax principles, despite California's mixed results. He moved, accordingly and in tandem with his desire to consolidate and dramatically expand state road-building efforts, to extinguish the Virginia state property tax, reserving that levy for the commonwealth's local governments. With his sights set on an extensive road-building campaign and the state takeover of county roads, and determined to leave the unwieldy property tax to the local jurisdictions, Byrd, following the path that Oregon had blazed in 1919, pushed for and won the passage of new state taxes on gasoline.[26] The regressive and outmoded character of the now retired state property tax appeared to render gasoline excise taxes as a suitably progressive alternative.[27] Recognized much later in his political career as a leading light of fiscal conservatism, especially when he came to chair the Joint Committee on the Reduction of Nonessential Federal Expenditures in 1941 and the Senate Finance Committee in 1955, Byrd's gubernatorial tax reform had at this point placed him squarely in the pantheon of progressive state leaders.[28]

Despite Byrd's use of excise taxes, most governors during the early decades of the century were searching for more equitable substitutes for the prevailing property tax. Along with his new gasoline taxes, even Byrd had pushed successfully for a small increase in the top bracket of the Virginia state income tax, a levy that had been adopted in the previous decade under the administration of Henry Carter Stuart. Though many states embraced moderately progressive income taxes and the concomitant ability-to-pay doctrine, there was hardly any consensus among lawmakers about the virtues of income taxes, especially after the federal government began to exercise its newly created taxing powers in World War I. Nonetheless, the Progressive Era was one in which governors frequently led their states away from state property taxes and toward the seemingly more equitable income tax. As the historian Jon Teaford has illustrated, the "income tax was the greatest contribution of the state tax reform movement. By 1920 most commentators agreed that it was the best answer to the states' problems, and during the course of the twentieth century it would be a major element in the transformation of the state revenue structure."[29]

The Great Depression, World War II, and the Turn to Consumption Taxes

In the 1930s and 1940s two broad historical forces compelled governors to strike out in new directions, away from the apparent political and theoretical ascendancy of the progressive income tax. The first of these was the Great Depression and the way in which it dramatically altered revenue streams. Magnified by the modest reach and limited progressivity of many of the era's income tax codes, the Depression hastened a renewed search for revenue, clearly dampening in the process the enthusiasm for progressive income taxes that had only begun to take hold. The advent of the New Deal, the financial demands of World War II, and the consequential revolution in federal power constituted the second set of historical factors that changed the trajectory of state-level tax reform. While some governors resisted this trend, others saw the revolution in federal power as a logical outgrowth of modernization and political complexity.

ECONOMIC CRISIS AND THE SEARCH FOR NEW SOURCES OF REVENUE

The dominant trend in the state tax policy of the 1930s was the widespread expansion of consumption taxes. Considered almost exclusively as an expedient source of new revenue in light of the Depression, sales tax legislation had begun to sweep through the nation's statehouses. The success of earlier state taxes on cigarettes and gasoline had convinced many that particular consumption taxes were uniquely stable sources of revenue, unlikely to decline in an economic downturn. Few governors, therefore, were able to resist the financial allure of sales taxes, despite possible misgivings about their distributional impact. In 1932, Mississippi became the first state to adopt a general sales tax; twenty-three other states followed suit between 1933 and 1938.[30]

More than most governors of the period, Franklin D. Roosevelt exemplified the attempt to balance equity and expediency in tax reform. Foreshadowing his actions as president, Roosevelt's attempts at tax reform in New York demonstrated a willingness to experiment and even reverse course while remaining committed to the broad principle of balancing fairness and convenience. Mounting his first tax reform effort in 1929, Roosevelt focused mainly on raising state gasoline taxes to pay for increased spending on roads and highways. Because these reforms were estimated to generate a significant surplus, Roosevelt proposed sweeping income tax relief while maintaining the state property tax. When Republican opponents in the New York legislature forced Roosevelt to explain his defense of the relatively small state property tax, he contended that property taxation conformed to the ability-to-pay principle. "I refer to the fact," Roosevelt declared, that the property "tax is paid in larger amounts by the big holders of real estate, the railroads and large business and industrial plants."[31]

Ultimately recognizing, however, the folly of what he called a "jerry-built tax system" and of his own less-than-coherent tax strategy, Roosevelt established a tax reform commission in March 1930. "It is time we consider," he declared, "a complete overhauling of our money-raising and spending governmental machine."[32] But the Great Depression exerted its influence as well; bewilderment combined with plummeting revenue forced many governors of the era, including Roosevelt, to consider little else but stop-gap tax policy changes. In February 1931, when Roosevelt's tax reform commission issued a preliminary report urging the state to find a replacement for the real estate taxes it still imposed, it was very likely, then, that New York would join other states in adopting new sales taxes.

Despite the imminent adoption of general sales taxes across the country and the vague pronouncements of the New York tax reform commission's initial report, Roosevelt quickly asserted his opposition to a general consumption tax. "I am against a sales tax," he declared in December 1931. "I have been in the past and I still am."[33] Although some tax experts supported excise taxes on luxury items such as tobacco and alcohol, Roosevelt believed that these, too, were unfair. Recognizing instinctively the regressive character of consumption taxes, Roosevelt stood his ground. "In the last analysis," he declared in January 1932, "these so-called luxury taxes are on the average individual, bearing nearly equally in actual cost on individual members of our population. They are not based on ability to pay and therefore bear far more heavily upon the poor than upon the rich."[34] His future Internal Revenue Bureau lawyer and Supreme Court nominee Robert Jackson noted that Roosevelt "viewed the taxation problem perhaps too exclusively as a social problem and not sufficiently as one in economics." Indeed, Roosevelt appeared to have placed front and center the ability-to-pay principle.[35]

With a fiscal crisis as the backdrop, however, Roosevelt could not ignore New York's growing demand for revenue, especially since he had recently introduced temporary works programs to combat swelling unemployment. Committed to balanced budgets, he began to consider raising income taxes and other levies to address the state's growing deficit, including a two-cent increase in New York's gasoline tax. Though he offered this gas tax proposal with very little reservation, it appeared to be a far less critical part of his emerging tax reform philosophy.

The ability-to-pay principle, on the other hand, was a critical component, and Roosevelt moved ultimately to make a more progressive income tax the mainstay of his last gubernatorial tax reform package. "This tax, better than any other," he declared, "measures ability to pay. That those who profit under a government and a given social and economic order shall contribute toward the support of government in accordance with their respective abilities cannot be questioned."[36] A banner headline on page one of the January 13, 1932, *New York Times* carried his proposal: "Roosevelt Asks 100 Per Cent Increase in Tax on Incomes and Gasoline Sales to Meet Large Deficit Faced by State."[37] Complying with Roosevelt's call for an increased and significantly more progressive state income tax, but accepting only half of his proposed gas tax increase, the New York legislature transformed their state code into one of the nation's more progressive and elastic tax systems.[38] Given the concentration of wealth and income in the Empire State, it was no surprise that these tax reforms led to significant revenue. By the end of World War II, New York's individual income tax collections accounted for more than half of the total income tax collections of all states.[39]

Roosevelt was an exceptional champion of progressive state taxation in a decade of sales tax ascendancy, but he did not stand completely alone. Utah Governor George Henry Dern, for instance, advocated the use of progressive income taxes to meet his state's growing demand for revenue. Elected in 1924 as the first non-Mormon and only the second Democrat to become the governor of Utah, Dern shared Roosevelt's political leanings. Indeed, while presiding over the 1930 Governors' Conference held in Salt Lake City, Dern struck up a friendship with New York's rising political star, an association that would ultimately bring him into Roosevelt's first presidential cabinet. On tax policy, in particular, the two progressive leaders found themselves very much inclined to favor the same political and economic approach.[40]

In his two terms as governor, Dern became preoccupied with several principal reforms including a major tax reform package that was introduced at the onset of the Great Depression and adopted in 1931.[41] The abundance of tax-exempt federal land, and the state's almost exclusive reliance on property taxes, meant that Utah faced perennial revenue limitations, even before the onset of the Great Depression. To combat this, Dern introduced progressive income taxes as part of a dramatic overhaul of the state's tax code. As contemporaries observed, Dern's tax leadership "was based on the fundamental ideals of economics—justice and the ability to pay."[42] Responding to critics who opposed this very visible tax increase, Dern declared: "New state activities which are created in response to a public demand, and which increase the taxes don't necessarily mean that the taxpayer's expenses are increased. It simply means that he is transferring a part of his expenses from his ordinary personal expenses to his tax account."[43]

Few state executives of the period, however, proved willing or able to follow the example of Roosevelt and Dern. Many other governors, particularly in agrarian regions where income taxes appeared to hold much less promise, tended to embrace a more expedient alternative for new revenue and property tax relief: the general sales tax. Following the lead of several European nations, Mississippi introduced the first general sales tax in 1932. Recently elected governor Martin "Mike" Conner depicted the new levy as a stable source of revenue that could also provide tax relief for farmers and other land owners. Retailers resisted the proposal, but many pragmatic Mississippi lawmakers understood that the plan would effectively shift the tax burden away from politically powerful land owners and onto the general public—including disenfranchised African Americans who comprised half of the state's population yet paid little directly in property taxes. Ultimately, Mississippi's 2 percent retail sales tax yielded what was for the Magnolia State relatively abundant revenues. Within five years, the sales tax was generating nearly $6 million annually, or roughly 20 percent of the state's total revenue, far outpacing the state's narrowly construed income tax, then producing only about $1.5 million per annum.[44]

Mississippi's apparent success with the sales tax led other states to follow suit. By the end of the decade, nearly two dozen states had begun collecting general sales taxes. At the height of the Depression in the mid-1930s, the gasoline excise tax remained the leading source of revenue for most states, but the sales tax had become popular enough to eclipse the property tax as the second leading source of state funds, far ahead of income tax revenues. By 1940, state governments in the aggregate raised nearly twice as much from the sales tax as the personal income tax.[45] Many tax experts, to be sure, disliked the regressive impact of the sales tax, even as a substitute for the much maligned property tax. As the Columbia University economist Robert M. Haig, Seligman's leading student, explained: "To propose the substitution of general sales taxes for taxes on real estate as a measure of relief for the small man is an insult to intelligence and an affront to common sense." Nevertheless, the political and financial lure of sales taxes during difficult times proved too strong for most chief executives to resist.[46]

With sales tax revenues beckoning, governors such as Louisiana's Huey Long, elected in 1928, often succeeded only in postponing their adoption. For Long, Louisiana's existing tax system—based principally upon a state property tax—was so regressive and so inadequate that ambitious reform could have conceivably taken many forms. Indeed, as one of Governor Long's tax commissioners recalled, his theory of taxation was to "cover everything in sight," to "throw out a network of taxes with low rates to catch everything."[47] Accordingly, instead of moving to institute an income tax, Long worked initially to broaden the existing severance tax on natural resources, first exploited under Governor John Parker in the early 1920s. Because state revenue was so inadequate, the state's inequality so marked, and the corporate exploitation of Louisiana's natural resources so profound, this change seemed to Long a very logical and progressive choice. Speaking to fellow governors at the 1928 Governors' Conference held in New Orleans, he urged the severance tax as a hedge against future losses, recommended it as a good way to compensate state citizens for the "taking" of their natural resources, and cautioned that broad education on the matter was a critical part of securing its even and efficient application.[48]

Only after Long became a U.S. senator and a national political figure, campaigning on the "Share our Wealth" slogan, did he begin to urge the creation of a Louisiana income tax. Driven by the force of Long's virtually unmatched political leadership and his emphasis on equity and redistribution, Louisiana instituted its first income tax provision in 1934. With Long in the U.S. Senate, Governor Oscar K. Allen, a key lieutenant in Long's political machine and his hand-picked successor, presided over the imposition of the new law. By 1936, however, one year after Long's assassination, Louisiana joined the rush to adopt a new sales tax, instituting a 2 percent tax on luxury items that would in 1938 be converted to a 1 percent general sales tax. After a brief repeal in 1940 under "reform" Governor Sam Houston Jones, and its reinstatement in 1942 as a "War Emergency Sales Tax," the general sales tax had become a mainstay of the Pelican State tax code by the late 1940s.[49] Like Mississippi, Louisiana could not count on the income tax to provide sufficient revenue, especially during a depression and especially since it was originally so limited in its scope and progressivity.[50]

California Governor Frank Merriam's path to tax reform was perhaps the clearest reflection of how the Depression affected the political economy of state taxation, and how different types of taxes exacted different political costs. After a brief tenure as acting governor and a watershed campaign in which he faced off against Socialist candidate Upton Sinclair and his End Poverty in California (EPIC) platform, Merriam began his administration amidst an ongoing labor clash between Bay Area police, striking longshoremen, and the strikebreakers hired by the region's shipping companies. No matter what policies he pursued, in other words, Merriam would be stamped almost permanently as a foe of California workers and progressive political activists, despite his own Bull Moose political origins. George Creel, for example, described Merriam as "reactionary to the point of medievalism."[51]

Unlike his immediate predecessor, James "Sunny Jim" Rolph, Jr., who vetoed a personal income tax and enacted a new sales tax in 1933, Merriam forged a different and somewhat surprising tax reform effort.[52] Given his reputation, most observers expected him to follow Rolph's lead by supporting an increase in the state's new sales tax. But Merriam sensed two things that set him on a decidedly different course: the resurgence of the state's Democratic opposition, and their commitment to a progressive income tax. Working closely with many of the Democrats who had supported Sinclair's EPIC campaign, Merriam campaigned for and ultimately signed California's first personal income tax law in 1935. Modeled after the federal tax law passed in the previous year, it was accompanied by the passage of a sales tax exemption for grocery purchases—an exclusion designed to reduce the regressive character of the sales tax introduced under Governor Rolph.[53] Yet, while these tax reforms would make the California tax code one of the nation's most progressive, they would also effectively end Merriman's political career and the dominance of his Golden State's Republican Party. The political lesson, for many state lawmakers, was difficult to forget. Few sales tax increases of the era, by contrast, including Governor Rolph's, exacted any similar political payment.

WORLD WAR II, THE NEW FEDERAL FISCAL ORDER, AND THE AMBIVALENCE OF GOVERNORS

After the Great Depression, the second set of broad historical forces to affect state tax systems from the 1930s through the 1950s was the rapidly growing influence and fiscal presence of the federal government. More than anything else, President Roosevelt's New Deal and World War II mobilization efforts forced states to view their tax policy alongside that of the increasingly powerful federal government. Of the thirty-one states that adopted an income tax by 1940, not one abandoned the measure as the federal income tax became much broader and more progressive. Yet, between 1938 and 1960, only the territory of Alaska implemented a new income tax. When states did implement tax changes during this period, usually under the pressure of economic contraction and fiscal crisis, they turned instead to the sales tax. Twelve states created new sales taxes over the same period, joining the twenty-three states and the territory of Hawaii that had done so in the 1930s. Although it is difficult to generalize, it appears that states largely conceded the use of an expanded income tax to the federal government, while keeping their existing taxes on income and consumption in place. In the calculus of state tax policymaking, expediency appeared to be taking precedence over equity.

While most governors reacted similarly to the extension of federal taxation, they often disagreed about the implications of the new fiscal federalism. Even before the federal government augmented its fiscal powers to finance the war, state executives had become wary of Washington's growing tax reach. As early as 1939, Nebraska Governor Robert Cochran prophetically warned his colleagues about the potential for an enlarged federal income tax system. "With reference to the income tax law," Cochran declared before the annual Governors' Conference, "I think it is a very proper method of taxation, but my position has been . . . that the field has already been preempted by the federal government, and it seems reasonably certain that that method of taxation will be extended by the Federal government as a matter of necessity."[54] Other state executives echoed Cochran's concern, as they pointed to the structural reasons why the federal government was in a better position to tax national incomes. At the 1940 Governors' Conference, Georgia Governor Eurith Rivers declared that the "Proper fields of taxation should be accorded the federal government free from invasion or duplication or pyramiding by the states or the local governments within the states."[55] Reminding his colleagues that the objective of any tax program "should be to tax those who have the greatest ability to pay," and that the federal government was clearly best situated to do this "on a basis more clearly approaching" this ideal, Rivers conceded that it was "interstate competition" that prevented states from doing what the federal government could accomplish more easily. New Jersey Governor Charles Edison, son of the famous Menlo Park inventor, seemed to sum up the popular sentiment when he announced that "The Federal government has already increased income tax[es], and may be expected to increase it further, so that state taxation of income does not seem to have a promising future."[56]

State leaders not only anticipated the growth of federal fiscal power, they also occasionally suggested ways that their constituents might benefit from this expansion. For Governor Rivers, "the most hopeful method of providing adequate funds" lay in "the further extension and development of variable grants to the states and from the latter to local governments." Belittling the notion that such grants would have any bearing at all on either the locus of authority or that they would encourage "state and local mendicancy," he urged the adoption of such grants as a way to correlate resources and needs and to exploit the progressive basis of the federal tax code.[57] Anticipating the revenue sharing proposals of the 1960s and 1970s, as well as the financing structure of what would become the federal Medicaid program, Rivers's proposal was, perhaps, as difficult to carry out as it was visionary. Speaking the following year at the 1941 Governors' Conference on the "Financial Implications of the Defense Program," Rhode Island Governor J. Howard McGrath endorsed Rivers's call for revenue sharing. "Since the Federal government is in a better position to raise revenues," he remarked, "it ought to share some of its revenues with the state governments."[58] Failing to catch on, however, in either 1940 or 1941, the revenue sharing idea was shunted aside. United States entry into World War II and the greatly enlarged federal presence that followed only intensified the related debate surrounding national power and local and state autonomy. Revenue sharing would be consigned to a twenty-five-year exile.

Just as state officials were conceding the income tax as the prerogative of federal authority, they were also cementing their own control over the sales tax. Ever since its adoption in the early 1930s, states anxiously guarded their jurisdiction over the general sales tax. When Congress considered a national sales tax in 1932, Mississippi's Pat Harrison, a ranking member of the Senate Finance Committee, led the charge in preventing the federal government from usurping what he and others saw as a tax base that ought to be "left exclusively to the States." As one Texas lawmaker explained, a national sales tax would "further trample upon the rights of the States." Enacting any such levy, he warned, would reduce a state "to the status of a province."[59] Throughout the 1940s, as Congress and the Roosevelt Administration reconsidered the idea of a national sales tax, state officials displayed their growing dependence on and jealous protection of this levy. When Congress proposed exempting war contractors from state and local sales taxes, for example, battle lines hardened and the 1942 Governors' Conference adopted a resolution objecting to such federal "interference."[60] As Harvard economist Alvin Hansen explained in 1944, "states cannot be expected to abandon sales taxes unless the productivity of other tax sources can be greatly increased."[61]

With most states and President Roosevelt opposed to a national sales tax, the federal government augmented its fiscal powers during World War II by revolutionizing the national income tax. The financial demands of underwriting a global conflict compelled lawmakers to transform the income tax from a "class tax" aimed primarily at the wealthiest Americans to a "mass tax" that reached a broader segment of the workforce. By dramatically lowering exemption levels, raising rates, and enacting the process of withholding, the national government quickly institutionalized the federal income tax in the mid-1940s. Both the number of citizens paying taxes and the amount collected skyrocketed during the war. Whereas less than 4 million individuals paid income taxes in 1939, that number grew to more than 42 million by 1945. Over the same period, income-tax collections mushroomed from roughly $2 billion to over $35 billion.[62] The process of financing the war, in the end, signaled a watershed in the development of U.S. tax policy, furthering solidifying the division of tax bases between the different levels of American governance.

After the war, governors were perhaps more divided than ever before over the new federal-state fiscal arrangements. The issues of fiscal federalism and tax competition soon became a salient part of Governors' Conference deliberations. In 1945, Governor Maurice Tobin of Massachusetts warned that "the present dominating position of the federal government in the realm of taxes must be superseded at the earliest possible moment by a fair reallocation of the spheres of taxation."[63] To develop proposals for federal-state coordination of tax policy, the Governors' Conference authorized a Special Committee on Tax and Fiscal Policy and in 1946 resolved that there was a pressing need for the "gradual elimination of tax competition between federal and state governments." Yet, when a number of governors attending the July 1947 Governors' Conference suggested that income taxes ought to be reserved solely for the use of the federal government, an even larger number of state executives objected, citing the instability of the kinds of taxes states would then be forced to rely upon. In September 1947, representatives of the Governors' Conference and Congress met to discuss the tax competition problem, after which they agreed only to divide inheritance and estate taxes more equitably and to reduce federal excise taxes, such as those placed on gasoline and local phone usage.[64]

Despite the attempts at intergovernmental coordination, governors remained divided over the growth of postwar federal taxing powers. One on side, there were those like Utah Governor J. Bracken Lee who anxiously believed that the centralization of taxing powers foreshadowed even greater consolidation of federal authority. "I'm worrying about the time when you won't even be Governor of your state," remarked Lee in 1949. "The Governor will be in Washington. . . . I think that a good majority of the Governors would be glad to give up [grants-in-aid] if they could get the taxing power back that the federal government now has."[65] Addressing fellow governors at the 1960 Governors' Conference, Christopher Del Sesto of Rhode Island recommended a constitutional amendment to "put in a realignment of the taxing power" between federal and state governments. "The thing that worries me more than anything else," added Governor Harold Handley of Indiana, "is that . . . this great American Eagle of ours, the American Eagle, is turning into the image of a mother hen." Stoked, perhaps, by such arguments, Mississippi Governor Ross Barnett lamented what he saw as a direct federal attack on the rights reserved for the states by the U.S. Constitution. Barnett contended that this attack was engineered by "power-mad politicians" who drew their inspiration from "foreign-written and communist-inspired sociology books."[66]

While some state executives feared the loss of what they saw as their political autonomy and fiscal sovereignty, others were more pragmatic about the centralization process. "We seem to forget," Governor Michael DiSalle of Ohio reminded his counterparts from around the nation, "that the people whom we accuse of all this subversive activity, who take these rights away from us, are men whom we elect to office in Washington. . . . What happens to these people when they suddenly leave their states and go to Washington? Is it because they get a different view on the problem than they had on the local level?"[67] Presiding over the 1956 Governors' Conference, Arthur Langlie of Washington informed his audience of what Illinois Governor Adlai Stevenson once referred to as the Industrial Age problems "which inexorably flow over state boundaries." Declaring that "these demands must be met" and "these services paid for," Langlie singled out the willingness to tell "your people" they must pay more taxes as "the greatest responsibility of Governors."[68] Such straight talk, of course, often came at a price. Like several others of the period, DiSalle became what North Carolina Governor Terry Sanford called "tax-loss" governors, voted out of office soon after raising state taxes.[69]

The "Era of Easy Finance" and the Advent of the Anti-Tax Movement

Between the Great Depression and the end of the 1940s, the federal government dominated American fiscal policy. But in the second half of the century, state governments once again regained a prominent place in the intergovernmental division of taxing powers. Buoyed by the postwar economic boom, subnational taxes witnessed explosive growth. Income taxes accounted for a large proportion of this growth, but sales taxes remained the dominant source of state revenue, and one that governors and state officials were still not eager to share with federal authorities. States used the increased revenue not only to address pending financial insolvency, both real and perceived, but also to underwrite new responsibilities, including those inherited from federal mandates and local demands. Ultimately, the financing of local education and new federal mandates such as Medicaid and the simultaneous desire to provide indirect local property tax relief placed great strain on state treasuries. When the stagflation of the early 1970s arrested the postwar economic boom and the growth in subnational tax collections, the calls for property tax relief became more strident. A newly invigorated anti-tax movement gained momentum, culminating in the property tax revolts of the late 1970s and early 1980s. This not only institutionalized limits on property tax increases, but also marked the start of a broader anti-tax movement that continued into the twenty-first century.

In the postwar decades, economic prosperity fueled the explosive growth in tax revenues. From 1946 to 1974, real U.S. gross domestic product (GDP) increased at an average rate of 3.3 percent, and government tax receipts grew accordingly, leading many scholars to characterize this period as an Era of Easy Finance. Subnational taxes, which accounted for a significant portion of the growth in total government tax receipts, rose from roughly 6 percent of GDP in 1954 to nearly 10 percent by 1972. Given the generally positive economic conditions, it is not surprising that state income taxes became an increasingly important source of revenue. But income taxes were only part of the incredible expansion in tax collections. Sales tax revenue also grew steadily during this period, as increased consumption followed economic growth. States not only increased rates, but also enacted new levies. Those that historically relied on income taxes such as Wisconsin, New York, and Massachusetts turned to sales taxes to bolster their treasuries. Conversely, states that already had sales taxes added income taxes to their fiscal mix. Overall, between 1961 and 1976, ten states adopted new sales taxes and eleven states adopted new income taxes.[70] With real incomes rising and American consumer culture taking hold, tax revenues flourished.[71]

Still, governors needed justifications for their desire to create new taxes and to raise existing ones. State executives relied on a variety of explanations. For many, claims of fiscal insolvency or crisis and the desire to provide local property tax relief by aiding municipalities proved instrumental. Demographic pressures and tentative civil rights reforms increased the demands for public education, and states responded by taking a greater role in funding education. This, in turn, provided local property owners with indirect tax relief but also placed increased pressure upon state treasuries. A perceived fiscal tightening and demands for increased educational spending, for example, compelled Massachusetts Governor John Volpe to enact a three percent sales tax in 1966, the first time that the Bay State was able to establish such a levy since the state commission first suggested it in 1935. Although Volpe's claims of pending financial ruin proved to be exaggerated, the perceived crisis was vital in expanding the Massachusetts budget and enacting a levy to support increased educational spending. The wide margin of voter approval for the sales tax and Volpe's reelection suggested, furthermore, that tax increases were not always harbingers of political defeat.[72]

In 1968, New Jersey Governor Richard Hughes responded to similar pressure by underscoring the need for his state to create more sustainable sources of revenue. Stumping for a progressive income tax increase, Hughes decried the ways in which he and others had previously evaded fundamental tax reform. "Like you," Hughes told his legislature, "I dislike taxes of any kind and, if such a thing were possible, might prefer to go on from year to year, stringing the beads and balancing the mirrors, a little excise boost here and a little gimmick here. But we have seen with our own eyes, in our political lifetimes, the result of such equivocation."[73]

By the mid-1960s, governors had also revived the call for revenue sharing first voiced by Governor Rivers in the early 1940s. Federal grants-in-aid had been a mainstay of subnational public finance since the 1950s, but governors now demanded general, "no-strings-attached" federal assistance that had providentially garnered the support of influential economists and federal politicians. Walter W. Heller, the chairman of the Council of Economic Advisers, told the Governors' Conference in 1965 that because of the "fiscal mismatch" between the federal and subnational budgets, "state and local governments have a commanding case for stronger federal financial support."[74] New York Governor Nelson Rockefeller also lent critical support, lobbying fellow Republican governors, assuaging the skepticism of municipal leaders such as New York's John Lindsay, and then taking his case aggressively to the Nixon White House.[75] The Nixon Administration enacted the State and Local Fiscal Assistance Act in 1972, which established a fixed disbursement of roughly $6 billion a year for states and localities. As state budgets grew, this figure was overshadowed by specific purpose federal grants-in-aid. And when budget woes began to hit Washington in the late 1970s and early 1980s, national lawmakers eliminated this general revenue sharing program.[76]

During the early 1970s, governors also urged federal support for subnational property tax reduction, as a means to more equitable education funding. Yet, while governors lent almost unanimous support to the general idea, they did not always agree on the form of such aid. In 1972, President Nixon's newly created Commission on School Financing recommended the abolition of the property tax and the use of a national European style Value Added Tax (VAT) to finance local education improvements. The VAT would be applied mainly to businesses in the form of a levy for the value added at each stage of production, but its ultimate incidence would likely fall on consumers. Viewing the VAT as a variant of sales taxes, state officials vociferously opposed the plan. The U.S. Advisory Commission on Intergovernmental Relations (ACIR), a bipartisan agency charged with examining the federal government's relationships with state and local government, also weighed in, using public opinion surveys and other data to oppose the proposal. The National Governors' Conference denounced the plan as a federal attempt to seize complete control of the sales tax. At the same time, governors could not ignore the potentially discriminatory connection between property taxes and local school financing. What they wanted was federal aid to reduce their reliance on the property tax, without having to give in to a national sales tax. Along with lingering opposition to the regressive character of any consumption tax, American fiscal federalism played a critical role, yet again, in defeating the proposal for a national sales tax.[77]

The biggest tax policy story of the 1970s, however, was one that originated not with governors or in the nation's statehouses but with a municipal tax reform movement that had broad implications for American politics. While the vagaries and inequities of the property tax had been political fodder for much of the twentieth century, a full-scale property tax rebellion emerged first in California, gradually in the late 1950s and 1960s and then with explosive force in the late 1970s. A confluence of historical factors contributed to this watershed moment in American tax history. First, a California real estate boom and dramatically increased property values awakened citizens there to the otherwise hidden evils and outmoded character of the property tax. In 1957, 30 to 50 percent property tax increases in California's San Gabriel Valley led to one of the nation's first rallies against the property tax, culminating in a mass meeting at the Los Angeles Coliseum attended by more than 6,000 homeowners. In 1965, a series of articles on the corrupt system of California property tax assessment, published by the *San Francisco Chronicle*, led to jail sentences for some municipal tax assessors and to the passage of the Petris-Knox Act, legislation which sharply limited the discretion of Golden State tax assessors. In the wake of the *Chronicle* expose, the San Diego assessor committed suicide. Protests there, and in Massachusetts in 1973, under the auspices of a group calling itself Massachusetts Fair Share, illustrated the rising tide of property tax rebellion that seemed evident throughout the country.[78]

Climbing property taxes tapped into the growing resentment of government power. This second factor had deep historical roots that stretched beyond taxes. By the 1970s, the popular faith in government that had largely been maintained in the postwar era had begun to recede. The Watergate scandal and rising inflation encouraged widespread antigovernment sentiment. Anti-tax advocates came to be portrayed, as a result, as populist crusaders defending individual interests against a bloated and misguided state bureaucracy.

Third, and perhaps most important, post–World War II demographic trends, particularly increased suburbanization, created a new electoral constituency of political moderates who identified with local, property-centered movements. Situated in places where they could ignore the problems of industrial cities and where large-scale, universal government programs could more easily be taken for granted, this new group of suburban warriors became wedded to low taxes and limited government services.[79]

These three factors combined to create the conditions that underpinned the success of Proposition 13, California's landmark constitutional amendment. The new rule capped property tax increases, constrained the reassessment process, and required a super-majority of the legislature for other tax increases. Although the amendment was aimed mainly at local property taxes, it also targeted state government. Despite Governor Jerry Brown's initial resistance to the measure, many critics claimed that he had done much to encourage the revolt. For Brown not only railed against big government, he also touted the inflation-induced state surplus as a mark of his fiscal conservatism. And when the ballot initiative passed by a magnitude of two to one, Brown readily embraced the tax revolt movement and its conservative leader, Harold Jarvis, riding the tax rebellion wave into a reelection victory.[80]

To be sure, there was nothing natural or inevitable about the particular contours of the California property tax revolt. California had several viable policy choices other than Proposition 13's draconian limits.[81] Property tax circuit breakers, for example, providing tax relief for certain lower income, retired, or disabled citizens came to be adopted by a majority of states in the 1970s and 1980s. By 1991 they had been adopted in thirty-five states.[82] Indeed, during the early stages of the California property tax revolt, circuit breaker proposals were a popular choice among progressive reformers. But the political power and perseverance of conservative proponents of Proposition 13's dramatic constraints eventually won the day, and in the process they ignited a broader anti-tax movement. Within a decade, sixteen other states had followed California's lead, with many of them taking their cues from Proposition 13. This tax revolt wave helped carry Ronald Reagan into the White House, and for many critics it signaled the end of the government activism that was the hallmark of New Deal liberalism.[83]

In its wake, this movement encouraged the devolution of authority to states and localities even as it placed new limits on their taxing authority. As a result, state-level tax reformers appeared to have less latitude for change than ever before. The increasing globalization of the economy, furthermore, added pressure on states to engage in the age-old practice of interstate tax competition, using their tax codes to lure and keep capital within their jurisdictions. As the labor leader John Sweeney noted at the National Governors' Association's 1984 annual meeting, states were engaged in "smokestack chasing," hoping to recruit industries battered by diminished markets (and more than a few supply shocks) by offering reduced corporate income tax rates.[84] Likewise, as the increasing prominence of the Internet has come to place increasing pressure on state sales tax revenue, governors and other state policymakers have clearly taken notice. In the era of globalization and electronic commerce, the interstate competition fostered by fiscal federalism seems to be more pronounced than ever.

During times of economic prosperity, states attempted progressive reforms, but many had learned how to exploit their heterogeneous tax base to limit political fallout from tax changes. As state and federal revenues mounted during the economic boom of the late 1990s, thirty states cut income taxes at greater levels than sales or excise taxes, while twenty

went in the other direction. Even more significantly, of the twenty-four
states whose income tax codes did not exempt families below the Federal Poverty Line at the beginning of the 1990s, twenty-three moved to
raise their income tax thresholds between 1991 and 2000. When economic fortunes declined in 2001 and beyond, and states moved to plug
revenue gaps, twenty-eight states raised sales and excise taxes at greater
levels than income taxes. In dollar amounts, the imbalance was even
more striking. Of the total net state tax increases in 2002 and 2003,
regressive consumption taxes comprised 54 percent while income taxes
comprised a mere 18 percent.[85] State officials had learned the political
benefits of less visible forms of taxation.

Still, some governors attempted to use tax policy not only to raise
much needed revenue, but to do so in an equitable manner. When Alabama Governor Bob Riley asked his constituents to look beyond the
state's considerable revenue problem in 2003 and to tackle problems of
equity first and foremost, he was fighting a strong popular impulse. Well
known as a conservative Christian, Riley had been persuaded to pursue
a more progressive tax code in the name of Christian morality, despite
the obvious political obstacles. "According to our Christian ethics," he
declared, "we're supposed to love God, love each other, and help take
care of the poor. It is immoral to charge somebody making $5,000 an
income tax."[86] Guided by Alabama law professor Susan Pace Hamill,
who had written widely on Judeo-Christian ethics and tax reform, and
by former congressional colleague Bobby Etheridge, a one-time North
Carolina school superintendent, Riley launched his crusade.[87]

To achieve this kind of reform, he proposed raising the income tax
threshold from $4,600 to $17,000, eliminating the full deduction for federal taxes paid, and raising the top income tax rate to 6 percent from 5
percent.[88] Alabama was also one of the few remaining states with a state
property tax, a rather unique variant in which timberland, comprising
approximately 70 percent of the state's landmass, was subject to an
exceptionally low rate classification locked into the state constitution. To
make wealthy Alabama landowners pay their fair share, Riley also proposed raising the state's property taxes. Yet, while Alabama timber bar-
ons would certainly have paid more under the Riley proposal, the same
proposal—relative to income—would have taxed working class homeowners at an even higher rate. "Our property taxes could go up as much
as fo' hundred percent," exclaimed the voice in a prominent radio ad
sponsored by the state's largest bank, a leading insurance company, two
timber and paper companies, and county farmers federations.[89] As the
contradiction became increasingly obvious, reform became far less
likely. In the 2003 referendum, 68 percent voted to reject the plan.[90]
When Riley returned in 2006, however, with a proposal that focused

exclusively on the state's low income tax threshold, he signed into law the state's first change in that category since 1935, raising the threshold from $4,600 to $12,500.[91]

As American governors surveyed their tax systems in the early twenty-first century, several began to launch modest reform efforts similar to Bob Riley's in Alabama. In 2007, Arkansas Governor Mike Beebe and Hawaii Governor Linda Lingle both proposed to join seven other states that had recently reduced sales taxes on groceries. "No one should be taxed for buying basic food necessities," noted Lingle.[92] Utah and Louisiana moved to eliminate or decrease itemized deductions exploited chiefly by their wealthiest taxpayers. Proposals to introduce personal and corporate income taxes in Tennessee and Washington—where none existed—both failed but also garnered closer consideration than ever before.

At the same time, regressive consumption taxes still account for a dominant share of the nation's state tax revenues. Despite trends indicating increases in interstate commerce and purchases of nontaxable services and the nearly complete nontaxation of remote sales (e.g., from the Internet and catalogs), states continued to collect significant sales taxes.[93] The Streamlined Sales Tax Project (SSTP), organized in March 2000 and designed to simplify rates and adopt uniform definitions of exempt and nonexempt items, was an ambitious attempt to mitigate some of these emerging challenges to sales taxes.[94] By 2007, fifteen states had signed on as full members of the SSTP, another seven had become associate members, and most of the other twenty-three states with sales taxes had joined the project as observers. Few states, however, moved to lessen their reliance on the sales tax, despite the rising difficulties. Instead, they frequently raised their sales tax rates to combat the challenges of taxing remote purchases. In 1970 the average state sales tax rate was 3.5 percent; by 2003 it had risen to 5.2 percent.[95]

Regressive fees and surcharges, highway tolls, and increased excise taxes have also become more common components in the nation's state tax codes, and, since 1979, the share of total state taxes contributed by the corporate income tax has declined steadily in all but three states: Delaware, Indiana, and West Virginia. Rigid supermajority requirements for tax increases prevail in sixteen states, and revenue limits have been written into the codes or constitutions of seven others. Unfunded federal mandates, steadily rising health care costs, and increased state aid to localities mark a system of fiscal federalism that makes sound state tax policymaking inherently difficult. Against this backdrop, American governors still preside over tax systems that collect approximately one half of the nation's revenues and their tax policy experiments have great bearing on the fate and trajectory of the nation's economy.[96]

Conclusion

Despite tremendous variation among states, efforts to balance equity and expediency within the institutional constraints of American fiscal federalism have significantly shaped the general development of twentieth-century state tax policies. From the Progressive Era to the present, governors and state lawmakers, in their constant search for revenue, have attempted to navigate between these two salient features of state taxation. On one side, their actions have been influenced by the institutional design of American governance. The decentralized, multilayered structure of American political power has fostered tax competition among states, and between states and the federal government. States and commonwealths thus have not only used tax policy to lure capital and jobs from other jurisdictions, they have also affected and been affected by national and local authority. In some cases, innovative states such as Wisconsin during the early decades of the century have served as quintessential laboratories of reform, testing new tax laws that other states and even the federal government have subsequently adopted. At other times, states and their leaders have exploited their fiscal autonomy to block fundamental tax reform.

The perennial search for revenue and the tradeoff between equitable and expedient tax sources had an equally important impact on the development of state tax laws and policies. At the turn of the twentieth century, when states and localities shared the general property tax as a principal source of revenue, tax reformers advocated the separation of sources, which not only relegated property taxes to localities but also hastened the state-level search for alternative tax bases. Initially, some states responded with the enactment of income taxes as a substitute for the dysfunctional taxes on personal property. But during the economic crisis of the Great Depression, when governors were forced to make more strategic choices, consumption taxes soon became a prominent revenue source. By 1950, the much maligned property tax had been left mainly to municipalities and counties, as states and commonwealths came to rely upon a mix of income and consumption taxes and upon increasing transfers from the federal government.

Amid a post–World War II economic boom that fueled incredible growth in subnational tax revenue, this intergovernmental division of fiscal sources proved increasingly resistant to change. Yet, while the discontent with the property tax may have subsided in the early stages of this period, it did not disappear. Displeasure with property taxes came to a head in the 1970s, when the emergence of stagflation triggered a shrill and nearly national property tax rebellion. Although there was nothing inexorable about how this revolt would be resolved, the growing public distrust of government and other structural changes during this period pushed property tax reform increasingly toward politically conservative anti-statist solutions, including California's Proposition 13, which severely limited the ability of state and local officials to raise revenue. Ultimately, the property tax revolts of the 1970s were politically pivotal, as they ushered in a new era of anti-tax popular sentiment. Together with recent legal constraints, this popular resentment of taxation continues to color state-level fiscal debates. While effective gubernatorial leadership remains critical for tax reform, the constraints of fiscal federalism, the convenience of the least visible and often most regressive tax vehicles, and the endurance of broad anti-tax sentiment, continue to exert significant pressure on state officials.

Chapter 3

Governors and the Development of American Social Policy

RON HASKINS

The history of welfare policy in the United States is in large part a story of the shift of responsibility for the health and well-being of Americans from families and local community organizations to government and from local and state government to the federal government. This process has occurred in fits and starts, and the division of responsibility between the public and private sector and between levels of government varies from program to program. Even so, the federal government has become the dominant force in policymaking and in financing the nation's social programs.[1] In this chapter, I trace this shift, and especially the dramatic last step in the welfare reform battle of 1995–1996 during which governors made a spirited and partially successful attempt to regain control of several major social programs.

These developments in social policy were shaped by powerful historical forces. Perhaps the broadest factor conditioning welfare policy after World War II was that the American economy grew relentlessly and produced goods and services beyond anything experienced by any previous society. Today, an American household in the middle of the income distribution typically owns a house, at least one car, several color television sets, radios, a DVD or VCR player, air conditioning, a computer, many appliances including a refrigerator and a washer and dryer, and clothes in style with current trends. There is, in short, a lot of stuff to divide up, and even the poor have goods that the middle class in previous generations did not enjoy.[2]

Perhaps this affluence, extending even to the poor, accounts for a second major condition surrounding American social policymaking. Decisions about specific policies, how they would be financed, and how they would be implemented were made with very little participation by the poor. With a few minor exceptions, America lacks a continuous tradition of a successful socialist party.[3] Thus, the debate about welfare policy in the United States has been between elites and has mostly taken place without organized lobbying—let alone threats of violence—from the poor themselves.[4] Rising affluence and the inherent strength of the American democratic system may have played a role in creating a national debate over the poor that seldom included their direct participation. Closely related to this lack of influence from the bottom of society is the fact that until around the late 1960s the thirteen states of the old Confederacy, whose representatives and senators usually exerted disproportionate control in Congress, were not democracies because racism and various "legal" strictures disenfranchised millions of blacks. Indeed, one of the few episodes in American history in which the poor played a direct role in politics was the overthrow of Jim Crow laws and the revolution in black power in the South and throughout the nation.

Another background factor, and one with a long and colorful history, has been the ongoing struggle between conservatives, who want to limit government and government spending while maintaining a minimalist welfare state, and liberals, who want to expand the role of government and especially the federal government while ensuring that individuals and families are protected against the hazards and risks of life. Much of the research, writing, and political activism connected with American social policy can be viewed as falling along a continuum that, moving from right to left, extends from a minimalist welfare state that would have government intervening only in emergencies all the way to a full-blown welfare state with programs, mostly federal, that would provide guaranteed benefits to cover the major—as Roosevelt called them in his message that accompanied the Social Security Act—"vicissitudes" of life.[5] Roughly speaking, Democrats tend toward the left end of this continuum and Republicans toward the right, although there are striking exceptions, such as the 2002 Republican initiative to spend $1.2 trillion over ten years on a prescription drug benefit for the elderly. Even in this case, however, prominent Democrats such as Senator Ted Kennedy criticized Republicans for not making the benefit generous enough and for retaining too little federal control over the benefit.

The battle over the division of responsibility for social programs between states and the federal government unfolded over the entire twentieth century, but four periods were particularly important. First, before the Social Security Act of 1935, states developed policies to counteract the individual risks created by industrialization and urbanization. Second, the Social Security Act of 1935 transformed—in a sense, reversed—the roles of the states and the federal government in social welfare. Third, the War on Poverty of the 1960s was the low point in state and gubernatorial authority in social welfare policymaking. Finally, the

1996 welfare reform legislation, in response to the initiatives of governors, returned some measure of autonomy over social policy to the states.

Social Welfare Policy Before 1935

Before the Social Security Act of 1935, families and local organizations had major responsibility for caring for the elderly, sick, and destitute. Five public policies, though fairly modest in scope, were instituted during this early period.[6] The first and most sweeping were pensions for Civil War veterans and their families. Both the federal government and most state governments funded various policies to help veterans and their families. The federal pensions were generous, extensive, and expensive, but as veterans began to disappear, so did veterans' benefits.[7] The second policy was workman's compensation, an all but exclusive domain then and now of state government, which provided cash income and medical care to workers injured on the job.[8] The third was labor regulations for women, including both limitations on hours of work and minimum wage laws, again the exclusive domain of states.[9]

The fourth public policy was the federal Sheppard-Towner Act of 1921. Passed by Congress at the instigation of the federal Children's Bureau and of influential women's groups at the local, state, and national level who lobbied on behalf of the legislation, Sheppard-Towner provided matching funds to states to establish programs to teach mothers about maternal and child hygiene. It is notable that the women who fought for Sheppard-Towner envisioned public clinics that would provide advice about care without a means test. In accord with this vision, all but three states had established programs by the late 1920s. In a turn of events that the women's groups and many others considered most unfortunate, the American Medical Association—whose House of Delegates officially proclaimed Sheppard-Towner to be a "socialistic scheme"[10]—lobbied successfully to not reauthorize the federal legislation in 1929. Even so, the premature death of Sheppard-Towner and its clinics did not obviate the fact that states had established a short but lively tradition of providing public help to mothers and infants to improve their health, a capacity which states would soon have the opportunity to use again.

Finally, and perhaps most important, nearly every state enacted mothers' pensions to provide benefits to widows—and, more grudgingly, to other single mothers—so they could stay home to rear their children. These programs, first enacted by Illinois in 1911 and then spreading to forty states before the 1930s,[11] allowed local jurisdictions to establish programs of cash assistance for poor single mothers. The characteristics of these pensions would greatly influence future social policy. First, the benefit was means-tested, providing support only for single mothers in financial need. As other industrialized nations established universal programs providing cash grants to all families with children, these American programs appeared unique. Second, each state established its own program leading to great variety rather than a single national set of requirements and benefits. Third, although the major purpose of the benefit was to allow single mothers to stay home with their children, the benefit was not given to all single mothers. At first the benefit was given primarily to widows who had been left destitute. Subsequently, although the exact qualifications varied from state to state, nearly every state allowed other single mothers to receive the benefit. In some states this included divorced mothers, deserted mothers, and mothers who had babies outside marriage. However, states did require the mothers to establish homes that conformed to community standards, thereby necessitating home visits and interviews by social workers or other officials to make judgments about whether the mother was providing an environment fit for rearing children. This concept of a "suitable home" environment was to have enormous consequences for future welfare programs.[12]

Thus, even before the Social Security Act, there was a surprising and often overlooked period of policy development that would influence the shape of national social welfare policy after 1935. With the exception of veterans' pensions, this period was the golden age of state-dominated federalism in social policy. It was also an era of extensive family responsibility for relatives and of reliance on private, community-based charities.[13]

The Social Security Act

The golden age of state control of social policy ended with passage of the Social Security Act of 1935. This revolutionary piece of legislation— still the centerpiece of American social policy—initiated a process of formalizing and expanding social programs and supplementing or, frequently, replacing state and local control with federal control. State and local governments remained important, but the federal government, formerly a bit player, now entered the field with flags flying.[14]

The Social Security Act featured several distinct types of programs, which in either their original or substantially revised and expanded form today constitute the bulk of American social policy. The Social Security Act, in a sense, opened the floodgates holding back a sea of social policies and spending. The 1935 act contained provisions for several programs that today would be called welfare because they provided benefits on the basis of means-testing and without any contributions by recipients. Welfare programs for adults included the Old Age Assistance program for the elderly and welfare programs for the disabled and the blind. In addition, Title IV of the act established the nation's leading welfare program for mothers and children, the Aid to Dependent Children program (later the Aid to Families with Dependent Children or AFDC program). All of these provisions offered states federal matching funds to establish programs that would give cash benefits to, respectively, the elderly, the blind, the disabled, and destitute children (and their mothers).

In 1935 it was widely believed that the Old Age Assistance program was the most important program in the entire act. However, this program became largely irrelevant as the retirement insurance program, established in Title II of the act, expanded to more and more people with bigger and bigger benefits. Today, the insurance benefit of Title II, usually referred to simply as "Social Security," stands as the nation's biggest social program and in almost every respect is the most important social program in American history. One effect of the growth of Social Security was to transfer control of cash benefits for the elderly from a partnership between the state and federal governments represented by the Old Age Assistance program to the exclusively federal benefit represented by Social Security. In effect, the role of states in providing cash assistance to the elderly was greatly reduced, leaving the field primarily to the federal government.

The categorical programs for the blind, the disabled, and children, all of which were partnerships between the federal government and the states, have had a longer and more important half-life than the Old Age Assistance program. The programs for the blind and disabled survived and grew for more than three decades until meeting the same fate as the Old Age Assistance program; namely, death by federal intervention. In this case, Congress enacted legislation in 1972 that created the Supplemental Security Income program. This progam replaced the state-operated programs for the blind and disabled with a universal program, providing benefits that were higher than those provided by most state programs and financed entirely out of federal general revenues, for all disabled and elderly people who met a means test. Moreover, the new program was administered by the federal Social Security Administration, thereby virtually cutting states out of the action.[15]

The federal-state Aid to Families with Dependent Children program survived even longer until it was replaced by the Temporary Assistance for Needy Families program in 1996, a historic event to which I will devote careful attention below. Over the years, a host of important welfare programs—including programs to force fathers to pay child support, to provide support for abused and neglected children, to provide medical benefits to mothers, children, and especially the elderly, and to provide social services to needy families—were added to the Social Security Act.

Yet another provision in the original Social Security Act created the Unemployment Compensation program, which provides a cash benefit to certain unemployed workers.[16] Like Social Security, the unemployment benefits are based on insurance principles, in this case taxes paid into trust funds by employers (and, implicitly, employees).[17] Though amended many times, Unemployment Compensation is still the nation's major program designed to replace the wages of unemployed workers.

The final program, mentioned briefly above, is the Social Security retirement benefit established by Title II.[18] This component, which has become the centerpiece of American social policy, made the federal government the source of security for life's greatest vicissitude, namely old age—a stage that increasing millions of Americans have come to occupy and for longer than in the past. Over the years, a series of presidents and Congresses helped many branches grow from this mighty oak. These include survivors' benefits in 1950, disability insurance in 1956, Medicare health insurance for the elderly in 1965, and a prescription drug benefit for the elderly in 2002. All these programs followed the Roosevelt playbook in that they were based, at least in part, on insurance principles, were predominantly self-financed by dedicated trust funds maintained by the federal government, and most important for our purposes, were controlled by the federal government.

The Social Security Act, both in 1935 and today, embodies what are still two of the major fault lines in American social policy: welfare versus insurance and federal versus state control. Broadly, the nation has two types of social programs: insurance programs that are based on the principle of beneficiary contributions and welfare programs in which the destitute—or at least those with low income—receive benefits based on largesse rather than insurance. By definition, the insurance programs provide benefits that are earned and are mostly paid to people who are not expected by the public to work—the elderly, the disabled, and workers temporarily unemployed.[19] Welfare, by contrast, is not based on work. Indeed, it is often provided precisely because people do not work.

It was Roosevelt's intention to establish Social Security retirement as a universal program that did not require a means test. Many New Dealers lived by the motto that poverty programs are poor programs. Thus, Social Security old age benefits, survivors' benefits, disability insurance, and Medicare are all based in part on the insurance principle, although the details of the trust funds for these programs differ. Of course, especially for its first half century or so, Social Security retirement benefits themselves were unlike insurance because beneficiaries received far more from the system than they had paid in (even if a reasonable rate of interest is added to the investment amount) and because lower-income earners, as a percentage of their tax payments into the system, get relatively more back in benefits than higher-income earners. All of these insurance programs are hugely popular and are not seen by the public as welfare, no matter what the facts of financing or of the exact relationship between contributions and benefits might be.

By contrast, welfare programs require a means test and are not based on previous contributions. In a distinction of immense importance to Americans, insurance benefits are earned; welfare benefits are not. In its wisdom, as early as 1935 the federal government claimed the former type of program almost entirely for federal control and administration and shared the latter with the states and localities. This fact raises the second fault line in the nation's social policy, federalism. Since 1935, the states and the federal government, with some participation by local governments, have conducted an elaborate Kabuki dance in which the federal government sometimes plays the lead and state or local governments sometimes play the lead. Federal control over insurance programs, first established in 1935, completely cut the governors out of the action, with the modest and partial exception of Unemployment Compensation.[20] The irony of this outcome is that the major ideas for both retirement benefits and unemployment insurance had been developed by the states before the federal government was involved with these programs. Indeed, deepening the irony, Roosevelt's legislation was written by the Committee on Economic Security, whose staff was headed by Edwin Witte,[21] a professor from the University of Wisconsin. Witte, who split his time between working in government and doing research and teaching, is a brilliant example of the value of experience in both scholarship and government service. Along with his colleagues at the University of Wisconsin, he designed Wisconsin's 1932 unemployment insurance program, the nation's first unemployment insurance program to be adopted by a state legislature. He subsequently joined the Roosevelt administration, where he played a direct role in developing the nation's unemployment insurance program that was then adopted as part of the Social Security Act in 1935. Witte's work shows yet again that many important ideas and programs were first conceived and implemented at the state level, paving the way for federal legislation at a later date.

The War on Poverty

If the Social Security Act of 1935 expanded the federal role in the nation's social policy, the War on Poverty of the mid-1960s solidified and extended the federal role. The War on Poverty had roots in the administration of President John Kennedy but was fully developed under President Lyndon Johnson. Johnson's proposals were enacted by Congress and implemented at a time of immense national fervor over civil rights. The fight against poverty was one that Johnson himself largely initiated, while the fight against racism blasted up from a host of local racial conflicts that, thanks to television, forced average Americans to face the ugly fact that the nation's historical claims of fairness and opportunity were false for a large segment of the population. In the midst of this growing antipathy between whites and blacks in the South and soul searching by the rest of the nation, Johnson initiated his War on Poverty. He cajoled Sargent Shriver, a member of the Kennedy family (he was married to President Kennedy's sister, Eunice) and an accomplished Washington operator who was already heading the immensely popular Peace Corps, into leading the effort to pass legislation and implement the War on Poverty. Shriver developed the programs by hiring and empowering a group of brilliant and tireless intellectuals, many with Washington experience, and by enlisting many others from federal agencies, with very little consultation with Congress or the governors.[22] Indeed, it was assumed from the beginning that the programs would have to be federal because so many of the southern governors and governments were racist and could not be counted on to faithfully implement anti-poverty programs which were, after all, aimed disproportionately at helping blacks. Shriver was a one-man army as he supervised the hatching of ideas, converted them to legislative proposals, and sold them to a skeptical Congress and public.[23]

Although the War on Poverty created many programs and a new federal agency (the Office of Economic Opportunity), perhaps the best known programs are Head Start, the Legal Services Corporation, the Job Corps, VISTA, and the Community Action Program, all of which are still operating.[24] These programs required virtually no involvement by governors. Head Start, a preschool program designed explicitly to avoid control by state or local government because of fear of racism, provided federal funding directly to local sponsoring organizations, often churches and local private entities created specifically to receive the Head Start money and design and run the programs.[25] In this way, the federal government created important and well-funded private agencies in the midst of many jurisdictions that would gladly have killed Head Start were it not for the federal support. Head Start is now a $7 billion program serving about 900,000 preschool children each year, and it is still usually operated at the local level by federally funded independent agencies. Although the public schools, largely controlled by local and state governments, operate a little less than one-fifth of Head Start programs, all must follow extensive federal regulations about administration and classroom quality. Similarly, the Job Corps, VISTA, and the Legal Services Corporation are directly controlled and operated by the federal government with virtually no role for state or local government.

The Community Action Program (CAP) provides an interesting example of how federal authority can sometimes impose unexpected burdens on local and state government. Shriver and many of the War on Poverty planners considered CAP to be the most important program in the War on Poverty.[26] The primary goal of CAP was to give the poor and minorities a voice in decisionmaking in their local communities, a voice that they sorely lacked. Shriver and his planners intended to give money to local organizations—YMCAs, educational, or other civic and non-profit organizations—that would then decide how best to spend the money to address poverty at the local level. They would also administer the funds, thereby giving these local organizations complete control over planning and implementing the programs. In many locations around the nation, the CAP became associated with stentorian complaints and agitation, usually directed at local officials and government agencies, about voting rights, discrimination, and many other long-festering issues. From the perspective of mayors, county commissioners, and other local and state officials, this new and often strident voice was at best a nuisance and at worst a threat to their political power—which of course was precisely the point. Senator Daniel Patrick Moynihan of New York, who was involved in administering programs at the Department of Labor during the initial days of the War on Poverty, wrote a scathing criticism of CAPs because they engendered so much controversy and conflict.[27] The point for my purposes is that states and localities did not especially want this controversy, but got it anyway because the federal government decided, almost entirely without consulting states and localities, that the poor actually did need a voice at the local level. The poor may well have needed more of a voice but in giving them one the federal government offended local and state authorities throughout the nation.

Finally, although not usually considered part of the War on Poverty, the Food Stamps program was enacted in 1964.[28] It had existed previously as a pilot program, but the 1964 legislation was the single most important law in creating the modern Food Stamps program. Food Stamps now provides beneficiaries with a debit card that can be used only for food purchases. Featuring benefits that are paid entirely by the federal government (the federal government and the states split the cost of administration), the program is the only federal or state welfare program that offers benefits to everyone below an income cutoff level—including men and women; single, married, never-married, separated, and divorced; children, adults, and the elderly.[29] Over time, Food

Stamps has become a welfare program run by states but within tight guidelines established by the federal government. At $35 billion in 2007, Food Stamps has also become one of the largest welfare programs.

The Welfare Reform Law of 1996

Perhaps in large measure because states had been losing control of social policy and programs to the federal government, the congressional battle over welfare reform of the mid-1990s saw a kind of counterrevolution on the part of governors.[30] A series of conditions prevailed in the mid-1990s that facilitated a major transformation in national social policy. After the congressional elections of 1994, the media and pundits focused attention primarily on Republican capture of the House of Representatives for the first time in four decades and on Republican capture of the Senate. But equally important, Republican governors had also scored major victories, capturing ten new governorships, bringing the total number of Republican governors to thirty, including the governorships of all the most populous states except Florida. The influence of governors on the formulation of social policy over the next two years was probably greater than at any time in the twentieth century. Governors, however, did not emerge as important players in welfare policy overnight; instead, the path to the 1990s welfare reform was blazed by reform efforts initiated within the states as early as the 1980s.

This movement had an inauspicious beginning with the Work Incentive (WIN) program enacted under President Ronald Reagan in 1981. Among other provisions designed to encourage work, the legislation authorized the WIN Demonstration program which gave states expanded authority to experiment with work-based reforms. Reagan was so serious about state demonstration programs on work that he sent a senior staffer named Chuck Hobbs to meet with governors in several states and personally encourage them to implement reforms. Not least because of Hobbs's ability to sell the importance of welfare demonstrations to governors and other state officials, many states took advantage of the opportunity to conduct welfare reform studies. But Wisconsin, primarily under Governor Tommy Thompson, was clearly the leader in conducting welfare demonstrations. Like other states, Wisconsin had struggled with rapidly increasing caseloads in the late 1960s and 1970s. The expanding welfare caseload was a special problem for Wisconsin because the state had high AFDC benefit levels, and because the benefits seemed to be attracting welfare recipients from other states.[31] The increase in welfare rolls, combined with Wisconsin's high payment level, put a serious strain on the state budget. As a result, legislators were focused on welfare reform by the 1970s. Early reforms included a state

Earned Income Tax Credit (EITC) and fundamental reforms of the child support enforcement program. The child support reforms eventually served as a model for national reform in both 1984 and 1988, illustrating again the tendency for social policy innovations to originate in states and then be adopted at the national level.

In 1986, just before Tommy Thompson was elected governor, Wisconsin enacted a reform program called Work Experience and Job Training. The program featured both education and training as well as more aggressive case management in helping recipients find jobs. But the most innovative feature of the legislation was a work program. Welfare recipients who did not find jobs, despite assistance from their case manager, could be assigned to work. It could be argued that this reform, expanded and studied in various guises over the next decade, was the seedling that grew into the sweeping federal welfare reform law of 1996.

The 1986 Wisconsin legislation, which was at first implemented in only a few counties, set the stage for Thompson's innovative administration. Upon taking office in 1987, he initiated a dizzying series of reforms based on waivers. At the time, it was rumored in Washington that Thompson, lobbying for his latest waiver, saw the secretary of Health and Human Services more than the secretary saw his wife. Thompson obtained waivers to experiment with ways to increase marriage rates, discourage nonmarital births, increase work incentives, and achieve a host of other goals. But in the end, he and his staff concentrated their efforts on mandatory work, proposing and implementing ever stronger work requirements. In 1993 Thompson asked the new Clinton administration to grant waivers for a program called Work Not Welfare. This program, which Thompson claimed was the first program to "absolutely require welfare recipients to find work," featured both mandatory work tests and time limits on the receipt of welfare benefits.[32] These features found their way into the 1996 federal reforms and were considered by all sides to be among the most dramatic and controversial features of the 1996 federal law.

This series of reforms, and Wisconsin's success in reducing its welfare caseload without increasing child poverty, became well known in Washington and the states. Encouraged by the Wisconsin example, nearly every state eventually conducted welfare waiver experiments. Thompson, in addition to chairing a task force on welfare reform of the National Governors Association (NGA), often testified before Congress.[33] Equally important, his county welfare staffers who actually implemented the reforms, most of whom were Democrats, testified before various congressional committees and compellingly expressed their enthusiasm for the work-based reforms. In addition, they brought data on the results of their programs, especially findings showing decreased welfare rolls and increased job placements.[34] There were also numerous articles in the national media about Thompson's reforms.[35]

As the Wisconsin reforms were building up steam in the mid-1980s, congressional Democrats began considering welfare legislation that was consistent with the emphasis on work being pushed by the Reagan administration in the states. Not since the era of the Works Progress Administration and the strong pro-work views of President Roosevelt had work occupied such a central position in Democratic proposals. Of course, Democrats were also committed to expanding welfare and included provisions in their 1987 bill, the Family Support Act, that required every state to offer AFDC to qualifying married parents if one parent was unemployed. Democrats also included about $1 billion in the law for states to provide education and training and other job-related services, as well as a child care entitlement to certain mothers on welfare, and significantly strengthened the child support enforcement program, not least by making more money available to states to expand their efforts to collect support and by imposing strong mandates on states to adopt specific child support policies. Although the actual provisions on work in the Family Support Act were modest, the rhetoric was unmistakably pro-work. Congress passed the Act with bipartisan backing in 1988.

Two additional factors associated with the Family Support Act turned out to be propitious. The first was a set of provisions on participation standards that House Republicans had managed to add to the legislation. Although the participation standards were weak, they established the precedent that a state could be required to place a certain percentage of its welfare caseload in work-related activities or receive a financial sanction. If subsequent legislation defined "activities" so that only—or primarily—work fulfilled the requirement, and if effective sanctions against recipients who did not meet the requirements were adopted, the AFDC program could be revolutionized by converting it to a program providing cash benefits contingent on work.

The second factor was that governors played a direct and vital role in the drafting of the bill and in providing the political support that was an essential part of getting the bill enacted. NGA, the Washington-based lobbying organization that represented all the governors, had an influential task force on welfare reform that was a presence in Washington throughout the debate on the Family Support Act. In fact, when Democrats on the Ways and Means Committee met with their Republicans counterparts in early 1987 to begin discussing welfare reform, they invited NGA's co-leads on welfare reform to address the subcommittee in private session. These co-leads were Republican Governor Mike Castle of Delaware and a Democratic governor from Arkansas named Bill Clinton.

When the Family Support Act was widely perceived to have failed because the AFDC rolls increased dramatically in the two years after the legislation passed in 1988, NGA's work on the Family Support Act proved to be only a warm-up. With a group of governors and effective staffers who understood the issues and had recent experience working on welfare reform with members of Congress, NGA was well positioned to play a continuing role. Moreover, its previous leader on welfare reform was elected president in 1992. More remarkable still, Clinton had in the meantime become the most distinctive Democratic voice of his generation on welfare reform. It was Clinton who helped create a national movement on the need for welfare reform with his rhetoric and promises during the 1992 presidential campaign. Whereas most Democrats wanted to expand welfare, which they in fact had done on several occasions during their four-decade control of Congress, Clinton spoke of "ending welfare as we know it." He also talked about allowing recipients to stay on welfare for only two years and then being required to work. Moreover, when he appeared before the National Governors Association in 1993 as the newly elected President, he promised to continue the policy of giving states wide latitude in conducting welfare waiver demonstrations.[36] Seldom had any Democrat talked this way, let alone a Democrat who happened to be president of the United States.

Despite his promises about ending welfare and requiring work, after moving into the White House in January 1993 Clinton delayed action on welfare reform for several months. Then he appointed a task force to study welfare and draft a proposal while he turned his attention and political capital to the single biggest item on the Democrat's long-term social agenda—creating a universal health insurance program.[37] The health insurance proposal met with failure, but it distracted the attention of the Clinton administration away from welfare reform. Meanwhile—and ominously for Democrats—House Republicans had been working quietly behind the scenes to write a welfare reform bill that would be supported by everyone in the House Republican caucus—and by Republican governors as well. In the process of writing their bill in 1993 and 1994, House Republicans and their staffers often consulted with Republican governors and their staffers. Governors John Engler of Michigan and Tommy Thompson of Wisconsin and their staffs were especially important in helping House Republicans draft their welfare reform bill.[38] Because of the emphasis placed on welfare reform by Clinton during his campaign and because of the task force working on his legislation, welfare reform was a high-profile issue in the media throughout this period and in a number of the House and Senate races in the congressional elections of 1994. While the work of Clinton's welfare reform task force was openly debated in the press—its latest recommendations often appearing on the front page of the *New York Times* and *Washington Post* before being denounced by various congressional Democrats, especially Senator Moynihan—House Republicans worked on their bill in almost complete obscurity.[39]

After Republicans won control of the House in the elections of November 1994, they continued working with the Republican governors to fashion a new and expanded bill that would have a chance to gain bipartisan support and be signed by the president. House Republicans again met frequently with Republican governors, especially Engler (who often participated directly in negotiating sessions), as they prepared their bill for introduction. Similarly, several House committees conducted hearings on welfare reform and the governors presented forceful testimony at the hearings in support of the central ideas in the Republican bill.[40] At some of the hearings, Republican governors were joined by Democratic Governor Tom Carper of Delaware who testified in support of many of the central provisions in the Republican bill.[41] The House bill passed in March 1995, but only a few Democrats voted in favor of the bill—despite the best efforts of the governors. The process was repeated in the Senate with the governors again participating directly in the writing of the bill and in the hearings held by Senate committees as part of the bill writing process. In fact, Engler's involvement in the writing of the Senate Republican bill led one Republican to complain that his participation was inappropriate.[42] The Senate, achieving what proved to be impossible in the House, enacted its bill on an impressive bipartisan vote of 87 to 12.

A compromise between the House and Senate bills was included in a massive budget bill that was sent to President Clinton, who vetoed the entire bill in December 1995. Determined to make it clear that Clinton would veto the welfare bill itself, Republicans pulled it out of the budget bill and sent it separately to the president. After some deliberation with his senior advisers, in January 1996 Clinton vetoed the welfare reform bill for the second time in a month.

At the height of this pitched battle between Clinton and congressional Republicans, with the Republican agenda in tatters and the president and Republicans stuck in cement on welfare reform and a host of other issues, the governors came to the nation's capital for their annual winter meeting in February 1996. Serving as a kind of deus ex machina, the governors came armed with a major proposal to break the welfare reform log jam. This was a compromise welfare reform bill that a small bipartisan group of governors, led by Engler and Carper, had been working on for several months. Better yet, the bill enjoyed the unanimous support of the governors. The governors unveiled their proposal at the beginning of their meeting amidst great fanfare. In response, leading congressional Republicans and Democrats publicly stated, some of them with enthusiasm, that the proposal was constructive and contained the outline of possible compromises that could get bipartisan support in Congress and a signature from the president.[43]

Working with the governors, primarily though Engler, House Republicans drafted a new bill that was somewhere between the last bill vetoed by Clinton and the governors' proposal on the most contentious issues. Core ideological issues were at stake in this debate over the welfare bill. Most conservatives believe that government should be limited and that freedom of individuals should be given maximum range. In cases in which government action is necessary and efficient, state and local government should be empowered and the federal role should be minimized. This view of government, usually subsumed under the term federalism, is embodied in Article IV and the Tenth Amendment of the U.S. Constitution. The Tenth Amendment reserves for state government powers not specifically given to the federal government by the Constitution. Despite this mandate in the Constitution, as we have seen, the history of American social policy witnessed almost continuous expansion of the role and power of the federal government—although state power remained extensive in administering programs in accord with state traditions and policy.

After 1994, Republicans controlled the House, the Senate, and the majority of governorships and the American conservative movement was in its ascendancy.[44] Thus, Republicans at all levels of government were determined both to reduce social spending—and the number of programs if possible—and to return as much control and authority as possible over social programs to state and local government. Many Democrats in Congress, scholars, and editorial writers were horrified by this agenda. The rhetoric against the Republican agenda, especially the cuts in social spending, knew almost no limits.[45]

One of the central policies that prompted this invective was the block grant. The basic idea of a block grant was to consolidate several programs that had a common purpose (for example, child nutrition, cash welfare, or support for abused or neglected children). The funding from the previous programs was put into one pot and distributed to the states for implementation. In place of the rules and regulations that had accompanied the constituent programs, the federal government would explain in broad terms what the block grant was expected to accomplish. Sometimes, but not always, the federal government could save money by reducing some of the funding that had been authorized under the original programs that comprised the block grant while justifying the cuts with the claim that states could realize administrative savings based on a reduction in red tape. From the perspective of Republicans, the two great advantages of block grants were that they greatly reduced federal control while increasing state control and that they presented a grand opportunity to reduce or at least tightly monitor federal spending.[46] Governors were strong supporters of block grants because they promised relief from federal oversight. When block grants did not cut federal funding, most Democratic governors also supported them; even when they cut funding, most Republican governors continued to back them. As Engler said on several occasions, governors were willing to sacrifice some funding in exchange for control over the programs.

What allowed block grants to cut or control both federal and state spending was the underlying logic of block grant funding, which differed from the logic of individual entitlement funding. In creating social programs, Congress had often defined specific eligibility criteria, or allowed states to define the specific eligibility criteria, and then stipulated that anyone meeting the criteria would have a legal right to the benefit.[47] Among others, Social Security pensions, Medicare, Medicaid, AFDC, Food Stamps, and SSI are entitlement programs of this sort. However, in creating a block grant, all individual entitlements are repealed and a flat sum of money is appropriated to achieve the purposes of the block grant (no matter how many recipients are involved).[48] Liberals, who were justifiably proud of their achievements in creating entitlement benefits for many groups that they defined as deserving, were strongly opposed to block grants, not least because they could be used to end entitlements.

Many of the entitlements, especially those for the elderly and disabled, enjoyed widespread public support, in large part because the public did not expect these groups to work. As outlined previously, the insurance entitlements in the Social Security Act were supported at least in part by individual contributions, making them resemble private insurance programs. Entitlements to welfare benefits, however, such as Medicaid and AFDC, were vulnerable to criticism because they were often given to able-bodied adults whom Americans expect to work and were simply transfers of money from one group of citizens to another—or to put it contentiously, as Republicans often did, transfers from productive to unproductive citizens. Although liberals were strongly opposed to using block grants to cut funds and reduce federal authority, many of them saw the reduction of entitlements as a much greater outrage because it struck at the heart of the traditional liberal agenda of providing guaranteed benefits to as many groups of Americans as possible. The stakes in the battle of the block grants were high because so many enti-

tlements were endangered: AFDC, Medicaid, at least three child nutrition programs, two day care programs, and six child protection
programs. Senator Moynihan even argued that by abandoning the New
Deal commitment to the AFDC entitlement, the federal government was
abandoning poor children.[49]

The entitlement battle of 1995–1996 represents one of the clearest
clashes in American history between two animating and incompatible
philosophies of American social policy. Most liberals, especially before
the rise of the third-way moderation of Bill Clinton and the Democratic
Leadership Council, wanted to expand guaranteed benefits, including
welfare entitlements for the poor.[50] These would include a cash grant to
all families with children (usually called a family allowance), unemployment insurance, old-age pensions, health coverage, funding for nursing
home care, as well as means-tested entitlements for nutrition, health
insurance, and housing. As we have seen, starting with the New Deal,
liberals enjoyed a series of major successes in moving the nation toward
cradle to grave entitlement benefits. All the elderly and disabled qualify
for cash, food stamps, and Medicaid. All the poor and near-poor qualify
for Food Stamps and Medicaid; and poor children also qualify for child
nutrition programs including school lunch and breakfast, food in child
care facilities, and infant formula and other healthy foods. But liberals
had never been able to pass a universal family benefit that would provide
a guaranteed income floor under all families like other industrialized
nations have. Moreover, the AFDC program—the nation's major cash
entitlement for the poor—was now under threat.[51]

Many conservatives, however, opposed welfare entitlements because
they undermined work. Similarly, conservatives wanted much less federal control than inevitably resulted from entitlements. Even in the case
of AFDC, in which states could determine eligibility and benefit levels,
the federal government could manipulate state programs and, as Democrats had tried to do in the past, enact a minimum national benefit that
would force many states to raise their benefit levels.[52] But above all, the
entitlement prevented states from requiring that recipients work or lose
their cash benefits.

The welfare reform battle of 1996 ended in compromise on many of
the major issues. AFDC was replaced by the Temporary Assistance for
Needy Families (TANF) program that featured strong work requirements, a five-year time limit, and sanctions on individuals and states that
failed to comply with the work requirements. In addition, the child support enforcement program was greatly strengthened; the SSI program
for drug addicts and alcoholics was repealed; the SSI program for children was reformed; several day care programs were converted to a block
grant and the funding expanded; there were numerous changes in the

food stamp program; and welfare benefits for noncitizens were dramatically reduced. By ending the entitlement to cash welfare, and for the first time repealing a New Deal entitlement, Republicans gained a step toward their goal of forcing individuals to rely on their own efforts rather than depend on government benefits. Further, by enacting a large block grant composed of AFDC and related programs and another block grant composed of several child care programs, considerable flexibility was given to states to run these programs as they saw fit.[53]

Social Policy and American Federalism: An Assessment

Having provided an overview of the creation of the nation's major social programs and basic information about many of the most important programs, we are now in position to assess the current nature of the relationship between the federal and state governments in the formulation and implementation of American social policy. My goal is to conduct an examination of the unique brand of federalism that characterizes intergovernmental relations in the United States, with an emphasis on the strengths and weaknesses of the system while anchoring conclusions in the characteristics of the actual programs that, taken together, constitute the American version of the welfare state.

Table 3.1, plus the historical record traced above, is the basic evidence on which to build conclusions about American federalism. The table summarizes descriptive information about the four major social insurance programs and eleven of the biggest and most important welfare programs or program clusters. The first point to emphasize is that the federal government controls the insurance programs with virtually no participation by states. As we have seen, states do set the tax and benefit levels in the Unemployment Compensation program, but the program is conducted under very strict federal guidelines and the states do not even control the taxes they impose on businesses located in their state because all the money is paid directly by employers to the federal government and retained in federal accounts. Whether counting by the total dollars spent, the number of people covered, or the popularity of the programs, the federal government's control over insurance programs makes it a far more powerful force in the nation's social policy than the states.

The second point is that the means-tested programs summarized in the bottom panel of the table come much closer to reflecting a division of responsibility between the federal government and state and local governments that gives important responsibility to each level of government. The eleven programs shown in Table 3.1 are only a fraction of all means-tested programs, but they are among the most expensive pro-

TABLE 3.1 CHARACTERISTICS OF MAJOR SOCIAL PROGRAMS

Program	Type of Benefit	Year of Origin	Financing	Administered by	Cost (billions 2007)	Number of Enrollees (millions 2007)
Insurance Programs						
Old Age and Survivors Insurance	Cash	1935	Federal	Federal	478.9	40.9
Unemployment Compensation	Cash	1935	Federal/State	Federal/State	32.0	7.6[a]
Disability Insurance	Cash	1956	Federal	State	97.3	8.9
Medicare[b]	Health Care	1965	Federal	Federal	381.9	115.3
Means-Tested Programs						
AFDC/TANF	Cash	1935/1996	Federal/State	Federal/State	16.5	1.7
Housing	Housing	1949	Federal	Federal/Local	38.9[c]	NA[d]
Medicaid	Health Care	1965	Federal/State	Federal/State	192.5	172.2
Head Start	Early Education	1965	Federal[e]	Federal/Local	2.8	0.9
Supplemental Security Income	Cash	1972	Federal	Federal	35.7	7.1
Earned Income Tax Credit	Cash	1975	Federal	Federal	37.6	20.5
Food Stamps	Nutrition	1970s	Federal	Federal/State	34.9	26.5[f]
Child Protection	Services	1980	Federal/State	Federal/State	6.3	0.7[g]
Child Nutrition	Nutrition	1980s	Federal	Federal/State	13.1	54.7[h]
Child Care	Child Care	Various	Federal/State	Federal/State	16.9	1.8
Title XX Social Services	Services	1981	Federal	State	1.7	NA

[a] In 2007, 152.7 million people were in the labor force and the average unemployment rate was 4.6 percent.
[b] Includes Medicare Part D prescription benefit.
[c] Estimate for 2004.
[d] In 2004 there were 3.4 million households in Section 8 housing, 1.2 million in public housing, about 347,000 receiving Section 236 interest reductions subsidies, and around 200,000 receiving other forms of housing assistance.
[e] With supplements by some states.
[f] Average monthly participation.
[g] Estimate from the Department of Health and Human Services.
[h] Many children receive benefits from more than one child nutrition program.
NA = Not available.

Source: Congressional Budget Office (www.cbo.gov/budget/factsheets/factsheets2007b.shtml), Administration for Children and Families (www.acf.hhs.gov/programs/hsb/about/fy2007.html), and Congressional Research Service, *Cash and Noncash Benefits for Persons with Limited Income*

grams and cover the most people.[54] Even in the case of welfare programs, however, the federal government plays a lead role. Two of the biggest programs—Supplemental Security Income and the Earned Income Tax Credit—are completely financed and administered by the federal government. The states play a modest role in the SSI program and almost no role in the EITC program. The states have also been completely cut out of two additional programs—Head Start and housing—because the federal government makes grants directly to local entities to run these programs. Both programs are financed entirely by federal dollars but are administered by local entities under often complex federal regulations.

Of the remaining welfare programs, all are administered by the states under guidelines established by the federal government. In most cases, the federal rules are elaborate and states frequently complain that the federal government has too much authority. Congress regularly passes legislation that changes the programs and has a direct impact on the states. In addition, the federal agencies that are responsible for seeing that states administer the programs in accord with federal rules have the power to change the rules and thereby impose new requirements on the states. With the exception of the Title XX Social Services Block Grant, every welfare program shown in Table 3.1 has federal statutory and regulatory guidelines.

Nonetheless, the fact that federal statutes give states leeway in designing most welfare programs—especially in setting eligibility requirements and benefit levels, two of the most important characteristics of any program—and the fact that states implement nearly all these programs means that the state role is of great importance. Moreover, by convincing the federal government to give them block grants in several vital areas of social policy, the governors moved the levers of control somewhat in their direction in 1996.

Perhaps the best analogy for the state-federal relationship in most types of domestic policy (including, in addition to social policy, transportation, the environment, energy, conservation, and many others) is Morton Grodzins's concept of "marble cake federalism." As Grodzins sees it: "Wherever you slice through [federal-state relations] you reveal an inseparable mixture of different colored ingredients. There is no neat horizontal stratification. Vertical and horizontal lines almost obliterate the horizontal ones, and in some places there are unexpected whirls and an imperceptible merging of colors, so it is difficult to tell where one ends and the other begins."[55] In fact, Richard Nathan of the Rockefeller Institute of Government argues that the struggle for power between the federal government and the states has gone through distinct cycles extending back as far as the Constitutional Convention. Even more to the point, Nathan argues that these cycles have had the effect of increasing overall government power. "American federalism is a growth machine for government," he says.[56] The typical pattern, shown by programs like child labor laws, Social Security, AFDC, Unemployment Compensation, and welfare reform emphasizing work, is as follows: a state develops an innovative program, the program spreads to other states, and then the federal government either nationalizes the program with substantial control at the federal level or requires each state to have its own version of the program. Nathan's theory is certainly consistent with the history of American social policy outlined above.

Although it seems clear that states often resent federal intrusion in social policies developed at the state level, I would argue that on the whole this marble cake federalism has served the nation well. Critics of federalism claim that the dividing government responsibility for social policy between states and the national government leads to low levels of spending on social welfare. One test of the efficacy of our form of federalism, therefore, would be whether our federalist system has maintained spending on social programs. The trend in social spending over the past several decades is also a test of Nathan's theory that federalism is a "growth machine for government."

Figure 3.1, based on data from the Congressional Research Service (CRS), traces the growth of federal and state spending on means-tested programs since 1968 in inflation-adjusted dollars. Spending on programs for the poor has grown in most years, beginning from a low base with President Johnson's War on Poverty in the mid-1960s. Not only has spending grown by a factor of 6.5 over the entire period, but the number and diversity of programs has grown as well. In constructing the time series of spending data that yielded the totals portrayed in Figure 3.1, CRS examined more than eighty programs divided into eight categories based roughly on the function of the program. The categories included medical, cash, food, housing, education, social services, jobs and training, and energy aid. Figure 3.2 shows spending on programs in each of these categories in 2004. The towering height of the medical bar graph dramatically portrays a development that is now the plague of federal and state budgets; namely, that spending on health programs is huge and growing rapidly. In recent years, the cost of health care has grown at about twice the rate of inflation, and there is no prospect for it to slow down any time soon.[57] Even so, spending on many other categories of programs is considerable and in most cases continues to grow.

Spending data like that in Figures 3.1 and 3.2 could be somewhat misleading because they simply tell us that spending on means-tested programs has been growing faster than inflation. But there are other important ways to judge spending growth. Two of the most important

FIGURE 3.1. STATE AND FEDERAL SPENDING ON MEANS-TESTED PROGRAMS, 1968–2003

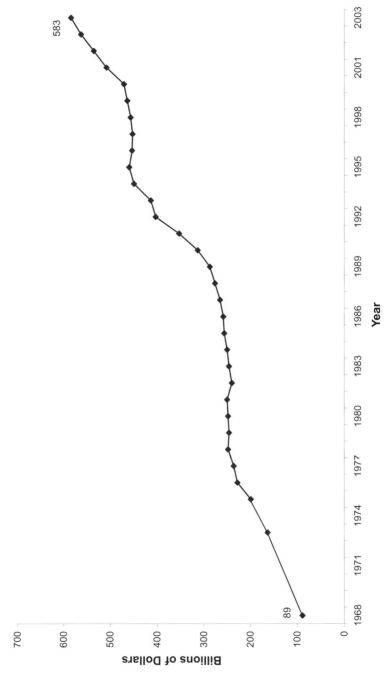

Source: Vee Burke, "Cash and Noncash Benefits for Persons with Limited Income: Eligibility Rules, Recipient and Expenditure Data, FY2002–FY2004" (March 27, 2006) Congressional Research Service.

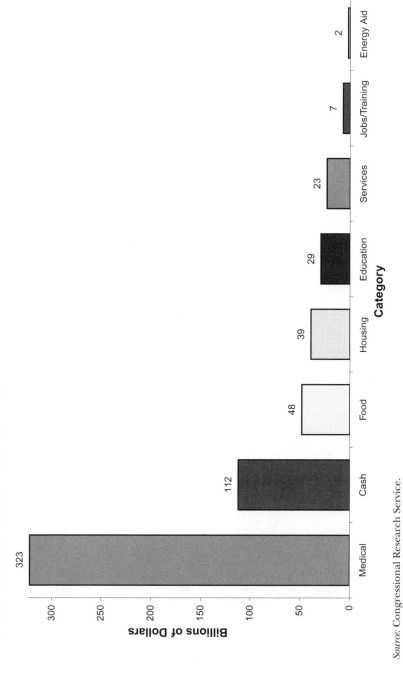

FIGURE 3.2. SPENDING ON EIGHT CATEGORIES OF AID

Source: Congressional Research Service.

are spending on means-tested programs as a share of all federal spending and as a share of the nation's GDP. The former allows approximations about the priority the federal government gives to means-tested programs; the latter provides a measure of whether the overall growth of the American economy above inflation is reflected in proportional increases in government spending on means-tested programs. Between 1968 and 2004, the CRS study shows, spending on the eighty or so means-tested programs increased from a little less than 10 percent to more than 25 percent of total federal spending and from 2.2 percent to 5.0 percent of GDP.[58] Clearly, judging by several measures, our federalist system has produced rising levels of spending on social programs.

Another important test of federalism is whether states have retained enough flexibility to serve as, in accord with the words of Supreme Court Justice Louis Brandeis, the laboratories of democracy. As shown above, most programs in the Social Security Act were first implemented at the state level, including cash welfare programs for the elderly, the disabled, and children, as well as unemployment insurance and pensions. This tradition of state experimentation was greatly expanded when Congress enacted Section 1115 of the Social Security Act in 1962. This amendment allows the Secretary of the Department of Health and Human Services to grant waivers to provisions of law in several programs established by the Social Security Act in order for states to test the effectiveness of innovative policies. A similar provision was added to Section 1915 of the Act to facilitate state experiments and demonstrations with the Medicaid program. In both cases, states have seized the opportunity to propose innovative demonstrations and have conducted hundreds of them, many of which have been replicated in other states and some of which have led to changes in national policy.[59]

In many respects, the historic 1996 welfare reform legislation was built directly on reform ideas that had been previously implemented by states under the WIN Demonstration authority or under Section 1115 waivers. Starting with the administration of Ronald Reagan and extending into the Clinton administration, almost all states had conducted welfare reform demonstrations, mostly to test ideas related to encouraging work.[60] A number of these demonstrations were based on scientific evaluation designs and yielded reliable information about work programs, not least that job search programs that required welfare applicants or recipients to look for work actually did boost employment and save money.[61] Many of the ideas tested by these state demonstrations were incorporated in the 1996 welfare reform law. Regardless of whether one likes its particular provisions, the 1996 law provides a model for successful state-federal policy innovation. Specifically, in large part because states were allowed and even encouraged to conduct demonstrations, many of which were scientifically evaluated, a body of knowledge on effective employment programs developed. This body of knowledge gave other states motivation to adopt similar reforms and informed members of Congress about the value of programs such as mandatory job search. In the end, Congress incorporated provisions in the 1996 law that had been tested and were already popular in many states. This sequence of events leading to federal legislation conforms to the sequence noted by Richard Nathan, with the additional point that the state innovations had been proven effective. Although Justice Brandeis could not have known about scientific experiments to determine whether specific reforms work, this virtuous sequence is surely an effective model for policymaking in a federalist system that allows plenty of range for state flexibility.[62]

Another advantage of the American federal system, which from time to time allows the federal government to impose requirements on states, is that it has been used to promote equity, one of the most important criteria of social programs. The federal government can bring a single set of standards to a given program and ensure that citizens in all states are treated the same, or at least more equitably than they would have been treated without federal requirements. Compare, for example, cash benefits provided by the TANF program with the cash benefits provided by the Supplemental Security Income program. The SSI program provides a uniform standard benefit of $623 per month to individuals and $934 for couples (in 2007) in every state (although many states supplement the federal benefit).[63] Compare these uniform benefits with the large differences across states in the TANF program for which states set the benefit level. The maximum TANF benefit for a mother and two children in Connecticut is $636, compared with a maximum benefit of $194 for the same family in Mississippi. Granted, there are differences in standards of living between these the two states, but the variation is modest compared with this huge disparity in benefits. Experience shows that any program that allows states to set program eligibility and benefit standards will result in major differences in benefit levels and eligibility across states.

Those who support states' rights argue that states should have the authority to set benefit levels because only in this way can the benefit reflect the traditions and policy goals of each particular state. By contrast, those who support uniform national benefits argue that identical families should have identical benefits, regardless of the state in which they live. Why should a mother and two children receive more than $600 in Connecticut but not even $200 in Mississippi? The point here is that our federalist system allows substantial differences in eligibility levels and benefit levels across states in some programs while providing uniform federal benefits in other programs. Though many critics would like universal federal benefits in all social programs, the federal system has maintained a balance between states' rights and universal program features. This balance increases the equity that would exist if the federal government played no role but does not maximize the parity criterion and in the process completely obliterate state flexibility.

An important aspect of the power of a centralized system to promote fairness in eligibility and benefit levels is fiscal capacity. The United States is characterized by major differences in the economies of its states. To continue using Connecticut and Mississippi as our example, the median incomes in the two states in 2004 were $73,500 and $39,300, respectively. Despite this huge difference, citizens in Mississippi enjoy the same benefits as citizens in Connecticut in many programs such as Supplemental Security Income, Food Stamps, Social Security, and Medicare.[64] Again, regarding benefit levels, the federal government imposes uniform federal standards in many of the most important social programs, in these cases by paying for the entire benefit. The federal government is able to promote interstate equity by transferring resources from rich states to poor states, just as the federal government transfers funds from rich individuals to relatively poor individuals via the income tax and distribution of social benefits.[65]

The concern that federal control of social programs is necessary because of unfair treatment of blacks in the South has, to a great extent, been resolved. There is no question that without federal direction, and even use of police and military power against citizens of southern states, the South would have taken much longer to overcome its racist system of government and its racist social practices.[66] The federal government forced southern states to integrate their schools, allow blacks to vote, and include blacks in their social programs on an equitable basis. Ironically, as pointed out by scholar Martha Derthick as long ago as 1987, the South's ability to overcome, at least in large part, its racist past, strengthens the argument that states should have more control over social spending. As Derthick put it: "Until now, arguments favoring the states' side in any dispute over federalism suffered fatally from the burden of the South's deviant social system. Whether or not blacks have been successfully integrated into American society (a separate question), there can be little doubt that the South as a region has been integrated. That change, even if achieved very largely by the instrumentalities of the federal government, holds the possibility that the case for the states can at last begin to be discussed on its merits."[67] While we still find racial and economic inequality in our society, these inequalities can no longer be attributed to the racist laws of a particular region and, therefore, no longer provide a cogent argument against state autonomy.

A final point about the American version of federalism is that the federal government is not inevitably successful in imposing its will on the states and localities. For one thing, as part of its budget procedure, Congress has adopted a rule that federal legislation cannot impose an unfunded mandate on the states. The tendency of the U.S. Congress to pass legislation that imposes costs on the states is widely considered by governors and other state officials to be unfair. The budget rule is a nod on the part of the Congress that the states are correct in this judgment. Both houses of Congress have procedures by which they can exempt themselves from this budget rule and regularly do so. Nonetheless, as a routine part of the legislative process, the Congressional Budget Office must write a section on state mandates as part of its report on every piece of legislation that goes to the floor in either house. This report alerts state officials and groups that lobby on behalf of states, including the National Governors Association, that Congress is about to impose a financial burden on them. Thus, states almost always know well in advance when Congress intends to impose costs on them and can orchestrate a campaign against the legislation. When this occurs, Congress is often willing to at least modify the legislation so that the cost to states will be reduced or eliminated.

Conclusion

As late as 1935, the federal government had very little responsibility for the well-being and social security of the American public. Local and state governments had only slightly more responsibility. But the Social Security Act of 1935, the War on Poverty of the mid-1960s, and other federal and state legislation over the period dramatically expanded government responsibility and spending. Although these waves of legislation vastly increased government power and responsibility at all levels, the federal government's power, relative to that of state and local government, grew the most. On numerous occasions the federal government created programs and funding mechanisms that expanded its own power to run social programs without assistance by state and local government. In other cases, the federal government created programs that required states to meet certain broad requirements if they wanted federal dollars. Even so, state governments retained considerable flexibility in establishing eligibility and benefit levels for numerous important social programs. States also retained enough flexibility to create and test new social programs and thereby preserve or enhance their reputation as the engines of social policy innovation. Because of the huge debt burden now facing the federal government—a burden that will expand exponentially as baby boomers begin to retire and health care costs continue to accelerate dramatically—it seems unlikely that the federal role in the nation's social policy will continue to expand at the rate it has in the past. The 1996 welfare reform law may be propitious in this sense. Innovation and implementation of social policy will continue to flourish at the state level—as it always has—but the state and local burden for financing social programs is likely to grow in the years ahead. This development will present states with the opportunity to enhance their power relative to that of the federal government in the ongoing redefinition of American federalism.

Part II
Laboratories of Democracy
PUBLIC POLICY IN ACTION

Over the twentieth century, governors achieved some of their greatest successes by working within their states. Faced with particular issues and demands unique to their polity, governors experimented with their own solutions. The chapters in this section focus on the work of specific governors in particular eras. Jon C. Teaford uncovers the role of governors, especially those in the South, in focusing new attention on economic development starting in the 1950s. Jason Sokol turns to an investigation of the governors of two states, Massachusetts and Virginia, during the 1960s and 1970s to demonstrate a convergence in the way governors responded to the problem of racial inequality in the late twentieth century. Finally, Brooke Masters examines four governors—Walter Roscoe Stubbs of Kansas, William John Janklow of South Dakota, and Pete du Pont and Mike Castle of Delaware—to suggest how governors, in very different historical contexts, made similar calculations about how to regulate business.

While all of these chapters focus on the roles of governors within their particular states, the fact that these states were part of a federal system shaped many of the decisions these governors made. Teaford explains how the drive to attract economic development by southern governors was met with disdain and later imitation by other governors as they competed to lure industries from other states and overseas. Governor Linwood Holton of Virginia, one of the primary subjects of Sokol's chapter, desired to recast the perception of the South in the rest of the nation. And Masters explains how policies to regulate business were developed by balancing the needs of the states with the economic well-being of the nation as a whole. Together, these chapters demonstrate that while governors toil to develop directions for public policies on their own, never far from their minds is the work of other governors. In fact, one of the contributions of the National Governors Association over its hundred-year history has been to provide a forum where governors can discuss and compare their efforts to deal with similar policy concerns.

The chapters in this section are focused on fairly narrow moments in the past and, often, on the work of individual governors. But the conclusions made in these essays about the transformation of the gubernatorial role in economic development, a convergence in public policies dealing with racial inequality, and the balancing of local and national concerns in business regulation can be applied to virtually every state. The states may act as the governors' "laboratories of democracy," but these are laboratories without walls that allow other governors to observe the experiments and fresh ideas to blow in across state borders.

Chapter 4
Governors and Economic Development

JON C. TEAFORD

Among the greatest changes in the gubernatorial role during the past century has been the emergence of governors as promoters of economic development. In 1908 voters did not expect their governors to provide jobs or generate business; regulation of corporate excesses took higher priority. Charles Evans Hughes of New York, Robert M. La Follette of Wisconsin, and Hiram Johnson of California were the great governors of the age, and they won their distinction by crusading for reforms that would curb exploitative business practices and protect the individual worker and consumer. Regulation of public utilities, child labor laws, maximum hours legislation, and workers' compensation were the chief economic issues of state government. At the beginning of the twentieth century attracting jobs and creating an optimal business climate for corporations were not on the gubernatorial agenda.

In 2008, however, economic development is decidedly a gubernatorial function. Governors have become the preeminent economic boosters of their states with a panoply of policies to promote business and create employment. They travel throughout the world in pursuit of investment and jobs, and they fashion initiatives to nurture new business and high-tech innovation that will supposedly pay off in the future. These economic initiatives can make or break a governor. New plant openings and thousands of additional jobs can ensure a second term and create a lasting political legacy. Sluggish growth might spell defeat for the incumbent and victory for a rival promising a more attractive economic panacea.

Pioneering Southern Efforts

Governors did not always assign a low priority to economic development. During the early nineteenth century executives such as New York's DeWitt Clinton sponsored expensive internal improvements aimed especially at creating state-funded canal systems to facilitate commercial development. Such programs, however, pushed some states to the brink of bankruptcy. For the remainder of the century wary governors shied away from such public initiatives and avoided the fiscal pitfalls of ambitious development schemes.

Yet in the early twentieth century some states were willing to take modest steps to promote their economies. This was especially true in the South. Since the Civil War the southern states had suffered second-class economic status, providing raw materials for northern industry while developing some low-wage, low-skill manufacturing. They were behind the rest of the nation economically, and their governors were well aware of this fact. Consequently southern governors were in the vanguard of state economic promotion. As early as 1923 Alabama created a Department of Commerce and Industries to promote the state's economy, and four years later it established an Industrial Development Board "to investigate and seek to ascertain the industrial possibilities of Alabama and to seek the development of the same."[1] In 1923 Governor Cameron Morrison of North Carolina likewise proposed the creation of a Division of Commerce and Industry that "would gather data and information upon which our hundreds of patriotic chambers of commerce and other commercial organizations could advertise our State's advantages in commerce and manufacturing." According to Governor Morrison, "It would be of very direct benefit to the whole State by the practical declaration its establishment would make that North Carolina is friendly to commerce and industry." The governor urged the state's general assembly to authorize the agency and thereby make "a declaration to all the world that North Carolina is hospitable to commerce, manufacturing and industry of every class."[2]

North Carolina established such an agency, which according to its annual report of 1927–1928 acted "in the nature of a state chamber of commerce." Yet at this time the idea of states and their governors presenting a sales pitch to boost economic development was offensive to many Americans and alien to prevailing concepts of government. In 1930 a Brookings Institution study of government in North Carolina expressed "some doubt whether a considerable portion of the work carried on by the Division of Commerce and Industry constitutes a legitimate state service." Reflecting prevalent notions of state government, Brookings questioned "the expenditure of public funds for the purpose of attracting industrial establishments and tourist travel, or in any way acting as an industrial bureau."[3] In 1930 promotion of business was deemed an illegitimate function of state government. By declaring to all the world that North Carolina was friendly to all manner of business, Governor Morrison overstepped the bounds of his office as defined by such an authoritative observer of government as the Brookings Institution. The governor and other public employees were not to sell the state like some chamber of commerce executives. Promotion of business was a responsibility of the private sector, not the public authorities.

Not until the mid-1930s did economic development begin to emerge as a major gubernatorial responsibility. One of the poorest states, Mississippi, took the lead. In 1935 Hugh L. White campaigned successfully for governor on a platform dedicated to promoting the "greatest industrialization in this state that has ever been known." In his inaugural address Governor White proclaimed that Mississippi must "balance agriculture with industry," a phrase embraced by the press as a name for White's program.[4] The Balance Agriculture with Industry (BAWI) scheme as enacted in 1936 authorized localities, subject to the approval of a state commission of gubernatorial appointees, to issue bonds to finance the building of manufacturing facilities for firms willing to locate in Mississippi. The public sector was committing itself to constructing and leasing manufacturing facilities and thereby luring jobs and income to cash-poor Mississippi. From 1936 through 1940, BAWI financed the creation of twelve new manufacturing plants in Mississippi which by mid-1943 employed 12,500 workers, 14 percent of the state's total number of manufacturing workers. More impressive, BAWI plants accounted for 24 percent of Mississippi's total manufacturing wages.[5]

Governor White's state-induced development offended laissez-faire thinkers opposed to government paternalism. An Alabama newspaper editorialized that BAWI was a "dubious experiment," a "step in the direction of government ownership and control of industry." "Economic growth can not be too highly stimulated; it comes best in response to natural laws," the newspaper concluded.[6] A Mississippi banker complained, "The thing was outright Socialism and should never have been attempted." Another more pragmatic banker remarked, "The BAWI plan was socialistic in its tendency, but it worked."[7] Though Mississippi remained among the poorest states, Governor White dismissed criticisms of his innovative scheme. "I can sit back and grin about the daily accomplishments made under BAWI," he later commented. "The plan was attacked as socialistic when it was first put into effect but now most people realize it has brought about a complete reversal of the state's economy."[8]

Through his BAWI program Governor White broke the ideological barrier to state enterprise. In future decades, governors were not willing to wait for "natural laws" to stimulate state economies. State financing of economic development might be socialistic in the minds of laissez-faire purists, but if it worked that was good enough for most governors and voters.

Though denounced as socialism by some, BAWI was representative of a growing commitment among southern governors to mold the economic future of their region. As early as 1934, southern governors met to discuss the discriminatory rail rate structure that favored northern manufacturers and, in effect, imposed a burdensome surcharge on southern industry. Known as the Southern Governors' Conference (later the Southern Governors' Association), this group led a challenge to these freight rates before the Interstate Commerce Commission. According to the *New York Times*, it was a "conference with the broad objective of industrial development of the Southeastern states."[9] Leading the conference and its rate reform crusade was Governor Bibb Graves of Alabama. Graves told the Interstate Commerce Commission that the existing rates were a "barrier to the free flow of commerce" and urged the commission to give the South "the right to have a full and fair opportunity in the commerce of the entire nation."[10] In a radio address Graves claimed that "if we can beat these barriers down you will see millions of dollars worth of southern products going into areas north of the Ohio River and west of the Mississippi."[11] Responding to a momentary victory before the commission in 1939, Graves proclaimed: "This is the supreme achievement of my life. It is the greatest victory for the South since the war between the States."[12]

The struggle, however, continued before the commission, in Congress, and before the United States Supreme Court throughout much of the 1940s. And southern gubernatorial rhetoric became even more heated as the battle dragged on. Addressing his fellow southern executives in 1943, Georgia's Ellis Gibbs Arnall proclaimed that "nothing but cold-blooded politics, waged with relentless unity, would rescue the South from its accepted role as a disfavored tomcat, prowling the political and economic backyards of a nation addicted to sectional snobbery."[13] In his book on the southern economic predicament, Governor Arnall wrote of the South and West as "colonial appendages" of the nation and argued that "the exploitation of whole regions, under a colonial system more wasteful than that practiced by the most greedy of European powers in Africa or the Pacific, must end." Arnall made clear that the South was in "shackles . . . because of the failure of a timid, reactionary Interstate Commerce Commission with its maddening jargon and ox-cart methods."[14]

The southern gubernatorial initiative also stirred a new concern about economic development issues among governors elsewhere in the nation. Seeking an economic alliance with the West, in 1943 the southern governors met with their western counterparts in a joint conference in Denver.[15] Meanwhile, governors in the Northeast had mobilized to oppose Graves, Arnall, and their colleagues. In the fall of 1937 the governors of the six New England states called for "united, cooperative action" to confront the southern challenge. The governors contended that "the need is greater than ever before . . . to contest the railroad rate cases initiated by the Governors of nine Southeastern States which threaten New England's industries." New England had "to meet the aggressive, organized, well-financed competition of these same nine States in the field of industrial development."[16]

To combat the southern threat, New York's Governor Herbert Lehman called a meeting of representatives of the governors of five Mid-Atlantic states. According to the *New York Times*, the Mid-Atlantic conferees feared that freight rate revisions "would encourage further the movement of 'runaway shops' from the industrial Northeast to the new centers of cheap labor in the South."[17] Testifying at an Interstate Commerce Commission hearing, Governor Lehman observed "that the South's efforts to build up its industry at the expense of New York for the sake of selling its products in New York market, may be a defeat for them, even if they win," for New Yorkers could not "remain purchasers of the products of industry, either in the South or in the North, unless their earning power is continued."[18] In other words, the South could not enrich itself by impoverishing New Yorkers.

Eventually the southern governors won their fight for freight rate equity. Yet perhaps the most significant consequence of the long battle was a heightened sense that southern governors could and should assume the lead in the economic development of their states. Similarly, northern governors were forced to become defenders of the economic wealth of their region. Promoting and perpetuating economic development was assuming a new significance on the gubernatorial agenda.

The Postwar Southern Initiative

The rail rate battle was only the initial strike in the southern gubernatorial offensive. During the two decades following World War II, Dixie governors stepped up their crusade for a fair share of the wealth of the nation. Recently enacted right-to-work laws added a new weapon to the southern arsenal. Northern manufacturers, tired of a unionized work force, could escape to the South where state law mandated open shops, thereby curbing the strength of labor and enhancing the position of management. In 1954 Governor James Byrnes of South Carolina recognized this when he asked the legislature to prohibit closed-shop contracts that required workers to join unions; he claimed that South Carolina needed to be able to compete with other southern right-to-work states in the pursuit of northern business. Other southern governors also believed right-to-work laws were essential to economic development. Mississippi's Governor Ross Barnett contended that "since the Right To Work law became part of our Constitution, capital investment in Mississippi has amounted to three and a half times more than the average in any one of the last ten years."[19] Fearful of a labor backlash at the polls, northern governors generally eschewed pandering to the anti-union sentiments of business leaders. Southern executives usually felt no such need to bow to the desires of labor. For them attracting business was the paramount concern, and they realized that cheap, nonunionized labor was a southern advantage that could be exploited.

During the postwar years one southern governor after another expressed the imperative of capitalizing on such advantages and catching up to the North economically. In his 1949 message to the legislature Georgia's Governor Herman Talmadge claimed that his state faced "limitless possibilities as an industrial state. We must work with might and main to bring new industrial developments to all parts of our state in order to strike a more favorable balance with our agricultural potential." Talmadge made clear: "We need more pay-rolls. We need job opportunities for our people." That same year South Carolina's Governor Strom Thurmond told the legislature: "We must continue to encourage in every possible way the industrial development of our state. This is necessary to raise the income of our people and to provide steady employment the year round."[20] In 1955 in his first inaugural address Governor Orval Faubus expressed this same imperative when he announced proposed legislation to establish an agency "with the specific task and duty of making an all-out effort to do whatever is possible to encourage industry in Arkansas."[21] The southern states had to do whatever was possible to industrialize. This was the message of the southern governors.

These governors did more than talk. Corporations considering industrial sites in their states received encouraging letters, telegrams, and telephone calls from the governors. Visiting industrial leaders were wined and dined at the governor's mansion. And state executives were willing to grant favors to prospective employers. For example, in 1948 Governor Sid McMath of Arkansas authorized a Texarkana businessman to promise the Eastman Corporation a four-lane highway to its plant if it agreed to locate in the Texarkana area.[22] Not willing to wait for corporations to contact them, southern governors took the initiative and embarked on a number of "raiding" trips to northern cities where they could use their political skills to win the favor of industrial moguls. State economic development agencies found their governors invaluable in the crusade to garner businesses and jobs. "If you send an industrial representative to these places, he talks to his counterpart in the business," commented Georgia's Governor Ernest Vandiver. "But a governor—any governor—

gets to the president and chairman of the board where the final decisions are made."[23]

The phone calls, trips, and incentive schemes became major elements
of the governors' lives. Albertis S. Harrison, Jr., Virginia's executive in
the early 1960s, estimated that he devoted one-third of his time as governor to his economic development effort, and Mississippi's Governor Barnett averaged one out-of-state trip to industrial prospects per month.[24]
In 1964 one observer summed up the new reality when he commented
that "Southern governors have become the *de facto* executive directors
of the state chambers of commerce, and spend their time competing
with each other as supplicants for new plants." Skeptical of this seeming
obsession with economic development, he remarked: "We have talked
of state socialism and state capitalism, but what do we call government
whose chief affair it is to entice and propitiate business?"[25]

The preeminent southern gubernatorial promoter, and a model for
later state executives, was Governor Luther Hodges of North Carolina.
Serving from 1954 to 1961, Hodges placed economic development first
on his agenda. He recognized that his state needed to wean itself from
dependence on low-paying employment in textile mills, furniture factories, and tobacco-processing plants and attract higher-wage industries. "It
became increasingly apparent to me," Hodges observed, "that low per
capita income was North Carolina's major problem—a bread-and-butter
problem that affected everyone in the state and every aspect of its
future." The answer to this problem was high-grade industrialization. In
his account of his gubernatorial years, Hodges reminisced: "My administration was considered by many to be 'industry hungry.' It was!"[26]

To nurture industrial growth, Hodges secured creation of the North
Carolina Business Development Corporation, a development credit
scheme that would supply long-term capital to those starting new businesses or expanding existing concerns. The capital for the development
corporation was raised through private stock subscription, not from
state appropriation. Hodges, however, was the first subscriber for the
stock and used his considerable sales skills to hawk the shares throughout the state. "Selling stock in the North Carolina Business Development Corporation was a wonderful experience," Hodges remarked.
"Never have I seen such interest, patriotism, and downright loyalty to
an idea, to an administration, or to a state as was evidenced by people
throughout North Carolina."[27]

To further promote industry Hodges secured a change in the state's
corporate income tax. Under Hodges's tax law North Carolina manufacturers would be taxed only on the share of their income derived from
property and operations within the state. Firms headquartered in North
Carolina would no longer pay the state tax on income earned outside

the state. Reporting on the change, the *New York Times* announced that "North Carolina is beginning to realize big dividends from a new tax law and the state is sparing no effort to tell industry about the tax package."[28]

Dedicated to ensuring that everyone heard North Carolina's pro-business message, Governor Hodges led a series of trips northward aimed at recruiting industry. In 1957 Hodges and a party of seventy-five North Carolinians descended on New York City where over the course of six days the governor hosted five luncheons and four receptions for more than six hundred persons, spoke on twelve radio and television programs, and delivered three major speeches.[29] "We are not a Cherokee war party trying to raid northern industry," Hodges told wary New Yorkers. "However, we are very much interested in securing new industries and expanding those already existing."[30] Yet, according to Hodges, the Tar Heel recruiting team was not so desperate for industry as to offer anything and everything to prospective investors in the state's future. They "made clear that special inducements, tax exemptions, public financing of industry, or other so-called give-aways were not offered by North Carolina." There was no BAWI in North Carolina and tax abatements were not part of Hodges's appeal. Yet the governor believed his state had a great deal to offer industrialists, including a labor force who "appreciated the opportunity to work" and who furnished "a full day's work for a fair day's wage."[31] This message appealed to union-plagued manufacturers, and the following year Hodges and his industry hunters hit Chicago and Philadelphia, reciting once again what the governor called "The North Carolina Story."[32]

Seeking to spread this story throughout the world, in 1959 the energetic governor led a two-week junket to Europe in search of industry. According to Hodges, the North Carolinians "made a great impression all over Europe" and at least 276 European business leaders expressed interest in investing in North Carolina.[33]

Hodges, however, not only charmed northerners and Europeans into locating plants in North Carolina, he also endeavored to build the entrepreneurial infrastructure of his state through creation of the North Carolina Research Triangle in the Durham-Raleigh-Chapel Hill area. Intended to attract and generate higher-wage, high-technology industry, the Triangle was to combine the expertise of three nearby universities in the pursuit of economic development. The governor again employed his skills as promoter and salesman to round up the necessary investors in the scheme and make sure it came to fruition. Hodges believed that the laboratories and facilities of this five-thousand-acre research park were "the heart and hope of North Carolina's industrial future." Expressing a faith in the link between research and economic growth that would underlie many gubernatorial proposals in the last years of the twentieth century, the governor observed: "Where there is research, there is industry. And if the Research Triangle develops as fast as I imagine it will, then more cities, towns, and communities across North Carolina will get their own industries, which in turn will supply more money locally."[34]

Hodges's efforts established the paradigm for future gubernatorial initiatives. Like Hodges, governors were increasingly expected to sell their states through personal contacts and junkets both within the United States and abroad. But in the last decades of the twentieth century state executives aimed especially at the expanding high technology sector and sought to create research incubators of industry comparable to the Research Triangle. Like Hodges, these latter-day executives needed both to sell and to create. They had to convince industry leaders that their state was a good place to do business, but they also sought to create the foundation for a high-technology future.

The industry hunting of Hodges and his southern colleagues did not endear them to many northern governors. In 1952 Rhode Island's Governor Dennis J. Roberts charged the southerners with conducting "raids" on his state's economy and claimed that manufacturers "in the long run will flourish best in the skilled industrial climate of New England in general and Rhode Island in particular." Roberts's charge elicited an angry response from Georgia's Governor Herman Talmadge. "If he wants war we'll give him war," announced the Georgia leader. He also suggested, "If Rhode Island wants to keep its industry I suggest it clean up its own front yard."[35] In 1954 Governor John Lodge of Connecticut advised a group of New England business and financial leaders: "The manufacturer who moves from New England or anywhere in the Northeast into a less developed region with the thought of obtaining lower labor costs is surely deluding himself." Criticizing the inducements offered by southern states, he contended that it was not good "for one region to be permitted to impair the economy of other areas at the expense of the general citizenry."[36] The following year Lodge's successor Abraham Ribicoff denounced southern efforts to lure industries from Connecticut following devastating floods that seriously damaged many industrial plants. South Carolina's Governor George Bell Timmerman, Jr., answered the irate New Englander: "I am shocked that you would issue such a statement. . . . You have been misinformed and I assure you that South Carolina's industrial development has never been, nor will it ever be, based on the misfortune of others."[37]

One factor that seemed to favor northerners was business fears of racial problems in the South. When southern governors threatened to close the public schools rather than desegregate and appeared to tolerate, if not encourage, the violent suppression of civil rights protests, this sent a message to northern business leaders that the South was not safe territory for investment. With economic development their preeminent concern, so-called moderates such as Hodges and Governor Leroy Collins of Florida failed to desegregate but also failed to issue fiery threats of defiance that might undermine the business image of their states. The more outspoken tactics of governors such as Alabama's George Wallace, however, possibly threatened the goal of economic development. "We do think the course you have chosen will lead to economic disaster," one Alabama business leader told Wallace. "I cannot emphasize this too strongly because I have already had many such reactions from prospects in the North who might have considered Alabama." Wallace responded that if Alabama surrendered its state sovereignty in the face of federal demands "we will have degenerated to a complete welfare state and Washington will be taking care of all of us." Moreover, his business prospecting trips convinced him that there would be "no major problem in bringing industry into the state of Alabama." Future Arkansas governor Winthrop Rockefeller perhaps summed up the situation best: "The industrial prospect doesn't give a hoot whether your schools are segregated or not, but he wants no part of disorder and violence."[38]

Criticism from the North might actually have added fuel to the southern drive to succeed. Suffering from longstanding colonial status as well as a rising wave of attacks from northern foes of racial segregation, southern leaders felt little compunction about pursuing with full force an economic counterattack on unsympathetic Yankees. After decades of economic subordination, the South was striking back.

Development Initiatives Spread Throughout the Nation

Though southern governors were in the vanguard of industry hunting, their counterparts elsewhere in the country gradually followed suit. During the last half of the twentieth century, the federal government took the lead in macroeconomic promotion, seeking to boost the national economy through tax policies and regulation of interest rates. In both North and South, however, the states assumed charge of microeconomic development. Attracting new industries and promoting the creation or expansion of individual businesses was largely a state responsibility. In 1948 the Conference of Western Governors (the present-day Western Governors' Association) recognized this when it adopted a resolution, asking commissions in the eleven western states "to jointly determine upon a program for advancing the industrial expansion of the West, to be presented to the next meeting of the Conference of Western Governors."[39] The West, like the South, was an underdeveloped region, seeking to catch up with the economic development of the Northeast.

Yet as deindustrialization struck first New England and later the Mid-Atlantic and midwestern rustbelt, governors in the northeastern quadrant of the nation also mobilized to protect their economies and create employment. During the 1940s and 1950s New England was clearly slipping economically. The first section of the nation to industrialize, it was also the first to suffer from serious signs of industrial obsolescence. In 1951 the New England Governors' Conference established a committee to investigate means for preserving the region's textile industry, which was hard hit by southern and foreign competition. Countering the southern offensive with ultimately unsuccessful defensive action, the New England governors discussed repeatedly how to protect this vital segment of their economy.[40]

One New England governor after another was awakening to the necessity of fashioning a new industrial future for their region. In 1950 Governor Chester Bowles of Connecticut asserted that the New England states were "a 'test' case to show whether a settled 300-year-old economy can, by realigning its sights, shifting its emphasis and developing new resources, industries and attitudes, continue to grow and expand rather than stand still." To aid this realignment Bowles's own "Governor's Steel Committee" was studying the possibility of creating a needed steel mill in Connecticut.[41] In 1952 Christian Herter ran successfully for governor of Massachusetts declaring that his "top priority Massachusetts issue is steady jobs, new jobs, better jobs"; he promised, "I will plan and fight to stimulate the creation of new industries that will offer new jobs for the jobless." On taking office Herter sponsored the creation of a cabinet-level Department of Commerce as well as a development capital corporation charged with making long-term loans to small and medium-sized firms.[42]

As the threat of deindustrialization spread in the 1960s and 1970s governors in both North and South competed increasingly for new branch factories and relocating plants. For example, Pennsylvania's Governor Milton Shapp and Ohio's Governor James Rhodes were the final contenders in the contest to land Volkswagen's first American plant. In March 1976 Rhodes led a fifty-person trade mission to Europe aimed particularly at convincing Volkswagen to choose Ohio for its plant site. Describing the Rhodes mission, the *New York Times* reported that "the atmosphere was a mixture of high-pressure sales and pre-game football rally."[43] But in May Shapp announced Pennsylvania's victory. Rhodes had been unable to match Shapp's hefty subsidy package that included $25 to $30 million from the state for highway and rail improvements, more than $3 million of state funds for a job training program for Volkswagen employees, as well as low-interest loans and tax abatements.

The indefatigable Rhodes meanwhile had embarked on a five-day visit to Japan to make a pitch for manufacturing investment.[44] Unabashed in his devotion to attracting new jobs, Rhodes claimed that "the greatest contribution I can make as governor is to try to get a job for every able-bodied person in Ohio."[45] The governor's efforts paid off in October 1977 when Honda announced the opening of its first American factory in Ohio. The state agreed to construct the water and sewer infrastructure for Honda and to reactivate a rail line and widen the highway leading to the new plant. Moreover, Rhodes asked local authorities for a fifteen-year real estate tax abatement to sweeten the deal. It was a relatively inexpensive incentive package, however, especially considering that this was just the beginning of Honda's investment in the Buckeye State. Providing thousands of jobs and spawning multiple suppliers in the next two decades, Honda became a major player in the Ohio economy.

Governor Shapp's initiative ultimately proved less successful. Volkswagen's Pennsylvania plant produced only half the jobs expected, and in 1988 after a mere nine years of operation it closed, leaving 2,500 Pennsylvanians without employment. Gubernatorial industry hunting was clearly a risky business. Much ballyhooed acquisitions might pay off or they might prove a bust. Pennsylvania's Volkswagen experience was a cautionary tale that governors throughout the nation needed to notice.

In fact, over the following three decades many critics decried the smokestack chasing of governors like Shapp and Rhodes, claiming that states were sacrificing too much in the form of incentives to lure industries. Tax abatements, infrastructure subsidies, and state-funded job training programs were all-too-common elements of the packages designed to attract business. But was the cost too high? In the case of Pennsylvania it seemed that it was. Yet if Volkswagen's management had proved more competent in manufacturing automobiles that appealed to the American public, then Shapp's package might have been judged a real bargain. Industrial recruitment was a gamble, but it was a gamble an increasing number of governors felt they had to take. In the underindustrialized South and West and the deindustrializing Northeast and Midwest, the clamor for high-paying jobs was growing, and the electorate targeted the governor as the person most responsible for attracting such employment opportunities.

The pressure for gubernatorial action mounted during the early 1980s as a national recession wreaked havoc with the economies of many states. Plant closings in the rustbelt accelerated, derelict steel mills symbolized the industrial decline of Pittsburgh and Youngstown, and few states seemed secure about their economic future. In the 1980s, however, state policymakers placed less faith in the pursuit of branch plants or the relocation of established facilities and became more committed to multifaceted programs to nurture new businesses and, especially, nascent high-technology companies. Governors talked more of creating businesses and jobs as opposed to attracting them; state governments were to become incubators of industry. States became venture capitalists dedicated to raising funds for potential high-growth industries that conventional lenders eschewed. They also sought to mobilize the scientific and technological expertise of their universities to aid entrepreneurs. With private-public partnerships aimed at jumpstarting their economies, many states and their chief executives proudly boasted of their new entrepreneurial posture.

The state many sought to emulate was Massachusetts. The home of high-tech establishments lining Route 128 west of Boston, Massachusetts launched a series of programs to promote further investment in less favored parts of the state. Most notably the state created a group of quasi-public financing bodies to channel capital into promising new businesses, emerging high-technology companies, and firms operating in poorer areas of Massachusetts.[46] Once known for its dying mills and obsolete industries, Massachusetts had turned around, a transformation known as the Massachusetts Miracle. Governor Michael Dukakis took much of the credit for this new prosperity, and his image as an economic wonder worker helped him to win the Democratic nomination for President in 1988.

Dukakis, however, was not the only governor placing economic development near the top of the policy agenda. The National Governors Association conducted a survey of governors and their chief aides in 1982 and found that in every region of the nation, except the West, "economy/jobs" was the top issue confronting the governors; in the West it ranked second.[47] That same year James Blanchard won the governor's office in Michigan by proclaiming three priorities—Jobs, Jobs, Jobs. The Blanchard administration appointed a task force to map a long-range economic strategy for the state. Its report, *The Path to Prosperity*, emphasized the importance of fostering innovation and new technologies; the state should invest in research and concentrate less on subsidies to relocating businesses. "We want to help our major industries redevelop for the future and be globally competitive," explained Governor Blanchard. "We want to diversify our economy as quickly as possible, and we believe that targeting small business as a growth sector is a good idea." Blanchard's goal was for Michigan "to once again be the center of complex manufacturing in this country—that's high-tech manufacturing, not low-skilled, low-paid manufacturing."[48]

Meanwhile, Pennsylvania's Governor Richard Thornburgh created the Ben Franklin Partnership; through four Advanced Technology Centers affiliated with major universities the Partnership funded applied research projects that were expected to reap new businesses and jobs. Criticizing the pursuit of giant auto plants that characterized the regime of his predecessor Governor Shapp, Thornburgh emphasized encouragement of new firms or small but growing existing businesses. "I'd rather have 50 new plants with a hundred employees apiece in different industries than five thousand new jobs in a one-industry operation," Thornburgh remarked.[49]

In the South governors were pursuing similar policies. North Carolina's Governor Jim Hunt was dedicated to making his state a powerhouse in microelectronics. Consequently, he successfully promoted the creation of the Microelectronics Center of North Carolina, a research and development facility to be located in the Research Triangle. With an enthusiasm reminiscent of his predecessor Luther Hodges, Hunt sold microelectronics as "perhaps the only chance that will come along in our lifetime" for a "dramatic breakthrough" in the struggle to boost wages and income in the state.[50] To the west, Tennessee's Lamar Alexander was nurturing a special relationship with Japanese business leaders and making plans for a Technology Corridor between Oak Ridge National Laboratory and the University of Tennessee that was intended to become the Volunteer State version of Hodges's Research Triangle.[51] Unlike his predecessors in the early twentieth century, Alexander not only needed to cater to constituencies in Memphis and Knoxville but had to extend his political skills to Osaka and Tokyo as well.

The blueprints for advanced technology centers and microelectronic research hubs did not preclude old-fashioned smokestack chasing. In 1985 General Motors embarked on a well-publicized search for a site for its new Saturn plant, a multibillion dollar facility that was expected to create six thousand jobs. One governor after another lined up to meet with General Motors officials and explain why their state would make the best location for the job-rich plant. And governors were unabashed in their competition to offer the optimal incentive package. Upon hearing that Michigan promised the best package, Illinois's Governor James Thompson responded: "Illinois will offer anything Michigan can and, in some instances, a bit more." The General Motors executive in charge of the Saturn project admitted: "With my first major decision I'm going to make 49 governors mad."[52]

The one governor who did not get mad was Lamar Alexander; General Motors chose Tennessee as its Saturn site. In cash value the Tennessee incentives in the form of access highways, industrial training, and property tax abatements did not equal those of some other states contending for the prize. Tennessee's central location and tradition of good labor-management relations seemed to influence General Motors more than the state's incentives. And possibly Governor Alexander's personal salesmanship had some effect. Acknowledging the Republican governor's sales skills, a Democratic leader admitted: "Alexander's the best governor we've ever had for economic development."[53]

Economic Promotion at the Turn of the Twenty-first Century

In the 1990s and the early twenty-first century governors continued their crusade for jobs with a focus on high technology development. Biotechnology became a favorite target, for that field seemed especially pregnant with the possibility of new employment. Moreover, state executives were not shy about identifying themselves as the figures most responsible for jumpstarting business. Governor's councils and conferences on economic development were commonplace; state executives proudly announced the acquisition of any major plant and appeared at business groundbreakings; and governors embarked on a multitude of trade missions with at least sixteen visiting Asia alone from September 2004 to September 2005.[54] In major metropolitan areas throughout the country, billboards bearing the visage of Governor Arnold Schwarzenegger announced, "Arnold Says: California Wants Your Business."[55] No one could doubt who was the chief pitchman for the Golden State.

By the early twenty-first century, the creation of jobs and advancement of the state's economy were being used to justify and support all manner of policy initiatives. Traditionally educators had justified public school expenditures as necessary to create an intelligent and informed electorate. In a democracy everyone needed the skills requisite for good citizenship. This was the rationale of early twentieth-century policymakers. A century later, however, state education initiatives emphasized the need to ensure a skilled workforce for the high-tech future, a trained citizenry that could attract jobs to the state. In 2006–2007, for example, Innovation America, an initiative sponsored by the National Governors Association, intended "to give governors the tools they need to encourage entrepreneurship, improve math and science education, [and] better align post-secondary education systems with local economic growth."[56] Emphasizing the significance of education as a tool for promoting economic development, Arizona Governor Janet Napolitano, co-chair of the Innovation America Task Force, asserted that "states must enable our students to gain the science, math and technology skills that support this new growth strategy—with an equal focus not just on what students are expected to learn but also on *how* knowledge is transferred in our classrooms and into local economies."[57] States needed to invest more money and effort in science and math education because such education spurred economic growth. Knowledge produced innovation and innovation produced good jobs, a prime goal of conscientious governors in the twenty-first century.

The arts and medical research were also promoted as boons to economic development. A National Governors Association issue brief reported that "states and communities have integrated the arts into their economic development arsenal to achieve a wide range of direct and indirect economic goals" and recommended that "governors can position their states to use the arts effectively . . . by harnessing the power of the arts and culture as tools that unite communities, create economic opportunity, and improve the quality of life."[58] When announcing Massachusetts's life science initiative in 2007, Governor Deval Patrick proclaimed: "Now is the time for us to invest in that talent and bring together the resources of our unparalleled research universities, teaching hospitals, and industry to work towards a common goal—to grow ideas into products to create cures and jobs."[59] Saving lives, creating beauty, and generating knowledge were justifiable not only for their intrinsic value but also because they would produce jobs. No matter the issue, economic development and job creation were ever-present concerns of twenty-first-century state governors.

Some scholars, however, questioned how much impact a governor realistically had on the trajectory of a state's economy. Billboards and trade missions could not wholly overcome the negative effects of rustbelt deindustrialization or generations of economic underdevelopment in parts of the South and West. At the beginning of the twenty-first century after decades of gubernatorial promotion, the southern states still had lower per capita incomes than the Northeast or Midwest. Some also doubted whether millions of additional dollars for math and science education could ever transform the majority of American teenagers into devotees of calculus and physics eager to outperform their Asian counterparts on the calculator and in the laboratory. Governors could not overcome the disadvantages of location or weather that might keep a state from winning the economic race. Alaska will never be within five hundred miles of a majority of American consumers, North Dakota will never lure those seeking a mild climate, and Arizona will always have an advantage over Pennsylvania in attracting lovers of sunshine. Moreover, governors are possibly of minor significance in winning job-rich plants. General Motors might well have chosen Tennessee as the site of its Saturn plant no matter who was governor. The state's central location and nonmilitant southern labor pool was of greater significance than the charm of Lamar Alexander or the attractiveness of the state's incentive package.

Yet there is evidence that governors can make a difference. Few would doubt that a first-rate promoter like Luther Hodges left an indelible imprint on his state's economy, shifting North Carolina from a low-wage textile center to the home of the famed high-tech Research Triangle. As the most high-profile figure in the state, the person who projects the state's image to the world, an effective governor can influence the attitudes of potential investors. And as the most potent policymaker in the state the governor can fashion a state investment strategy and reform a state tax structure in order to foster and attract business. A Luther Hodges can make a permanent contribution, but any governor has an arsenal of weapons useful in the fight for economic development.

In any case, in the early twenty-first century the question whether a governor can significantly impact a state's economic growth is politically moot. In 2008, unlike in 1908, governors are expected to promote their states' economies, and they have to make the attempt no matter the potential for success. State economic development efforts are no longer regarded as inappropriate or socialistic. In the public's mind, state intervention is definitely legitimate; it is unconscionable for the state's highest elected official to preside over economic decline without at least proposing an incubator for high-tech business or embarking on a trip to Asia. No governor, no matter his or her ideology, can afford to leave the economic future of his or her state up to the natural laws of the market. Hugh White, Luther Hodges, James Rhodes, and Michael Dukakis have long since trumped Adam Smith in the gubernatorial game. Governors are held responsible for their states' economies and charged by the public with the task of creating jobs. In the early twenty-first century economic promotion is a most significant part of a governor's job description.

Chapter 5

Uneasy Executives
Governors and Civil Rights from the Bay State to the Old Dominion

JASON SOKOL

The history of American governors almost always appears—in scholarly works, in popular images, and in statistical sketches—as a tale of white men and women. Among more than 2,300 governors of American states, just sixteen have identified themselves as racial minorities. The annals of U.S. history include eight Latino governors, five Asian Americans, and three African Americans—one of whom inherited Louisiana's state-house during Reconstruction.[1] Only Massachusetts and Virginia have elected African American governors, a pairing of states infused with deep historical irony. From Jamestown and Plymouth to Douglas Wilder and Deval Patrick, Virginia and Massachusetts continue to act as political mirrors. Their colonial experiences remain subjects of constant comparison; almost every "Founding Father" hails from either Massachusetts or Virginia. In concord or in combat, the two states helped forge the nation: their compromise placed the White House in Washington, D.C., and their leaders assumed prominent roles in the republic-rending debate over slavery. Civil War shrines grace both state capitals. Robert E. Lee's likeness dominates Richmond's Monument Avenue while the Robert Gould Shaw Memorial looms over Boston Common. Political observers now speak of Wilder and Patrick in the same breath.

The tangled racial pasts of Virginia and Massachusetts paint stunning backdrops behind Wilder's and Patrick's elections. While Virginians might cherish tropes about cavalier gentility and Massachusetts residents may fancy themselves the heirs of the abolitionists, both states grappled uneasily with struggles for black civil rights. Both witnessed massive confrontations over school desegregation. Virginians mounted legal obstructions to block African American children from the schoolhouse door, while whites in Boston flung rocks, bricks, and epithets at black students.

To compare governors' responses in Virginia and Massachusetts is to probe northern and southern policies side by side. Virginia's "massive resisters" closed public schools a decade before Governor Linwood Holton counseled citizens to abide busing plans. Massachusetts governors initially supported the Racial Imbalance Act—the state's pioneering civil rights law—before a grass-roots movement against busing forced Francis Sargent into an uncomfortable evasion. At some moments, the North and South displayed sharp differences, fulfilling their regional stereotypes. Yet Massachusetts and Virginia also illuminated a national convergence on race in the late 1960s and early 1970s—a time characterized by urban riots, spirited opposition to school busing, the "white backlash," and a host of racial controversies that thrust governors into burning political fires.

In the end, a comparison of Massachusetts and Virginia pictures governors as more than mere responders to the civil rights movement. They shaped its destiny, and in the Bay State and Old Dominion, emerged as products of its triumphs. The specific racial histories of these two states also shed important light on a scholarly debate about black candidates and their prospects in statewide elections.[2] Whites in both Virginia and Massachusetts experienced immense crises over integration long before they sent African Americans to the statehouse.

In the popular mind, the words "governors" and "civil rights" conjure images of southern politicians who spewed segregationist venom. Orval Faubus gave life to the mob at Little Rock's Central High School. George Wallace defied the federal government at the University of Alabama, encouraged the violence of Bull Connor and Jim Clark, and wrote himself into the civil rights narrative with the line, "segregation forever." Ross Barnett whipped Ole Miss football fans into a frenzy one day before thousands violently resisted the integration of that institution. Louisiana's Jimmie Davis, Georgia's Marvin Griffin and Lester Maddox, and other governors both led and followed the resistance to black civil rights. While these stories may be well known, scholars have also drawn more complicated portraits: they explore the varieties of response, and narrate politicians' transitions from outright resistance to more ambivalent "strategic accommodation" and even overt embraces of black equality.[3] Earl Black's *Southern Governors and Civil Rights* (1976) divides Dixie's governors into "segregationists" and "non-segregationists," exploring their divergent strategies and the environments that encouraged each type of leader. More recently, Matthew Lassiter's *The Silent Majority* and Randy Sanders's *Mighty Peculiar Elections* emphasize the "New South Governors"—that group of officeholders elected in and around 1970 whose ambiguous stances on race represented clear steps toward progress.[4]

No comparable literature examines northern governors and civil rights.[5] By the late 1960s, however, desegregation policies became a vital national concern and pressed politicians above the Mason-Dixon Line as much as below. While southern governors shook off a history of blatant race-baiting, officeholders elsewhere in America navigated the terrain between the North's self-image (as a progressive beacon) and a more sobering reality. Their public policies centered on—or tiptoed around—large urban centers with rampant segregation, restive African American populations, and mounting white resentment. Frequently during the civil rights era, southern governors fed the stereotypes of rabid racism while northern politicians charted plans for peaceful integration. At other times, the regions reversed. Southern leaders enacted desegregation proposals while governors in the North muddled through racial quagmires.[6] Yet they were all beholden to substantial white majorities, and in the 1970s leaders stayed far away from explosive racial issues. When pleas for legal rights and token desegregation morphed into proposals for school busing and demands for residential integration and affirmative action, the last years of the civil rights struggle exposed a body of political leaders—North and South—unified in their caution.[7]

Massive and Passive Resistance in the Old Dominion

Temerity, and not timidity, characterized Virginia's response to the Supreme Court's *Brown v. Board of Education* decision. Governor Thomas Stanley first created a commission to study the problem of desegregation, and thus to delay any action. On February 24, 1956, U.S. Senator Harry Byrd trumpeted a "massive resistance" and led the southern charge against integration. Meanwhile, the state's General Assembly adopted a package of anti-integration bills. Byrd's Democratic Party had dominated state politics for years, and it supported Attorney General Lindsay Almond for governor in 1957. Described by *Time* as "one of segregation's ablest legal advocates," Almond's platform pulled no punches: "We dedicate our every capacity to preserve segregation in the schools."[8] Against the federal government's "massive attacks" on the states, Almond declared in his 1958 inaugural, "We must marshal a massive resistance." In the uppermost reaches of the South, Almond's rhetoric matched that of leaders from Mississippi, Alabama, and other citadels of white supremacy. While the *New Republic* pronounced it "inconceivable that the white people" of the Old Dominion would close schools rather than integrate them, Virginia's governor transformed the unimaginable into the stuff of public policy. Facing orders to desegregate nine schools in Norfolk, Newport News, Charlottesville, and Warren County, Almond closed them in September. To avoid the prospect of makeshift "segregation academies" for their own children, thousands of white parents gathered in a statewide movement for open public schools. On January 19, 1959, the Virginia Supreme Court of Appeals struck down the school closing laws. The governor raised his voice in defiance one last time on January 20, but soon buckled to the court ruling. Almond traded "massive resistance" for a subtler opposition to integration. Later in 1959, Prince Edward County closed its public schools. While many whites enrolled in private schools, African American children languished without education. In turn, Almond's administration embraced inertia. By 1962, when Almond left office, his strategy of "passive resistance" enabled only 1 percent of Virginia blacks to attend integrated schools.[9]

Virginia's era of "massive resistance" seemed ephemeral, but it deposited a legacy of closed public schools and private "segregation academies," and spawned a quieter resistance to integration. After the state's pitched confrontation with the courts and the federal government died down, desegregation still remained a threat—not a goal.

Democratic governors Albertis Harrison and Mills E. Godwin, Jr., followed in Almond's footsteps. As Almond's attorney general, Harrison had supported the governor through the school closing crisis. Yet after that episode, as Earl Black argues, "a certain corner had been turned."[10] Virginia's governors gradually deemphasized civil rights issues. Before his tenure as governor, Godwin waged futile battles against the *Brown* decision, the 1964 Civil Rights Act, and the 1965 Voting Rights Act. When Godwin took office in 1966, however, he seemed ready to replace the overt tactics of his segregationist past with more innocuous evasions. Such machinations could not stave off change, for Richmond had already become the epicenter of the Old Dominion's saga of race, civil rights, and school integration.

Since 1956, the state's Pupil Placement Board had assigned students to schools. The board's authority ended in 1965, and a freedom-of-choice plan took hold in Richmond. As in other American cities, Richmond's residential segregation hindered such voluntary plans. Richmond later experimented with suburban annexation, and finally, school busing. Godwin remained aloof from such concerns. Civil rights issues defined the tenures of neither Godwin nor Harrison. But the prospect of busing came to polarize residents of Richmond in 1969. That year, Linwood Holton won the statehouse for the Republicans and offered himself as the face of a racially progressive "New South."

The Bay State's Brand of Segregation

Rivalries of ethnicity, geography, and class marked Massachusetts politics. Conflict flared between Irish Americans and Yankees, between Boston and its suburbs. Yet on the issue of race, Bay State voters—over 95 percent of whom were white—could appear enlightened. They elected Edward Brooke, an African American and a Republican, as attorney general in 1964. Two years later, voters sent Brooke to the U.S. Senate—the first African American since Reconstruction to hold that position.[11]

In Boston, like many northern cities, civil rights issues centered on the de facto segregation that African Americans encountered in city housing and schools.[12] The Second Great Migration, coupled with the rising black freedom struggle in the South, lent an immediacy to issues of inequality nationwide. In the 1950s alone, Boston lost 100,000 whites to the suburbs and gained 25,000 blacks, many of whom crowded into the South End and lower Roxbury.[13] Segregated neighborhoods combined with the Boston School Committee's machinations to achieve a school system almost complete in its racial separation.

In 1963, Boston's NAACP requested a School Committee hearing on de facto segregation. Louise Day Hicks, as head of the Boston School Committee, presided over the June 11 meeting—and agreed to compromise on some of the NAACP's suggestions. But the committee refused to acknowledge that de facto segregation existed. On June 19, over one-quarter of Boston's African American students boycotted the schools. Both sides hardened their stances during the ensuing months, and Hicks won reelection in November with almost 70 percent of the vote. If over two-thirds of Bostonians agreed with Hicks, African Americans realized, they would have to look toward the state government and the courts—instead of city officials—for redress.

Governor Endicott "Chub" Peabody responded to the standstill in Boston. The state Board of Education acted at Peabody's behest, and in March 1964, formed a twenty-two-member committee to study school segregation. The board soon announced its findings—that racial imbalance existed in several of the commonwealth's school systems—and released an official report on August 19. That summer, Peabody lost in the Democratic primary to his own lieutenant governor; in the fall, voters returned Republican John Volpe to the statehouse after a two-year hiatus. Volpe inherited the growing battle over school integration in Boston.[14]

The state Board of Education published its final report in the spring of 1965. The board defined as "racially imbalanced" any school where over half of the student body was nonwhite.[15] It identified fifty-five such schools, forty-five of them in Boston. Volpe declared that if the cities did not correct this imbalance, he would urge the state legislature to act.[16] Martin Luther King, Jr., attracted thousands to a civil rights march on Boston Common, and on April 26, the state Board of Education submitted a bill to address racial imbalance. Volpe offered his own bill on June

1 and advocated "putting the force of our state government solidly behind the fight for equal rights."[17] Legislators from both parties filed racial imbalance bills. Volpe backed the Democratic measure, and the cause became a bipartisan juggernaut. To politicians from the suburbs, "who knew the bill would have no effect on their constituencies," scholars J. Michael Ross and William Berg write, "the Racial Imbalance Act was hard to oppose."[18] Boston representatives attempted to weaken the bill, but their antibusing amendments failed by small margins. In August 1965, the legislature passed the Racial Imbalance Act. Volpe signed it on August 18. Massachusetts took the lead on civil rights policy, enacting the first such state law in the nation. The Bay State's mystique as a progressive bastion appeared alive and well.[19]

While Virginia's governors chafed under federal laws and court orders, Peabody and Volpe positioned the Massachusetts state government as the initial shaper of desegregation policy. If defiance was to be found in the North, urban politicians—like those on Boston's School Committee and legislators from Boston and Springfield—led the charge against the power of the state. In Massachusetts, "states' rights" was no rallying cry; Boston leaders saw the state government as the domineering force.

In the North, the black freedom struggle struck at inequalities not so much in the letter of the law but in the texture of society. Shortly after Watts exploded in California, a series of small riots and demonstrations gripped Springfield, Massachusetts, during the summer of 1965. Despite the existence of the Racial Imbalance Act, Boston officials delayed any meaningful action on integration. Like Richmond residents, they waited for gavels to pound. As the prospect of court-ordered busing approached, the two populations—North and South—came to grapple with similar fates.

A Face of the New South

Linwood Holton won the Virginia statehouse in 1969. From the beginning, Holton's campaign sought to alter the nature of Virginia politics. Even his ads pulsed with a new spirit. They pictured the Republican candidate in streets and parks, vying for the votes of African Americans. One-party rule stifled competition and constrained choice, Holton told onlookers. Moreover, "there are no Negroes in our government; they are all white." Five years after the Prince Edward County schools finally reopened, the candidate spoke a bold language. Once Holton won the election, he became bolder. His 1970 inaugural address moved the issue of race back to the center of state government. "No more must the slogan of states' rights sound a recalcitrant and defensive note for the

South . . . for the era of defiance is behind us." Holton engaged in a conscious attempt to position Virginia at the forefront of a "New South." Motivated by a moral conviction that racial equality was right and by a political realization that African American voters composed an important bloc, Holton continued in this new vein. "As Virginia has been a model for so much else in America in the past, let us now endeavor to make today's Virginia a model in race relations." In the city that honored Robert E. Lee, Holton channeled Abraham Lincoln. "Let us . . . insist upon an open society 'with malice toward none; charity toward all.'" Jarring in its rhetoric, Holton's first speech as governor announced a new force afoot in Dixie.[20]

Other southern politicians followed Holton's lead. Jimmy Carter won Georgia's governorship in 1970 with a moderate stance on civil rights issues, while progressive racial views animated the campaigns of John West in South Carolina, Reubin Askew in Florida, Dale Bumpers in Arkansas, and a year later, William Waller in Mississippi and Edwin Edwards in Louisiana. Carter appeared on the cover of *Time*, headlining the class of 1970.[21] During an interview three years later, Holton highlighted his own place in that history. "I set the pace. I was the first guy that had the initiative, and in . . . a . . . former Confederate state, the courage to get up with his inaugural address and say, 'I want this state to be a model of race relations and an aristocracy of ability.'" More astonishing, Holton's actions over the next four years matched the novelty of his promises. Holton's first executive order banned any bias in the hiring and promotion of state employees. He supported a successful open housing bill and later declared it "the most important piece of legislation to pass this Assembly since the Civil War." Yet the conflict over school integration—and specifically, busing in Richmond—defined Holton's term. Holton shaped the course of desegregation more by the court orders he refused to denounce than by any laws he enacted. As much by his personal actions and words as his public policies, Linwood Holton forged a new racial path for Virginia.[22]

Shortly before Holton took office, an annexation plan redefined the city of Richmond. The proposal took effect on New Year's Day 1970 when suburbanites in Chesterfield County became residents of Richmond. The city added twenty-three square miles across the James River and lost its black majority overnight. Annexation enabled Richmond's leaders to craft a white majority city. They hoped to revive the tax base and retain political control. Richmond's African American population plummeted from 52 percent to 42 percent.[23] The city's public schools still contained almost two black students for every white. Ineffectual "freedom-of-choice" plans, and an influx of Chesterfield whites, failed to remedy the segregation that characterized Richmond schools.[24] As

U.S. District Court Judge Robert R. Merhige, Jr., considered busing to desegregate the schools, white fears deepened. During the summer of 1970, controversy flared and anti-busing groups materialized. The possibility of court-ordered busing "caused more apprehension among parents," the *Washington Post* reported, "than anything since the U.S. Supreme Court's decision in 1954."[25] Demonstrations attracted tens of thousands of white protesters. "The tone of the late 1950s is back," the *Post* editorialized. While a growing grass-roots movement supported defiance of the courts, few could mistake this for Lindsay Almond's Virginia. Holton called a press conference and urged "a calm, reasoned approach to busing." Holton's leadership distinguished Virginia during the busing crisis from the days of "massive resistance." With an appeal to calm, Holton set himself apart from his predecessors in Virginia and his contemporaries around the South.[26]

The U.S. Supreme Court's October 1969 ruling in *Alexander v. Holmes County* had mandated immediate integration in fourteen states. It penetrated rural southern fortresses of segregation. Across the region, governors deplored the idea of sudden desegregation. In February 1970, Georgia's Lester Maddox, Louisiana's John McKeithen, Alabama's Albert Brewer, and Mississippi's John Bell Williams gathered in Mobile and agreed to defy the integration ruling. Quickly, governors turned yellow buses into straw men. In April, Claude Kirk of Florida seized Manatee County's school system and installed armed troopers to block busing. Williams later cut off funds to Jackson schools when the city drew up a busing plan. In September, the Southern Governors' Conference drafted a resolution opposing "the busing of school children from one neighborhood to another for the avowed purpose of attempting to achieve numerical balancing of the races." Linwood Holton voted for the statement. Yet if Holton opposed busing to "achieve numerical balancing," he had already supported Richmond's plan. This seeming contradiction exposed the nuances and complications inherent in battles over integration policies.[27] For Holton, as for many governors, school busing produced enormous strain. When it mattered most, however, Holton's actions betrayed little internal conflict.[28]

Richmond schools opened their doors on August 31, 1970, and buses rolled along the James. The initial busing plan involved 13,000 of Richmond's 50,000 students. Holton became the plan's most powerful proponent and the city's daily newspapers his most visible antagonists. The *Times-Dispatch* and the *News-Leader* waged personal attacks against Holton.[29]

Holton rose to the occasion. On the last morning in August, the governor escorted his thirteen-year-old daughter Tayloe to John F. Kennedy High School. Situated in Richmond's East End, the previously all-black school contained a vast African American majority. Holton not only backed desegregation in theory but seized the opportunity to support it in practice. He became the opposite of the reviled "limousine liberal." Meanwhile, Holton's wife took their two other school-age children—eleven and twelve years old—to Mosby Middle School, where they were two of the only white students amid a sea of black faces.[30] The resolve of the governor's family impressed even the local papers, but made busing no more palatable to Richmond's white majority.

On September 1, photos of Virginia's governor and his daughter graced front pages across the nation. Newspapers featured southern governors many times in the 1960s and 1970s, but rarely as the champions of integration. "Here was a ready-made situation where I could walk onto the front page of the *New York Times*," Holton explained in a 1987 interview with historian Robert Pratt. Holton could "say to the whole world, 'You see, we're law-abiding here in Virginia, and this is right.'" Holton's actions created a mighty dissonance in the minds of those Americans who continued to view white southern leaders as intransigents. "I could see that picture of my daughter and me juxtaposed against the Ross Barnetts and the George Wallaces saying, 'You ain't a coming.'" For the rest of his life, Holton remembered that hour as the finest of his political career.[31]

As the years wore on, Judge Robert Merhige's various rulings became harder for Holton to abide. Merhige's support for the idea of metropolitan consolidation was particularly nettlesome. On November 4, 1970, the Richmond School Board argued that white flight to the suburbs rendered desegregation increasingly impossible. Merhige advised that the suburban counties of Henrico and Chesterfield should become parties to any litigation. In this line of thinking, the geography of race in urban America demanded that integration plans extend beyond a city's bounds to encompass an entire metro area. Holton opposed such a remedy. Yet in the spring of 1971, at roughly the same time as the Supreme Court's pro-busing ruling in *Swann v. Charlotte-Mecklenburg County*, Merhige expanded the reach of the existing busing plan. As a result, 21,000 pupils would be bused throughout the Richmond metropolitan area over the 1971–72 school year.

As circumstances changed around him, Holton adapted. Holton still stated that Virginia could provide "leadership to the rest of the nation" and accept court busing plans.[32] As a matter of personal opinion, however, Holton opposed busing. He drew a sharp distinction between a governor's personal views and his public policy, and he vowed that as long as school busing remained the law of the land, Virginians would comply. In August 1971, as the election for lieutenant governor neared, Holton felt increased pressure. He supported an anti-busing plank as part of the Republican Party's platform. Seemingly antagonistic positions mingled within the same public figure.[33]

Holton's stance mixed a respect for court rulings, a genuine desire for school desegregation, a moral belief in racial equality, a personal distaste for busing, and a recognition of the political fact that millions of Americans—North and South, from Richmond to Boston—loathed judges' attempts to wrest their children from "neighborhood schools." Muddling through this amalgam of views, Holton urged compliance with court orders but continued to hope for alternate policies. "The governor knows most people are against busing," according to Ed Shull, Virginia's executive director of the Republican Party in 1971. "But the courts of the land have established the criteria, not Linwood Holton. All the governor has done is to adopt a statesmanlike position and obey the law." If Holton resisted busing, he would acquiesce to the ghosts of Virginia's past rather than help to create its future. "The busing issue is the same one that has gone by different names—segregation, integration, massive resistance, interposition—for 100 years," Shull said. Holton meant to lift Virginia up and over that ugly history. While Holton voiced support for the law, the Nixon administration criticized busing orders and George Wallace scored victories in the presidential primaries on the strength of his anti-busing attacks. Across the nation, the political tide was turning against Holton's stance. In February 1972, a committee of Virginia's General Assembly approved two anti-busing amendments. Grass-roots movements grew in Richmond and in other American cities confronting the possibility of busing. Through it all, Holton continued to support compliance with the court.[34]

On February 11, 1972, a crowd of 4,000 anti-busing protesters gathered at the state capitol, demanding that Holton officially oppose busing. The governor responded, "Although I am opposed to the principle of busing for the purpose of maintaining a racial balance in our schools . . . it is my duty as Governor of the Commonwealth to provide the leadership to comply with the mandate of our Virginia Constitution." Holton remained resolute.[35] The U.S. Congress began to consider a constitutional amendment that would ban busing. On March 30, Holton called a press conference and asserted that such an amendment would be "tragic." Furthermore, it would "take this nation back from a position it has finally reached of recognizing that black people are citizens of this country and are entitled . . . to all of their rights." Holton waded through any contradictions in his private views and issued a ringing statement. Busing was not primarily about "neighborhood schools," class, or "social engineering"—it concerned African Americans' rights to attend desegregated schools.[36]

Metropolitan consolidation presented an even thornier issue. In January 1972, Merhige ruled that Richmond would merge with Henrico and Chesterfield counties, forming a single school district. An appeals court overturned this ruling in June, and in the spring of 1973, the case divided the U.S. Supreme Court. One justice recused himself, the other eight of them split evenly, and the appellate court's ruling triumphed. Busing would stop at the city lines. In large part, this reality corresponded to Holton's political vision. Through four stormy years, the governor consistently supported school desegregation and busing, while he raised his voice against plans for metropolitan consolidation. He remained wary of proposals that sought "numerical racial balance" or the obliteration of city boundaries; such policies often attracted the rage of powerful suburban voters. Yet when the court ordered integration and used busing as an instrument to achieve it, Holton expressed firm support. The same qualities that placed Holton in the southern vanguard also defined him as a prototype for the nation. This showdown over busing and civil rights shaped Holton's short political life; he departed from office in January 1974.

Francis Sargent's Torment

Racial tensions eventually engulfed Massachusetts, and the political tempest subsumed Governor Francis Sargent. Sargent was first elected as John Volpe's lieutenant governor in 1966. He became acting governor in 1969, after Volpe accepted a position in Richard Nixon's cabinet. As Sargent ascended to the office of chief executive, the Boston and Springfield school committees continued to delay any desegregation efforts. A growing campaign against the Racial Imbalance Act rooted its power in the resistance of these cities. Early in 1970, the state legislature filed three bills to strike down—or water down—the law. In response, Sargent declared that the Racial Imbalance Act had begun to achieve the progress that it promised, and he requested "cooperation to make it move faster." Sargent cited new schools in Springfield and an expansion of METCO—the voluntary program in which suburban schools welcomed racial minorities from the cities. He urged rejection of all attempts to repeal the Racial Imbalance Act. While the jousting between Sargent and state legislators seemed tame in 1970, the controversy gathered steady steam.[37]

Sargent won election to a full term in 1970, and shortly after his January inaugural the fight brewed again. The city of Springfield faced a cutoff from state funds on April 1, 1971, if it failed to present a plan for reducing racial imbalance. Springfield representatives filed a bill to prevent the funding cutoff; it passed the house and the senate. Sargent vetoed the bill on June 21. "I veto this bill with a moral conviction that

I hope will jolt those who assume the law applies to everyone but themselves," Sargent declared, and his veto was sustained. A similar dance occurred the following year, in 1972, when the governor opposed eleven different bills aimed at the Racial Imbalance Act. Neil Sullivan, the head of the state Board of Education, dubbed Sargent "the state's strongest proponent of the law." Against rising opposition, Sargent dug in his heels.[38]

Massachusetts's national reputation as a progressive stronghold, together with residents' perception of their state, played no small part in this story. If politicians in Virginia conducted their business under an ever-present historical cloud, it rained memories of slavery and Sambo, of segregation and Jim Crow. In Massachusetts, leaders grappled with very different—though equally powerful—images of their own history. Sargent invoked a mystique about the Bay State's past, a belief that Massachusetts led the nation, that it looked ever forward, exuded tolerance, and spearheaded progress. Like many popular tropes, this vision contained threads both factual and fictive. In a speech before the League of Women Voters on May 24, 1973, Sargent placed the state's passage of the Racial Imbalance Act within a broader triumphal narrative. He invoked John Winthrop, the Puritan who declared that "the eyes of all people are upon us." Sargent portrayed Massachusetts as a beacon: "When this nation cried out for leadership during the uneasy period of the civil rights struggle, Massachusetts, in its great tradition, stepped forward and provided that leadership. We adopted the historic Racial Imbalance Act that guaranteed equal and integrated education for *all* our citizens. A nation looked at us and was inspired and began to follow suit." As conflict heightened over the racial imbalance law, Sargent argued that Massachusetts must lead. "Governmental leaders all over the country are watching to see if Massachusetts has the true commitment to equality for which it is so widely known and admired, or whether it has, for over 100 years, simply paid lip service to this doctrine." Sargent was asking whether the mystique possessed any basis in reality.[39]

In October 1973, both houses of the legislature passed a one-year suspension of the Racial Imbalance Act. Sargent answered with a veto, one the senate barely upheld. Anti-busing leaders voiced their outrage over a string of close defeats. Louise Day Hicks denounced the governor; Boston School Committee member John McDonough blasted Sargent's "insensitivity to the people of Boston" and called for his impeachment. Through Sargent's first four years in the Massachusetts statehouse, he stood as the last line of defense—a crusader for black equality and school desegregation, even if that meant support for "racial balance" and the politically toxic busing it might entail.[40]

By the spring of 1974, Boston was a center of anti-busing ferment. The movement included working-class Irish Americans in South Boston and Charlestown, and Italian Americans in East Boston, but it also gained wide support among middle-class parents in neighborhoods like West Roxbury and Roslindale. Buoyed by the state legislature's opposition to the Racial Imbalance Act and by a vote in the U.S. House of Representatives that favored an amendment to ban busing past one's nearest school, the anti-busers grew more active. Especially in South Boston, this opposition had germinated for years. Since the mid-1960s and before, Southie residents had rallied against the encroaching "black threat." On April 3, about 20,000 demonstrators gathered on Boston Common. Later in the month, the legislature offered its boldest gesture. Both houses passed a repeal of the Racial Imbalance Act. When the first day of May arrived, the repeal landed on Frank Sargent's desk.[41]

State laws allowed the governor ten days to consider the bill. During that period, the *Boston Globe* reported that Sargent was contemplating alternatives to the existing policy. On May 10, television stations beamed Sargent's statehouse address into living rooms across the commonwealth. Sargent thought long and hard about what "caused one of the most progressive legislatures in America to vote repeal of one of the nation's most historic efforts to further social justice."[42] He organized such reflections into a dichotomy. Sargent asked whether "this resistance rising all around us" constituted the stuff of "racism, of bigotry, the resistance that would perpetuate two educational systems, one black, one white?" Was this the same type of activism that propelled "massive resistance" and the horrific violence against civil rights activists? If such actions were not "the blindness of the sixties," Sargent countered, "but the reality of the seventies, if the resistance comes because in pursuit of equality we ride roughshod over other equally important values—then we face a very different situation."[43] Sargent mollified the anti-busing movement when he declared, "Those who resist have not made their life's work blocking a good education for *other* children. Rather, they seek to insure a better education for their own." At long last, Sargent cast his lot with those who opposed the Racial Imbalance Act.[44] While Sargent told citizens that he had vetoed the repeal, he also presented an alternative. The governor's package came to be known as the Sargent Plan. After four years of support for a firm desegregation policy, Sargent finally caved.[45]

Sargent advocated voluntary busing, magnet schools, and incentives to promote better education. He asked the suburbs to become involved—by choice, not by decree. He stressed that parents, not politicians, should assume responsibility for their children's education. These sounded like admirable goals in principle. Up against the many whites in Massachusetts who expressed opposition to everything but their children's "neighborhood school," however, the plan seemed decidedly lackluster.[46] Sargent noted that if the court demanded a "compulsory plan of the sort I have rejected tonight. . . . I shall, as governor of this Commonwealth, be bound by it, obliged to execute it and firm in enforcing it." He sounded like few public officials so much as Linwood Holton. "It will be the law, then—and above all I am sworn to carry out the law. I shall be true to that oath, whatever my personal views." However, "I choose, I propose, I urge a different way." Holton and Sargent both hoped for alternatives to court-ordered busing.[47] Yet both governors vowed they would support the courts, if busing was so ordered. Sargent provided the details of his plan on May 29. One day prior, he had announced his intention to seek reelection. In this light, the Sargent Plan seemed more like an election-year attempt to elude explosive issues than a thoughtful policy to lead his state out of a morass.

Many Bay State residents viewed Sargent's plan with confusion; the anti-busers celebrated a victory. Across the political spectrum, observers could agree that it stripped the state government of vital powers. The Board of Education would lose the authority to redistrict or bus students.[48] The legislature's Black Caucus raised its voice against the governor's plan. State Representative Mel King perceived Sargent's proposals as "reactions to a hostile white majority."[49] Sargent signed into law an amended version of the Racial Imbalance Act in July, but by then the matter had traveled far from his own hands.

U.S. District Court Judge Arthur Garrity issued his ruling on June 21 and set off a chain of events that transformed the "cradle of liberty" into the embodiment of northern racism. Garrity ordered extensive school busing in select Boston neighborhoods. The plan's initial onus fell hardest on working-class enclaves like South Boston. In a pairing of neighborhoods perfectly suited for violence, Southie students traveled on buses to Roxbury, and black children from Roxbury were bused into South Boston. The resulting scenes—of stoned buses, stabbed students, and a wave of racially charged violence—need little more description.[50] Yet such violence did not typify reaction to integration in northern cities. "The picture of hatred and violence outside some Boston schools, is misleading," writes school desegregation expert Gary Orfield. "It does not portray the normal pattern but rather the worst failure of local leadership."[51] And yet if the awful violence in Boston seemed an anomaly, the gamut of reactions that Massachusetts governors embraced—from Volpe's signing of the Racial Imbalance Act to Sargent's changing stances over the years, and later, Michael Dukakis's evasion of the issue—proved representative of northern political leaders. Many northern governors advocated laws in favor of school desegregation. Yet these politicians kept their distance from the most controversial issues and rarely instigated school busing plans. They left that task to the courts.

Governors could not help but react to the massive groundswell against school busing. The most virulent activists often captured headlines. Their violence played into arguments about the white backlash. For various acts of anti-busing outrage, no term can define them better than "racism"; no word better captures the hate and fear, the viciousness and loathing. Yet even in Boston, according to historian Ronald Formisano, the majority of anti-busers possessed moderate racial attitudes.[52] The anti-busing movement enveloped thousands of Boston residents from various backgrounds, stretching far beyond hard-scrabble neighborhoods like Southie and Charlestown. Opposition to busing often centered on race, but also stemmed from displaced resentments over class and urban space. The middle and working classes inhabited a city that had been deteriorating for decades—a decline due partially to the policies, plans, and neglect of powerful suburbanites. When a Harvard-educated judge from Wellesley issued his order, city residents came to further feel that busing was foisted upon them from the outside. Garrity's solution—to pair South Boston with Roxbury—stung even more. The plan seemed either callously shortsighted or it displayed an idealism that smacked of whimsy. And yet Boston's anti-busing movement did not arise from Garrity's ruling; the court decree only added to an already bustling discontent. In Massachusetts, the first state to pass a Racial Imbalance Act, that law stirred years of resentment. By 1974, Boston's anti-busing struggle enlisted a citywide army.

In the 1970s, most northern and southern governors generally supported the principle of black civil rights. But when those principles required whites to sacrifice—or generated the perception of sacrifice—governors backed off. When Linwood Holton first supported integration and busing in 1970, he could almost sense his place in the future history books. Similarly, Francis Sargent's initial vetoes always came with rhetorical grandeur—with flourishes about morality, principles, and progress. Over time, however, both governors gradually stepped out of the hot light of controversies regarding school busing and metropolitan consolidation.

The busing dilemma ensnared many northern politicians. In 1969, New York's state assembly passed a law that stripped the state education commissioner of his power to authorize measures for racial balance. Governor Nelson Rockefeller, a moderate Republican, signed the bill. Rockefeller reflected that though he would not have "initiated the bill," it possessed "very strong support . . . reflective of a trend which has grown in communities of the state." After Nixon came out against busing in March 1972, politicians were pressed on their own stances. Many northeastern governors (almost all of them moderate Republicans) opposed busing. Connecticut's Thomas Meskill supported a moratorium on busing and stated his opposition to the policy "as a means of achieving racial balance." Seventeen Republican governors "deliberately left out" the issue at their annual spring conference on May 2, 1972, testament to busing's emotional strength.[53]

New Jersey Governor Thomas Cahill became one of the few to speak in favor of busing. At that time, in 1972, Cahill's position aligned with Sargent's. On March 22, Cahill opposed "rollback" of local busing plans. His declaration "underscored how . . . the busing issue has had the effect of separating the men from the weather vanes," the *New York Times* editorialized. While many governors tilted with the political winds, Cahill—and initially Sargent—backed firm integration policies. In late April, the New York State Assembly imposed a one-year moratorium on "the compulsory assignment of public school pupils." Such wording not only suspended busing proposals, but hamstrung almost every attempt at school integration. Rockefeller vetoed the bill, noting that the 1969 legislation had been deemed unconstitutional—and that the 1972 version likely smacked of the same violations. If a veto could be couched in the cover of the constitution, New York assemblymen and constituents might abide it. Yet Frank Sargent's vetoes enjoyed no such reception.[54]

In light of the delicate balancing acts that governors practiced the region over, Sargent's ordeal seems representative. Discomfort with busing proposals bound northern governors. They devised policies with an eye on the polls and an ear to the ground. Such senses told them to heed the anti-busing movements in their midst. In rare moments when governors supported busing—or, more frequently, when they refused to defy it—few displayed any enthusiasm. "Forced integration" was a pill to swallow, not a policy to champion. Almost as one, governors walked gingerly around issues of race.

When the first school buses transported blacks into South Boston in September 1974, whites met them with violence. The events stunned much of the nation and inverted popular conceptions about race in the North and South. "The rest of the republic, believing all the clichés it had ever read about the city," journalist Alan Lupo wrote, "was confused or shocked or, in the case of the South, delighted." One Virginia woman broadcast her euphoria in a letter to the *Boston Globe*: "My eyes and ears must be deceiving me! Is it really true that Boston, the cradle of liberty, freedom and democracy, is experiencing integration difficulties?"[55] On October 15, during the fifth week of busing, an African American stabbed a white student at Hyde Park High School. As tensions rose, Sargent mobilized the National Guard. Many Massachusetts citizens agreed with the move, and Sargent enjoyed a fifteen-point bump in support in the gubernatorial race—a campaign that neared its home stretch.[56]

The Democrats offered Michael Dukakis, a state representative from Brookline. Like Sargent, Dukakis long supported the Racial Imbalance Act—up until the spring of 1974. In May, Dukakis proposed a plan that emphasized "community control of the schools" and criticized busing.[57] Dukakis's proposal, like Sargent's, seemed weak in a city so shaped by school and neighborhood segregation. It was understandable if politicians did not wish to cross the anti-busing movement. But Sargent's and Dukakis's plans possessed, on their face, very little chance of lessening segregation. In a September 10 editorial, the *Boston Globe* slammed Dukakis. "Mr. Dukakis has developed a plan for community schools in Boston which would have the effect of preserving segregation."[58] Through the campaign, Dukakis and Sargent tried their hardest to avoid any mention of school busing—the very issue that was defining political life in the Bay State. On November 5, Dukakis triumphed with nearly 56 percent of the vote. Blacks in Roxbury favored Sargent by a margin of two-to-one, rewarding the liberal Republican for years of support on school integration.[59] Yet by the fall of 1974, neither Massachusetts candidate embraced a strong desegregation policy.

Dukakis's predecessors worked to strengthen the office of Massachusetts's chief executive. Volpe passed legislation that extended the governor's term to four years, and Sargent created a full-scale cabinet. Dukakis inherited unprecedented power, but on the issue of integration he wielded little of it.[60] During the busing crisis, as the *Boston Globe* reported, "Dukakis the governor was largely invisible."[61] If Linwood Holton injected himself into Virginia's ordeal, and Sargent at first signed courageous vetoes, Dukakis often remained silent on busing. The *New York Times* published Anthony Lewis's scathing critique on December 16, 1974. "The politicians have left it to one federal judge to uphold the law. The Governor-elect of Massachusetts, Michael Dukakis, a supposed liberal, advanced a school plan . . . to legitimize segregation forever."[62] In both time and space, Dukakis's Massachusetts stood far away from George Wallace's Alabama. Yet for his policies on busing in 1974, Dukakis endured similar criticism. Dukakis suffered such barbs in part because of unfortunate timing. As the 1970s wore on, busing became less and less tolerable to the American majority. Dukakis took office just after Boston's anti-busing movement began to crest—and his political career seemed to have a high ceiling. Across America, the issue assumed such power that Delaware Senator Joseph Biden termed it a "domestic Vietnam."[63] For Dukakis and many others, "forced busing" was too divisive an issue to touch. It afflicted executives with the deepest unease and forced profound conflicts to the fore. On this landscape, pragmatism warred with principle, politics dueled morality, class battled race, the cities fought the suburbs, and the white backlash had it out with the civil rights movement's emerging legacy—malleable and contested as it was.

Civil Rights Legacies: Electing Black Governors

The busing battle dominated Boston's landscape through the mid-1970s. In 1975, the city implemented the "Masters' Plan." This citywide plan featured more local involvement in the design and bused fewer total students than Garrity's first order. The 1977 elections witnessed Louise Day Hicks's final defeat and the triumph of John O'Bryant, the first black candidate elected by a citywide vote to the Boston School Committee. Dukakis lost the statehouse in 1978 to conservative Democrat Ed King, but regained it in 1982 and served for the remainder of the decade. He built an innovative and active state government, and won the Democratic Party's presidential nomination in 1988.

During his bid for the White House, Dukakis could not outrun the prodigious legacy of racial politics. If Dukakis's integration policies had previously been hammered by the *New York Times* and *Boston Globe*, in 1988 Republicans attacked him for liberal policies on race—or more specifically, on the proxy issue of crime. Before this assault, Dukakis nursed a lead in the polls. But Vice President George Bush soon aired an unforgettable advertisement. It featured the unkempt visage of Willie Horton, a black convict. While on furlough, Horton raped a Maryland woman; Dukakis had supported a prison furlough program. Thus linked in the popular mind to this African American rapist, Dukakis saw his lead in the polls vanish almost overnight.[64] Bush went on to brand Dukakis as a "Massachusetts liberal" who was "soft on crime," pejoratives that would doom Bay State Democrats for decades. Dukakis left the Massachusetts statehouse in 1990, and no Democrat occupied it again until Deval Patrick in 2006. Patrick not only wrested the governor's mansion from Republicans; he also became the nation's second African American elected governor.

The first was Douglas Wilder, who won Virginia's statehouse in 1989. Some observers drew a straight line to connect Linwood Holton's leadership on civil rights in the early 1970s with the election of Douglas Wilder less than two decades later. The image of racial moderation that Holton plastered on the front page of the *New York Times* "stuck with Virginia for almost 20 years," commented political scientist Larry Sabato.[65] Between the Holton administration and Wilder's election, race helped to realign the Republican and Democratic parties. Mills Godwin won another term in 1973—this time as a Republican, and an exponent of

the party's "Southern Strategy." Godwin soared to victory despite carrying just 8 percent of the black vote. This trend held firm, as Republicans
occupied the statehouse until 1981, winning little black support along
the way. Democrats held office from 1981 to 1989, when Charles Robb
and Gerald Baliles enjoyed high favorability ratings statewide. Both candidates received over 90 percent of the black vote. In 1989, after serving
as Baliles's lieutenant governor, Wilder positioned himself as next in
line for the party's nomination.[66]

Wilder grew up in a segregated Richmond neighborhood during the
1930s and 1940s. Despite an upbringing of self-described "gentle poverty," Wilder later built a thriving law practice. In 1969, he won election
to the state senate. Wilder immediately attacked Virginia's anthem,
"Carry Me Back to Ole Virginny," for its lines about "contented dark-
ies." From the beginning, Wilder's presence was palpable—and polariz-
ing. "I walked out of a meeting [where] they were singing the song,"
and the next day, from the senate floor, "read a speech of protest. And
you would have thought I touched the atom bomb. All hell broke
loose." Deluged by a slew of angry mail, Wilder wondered why "men
have to stand and wax nostalgic about that shameful period in our history. . . . What is there to boast about?" By the time of Wilder's gubernatorial candidacy, he had honed a more conciliatory approach. He also
gave white Virginians an event worthy of their boasts. In the Old Dominion of Robert E. Lee, and more recently of Harry Byrd, Lindsay Almond,
and Mills Godwin, Wilder's campaign raised an enchanting prospect.[67]

Many scholars have examined black candidates' campaigns for statewide office. Political scientists analyze many factors: media coverage,
candidates' attempts to "transcend race," the effects of light skin color,
and the varying importance of centrist policies, wedge issues, and the
candidates' political resumes.[68] But voters in Virginia and Massachusetts
also acted on perceptions about their states' pasts, and reacted to their
own historical experiences.

The election of African American governors makes sense only in this
context. During the civil rights years, Virginia and Massachusetts both
confronted school desegregation, both developed forceful anti-busing
movements in their capital cities, and in both places, thousands of
whites eventually experienced busing and school integration—if often
against their will. Moreover, residents of both states seemed to acknowledge that they were waging battles for the future on the terrain of a sto-
ried past. These factors help explain why whites in Virginia and
Massachusetts were ready, before voters in other American states, to
elect black governors. Their racial histories, charged and conflicted, and
their own awareness of their states' places in the union—hallowed and
high-minded—gave them a sense that they could and should elect Afri-

can American leaders. With halting steps, white voters thus attempted to overcome their own racial demons and resume their places at the American forefront.

When Virginians elected Wilder in 1989, they leapfrogged Massachusetts, New York, California, and every other state. For many Virginia voters, "the election of Douglas Wilder was a cathartic event," journalist Margaret Edds wrote, "allowing the state to at long last resume its eighteenth-century role as a force of political enlightenment for the nation."[69] If Linwood Holton's racial moderation had whacked away at an ominous past—one that included slavery and Reconstruction, Jim Crow and "massive resistance"—many thought that a black man's victory might dissolve the final remnants of that history.

In the 1989 general election, Douglas Wilder squared off against Republican Marshall Coleman. The campaign attracted worldwide attention. German television stations and British newspapers followed Wilder from Richmond to Norfolk, Williamsburg, and Virginia's "Southside." But Wilder downplayed his own race. Instead, he highlighted the issue of abortion. While Coleman embraced the Republican Party's pro-life position, Wilder fashioned himself as the defender of a woman's right to choose. This helped place him in a progressive "new mainstream," Wilder claimed. "Keep Virginia moving forward," declared Wilder's campaign slogan. "Don't let Marshall Coleman take us back." A savvy politician, Wilder aimed for the affections of Virginia moderates. He took up the abortion issue mainly for its potential to win over female voters. Wilder had long since shorn his Afro of the 1960s and 1970s, and he kept the divisive Jesse Jackson away from Virginia during the campaign. Still, Wilder did not completely bury the fact of his race. While Wilder's speeches and television ads rarely carried any language about race, they contained an implicit message that "the rejection of a black man would amount to regression," as R. W. Apple wrote in the *New York Times*. "Mr. Wilder kept reminding people that it was too late to turn back. The phrase reminded the state's voters of the days of massive resistance to integration, when schools were closed and the proud old commonwealth's reputation was corroded." Wilder navigated the specifics of Virginia's past—the blemishes of slavery and closed schools on the one hand, as well as the celebrated tradition of the Founding Fathers on the other. His very presence would help Virginia overcome the pain and reassert the pride.[70]

A typical Wilder television ad began with shots of the American flag, Monticello, and Thomas Jefferson. "Virginia—Birthplace of the American dream, American values," intoned the voiceover. As a shot of Wilder appeared on the screen, the narrator continued, "And in the best Virginia tradition, an extraordinary leader." In the only campaign speech where Wilder dealt in depth with race, he drew on wells of the Old Dominion's heritage. "Can it really be taking place in Virginia?" he asked a Virginia State University crowd on October 4. "Are they really going to do that there? What sort of poison have they poured in the water down there?" According to the *Washington Post*, Wilder then cited "the revolutionary and constitutional writings of colonial Virginians such as Thomas Jefferson, George Mason and Patrick Henry." He played on a view of Virginia as the land of liberty, and asked voters whether they wished to move toward increased political freedom or turn back. "I believe that the breath of freedom that was infused in this nation started in Virginia," Wilder continued. He was giving voters a chance to extend that history.[71]

On Election Day, November 7, some Virginians reveled in their chance to help write a new chapter in American politics. "It will be like a miracle," reflected Portsmouth voter Carolyn Simons. "I just feel like I'm making history this morning whether he wins or not." After all the votes were counted and recounted, Wilder eked out a victory. On November 8, a Virginia governor reclaimed the front page of the *New York Times*; his parents were the children of slaves. And fully 41 percent of Virginia whites voted for him.[72] Some observers were stunned not by Wilder's victory but by its narrowness. Political scientists cited polls that had placed Wilder well ahead in the weeks before the election, and they blamed persistent white racism for the fact that it remained so close. Others emphasized the victory itself. Frank Greer, Wilder's media consultant (and a white Alabamian), called it "a proud moment for his native South," and a "moment of redemption." *Washington Post* columnist Jonathan Yardley marveled that Wilder's win "borders on the miraculous." Even ten years prior, if one had predicted a black governor for Virginia, "he would have been laughed out of the room; if the same had been said in 1949 . . . the speaker would have been wrapped in a straitjacket and given a one-way ticket to a hospital for the terminally insane." Historically, "racial prejudices have been deep, entrenched, and bitter; what the election of 1989 tells us is that somehow, that history has been overcome." If Linwood Holton's acceptance of busing flowed against popular opinion in the 1970s, Wilder's election now involved the majority of Virginia citizens. The fact of his race alone proved startling.[73]

Because Douglas Wilder's election took place in a former Confederate state, it stunned Americans. Deval Patrick's victory seemed more understandable—occurring as it did in Massachusetts, the home of William Lloyd Garrison's *The Liberator*. But if African Americans constituted more than 15 percent of Virginia's voters, they counted only 6 percent of Massachusetts's electorate. The white majority's votes were even more crucial in Patrick's run against Lieutenant Governor Kerry Healey.

Patrick grew up on Chicago's South Side, attended Milton Academy on a scholarship, and graduated from Harvard. His up-by-the-bootstraps tale took him to the boardrooms of Texaco, Coca-Cola, and Ameriquest, and to Bill Clinton's Justice Department. Healey's television ads painted Patrick as soft on crime, and wielded the issue of race. The most unseemly ad depicted Patrick as a friend of rapists. Filming from the potential attacker's point of view, the camera followed a woman walking through an empty parking garage. The ad then replayed an interview in which Patrick described a convicted rapist—whose guilt was then in dispute—as "thoughtful" and "eloquent." Almost a century after D. W. Griffith's *Birth of a Nation*, the Healey campaign transported the darkest racial fear of the white American mind—the interracial rape night-mare—onto Massachusetts television screens. In a National Public Radio interview, Michael Dukakis reflected, "It's Willie Horton all over again."[74]

Patrick countered with a hopeful message, a compelling life story, and a well-organized grass-roots operation. He scored a twenty-one-point victory. Patrick garnered overwhelming support across the state, from W. E. B. DuBois's Great Barrington to Louise Day Hicks's South Boston. He carried Boston by a three-to-one ratio, and Springfield by almost as large a margin. Patrick fared well in middle-class white neighborhoods as well as minority enclaves. Three decades after Southie erupted in violence, the neighborhood supported a black gubernatorial candidate.[75]

Patrick took the oath of office in January 2007. The inauguration was rife with symbolism. Patrick placed his right hand on the Mendi Bible, an item invested with the legacies of both liberty and bondage. A group of Africans had bestowed the Bible as a gift to John Quincy Adams, who represented them in the *Amistad* court case and "saved them from slavery."[76] In the 1970s, Boston's image as a hotbed of racism was burned into the American mind. Three decades later, as the *Boston Globe* opined, "Patrick's elevation is one of many reasons to be optimistic that Massachusetts and especially Boston are overcoming the reputation for . . . hostility that has haunted the region for decades." Patrick's election eased the legacy of Boston's busing crisis.[77]

In 1976, that busing crisis produced an indelible image. Ted Landsmark, an African American, found himself rushing across City Hall Plaza while late for a meeting. At that moment, an anti-busing march rounded the corner. In the resulting frenzy, white youths attacked Landsmark with fists and feet, and with the only weapon at their disposal—an American flag. The image appeared on front pages of newspapers, and its photographer won a Pulitzer Prize. J. Anthony Lukas wrote, "In America's Bicentennial year, its symbolism required no commentary." To Bostonians and residents of the Bay State, no single event so tarnished the region's image—and it possessed enormous staying power. On the day of Deval Patrick's inauguration, the American flag waved over Beacon Hill. This time, Bostonians could celebrate the flag's symbolism. And yet Patrick himself would be more than a mere symbol, Charles Pierce argued in the *Boston Globe Magazine*, "and he would not be the repository of anyone else's redemption." Patrick "did not run to make white people feel good about themselves."[78] That such feelings may have factored into some white voters' decisions does not diminish Patrick's accomplishment but helps to explain it.

As in the election of Douglas Wilder, Patrick's victory carried deep historical implications. Voters in Virginia and Massachusetts bore the burden of difficult racial pasts as well as high conceptions of their own histories. Significantly, both states termed themselves commonwealths. "To call your state a commonwealth is to recognize the interdependence of citizens essential to self-government," Pierce wrote. "It is to leave a great bluff out there to be called. Virginia called it first with Doug Wilder. More than anything else, Deval Patrick and his campaign asked Massachusetts to call it this year." The racial traumas of the 1970s did not directly lead to the elections of Douglas Wilder and Deval Patrick decades later. Yet the crises of the civil rights years constituted a vital part of the historical fabric in both states. The memories of closed schools in Virginia, and waves of racial violence throughout Boston, weighed heavily on voters. Such histories mingled uncomfortably with voters' understandings of their own states' positions within the American nation. Children in both places learn about their commonwealths' celebrated histories; the racial conflict of the 1970s fits awkwardly into these tales. Once voters in Virginia and Massachusetts complemented their rhetorical traditions with electoral actions, the notion of the commonwealth became more than just a fanciful idea.[79]

Yet the meaning of these elections remains an open question. Immense racial inequalities continue to characterize the United States in the twenty-first century. In Virginia and Massachusetts, as in every other state, African Americans are the most impoverished, imprisoned, and undereducated. If the elections of black governors wrote the first lines of a new chapter in America's racial politics, they did not spell automatic progress.

In the realm of race relations, high politics have rarely been separable from social conditions or social movements. Political leaders like Sargent and Holton both responded to pitched protests from below. They embraced the legacy of the black freedom struggle at some moments; at other times, grass-roots anti-busing movements molded their policies. Suspended between two warring social struggles, these governors became racked with unease.

In a similar vein, the significance of Douglas Wilder's and Deval Patrick's elections remains tied to the plight of blacks in America. One could not celebrate these governors' triumphs, either in 1989 or 2006, without exploring how much racial progress had actually been achieved. Their incredible victories highlighted America's drastic changes over the years, from the days of slavery and segregation to civil rights. At the same time, these elections shined a spotlight on the ambiguous contours of racial change. After years of struggle, the civil rights movement expunged segregation from the law and the signs that declared "Whites Only" and "Colored Entrance" dissolved into southern air. Black and white children soon attended school together. The grandchildren of slaves ran for, and won, political office. Yet many who were impoverished before the civil rights movement remained so afterward. They may have gained the vote, but ballots could not always bring money or power. In many phases of life, and in many forms, racial inequity persisted. Joseph Lowery, former president of the Southern Christian Leadership Conference (SCLC), spoke to this ambivalent legacy in 1985: "Everything has changed, but nothing has changed. In the 1960s Bull Connor . . . threw us in jail, sicked dogs on us, turned the water hose on us. Today Birmingham has a black mayor. Last year he . . . gave me a key to the city. But in the shadow of City Hall I saw black people still living in slums, still suffering from ill housing and empty stomachs. Downtown I met blacks of the expanding middle class. In the shadows of downtown I observed a growing underclass." Even as black governors took office, the lives of many African Americans still resonated with a sobering familiarity.[80]

On June 28, 2007, Deval Patrick introduced the Democratic Party's presidential candidates for a debate at Howard University, where they addressed issues of race and courted black voters. Among the front-runners stood Illinois Senator Barack Obama, seeking to become the first African American president. One who looked at American race relations through the prism of presidential politics would glimpse magnificent progress. On the day of the debate, however, the Supreme Court struck down school integration plans in Seattle and Louisville. In the opinion of *New York Times* columnist Bob Herbert, "a malevolent majority on the U.S. Supreme Court threw a brick through the window of voluntary school integration efforts."[81] Thirty years after Louise Day Hicks lost her final election, Massachusetts inaugurated a black governor, Democrats considered nominating an African American for president, and the Supreme Court outlawed modest integration efforts. This amalgam of events revealed a hazy reality, befitting the knotted legacy of racial politics. From the civil rights era to the first years of America's black governors, struggles for racial equality have been uneven: the stuff of partial triumphs, ambiguous defeats, and ever-evolving visions. Few political leaders will greet the Supreme Court's latest verdict either with celebration or hysteria. If their predecessors offer any clues, today's governors will tread lightly around the court's decision. As Americans learned during the civil rights years, and many times before and since, such a ruling will mean only so much as its results are lived—filtered through statehouses and city halls, finally experienced in the nation's classrooms and neighborhoods, in its schools and on its streets.

President Theodore Roosevelt and Gifford Pinchot stand on the deck of a steamboat during Inland Waterways Commission Tour in 1907. Pinchot, the first chief of the U.S. Forest Service, was instrumental in organizing the gathering of governors in 1908 to discuss on the importance of conservation. Roosevelt, who led the conference at the White House, called Pinchot "the man to whom the nation owes most for what has been accomplished as regards the preservation of the natural resources of our country." Pinchot become Forester of Pennsylvania in 1920. Two years later he won the governorship. U.S. Forest Service.

Franklin Delano Roosevelt is sworn in to his second term as New York governor in Albany on December 30, 1930. During his second term, he passed significant tax reform legislation, including a more progressive income tax. Roosevelt's approach was unique in this period; most governors turned to the general sales tax as a way of relieving the fiscal crises of the Great Depression. In New York, however, with significant concentration of income, Roosevelt was able to rely on the income tax to provide sufficient revenue and create a measure of equity in taxation. Franklin D. Roosevelt Presidential Library.

Health and Human Services Secretary and former Wisconsin Governor Tommy Thompson speaks at a special session on Medicaid reform during NGA's 2003 Winter Meeting. NGA vice chair and Idaho Governor Dirk Kempthorne looks on. As governor, Thompson took the lead in providing state level innovation in welfare reform. Many of the initiatives implemented in Wisconsin later became part of the 1996 federal welfare reform legislation. NGA.

Commerce secretary and former North Carolina Governor Luther Hodges (second from left) meets with President John F. Kennedy, Federal Highway Administrator Rex Whitton, and governors John M. Dalton of Missouri, Frank G. Clements of Tennessee, Otto Kerner of Illinois, and Bert Combs of Kentucky. As governor, Hodges had initiated a program of economic development in an attempt to transform North Carolina. Among his accomplishments was the creation of the North Carolina Research Triangle. Hodges's efforts, along with other governors, made pursuing industrial development one of the roles governors were expected to fulfill. John F. Kennedy Presidential Library, Credit: White House photographer Abbie Rowe.

Governor L. Douglas Wilder of Virginia, the first African American to be elected governor, is inaugurated in Richmond in 1990. A decorated Korean War veteran, Wilder was elected to the Virginia Senate in 1969, became lieutenant governor in 1985, and served as governor from 1990 to 1994. Courtesy the Library of Virginia.

Delaware Governor Mike Castle speaks at the 1987 meeting of the National Governors Association in Traverse City, Michigan. In Delaware, Castle worked to preserve the state's leadership in incorporations. This included passage of an anti-takeover measure intended to protect both corporations and shareholders. NGA.

Vice President Richard Nixon waves after a speech at the 1954 meeting of the Governors' Conference in Lake George, New York. Colorado Governor Dan Thornton, Governors' Conference chair, is to the left of the photo. In his remarks to governors, Nixon called the nation's network of roadways obsolete and promoted a program initiated by the federal government, with state cooperation, for the planning and construction of a modern interstate highway system. Nixon told the governors that President Eisenhower "believes that only with cooperation, and with the maximum of state and local initiative and control can we have a program which will deal with the problem and deal with it effectively." Photo by Richard K. Dean.

President George H. W. Bush attends a working session at the 1989 Education Summit in Charlottesville, Virginia. Bush is flanked by (left to right): Washington Governor Booth Gardner, Iowa Governor Terry Branstad, Secretary of Education Lauro Cavazos, and Arkansas Governor Bill Clinton. The president later recalled: "In September, I met with the Nation's Governors in an historic Summit to discuss the challenges facing us in working toward excellence in education. The President's Education Summit with the Governors brought forth unanimous agreement on the significance of this issue to the future of the Nation and to the quality of life for every American. We will build upon the vision of our Founding Fathers in establishing national education." George Bush Presidential Library.

New York Governor Nelson Rockefeller arrives at the 1968 Winter Meeting of the National Governors' Conference in Washington, D.C. In his fourteen years serving as governor, Rockefeller shaped public policy both within New York and across the country. In 1966, for example, he oversaw an expansionary implementation of the new federal Medicaid program. Although Congress eventually revised the law closing the broad availability of Medicaid in New York, the tensions between the states and federal government over who should receive publicly supported health care have continued until today. An unsuccessful Republican candidate for the presidency in 1964, 1968, and 1972, Rockefeller was nominated by President Gerald Ford for the vice presidency, an office he held from 1975 to 1977. Library of Congress/U.S. News & World Report collection.

Chapter 6

Balancing Economic Development with Investor Protection

BROOKE MASTERS

When it comes to regulating business, governors have often had to reconcile the contradictory pressures inherent in a federalist system. On the one hand, they need to look after their states by attracting and nurturing businesses that can generate badly needed jobs and tax revenue. On the other, they must be mindful of their impact on the country at large and make sure that their actions do not stifle economic growth or lead to a regulatory "race to the bottom" that could leave consumers and investors vulnerable to sharp practices and fraud. This chapter will look at how governors of three states have approached this difficult area and how the growing gubernatorial emphasis on economic development has prompted some governors to take actions that clearly benefited their own states but drew criticism elsewhere for their effects on the broader economy.

In the first decades of the twentieth century, Kansas's governor Walter Roscoe Stubbs and the state's enterprising banking regulator J. N. Dolley put the state at the forefront of the Progressive movement, which tried to rein in business and protect consumers, labor, and investors from the growing power of multistate corporations. They pushed through a first-in-the-nation investor protection law that sought to limit the sale of fraudulent and highly speculative securities. Though Kansas's law was seen as a blow on behalf of small investors and widely imitated around the country, there was also an economic motive behind the move. Unlike many eastern states, Kansas was home to very few investment firms, and some historians argue that the main support for the bill came from local banks and businesses that were seeking to keep investment capital from flowing out of Kansas to New York and other financial centers. Stubbs and Dolley saw their law as a potential national model, but the federal legislation that ultimately passed had to take into account the needs of a broader range of states and therefore took a rather different form.

In 1980, South Dakota Governor William John Janklow had an entirely different problem: South Dakota's economy was going bust. Wheat prices were low, a local railroad had recently gone bankrupt, and the state budget was facing a $6 million shortfall. Out of the blue, Citibank called and offered to move its credit card business to Sioux Falls. The new outpost would employ four hundred people initially with more jobs to come later if the experiment worked. But there was a catch. The bank was interested only if the state was willing to repeal its usury laws, a move that would allow Citibank to charge whatever rates it wanted to credit card holders around the country. As it happened, the state's local bankers were already pushing to remove the rate cap because national interest rates were so high that they were losing money by making loans. So Janklow jumped at the chance, and the credit card industry became one of South Dakota's biggest employers—at one point employing one out of every seven people in the state.[1]

Later that same decade, Delaware's governors also found themselves grappling with the issue of balancing investor protection with the need to preserve and attract business. Though the First State is tiny, with little in the way of homegrown industry—except DuPont, the international chemical conglomerate—Delaware has long been the state of choice when American businesses incorporate, and taxes on Delaware-incorporated companies are a crucial part of the state's revenue base. The companies were drawn to Delaware by the state's tradition of hands-off business regulation and its widely respected Court of Chancery, which specializes in business cases and emphasizes efficient, practical solutions rather than just strict application of laws. But in the 1980s, Delaware's preeminence was under threat. The takeover boom was hitting Wall Street, and some companies sought to resist the raiders with tactics that left them open to lawsuits. The resulting litigation blizzard threatened to overwhelm the court's personnel and undercut its reputation for timely opinions, often issued within a few days. At the same time, other states were trying to steal some of Delaware's incorporation business by adopting anti-takeover statutes that purported to offer management more protection against corporate raiders. Delaware governors Pierre S. "Pete" du Pont IV and Michael N. Castle helped keep the court on track by increasing the size of the judiciary, appointing respected judges who gave the Court of Chancery higher visibility and—in Castle's case—signing an amendment to the state's corporation laws that provided some, but not all, of the protections that companies were seeking. Partly because of their efforts, Delaware's courts remain to this day the most important arbiters of acceptable corporate behavior outside of the U.S.

Supreme Court. Taken together, these examples will show that twenti-eth-century governors were active participants in the federalist system. They stepped up when they believed their states needed help, but they also kept the larger picture in mind and considered national interests alongside more parochial concerns.

Investment Protection in the Progressive Era

As the twentieth century dawned, governors and their states found themselves grappling with the consequences of rapid industrialization and urbanization. Giant corporations dominated the economy and tried to control the political process as well. Factory workers lived and worked in appalling conditions. Con men abounded in the fledgling financial services sector, tricking innocent people out of their savings with prom-ises of high-yield investments. Growing numbers of outspoken reformers fought back—first by exposing the ills and then by turning to govern-ment to pass laws protecting workers, the environment, and investors. Governors and state legislators were often at the forefront of this move-ment, often known as Progressivism, proposing and pushing through laws to break up monopolies, set minimum wages and maximum hours for workers, and protect investors from what was widely seen as a wave of corporate fraud. Individual states often served as laboratories for experimentation and the most successful statutes were copied across the country and, in some cases, enacted on the national level. In the investor protection area, New Jersey's Woodrow Wilson served as a pioneer. Elected governor in 1910, he cemented his reputation as a reformer by significantly tightening the rules for trusts—then the most common cor-porate form—and enacting banking reforms.[2] A few years later, New York Attorney General Albert Ottinger made his crackdown on securi-ties fraud the centerpiece of his 1928 run for governor.[3]

But it was in the Midwest and in Kansas in particular, where investors far outnumbered financial services firms, that the drive for tough inves-tor protection laws reached full flower. Recognized as the first Kansas governor to be nominated by primary election, Walter Stubbs was elected in 1908 on a platform of progressive reform and prohibition. A native of Indiana who lived in Lawrence, Kansas, he was a millionaire who had grown wealthy building railroads in his adopted state. His rapid rise in the Kansas Republican party—from the time he was first con-vinced to seek public office in 1902, to the chairmanship of the state party by 1904, and to his selection as House Speaker in 1905—compelled many to view him with great admiration and respect but also with no small measure of bewilderment and suspicion. Some referred to him as "the redheaded governor," a nickname bestowed at least partly because of his reputation for irascibility and for his willingness to agitate for reform.[4] Others, such as his colleague in the Kansas "boss-busters" movement, U.S. Senator Joseph L. Bristow, deemed him incapable of practical political organization. Governor Stubbs "seems to be making a good impression with his speeches," Bristow once noted, "but he has not the slightest conception of perfecting an organization. He simply goes into a county, disturbs the atmosphere, creates a good impression, and goes away and permits things to aimlessly drift or evaporate."[5] Writing in 1911, the "Sage of Emporia," William Allen White, characterized Stubbs as "awfully square and fine and true, but he is not a friendly man."[6]

As one historian surmised, however, Stubbs appeared to represent, more than anything else, the reform impulse that swept the nation in the early twentieth century, but that was shaped in Kansas by a traditional utilitarian attitude.[7] "I would not have you confuse, in any sense whatever," House Speaker Stubbs declared in 1905, "the honest, sterling banker, merchant, corporation, or business man, who has grown rich out of legitimate profits . . . with these greedy, money-mad, lawless concerns. The one is a necessity and blessing to a community, the other a law breaker and a menace to the perpetuity of popular government."[8]

When the Kansas legislature clashed in 1905 with Standard Oil—then operating a $3.5 million refinery in Neodosha, Kansas—and moved to appropriate $410,000 for a state-owned oil refinery with which to threaten the Rockefeller monopoly, Stubbs called the scheme "wild-eyed legislation and Socialism."[9] Stubbs and his allies—calling for what they termed a "square deal"—had, nonetheless, issued a broad enough call for reform to unsettle many conservative opponents. On his way to Kansas early in the Stubbs administration, Illinois congressman and Speaker of the House Joe Cannon reminded a group of Kansas City reporters just how radical Stubbs and his "square dealers" had become. "Kansas is the insurgent country, you know," Cannon declared. "I understand that the mothers in that state send their sons to Congress with instructions to fight everything that comes up, just as the old Spartan mothers used to tell their boys to come back from the war a victor or a bloody corpse."[10]

Stubbs's first message to the Kansas legislature, issued on January 12, 1909, drew on progressive reforms and experiments in other states but also placed Kansas at the foreground of a movement to establish a new and potentially useful state-level regime of business regulation. Recommending the enactment of a Kansas public utilities law, Stubbs noted the leadership of governors Charles Evans Hughes in New York and Robert La Follette in Wisconsin, where "public utilities laws have been enacted which have resulted in great practical benefits" to the citizens of those states.[11] With a focus on what he called "equitable rates and adequate service," he urged his legislature to utilize "the present railroad law" and to add "the best features of the New York and Wisconsin public utilities laws" but also to extend public supervision beyond the railroads and principal gas and electric and communications utilities to the issuance of the stocks and bonds of all public utility corporations. He urged the legislature to prescribe as well a system of "proper and uniform accounting methods."[12] Recommending the passage of new laws for the establishment of savings banks and a state-backed bank deposit guaranty, Governor Stubbs hoped to spark a general movement in the Kansas legislature toward a new regime of state-level business regulation.

Successful in his attempt to pass freight rate legislation and a bank guaranty law in 1909, Stubbs urged a second round of reforms in 1911. His 1911 proposals included a workman's compensation law, the ratification of the Sixteenth Amendment to the federal Constitution (federal income tax), and—what was perhaps the most singular of his administration's progressive reforms—legislation that would ultimately come to be known as the Kansas "blue sky" law because it sought to protect investors from fraudulent securities that offered investments as ephemeral as the air overhead. Spearheaded by State Banking Commissioner J. N. Dolley, an old Stubbs friend and ally who had previously succeeded him as state party chairman and speaker of the state House of Representatives, this legislation was designed to regulate the sales of "wildcat" securities within the state, corporate stock sales that had been deemed responsible for losses in the previous year estimated to be between $3 and $5 million.[13] Put into effect on March 15, 1911, the Kansas "blue sky" law was the first of its kind in the nation, and its impact was both substantial and immediate. Unlike today's regulatory regime, which emphasizes full disclosure of risks and punishes fraud after the fact, Kansas's law gave Commissioner Dolley the power to review—and in some cases reject—securities that he believed were too risky or simply bad investments. In practice, this legislation appeared to force many agents out of the state altogether, while many more, forced to register for the first time under the act, saw their requests for licensure rejected. Of the more than five hundred applications received by Commissioner Dolley in the first six months after the bill's enactment, only forty-four were approved.[14]

Some commentators argue that the state's enthusiasm for the blue-sky law was based as much on protecting entrenched economic interest as investors. Most notably, Jonathan Macey and Geoffrey Miller write that the driving force behind Kansas's blue-sky law came from small banks and savings institutions who believed that cracking down on out-of-state securities offerings would reduce competition for depositors' funds. They argue that farmers and small businessmen also supported the effort, thinking it would increase their access to bank credit because the lending institutions would have fewer customers for their loans.[15] Dolley himself had served as director of a local bank and later boasted that the blue-sky bill had stopped the flow of millions of dollars that were being "taken from Kansas."[16]

Although investor protection may not have been the sole motive for the Kansas laws, there is no question that Stubbs and Dolley had hit a nerve. By 1913, ten states, mostly in the Midwest, had adopted blue-sky laws based on the Kansas model. In each case, the statutes allowed state officials to ban investments on the grounds that they did not offer a fair rate of return. Reformers in other states also agitated for investor protection laws, but the statutes tended to take a different form in states with financial centers and large numbers of investment banks and stockbrokers. In a pattern that tends to support Macey and Miller's hypothesis, states like New York, Pennsylvania, and Delaware opted for laws that relied on licensing and disclosure and punished fraud after the fact rather than requiring prior clearance of an offering based on the merits and proposed rate of return. By 1931, forty-seven of the forty-eight states had adopted some sort of blue-sky law. The federal government soon followed suit with the 1933 Securities Act and the 1934 creation of the Securities and Exchange Commission to enforce it.[17] But in the end, the federal law, which had to balance the interests of investor-heavy states with the needs of the financial centers, rejected Dolley's model in favor of a more hands-off approach. To this day, the SEC emphasizes disclosure beforehand and punishes fraud afterward rather than trying to review the merits of investments before they go on the market.

South Dakota Courts the Credit Card Industry

William John Janklow, routinely dubbed "Wild Bill" in media accounts, was one of South Dakota's most successful and most controversial politicians. A U.S. Marine and a lawyer, he got his professional start defending Native Americans involved in criminal cases on the Rosebud Sioux reservation. Janklow then changed sides and drew attention for prosecuting twenty-two people, mostly associated with the American Indian Movement, for rioting in an incident leading up to the 1973 standoff between the group and law enforcement at Wounded Knee. At one point, his house was firebombed. Elected attorney general in 1974, he often boasted that he slept with an M-16 assault rifle beside his bed—and a 1976 incident lent support to his story. As Janklow later explained it, he was working at home when he heard that a man had taken hostages at the state capitol, where several of his secretaries worked. He grabbed a machine gun and headed over. But when he was told that the hostages were not his employees, he backed off and let the police handle it. "That was it," he told the *New York Times,* "no drama in the reality. My machine gun days are over."[18]

Elected governor in 1978, he ultimately served four terms as South Dakota's governor in two eight-year stretches with a break in the middle because of the state's term limit law. A populist who routinely decried the federal government, Janklow had a reputation for colorfully blunt language—he changed the name of the state's "correctional facility" to "prison" and said that as a youth, he had been "your average juvenile delinquent."[19] A rapid, and by some accounts reckless, driver, he amassed speeding tickets and dozens of police warnings, and he also lounged around the governor's mansion in pajamas with feet and, by some accounts, a bunny tail sewn on. Between his stints in the governor's mansion, he irked the Republican Party by challenging a sitting GOP senator, James Abdnor, saying the incumbent was ineffective and couldn't win. "Every problem we have here is the result of federal government policies or lack of them—high interest rates, trade, farm foreclosures, water," he said to the *Washington Post* during that campaign. "Those good old boys in Washington got us into this mess, and they're like a team in last place that never drafts new guys because they like the old guys."[20] Though Janklow lost—his only loss in seven statewide races—he so wounded Abdnor that Democrat Tom Daschle won the fall election. Janklow returned to the governor's mansion in 1995 after knocking off the Republican incumbent, Walter Dean Miller, in a primary and served two more terms.

At the end of his fourth term as governor in 2002, he ran for Congress and won, but then his passion for fast driving caught up with him and all but wrecked his career. South Dakotans had known of his driving troubles for years—he even alluded to it in his 1999 state of the state address. "Bill Janklow speeds when he drives—shouldn't, but he does," Janklow explained speaking in third person. "When he gets the ticket, he pays it, but if someone told me I was going to jail for two days for speeding, my driving habits would change."[21] But the state's patience ran out in August 2003, when Janklow ran a stop sign, hit a motorcyclist, and killed him. Though he tried at first to blame the crash on a nonexistent third motorist and then claimed he was disoriented by low blood sugar, a jury convicted him of manslaughter and he resigned his House seat. He was later sentenced to one hundred days in jail.[22]

But all those issues and his penchant for picking intraparty fights were still ahead of Janklow in 1979. Back then, he was a relatively new governor facing a serious fiscal crisis. For the first time in South Dakota's history, the state's economy was shrinking. Year after year, farms, railroads, and businesses went belly-up, and sales tax collections continued to diminish. After the Chicago, Milwaukee, St. Paul & Pacific Railroad went bankrupt, South Dakota's leaders found themselves having to spend $30 million on eight hundred miles of track, in a desperate bid to save the state's crucial freight railroad system.[23] In the waning days of the 1970s, the state government was $6 million in the hole and Janklow was reduced to proposing a tax on the state's major goldmine in an effort to cover the shortfall. "The economy was, at that time, dead," Janklow remembered in a 2004 interview on the *Frontline* television program. "I was desperately looking for an opportunity for jobs for South Dakotans."[24]

The state's banking association was equally desperate in late 1979. Short-term interest rates were rising rapidly because the Federal Reserve under Paul Volcker had recently begun allowing rates to float, but South Dakota's usury laws put strict limits on what banks could charge. Local banks soon found it prohibitive to lend money for mortgages, cars, and farms. "It stopped credit. In this city, in Sioux Falls, there were only . . . seven houses built in 1981. That's all. There were only seven housing permits, because nobody could afford the financing for a home," Janklow remembered.[25] Douglas Hajek a young banker at the time, later recalled that "it was clear something needed to be done with South Dakota's usury limit so lending rates could keep pace with the rapidly increasing cost of money."[26] So Thomas Reardon, the founder and long-time chairman of Western Bank in Sioux Falls, convinced the state banking association to take the unpopular step of asking the legislature to lift the interest caps. Though the bankers were worried that the public might see them as greedy, they were able to convince some legislators to sponsor the proposal, and a bill that effectively raised the annual interest rate cap for national and state-chartered banks to 24 percent passed the state legislature in early 1980.

Halfway across the country, someone else was worrying about interest rate caps. Citibank, one of the nation's largest lenders, and one of the biggest players in the credit card market, was in deep trouble. Caught between rising short-term interest rates and tough usury laws in New York, where the bank was headquartered, Citibank was quite literally "going broke," remembered Walter Wriston, then the bank's chairman and chief executive. "If you are lending money at 12 percent and paying 20 percent, you don't have to be Einstein to realize you're out of business."[27] Citibank first tried an appeal to New York Governor Hugh Carey. "We said: 'Look, we want to continue our credit card, but we can't do it because we're losing too much money. And all you have to do is lift the usury ceiling to some reasonable amount and we'll stay here,'"

Wriston remembered.[28] Carey and the New York legislature were less than sympathetic. Concerned about protecting their citizens from high interest rates, they thought Citibank was bluffing and flatly rejected the bank's request for a higher usury ceiling. But the U.S. Supreme Court had unexpectedly offered the bank a way out with its 1978 decision in *Marquette National Bank v. First of Omaha Service Corp.*, which held that nationally chartered banks could charge whatever interest rates were permitted by the state where they were chartered and were not limited by the usury laws in the states where their customers lived.[29] So Citibank was on the lookout for a state with very high interest rate caps, or no caps at all.

But there was a catch. Under the federal banking laws, a national bank cannot simply move into a state and set up shop. It has to be specifically invited by the state legislature, and bankers in most communities would fight tooth and nail against such a move.[30] So the action of the South Dakota house caught the bank's attention. There were several advantages to South Dakota—it was closer to New York than Hawaii, one of the other options, and its legislature was still in session, unlike Nebraska, another choice. The state was desperate for economic development and it had a reputation for being friendly to business, with weaker consumer protection laws than states like New York and California.

All of a sudden, Bill Janklow's phone started ringing. There were four phone calls in a single day; all of them told him that Citibank was interested in moving its credit card operations to the state. "I'd never heard of all this credit card stuff," he remembered. But Citibank put on the full-court press. Charlie Long, then a senior vice president in charge of credit cards, flew to South Dakota for a visit a few days after the first calls and Wriston followed soon after. "They were really dying, and they were desperately looking for someplace where they could be rescued. They were in the water adrift; that's what they were," Janklow remembered.[31] The bank offered Janklow a deal. If he could get the legislature to pass a law inviting Citibank into the state, they would bring four hundred jobs to Sioux Falls, with two thousand five hundred more to follow, if the bank received permission from the Federal Reserve to move its credit card operations to South Dakota. To reassure the state's banking establishment, Citibank agreed to put strict limits on its South Dakota operations. "We said: 'Well, we'll open a limited national bank in which we will not compete with the local banks, and we'll put the facility in an inconvenient place for customers, and we'll pay different interest rates than you guys, and you can be happy. All we want to do is use it to issue cards,'" Wriston remembered.[32]

The promised jobs and Janklow's enthusiasm did the trick. The South Dakota legislature passed what was widely known as "Citibank bill" on

March 12, 1980. While the bill did not mention Citibank, it basically invited any nationally chartered financial institution to open special purpose banks within the state in order to issue credit cards there.[33] Janklow and the legislature also took the additional step of declaring the bill an emergency measure, so that the law would go into effect immediately rather than the first of July, as was customary for laws in South Dakota. "We declared it to be a shortage of financial capital in South Dakota, the inability of our people to get more and better jobs," Janklow remembered. "The inability of our people to get the capital they need at a price they could afford to pay, or at any price, made it so that this was an emergency situation. And so that had an emergency clause on it."[34]

Citibank applied for a charter within weeks, and some of its major New York competitors, including Chase Manhattan and Chemical, let it be known that they were exploring the South Dakota option as well.[35] By the end of June, Citibank had signed a lease for two floors of Thomas Reardon's Western Bank building, and the *New York Times* was writing articles about "the birth of a banking center" in Sioux Falls, then a city of 78,000 people. "Everybody is talking about it. It's a good, clean industry," Mayor Rick Knobe told the newspaper.[36] Janklow won reelection by a record margin in 1982 and, by 1984, the governor had won national attention for his economic development skills. The *Wall Street Journal* reported that he had lured nearly one hundred businesses away from neighboring Minnesota, and he also raised hackles by trying to make South Dakota the first state where out-of-state banks would be allowed to sell insurance.[37] By the time Janklow left the governor's office, half a dozen large out-of-state banks had brought their credit card operations to South Dakota, and 16 percent of workers in the state were employed by the financial services industry.[38] The numbers might have been even more dramatic, but several other states rushed to emulate South Dakota by lifting their interest rate caps and inviting out-of-state banks to come in. The U.S. Comptroller of the Currency also proved reluctant to approve so many relocations to South Dakota. "I was going to sleep at night thinking that we were the new financial center of America," Janklow remembered. "I was just praying that we could go about one more year—about six more months is all we needed—where other states would really not make this move. I mean, Alaska made the move. Even Alaska changed its laws. California changed its laws. But if they'd have waited just five or six more months, we'd have had 20,000 more jobs in this state. We would have had to import workers."[39]

Other state leaders were happy the state got as far as it did. "In my humble opinion, South Dakota's image changed with Citibank coming to the state," Reardon, the state banking leader, wrote later.[40] Hajek, the young banker, agreed, writing in 2004, "After two and a half decades as the engine transforming South Dakota's economy, it is clear that Citibank's move to South Dakota was one of the most important events, economic or otherwise, in the state's history. . . . The reward has been a dramatic growth in personal income, and a substantial modernization and diversification of South Dakota's economy."[41]

Others have been more critical about the national impact of Janklow's move. Other states copied South Dakota and credit cards carrying high interest rates—and later high fees—spread rapidly across the country. Consumer debt in the United States topped $2 trillion in 2004, not including home mortgages, and by 2007, it had reached $2.4 trillion, according to the Federal Reserve.[42] At that time the average total debt payment had reached 19.4 percent of household income.[43] "The Depression generation is passing on, and we're losing their values," Howard Dvorkin, president of the nonprofit Consolidated Credit Counseling Services, told the Associated Press. "Now we've got an entire generation that doesn't know anything about thrift and careful spending. It's tearing the fabric that made this country great."[44]

Still, Janklow had no regrets for his role in enabling the growth of the high interest credit card industry, even though some South Dakotans have become sunk in debt along with everyone else. The expansion of the credit card industry "was going to happen. It may not have happened then, but it was going to happen," he told *Frontline*. "I'll accept my responsibly as one of the performers. . . . I still like what we did, and I still think it was a huge opportunity for my state. If you knew the upward mobility that South Dakota's kids have gotten from the opportunity to intern and to work and to be employed and to have upward mobility in that company and move on, it's been phenomenal for South Dakota."[45]

Delaware Tends Its Corporate Garden

When Woodrow Wilson tightened New Jersey's banking and securities laws in the early 1910s, Delaware was the major beneficiary. Companies and investment trusts decamped across the state line by the dozens in an effort to avoid the new laws as well as a new employer-liability statute passed around the same time. It was one of the early examples of how lax regulation can help swell a state's coffers.[46] Once in Delaware, corporations found themselves under the mantle of the state's highly unusual court system, which sent lawsuits involving issues of fairness and equity to a specialized Court of Chancery. There, judges, rather than juries, held sway, and they emphasized speedy and narrowly tailored rulings that were relatively predictable and tended to give management the benefit of the doubt. Eager to benefit from what some regulators viewed as a race to the bottom, businesses based all over the country flocked to incorporate in Delaware. That gave the state a steady stream of new tax revenue and became a vital source of high-level jobs for lawyers, accountants, and other business professionals. By 1929, corporate fees and taxes provided 42.5 percent of the state government's revenue.[47] Not bad for a tiny state dwarfed by much larger neighbors. Once the companies got to Delaware, they liked what they found. In the middle part of the century, more than half of Fortune 500 companies were incorporated in Delaware, as well as 45 percent of the companies listed on the New York Stock Exchange.[48]

But that success came under threat from several directions in the late 1970s and 1980s. At the start of the period, Delaware's economy was deeply troubled. Years of back-of-the-envelope budget forecasting and out-of-control spending had produced monster deficits and one of the highest personal income tax rates in the nation, 19.8 percent.[49] At the same time, corporate litigation around the country was increasing, causing concern in the business community that the tiny, three-judge Court of Chancery would not be able to keep pace with the blizzard of lawsuits and might lose its reputation for timely, well-thought-out decisions. Incorporation fees had dropped steadily through the decades. By 1955 they accounted for only 7.2 percent of the state's budget and showed little sign of rebounding.[50] At the same time, other states were making bids to attract the incorporation and financial services businesses on which Delaware had come to rely. South Dakota, as described above, was wooing the credit card industry, while Indiana sought to parlay the 1980s takeover boom into a source of new revenue by passing an antitakeover law that made it all but impossible to mount a hostile takeover of a company incorporated in Indiana.[51] The businesses already based in Delaware were growing restless. In April 1978, Alexander Giacco, president of the state's second-largest employer, Hercules Inc., mused publicly about moving the company's headquarters out of state. "Delaware's got too much government. The income tax is just the end result," he told the Wilmington Rotary Club. Two days later, Irving Shapiro, chairman of DuPont Company, the largest employer, added his voice to the criticism, telling the *Wall Street Journal* that he couldn't support efforts to recruit new businesses to the state.[52]

But two successive Republican governors, Pete du Pont, scion of Delaware's best known and wealthiest family, and Mike Castle, a close du Pont ally, made restoring Delaware to corporate primacy their top mission. They set out to change the state's anti-business image. Du Pont would tackle Delaware's tax and budgeting problems and professionalize the process of filling seats on the chancery court, while the judges he and Castle selected would raise the court's profile and tackle the increased workload created by the takeover frenzy of the 1980s. During

Castle's governorship, Delaware also beat back one of the strongest challenges to the state's primacy among incorporation locations. The legislature passed and Castle signed an anti-takeover law that protected corporate management from most raiders but did not completely sacrifice investor protection. That balance would later be seen as important because it helped preserve Delaware's reputation for fairness and made activist shareholders more comfortable with companies that remained incorporated in the state.

Du Pont had grown up in Delaware, though he left the state to attend Phillips Exeter Academy and Princeton. By his own lights, he was not much of a scholar—"I was just a lousy student," he told his official state biographer—and he majored in mechanical engineering because he thought it would help in his career at the family chemical company.[53] Naval service and Harvard Law School briefly interrupted his plans, but by 1963 he was back in Delaware working at DuPont. He then served a term in the state General Assembly and three terms in Congress before running for governor in 1976.

When du Pont took office in 1977, Delaware was a mess. "We had just about the worst economy in the country," du Pont remembered in an interview. "We had an inner-directed political system; we had major lawyers saying I wouldn't advise any company to come here because the taxes are so high."[54] After briefly terrifying the bond markets by including the hyperbolic statement "Delaware is bankrupt" in his first budget address in 1977, du Pont made cutting taxes and professionalizing the state government his top priorities.[55] He reached outside the Delaware establishment for Pete Nellius, his secretary of finance, and Jim Decker, the new budget director. The governor also established the Delaware Economic and Financial Advisory Council, which publicly voted on the state's revenue forecasts, a process that forced the state legislature to stop relying on inflated revenue estimates to make the budget balance. By the time du Pont left office, the state income tax rate had dropped to 5.95 percent.[56]

To protect and preserve the all important chancery court and the state's ability to attract national companies, du Pont firmly rejected Delaware's tradition of political patronage. "When the Democratic leader of the Senate said, 'we'd like to come tell you who you should appoint,' I said, 'we're going to have a commission to do that.' There was a dead silence and he said, 'we've always done it.'" I said, "I know. But now we're going to have a commission.' It brought professionals into picking judges."[57] There was a political element to this move—du Pont was a Republican and the legislature was controlled by Democrats, but the end result was a court made up of lawyers who were respected by the corporate establishment both in and outside Delaware. Du Pont and the legislature also agreed to expand the court from three judges to four, giving the governor the opportunity to appoint the first female judge, Carolyn Berger.[58] "The belief simply was that a three person court was way overworked," du Pont said.[59] Under Castle, the court would expand again, to five jurists.

The expansion of the court and the creation of the judicial appointments commission were critical for Delaware because they helped the chancery court keep up with the needs of modern business in a period when the takeover boom and the rise of class-action securities lawsuits had raised all kinds of new questions about the responsibilities of boards and management. Businesses around the country needed quick, decisive judicial opinions to guide their responses to hostile bids and angry investors. du Pont's actions made it clear that they could continue to count on Delaware to provide them. "The court had really great precedents and business really loved it," du Pont remembered. By investing in the court and professionalizing it, "we were sending all sorts of messages across the country."[60] For example, this period saw a flood of so-called derivative lawsuits, in which plaintiffs' lawyers claimed to be acting in the best interest of companies because the management had failed to do so. Delaware's courts responded by revitalizing the legal concept of "demand requirement" that insisted that angry investors go to company's management first with their complaints before turning to the courts. The chancery court then had to issue more than one hundred opinions on whether the demand requirement had been satisfied by particular plaintiffs, increasing its workload significantly.[61]

Mike Castle succeeded du Pont in the governor's mansion in 1985, but Delaware continued to carefully feed its incorporation cash cow. A Republican like du Pont and the son of a DuPont Company patent attorney, Castle served in the state legislature and then as Pete du Pont's lieutenant governor from 1981 to 1984. A believer in supply-side economics, Castle was a firm supporter of his predecessor's tax cuts and believed strongly in preserving Delaware's status as a haven for corporations seeking an efficient, predictable, and business-friendly environment. In his case, that meant providing full funding for the courts, selecting judges who would reach out to the business community, and passing laws that offered companies incorporated in Delaware the full measure of protection from investor lawsuits and corporate raiders. "If you come to Delaware, you are confident in what you are dealing with. Other states have tried to copy our laws but they don't have the history we have or the professional community," Castle said in an interview. "Decisions are made to benefit Delaware. This is a true revenue-driver."[62]

As governor, Castle appointed William T. Allen to be chancellor of the chancery court, a lucky choice that helped solidify the court's national reputation as a good place to resolve complicated commercial disputes. Allen "was the first chancellor to start appearing on panels at seminars around the country," said Michael Hanrahan, a Delaware attorney who co-wrote a history of the court. "Before that there were wonderful chancellors, but it was really a sleepy place. . . . The visibility of the court rose tremendously in the 1980s."[63]

But it wasn't just increased visibility. Delaware authorities took several concrete steps to keep the state attractive as an incorporation site for large companies. In 1986, the state comforted corporate boards by explicitly allowing corporations registered in Delaware to reimburse directors for most court-ordered damages in investor suits.[64] But it was the battle over anti-takeover laws that really solidified Delaware's position. During the mid-1980s, several states, including Indiana, passed laws that made it all but impossible to mount a hostile takeover against a corporation headquartered in their states, either by requiring a would-be raider to seek approval from disinterested (nonmanagement, nonraider) shareholders rather than simply snapping up shares on the open market or by imposing a freeze period.[65] Delaware officials were initially unconcerned about the new laws—state law required Delaware companies to seek shareholder approval to reincorporate in another state, and the anti-takeover laws were widely seen as unconstitutional restraints on interstate commerce.[66] But the U.S. Supreme Court confounded those expectations in April 1987 by upholding Indiana's law. By the end of the year, twenty-seven states had enacted anti-takeover provisions, and the Boeing Corporation, which feared a bid from famed raider T. Boone Pickens, had threatened to change its incorporation from Delaware to Washington state.

Fearing a major outflow, Delaware's corporate bar, its legislature, and Governor Castle sprang into action. "With all of the takeover fever, there was a feeling Delaware needed to do something, but there needed to be balance because some of the laws [in other states] were really draconian" and unfairly penalized investors, remembered Hanrahan, the chancery court historian.[67] Law firms from around the country weighed in on the debate. So did the SEC. Delaware lawyers and legislators ultimately opted for a law that would allow hostile takeovers but sharply limited the circumstances. The law prevented raiders from gradually accumulating stock on the public market by requiring a would-be buyer to leap from owning less than 15 percent of a company's publicly traded shares to more than 85 percent in a single transaction. Otherwise the raider faced a three-year waiting period to complete a hostile takeover. But investors weren't completely forgotten. Delaware officials wanted to avoid alienating unions, pension funds, and other institutional investors who would have taken it amiss if the state completely caved in to the demands of corporate management. Delaware's anti-takeover bill instructed boards of directors to try to maximize shareholder value—rather than simply consider the more nebulous "long-term interests of shareholders"—when deciding whether to approve an outside bid.[68]

As in the prior cases, Delaware's activities had a significant impact on the national regulatory debate. The SEC viewed the proposed law as too protective of management and eventually filed a brief in federal court seeking to have the statute overturned. But some business interests complained that Delaware's law was weaker than similar statutes elsewhere. Castle said he relied on Delaware's corporate bar to help the state strike the right tone between keeping the it attractive to business and making sure that Delaware did not lead a regulatory "race to the bottom" that would have harmed investors. "The key to Delaware has been the legal community, which has kept a very watchful eye on corporate affairs," he explained. "You're getting good suggestions [that are] pretty well-balanced."[69] He ultimately signed the takeover bill in February 1988, and the resulting law helped preserve Delaware's stature as a state where companies could go for a fair hearing but where investors also received some measure of protection. "I do not think there is anything in Delaware law that is punitive to regular stockholders, as opposed to those who are trying to acquire corporations," said Castle, who now represents Delaware in Congress. "Most people want their companies to be incorporated in a state where the laws are fair and the corporation can go about its business" without being second-guessed by courts or disgruntled investors.[70]

Balancing State Needs with the Impact on the National Economy

As these case studies demonstrate, governors have generally approached the arena of business regulation on two levels. As the titular heads of their states, they were often focused on creating and maintaining a business-friendly environment. But they were also part of a larger federalist system and had to be wary, lest their actions undermine the entire American economy or ignore serious public policy issues that could in the end harm the interests of their states. In the Progressive Era Midwest, promising to rein in business was an easy way to draw votes. But the particular investor protection laws pushed by governors like Kansas's Roscoe Stubbs also dovetailed with the needs of each state's existing business elites. It is no accident that the small states most threatened by the flow of investment capital to Wall Street were also the states most likely to require would-be securities issuers to get a stamp of approval from the state. The pressure on governors to protect and promote revenue-generating industries only grew during the twentieth century as economic development became a larger and larger part of the guberna-torial portfolio. In the 1980s, South Dakota's William Janklow spent little or no time worrying about the implications for consumers of the state's decision to repeal its usury law. Job creation and attracting new industry were paramount in his calculations, and Janklow paid little mind to the long-term problems of a nation awash in high-interest consumer debt. Neither governor had as long-lasting an impact as they might have hoped. South Dakota eventually lost its edge in the credit card business because other states also repealed their usury laws, and the federal gov-ernment turned away from Kansas's example and used other states' laws as the models for national securities regulation. Delaware's Mike Castle was the most active practitioner of federalism considered in this study. When deciding whether to sign the state's anti-takeover legislation in 1988, Castle explicitly worried about the potential impact on the larger national economy. As a result, he appears to have been more successful at achieving his main goal of preserving Delaware's reputation as a fair arbiter of corporate disputes. The state has continued to attract the incorporation business and its chancery court remains one of the most important arbiters of business disputes today. These three examples sug-gest that when it comes to business regulation, the best way for gover-nors to look after their states' interests may be to keep one eye focused on the demands of the national economy.

Part III
Collective Action
GOVERNORS AND FEDERAL POLICY

The history of the federal system in the United States has largely been written as a history of conflict. There is good reason for this; contention among the states and between the states and the national government has typified much of our history. Even the history of the twentieth century is often portrayed as a story of states opposing the mandates of a newly powerful federal government. This focus on conflict, however, has overshadowed a long-standing and equally important history of cooperation between the various levels of American government. The following chapters reveal this process of cooperation at work. Furthermore, these chapters demonstrate that the development of public policy has not been shaped by the proclamations of a distant federal leviathan; instead, states have, at times, pushed for federal intervention and negotiated the role of the federal government. Robert Jay Dilger explains that it was state highway officials who first looked to the federal government for support and coordination in transportation. When the Federal Road Act of 1916 was passed it required every state to set up a department to oversee highway construction. This requirement expanded the constituency for transportation aid and placed new pressures on the federal government. Similarly, Maris Vinovskis implies that the long-term effect of federal intervention in education policy has been to make states, or more specifically governors, the prominent players in education policy. Colleen Grogan and Vernon K. Smith argue that even before the passage of Medicaid, governors urged the federal government to provide more assistance for the ever-burgeoning population that could not afford medical care.

The essays in this section portray the prominent role played by governors in this give and take with the federal government over the shape of public policy. Governors emerged, over the twentieth century, as the prime negotiators for their state's interests vis-à-vis other states and the federal government. Much of the negotiation between governors and the national government has occurred through the National Governors Association (NGA). Among the other roles it has performed over the last century—providing a forum for policy discussion, pushing best practices, and professionalizing the office of governor—NGA has also emerged as a successful representative of the collective interests of the governors. These chapters demonstrate some of the specific instances in which NGA has performed this role. When the Eisenhower administration wanted to gain the cooperation of the states in developing the interstate highway system, it appealed directly to the governors at the 1954 meeting of the Governors' Conference, the predecessor organization to NGA. This revised the sometimes tense partnership between the states and the federal government and, in the process, revolutionized transportation in this country. When governors wanted to increase federal support for education reform in the 1980s, they turned to NGA to pressure President George H. W. Bush to fulfill his stated commitment to be an "education president." In the early 2000s, when the states faced virtually unprecedented fiscal crises, governors, through NGA, pushed for Congress to provide relief from the near crippling costs of Medicaid. As these chapters demonstrate, some of NGA's greatest accomplishments in its hundred-year history have been in the areas of transportation, education, and health care. It is in these areas, as well as the others covered in this volume, that NGA promises to remain an active participant representing the collective voice of America's governors.

Chapter 7

Moving the Nation

Governors and the Development of American Transportation Policy

Robert Jay Dilger

Every American confronts issues of transportation: their daily commute, the products they buy and sell, the place where they work are all intimately connected with the nation's transportation infrastructure. Most of us take this system of roads, rails, and planes for granted. It is only when this transportation system fails—as the collapse of a bridge in Minneapolis in 2007 tragically demonstrated—that transportation policy makes the front page.

For governors and other state government officials, however, transportation policy must remain a constant concern. Of the many issues on governors' policy agendas, however, transportation policy is exceptional. First, transportation is virtually universal in its effect on constituents. Governors recognize that transportation shapes both social and economic relationships throughout the nation. They share a keen awareness of transportation's importance to their state's economic competitiveness. They also know that transportation is a salient political issue for businesses seeking competitive advantage, for drivers interested in maximizing the ease of their daily commute, and for thousands—and in some states millions—of constituents who rely on a transportation-related industry for their livelihood. Second, transportation is exceptional because it is perceived in distributive terms, where everyone is thought to contribute to and benefit from new highways or improved public transit. Unlike redistributive issues like social welfare policy, in which there are identifiable shifts in resources or opportunities among winners and losers, distributive issues are typically not subject to partisan conflict, with disagreements focusing on resource allocation, rather than fundamental approaches. For these two reasons—its universality and its distributive nature—transportation has provided unique opportunities for cooperation among governors. Much of this cooperation has occurred through the National Governors Association (NGA). Because transportation is both complex and of mutual concern, governors have looked to one another for advice on how to proceed, using NGA as a forum to learn from each other's experiences. In the absence of partisan division, governors have historically shown a united front on most transportation issues, using NGA as a vehicle for collective action to advocate policies that align with their shared goals of maximizing federal transportation assistance and minimizing federal interference in the use of those funds. When governors have disagreed over national transportation policy, the grounds have not been based in partisan ideology or even in views of federalism. Instead, as this chapter demonstrates, these disputes are between states that pay more into federal coffers and states that receive more in transportation funding.

The Historical Context

To provide the best transportation system for their constituents, governors must dedicate enormous financial resources. Currently, about $250 billion is spent on transportation infrastructure annually in the United States, with the federal government providing $80 billion, states $76 billion, local governments $68 billion, and the private sector $25 billion.[1] Transportation is the states' fourth largest budgetary item, trailing only vendor payments for Medicaid and other public welfare programs, higher education, and employee retirement. Yet, in spite of the significant spending on transportation, many highways and bridges are in need of repair or replacement, and traffic congestion on highways and in many seaports and airports remains a serious public policy problem.

Over the course of American history, the nexus of decision-making authority in transportation policy has shifted. In the nineteenth century, transportation policymaking moved from the private sector to local governments. Then, in the mid-twentieth century, federal and state governments emerged as the dominant forces in transportation decisions. Today, there is a diffuse system of transportation decision-making, with local governments leading in some areas, states in others, and the federal government in still others. Governors' growing interest and involvement in transportation resulted primarily from the same factors that led to the public sector's growing influence. First, and foremost, technological innovations—the diesel locomotive, automobile, and jet engine—made intercounty, then interstate, and now international travel economically feasible for both goods and passengers increasing constituent pressure on governors to enhance transportation infrastructure. The national economy's maturation into a global market that is increasingly dependent on a nationally cohesive intermodal transportation system to maintain economic competitiveness also played an important role.

The Early Automotive Era

At the turn of the twentieth century, few predicted the dramatic increase in automobile and truck ownership in the United States that would occur in the coming decades. From 1900 to 1908, about 50,000 automobiles were hand built each year in the United States. Most cars cost between $2,000 and $3,000, limiting ownership to the wealthy. Henry Ford's October 1908 release of the Model T for $850 expanded car ownership to the middle class. Ford sold 12,176 Model T cars in 1909, and continued to experience sales growth, reaching 78,610 cars in 1912. In 1913, production efficiencies realized from introducing the moving assembly line to the automotive production process allowed Ford to reduce prices. As prices fell, Ford's sales increased exponentially, reaching 783,188 cars in 1917.[2]

Public officials, however, largely failed to anticipate this explosion in the number of automobiles and the pressures it would put on the transportation infrastructure. For example, when governors met in Washington, D.C., in May 1908, in what is generally regarded as the National Governors Association's initial meeting, Governor John Franklin Fort (R-N.J.) lamented "the inability of our railroads to keep step with our rapid industrial growth" and erroneously predicted that "our waterways were meant to serve as highways for our commerce."[3] The need for road improvement and expansion, however, could only be ignored for so long. By 1915, over two million motor vehicles were on America's roads. Importantly, trucks replaced horse drawn wagons as the primary means of transporting goods over short distances. As automobile and truck ownership increased the public began to drive out into the countryside and the demand for improved roads intensified.[4]

In the early twentieth century, the federal government played a limited role in transportation funding. In 1912, for example, Washington authorized a $500,000 state and local government grant program to cover one third of costs to improve rural free delivery (RFD) postal roads. It also established a Joint Committee on Federal Aid in the Construction of Postal Roads to consider proposals to expand federal highway assistance. Among state officials, however, there was little expectation of or demand for federal assistance. Responding to a survey by the Joint Committee, most governors indicated that they had little or no role in road construction. In most states, either counties or a state highway commission oversaw highway construction and improvements.[5] Of the forty-five governors who responded to the survey, only seven indicated support for federal highway assistance, and several of these governors worried that such assistance might violate the Tenth Amendment's protection of state rights. For example, Governor John Burke (D-N.D.) wrote that he was "in favor of Federal participation in the building of highways throughout the country as far as Federal assistance can go under the Constitution."[6]

Given their perspective, governors were not actively involved in congressional deliberations concerning the establishment of federal assistance for highways. Still, state officials appealed for federal support though various national interest groups. For instance, the American Association for Highway Improvement (AAHI), comprised of state and local government highway officials, railroads, and good-roads civic associations, called for improvements to U.S. postal roads. Similarly, the American Association of State Highway Officials (AASHO, later the American Association of State Highway and Transportation Officials), comprised of state and federal highway officials, initially cosponsored an American Automobile Association (AAA) proposal to establish a federal program to construct a cross-country system of hard-surfaced roads. However, AASHO members from the Midwest, where road networks were less developed than on the eastern seaboard, objected to the proposal and AASHO subsequently shifted its support to AAHI's proposal.[7] This proposal to bolster postal roads would form the basis for the first significant federal involvement in highway policy.

The Federal Road Act of 1916, signed into law by Woodrow Wilson (former Democratic governor of New Jersey), fulfilled the desires of both AAHI and AASHO. The act authorized $75 million over five years to improve rural postal roads. The federal government allocated funding to states according to a formula based on state population, area, and road mileage. Program costs were shared on a fifty-fifty matching basis, up to $10,000 per mile. The law prohibited expenditures in communities with populations exceeding 2,500, thereby excluding urban roads. The law enhanced state transportation administration by requiring states to establish a highway department or commission to oversee program operations. At that time, nine states lacked a state highway department. In order to receive federal funding, advanced examination of projects, detailed progress reports, audits of expenditures, and examination of finished work were also required. Foreshadowing future transportation policy debates, representatives from wealthier states, which contributed a disproportionate share of federal revenue, and those representing cities, which received no funding, argued that the funding formula failed to provide them a fair share.[8]

The Federal Road Act of 1916 marked the beginning of the centralization and professionalization of highway policy in the United States. At the time of the act's passage, in most states highway planning was a county responsibility. By the mid-1920s, federal and state road engineers were increasingly requiring county and city government officials to apply planning standards based on the premise that highways were financed by users and, consequently, should serve traffic, not bolster local property values.[9]

One of the early tensions that emerged was whether states or the federal government should supervise the nation's growing highway network. During the Federal Road Act of 1916's reauthorization process, AASHO endorsed continuation of federal highway assistance to states and opposed AAA's proposal to create a federal highway commission to oversee construction of a 50,000-mile federally constructed highway system. Governor Henry J. Allen (R-Kan.) was instrumental in AASHO's opposition to AAA's proposal. In July 1919, he invited state highway officials from seven surrounding states to meet with him to plan a campaign to defeat it. They circulated a petition opposing the national highway plan. By the time AASHO held its annual conference in December 1919, three-quarters of the states had signed the petition.[10]

The Federal Highway Act of 1921 generally reflected AASHO's state-centered approach. However, it broadened the program's focus on RFD postal roads to include roads that were interstate in character and expedited the completion of "an adequate and connected system of highways."[11] Funding was limited to 7 percent of each state's road mileage, with 3 percent designated by the state as primary, or interstate, in character. Up to 60 percent of the state's funding could be used on primary highways. Federal funding was increased to $75 million annually on a fifty-fifty matching basis, up to $20,000 per mile.

Governor Allen's opposition to AAA's national highway proposal was indicative of a new trend for governors. Previously, most transportation decisions were made by state and county highway officials. This helps to explain why Governor Allen invited his surrounding states' highway officials, rather than those states' governors, to meet with him. However, as Governor Allen's actions attest, as constituent demand for highways increased and state highway networks and associated expenses expanded, governors were increasingly being drawn into transportation policy debates.

The 1920s became known as the golden years of highway construction as governors, state legislators, and local government officials responded to increased constituent demand for new and improved roads. About $15 billion was spent on highways, with the federal government providing $800 million, states $5.8 billion, and local governments $8.6 billion. By the decade's end, there were 26.5 million registered motor vehicles in the nation, state highway systems had expanded to 314,136 miles, and total surfaced roads increased to 662,435 miles.[12] Importantly, the nature of intercity travel changed during the 1920s. Most intercity travelers now rode in buses or cars rather than on trains. In addition, most short-haul shipping, especially of perishable goods, was completed by truck. Railroads dominated long-haul shipping, particularly for heavy items such as coal, but even in that category they faced increased competition from trucks and the fledgling airline industry.

Recognizing the growing demand for new and improved roads and bridges, in 1919 Oregon, New Mexico, and Colorado adopted a state gasoline tax to support transportation costs. These taxes supplemented revenue drawn from property taxes and highway bond issues. By 1929, every state had a gasoline tax, ranging from two to six cents a gallon. In that year, state gasoline taxes generated about $431 million.[13] In addition, where just a decade before most governors paid relatively little attention to road construction, that issue was now one of their highest priorities.

Governors faced many challenges during the Great Depression of the 1930s; their ability to provide services was severely undercut by stagnant state revenue growth. Constrained by balanced budget requirements and reluctant to raise taxes during an economic downturn, governors were forced to seek ways to curtail state spending. Because road construction generated jobs, state highway spending was spared major reductions. For example, state highway spending increased from $841 million in 1929 to just over $1 billion in 1930, and stayed near that level throughout the decade. In spite of their budget woes during the Depression, states typically had more robust revenue systems than localities. Local government officials, therefore, were forced to reduce highway spending from $8.6 billion during the 1920s to $6.3 billion during the 1930s. Recognizing the states' fiscal difficulties, the federal government loaned, and later waived, the state matching requirement in the federal aid to highways program, saving states around $200 million from 1932 through 1936. In addition, federal highway spending increased to $3.8 billion during the 1930s, up from $800 million the previous decade. About $1.6 billion of that amount was through various employment relief programs targeted at local roads and railroad grade crossings.[14]

The federal gasoline tax's enactment in 1932, coupled with the federal government's expanding role in funding highways, led governors to become active participants in federal transportation policy. Previously, governors used the Governors' Conference—now known as the National Governors Association—primarily as a forum for the exchange of best practices. Now, governors also used it as a vehicle to exert their collective influence on Congress and the president as they deliberated the federal role in transportation.

Most governors viewed the federal gasoline tax as an infringement on their taxing authority. The tax generated $125 million in 1933 and averaged about $200 million annually through the decade, revenue that the governors believed should be in state coffers. Governors also objected to the diversion of federal gasoline tax revenue to nonhighway purposes. Ironically, the Hayden-Cartwright Act of 1934 penalized states up to one-third of their federal highway assistance if they diverted state gasoline tax revenue to nonhighway purposes.[15] At that time, several states had legislation or a state constitutional amendment to prevent the diversion of these funds to other purposes, but most did not. For example, in 1936 about 19 percent of state gasoline tax revenue was diverted to education. In 1937, Maryland, Massachusetts, and New Jersey lost federal funds for this reason.[16] Such actions exacerbated tensions between the state and federal governments over transportation policy.

During the 1940s, with the economy recovering and the federal government focused on defense, states again contributed the predominant portion of highway spending. States spent $11.4 billion on highways, up from $9.6 billion during the 1930s, local governments spent $8.4 billion, up from $6.3 billion, and the federal government spent $2.1 billion, down from $3.8 billion. A new development was an increased focus on highway maintenance. By the decade's end, there were 3.3 million miles of roads in the nation, with 564,000 miles under state control. About 55 percent of roads were surfaced (1.8 million miles). Most surfaced roads had been built during the 1920s and 1930s and needed repair or upgrading to accommodate higher automobile and truck speeds.[17]

This increase in state transportation spending, however, did not resolve tensions with the federal government. In 1940, the federal gasoline tax was increased to one and a half cents per gallon. It generated about $300 million annually during the early 1940s and more than $800 million annually following World War II. Governors continued to object to what they viewed as a federal intrusion into their taxing territory. They also continued to oppose the diversion of federal gasoline tax revenue to nonhighway uses. For example, at the 1948 governors' conference they approved a resolution that "all revenue from these sources should be used for the purpose of expanding and improving the highway system of the nation."[18] Another issue of gubernatorial interest was a 1939 proposal by Thomas MacDonald, commissioner of the U.S. Bureau of Public Roads, to construct a 30,000-mile national expressway system to improve traffic flow, eliminate urban and rural decay, and create thousands of jobs.[19] The highway lobby (oil, gasoline, and automotive manufacturers; trucking firms; and associated unions) endorsed the proposal enthusiastically. Most governors opposed it as a further infringement on state prerogatives. The Federal-Aid Highway Act of

1944 authorized $20 billion for a 40,000-mile national system of interstate highways. However, World War II precluded spending billions on highways and only token amounts were appropriated for the system's construction.

The nation's governors, through the Governors' Conference, also influenced the Federal Airport Act of 1946, and, in turn, the shape of the nation's air transportation system. The act created a $234 million, ten-year Federal-Aid to Airport grant program that provided half of airport development project costs consistent with needs identified annually by the Civil Aeronautics Administration (CAA). Governor Herbert B. Maw (D-Utah), testifying on behalf of the Governors' Conference, urged Congress to allocate the airport program's funds directly to states. He opposed a CAA recommendation to allocate funding for noncommercial airports to states and funding for commercial airports to municipalities. Forty-four governors sent telegrams to the Senate Commerce Committee, urging it to adopt the Governors' Conference position.[20] Congress chose CAA's approach but specified that program funds be allotted to states if state law required it. Governors subsequently reaffirmed a 1945 resolution at their 1946, 1947, and 1948 annual conferences, urging the federal government to allocate the program's funds through the states.[21] By 1947, about half of the states had adopted laws requiring local airport authorities to receive state government approval before applying for and receiving the funds.

The relationship between the federal government and the states over transportation policy shifted over during the 1950s. As the decade opened, controversy continued to surround the federal gas tax. Ten years later the states and the federal government had reached a consensus on the creation of an interstate highway system to ease traffic congestion, promote interstate commerce, and move troops and supplies in the case of an emergency. Congress fired the first volley of the decade in the ongoing skirmish with states by raising the gasoline tax two cents to offset the costs of the Korean conflict. Once again, governors were united in their opposition to the federal gasoline tax, adopting resolutions at their 1952 and 1953 national conferences asking for the federal gasoline tax revenue and freedom to build highways and bridges without federal interference.[22] In 1952, Governor Walter J. Kohler, Jr. (R-Wis.), stated at the Governors' Conference that he was "sick to death of Federal interference in the administration of programs which should be, and have traditionally been, the responsibility of States."[23]

In 1954, Congress authorized $2 billion for federal highway assistance, including $175 million in start-up money for an interstate highway system. Many governors expressed outrage that their objection to the expansion of federal aid for highways was ignored. At their 1954 annual meeting, Governor Robert B. Crosby (R-Neb.) urged the conference to "double and triple and quadruple its efforts in the next Congress" to get federal highway revenue returned to states.[24]

The governors' view of federal interference in transportation policy, however, would change dramatically after 1954. On July 12, Vice President Richard Nixon, filling in for President Dwight Eisenhower (absent because of his sister-in-law's death), announced to the Governors' Conference the creation of a massive interstate system of highways. Nixon presented a $50-billion, ten-year highway program, based on a pay-as-you-go system financed in part by tolls, an unspecified increase in federal gasoline taxes, and—"where the national interest demands it"—additional federal spending.[25] He invited governors to participate in the program's planning. A special gubernatorial highway committee, chaired by Governor Kohler, was formed to examine the proposal. The President formed an Advisory Committee on a National Highway Program, chaired by General Lucius D. Clay, to hammer out the program's details.[26]

Financing the interstate system was a key sticking point. Motorists and trucking industry organizations opposed tolls to finance the system. All interested parties, especially governors, were reluctant to raise federal fuel taxes to pay for it.[27] Clay's committee subsequently recommended the creation of a Federal Highway Corporation that would float thirty-year bonds to finance the system. Federal gasoline tax revenue, which generated about $800 million annually at that time, would be used to finance the bonds. However, Senator Harry Byrd (D-Va.), chair of the Senate Finance Committee, wanted a pay-as-you-go plan that avoided interest charges. His opposition prevented legislative action during the 1955 legislative session.

The solution that ultimately allowed for the creation of the interstate system was a federal Highway Trust Fund. A relatively small increase in federal fuel taxes, from two to three cents per gallon, to fund the Highway Trust Fund appeased governors and AAA. Governors continued to oppose the federal gasoline tax in principle, but recognized that using federal gasoline taxes to fund the interstate highway system was the only viable political solution. One factor contributing to the governors' support was that all Highway Trust Fund revenue was dedicated to highways, whereas in the past one-third to one-half of federal gasoline tax revenue had been diverted to other uses. Prohibiting tolls on federally financed interstate highways, with an exception for the 2,447 miles of toll expressways already in operation, appeased motorist and trucking organizations.[28]

The Interstate Highway System Era

The Federal-Aid Highway Act of 1956 was a defining moment in American transportation policy. It created a $27 billion, 41,000-mile project, formally titled the National System of Interstate and Defense Highways, with a 1972 target completion date. For the next thirty-five years, federal transportation policy focused on the interstate highway system. During this period, governors paid particularly close attention to proposals addressing escalating costs, efforts to divert Highway Trust Fund revenue for nonhighway uses, particularly for mass transit, and the proliferation of intergovernmental crossover sanctions requiring states to take specific actions—such as limiting highway speed limits, removing certain highway billboards, and imposing uniform alcohol standards for determining drunk driving—or lose federal highway funding.

Contention over the costs of the interstate system began within a year of the passage of the 1956 act. In 1957, federal highway administrators reported that it would take at least $37 billion, $10 billion more than initial estimates, to complete the interstate system. Most of the additional expenditure was due to escalating land costs and incorporating improved, and more expensive, highway design and safety features. Congress was faced with four options: reduce the system's size, delay the system's completion date, increase revenue by increasing federal fuel and transportation excise taxes, or provide additional funding from the general treasury.

Governors hoped that the federal government could remain on schedule with highway construction without further encroachment into their revenue sources. For example, the Governors' Conference adopted a resolution at its 1960 meeting urging the federal government to complete the interstate system on time without increasing the federal gasoline tax. They also created a standing Committee on Roads and Highway Safety to provide "continuous scrutiny" to highways and highway safety issues.[29] The formation of this committee elevated the governors' presence on Capitol Hill. Nevertheless, the federal gasoline tax was increased temporarily in 1959 to four cents a gallon to prevent the interstate highway system from falling behind schedule. This increase, coupled with rising traffic volume, nearly doubled Highway Trust Fund revenue from about $1.5 billion annually to $2.9 billion annually. In 1961, the temporary one-cent increase was made permanent through 1972, excise taxes on inner tubes, tires, tire retreads, and other automotive products were increased, and an additional $900 million annually was authorized from the federal treasury to complete the system on time.[30]

By the mid-1960s, then, most policymakers, including governors, believed that the interstate highway system's funding problem was resolved. In 1966, governors replaced their standing Committee on Roads and Highway Safety with a subcommittee on highway safety within their standing Committee on Public Safety. However, interstate highway system costs continued to rise. In 1966, the interstate system's completion date was pushed back a year to 1973. Governors responded by adopting a resolution at their 1967 conference urging Congress to provide additional revenue to "meet the future highway needs of the nation."[31] In 1968, the interstate highway system's completion date was pushed back another year, to 1974. Sensing that the federal government's commitment to the interstate highway system might be waning, the governors created, in 1968, a new standing Committee on Transportation chaired by Governor Ronald Reagan (R-Calif.).

The committee examined all transportation modes as part of a collective system, reflecting a growing consensus that a comprehensive, unified transportation policy was needed to address traffic congestion. As part of this comprehensive approach, the committee lobbied Congress and the White House to complete the interstate highway system as scheduled without increasing federal gasoline taxes.[32] Governors, however, also looked beyond highways, adopting resolutions in 1969 and 1970 advocating a National Airport/Airways Trust Fund, supported by appropriations from the federal general treasury and revenue from aviation taxes and users' fees, to increase airport capacity. Furthermore, governors also adopted resolutions in 1969 and 1970 advocating a National Urban Mass Transit Trust Fund for capital improvements, provided that states retained primary responsibility for statewide and regional transportation planning and its funding was not taken from the Highway Trust Fund.[33]

The efforts of the National Governors' Conference to secure airport funding came to fruition in the Federal Airport Act of 1970. It increased federal funding for airports from $75 million annually to $250 million annually from FY 1971 to FY 1980. It also created the Airport and Airway Trust Fund to finance the Federal Aviation Administration's other activities, including the automation of its air traffic control system. The Airport and Airway Trust Fund's revenue was generated by increasing the existing passenger ticket tax from 2 percent to 8 percent, imposing a $3 per head tax on passenger tickets for most international flights departing the United States, and increasing various aviation fuel taxes and other assorted fees. Annual Airport and Airway Trust Fund revenue exceeded $1 billion in 1970, $2.2 billion in 1980, $4.9 billion in 1990, $10 billion in 2000, and $11.8 billion in 2007.[34]

As they had since 1959, governors continued to advocate the interstate highway system's on-time completion without an increase in federal gasoline taxes. However, cost estimates for finishing the interstate highway system continued to escalate. In light of strong opposition from both governors and the highway lobby to increasing the federal gasoline tax, and lawmakers' reluctance to draw additional resources from the general revenue fund for highways, in 1976 the interstate highway system's completion date was pushed back to 1990.[35]

The interstate system faced an additional challenge from efforts to divert Highway Trust Fund revenue to mass transit during the 1970s. In most cases the highway lobby, with the support of governors, was able to prevent such a diversion. However, the Federal-Aid Highway Act of 1973 provided a symbolic victory for mass transit advocates by allowing Highway Trust Fund revenue to be used to purchase buses after mid-1975, and facilities and rolling stock for fixed rail systems after mid-1976. The act also allowed local government officials to eliminate interstate routes and use the funds saved for mass transit. However, if such a substitution was made, the funds available for mass transit had to come from the general treasury, not the Highway Trust Fund. As a result, the vast majority of the Highway Trust Fund's revenue remained dedicated to highway construction and repair.[36]

In 1980, in a significant departure from past resolutions, governors dropped their long-standing resolution opposing federal gasoline tax increases. This did not mean that NGA was no longer an active participant in transportation policy debates; governors insisted that any new federal energy-related tax revenues be used for highways.[37] Additionally, over the 1980s governors advocated for the interstate highway system's completion by 1990, opposed diversion of Highway Trust Fund revenue to other purposes, and requested additional flexibility in the use of federal highway assistance.[38]

In 1981, the U.S. Department of Transportation reported that 95 percent of the now 42,500-mile interstate highway system was complete at a cost of $70 billion (including $7 billion from the states). It also reported that it would cost $48 billion to finish the system. Initially, President Ronald Reagan recommended scaling back the interstate highway system to reduce expenses. Many members of Congress, viewing highway construction as a means to generate jobs and an opportunity to gain electoral credit by providing visible benefits for constituents, supported increasing federal gasoline taxes to generate the funds. In 1982, President Reagan, who generally opposed tax increases, reluctantly agreed not to veto a bipartisan congressional effort to increase Highway Trust Fund revenue about $5.5 billion annually by raising the federal gasoline tax from four cents to nine cents a gallon. Revenue from one cent of the five-cent increase was earmarked for mass transit capital construction projects (approximately $1.1 billion annually).

Transportation-related sanctions, which required states to adopt certain policies or forfeit a portion of the federal system, proved particularly bothersome to governors. Throughout the 1980s and 1990s, NGA urged Congress to repeal these sanctions and replace them with financial incentives that encouraged states to adopt particular policies.[39] One of the most controversial issues, especially for governors from western states, was the federal speed limit. The Emergency Highway Energy Conservation Act of 1974 had prohibited the Federal Highway Administration from approving federal highway projects in states with speed limits over fifty-five miles per hour. The states, however, found some relief in the Federal-Aid Highway Act of 1987, which allowed states to increase speed limits up to sixty-five miles per hour on rural interstate highways without penalty. Within twenty-four hours of the law's enactment, New Mexico and Arizona raised their speed limits on their rural interstate highways, and within a year another thirty-six states had raised speed limits on at least a portion of their highway system. In 1995, Congress repealed the speed limit sanction entirely, providing relief for the states from at least one federal sanction.[40]

The Intermodal Era

In 1991, with the interstate highway system finally finished, governors pushed for more programmatic flexibility in federal highway and mass transit policy. The six-year, $151 billion Intermodal Surface Transportation Efficiency Act of 1991 (ISTEA) continued separate programs for highways, bridges, interstate maintenance, and mass transit. However, it decentralized control over highway and mass transit decision-making by creating a $24 billion Surface Transportation Block Grant and provided state and local government officials added flexibility to transfer funds from one program to another. Furthermore, the act strengthened the role of local metropolitan planning organizations (MPOs) in project selection and placed greater emphasis on intermodal transportation solutions to reduce traffic congestion, combat air pollution, and enhance economic productivity. Governors applauded the increased funding authorization level and ability to shift funds between transportation modes. They objected to the expansion of MPO authority as an intrusion on state prerogatives and the continued diversion of Highway Trust Fund revenue for deficit reduction, and they urged full program funding in subsequent appropriations.[41]

While they argued for more flexibility in federal transportation funding, governors were also concerned that the national funding mechanism for transportation was being undermined. In 1990, the federal gasoline tax was increased a nickel, from nine cents to fourteen cents per gallon, with half of the revenue directed for deficit reduction.[42] In 1992, the federal gasoline tax was increased again, to 18.4 cents per gallon. All of the additional revenue was earmarked for deficit reduction. Outraged, governors testified before congressional committees, urging the federal government to fully fund ISTEA and to end diversion of Highway Trust Fund revenue to nontransportation purposes. For example, on January 31, 1995, six governors—Edward T. Schafer (R-N.D.), Terry V. Branstad (R-Iowa), Howard Dean (D-Vt.), E. Benjamin Nelson (D-Neb.), Tommy G. Thompson (R-Wis.), and Christine Todd Whitman (R-N.J.)—testified before the House Committee on Transportation and Infrastructure on behalf of the National Governors' Association. During their testimony, Governor Schafer advocated fully funding ISTEA at authorized levels and returning "the diverted Federal gas tax from the general revenue fund to the Highway Trust Fund."[43]

In this fight, governors found an ally in Representative Bud Shuster (R-Pa.), chair of the House Transportation and Infrastructure Committee. Advocating full funding for ISTEA and an end to the diversion of Highway Trust Fund revenue, Representative Shuster played a key role in congressional deliberations on ISTEA's reauthorization bill, the six-year, $203 billion, Transportation Equity Act for the 21st Century (TEA-21). TEA-21, signed into law on June 9, 1998, by President Bill Clinton (former Democratic governor of Arkansas), authorized $167.1 billion for highways and $36.3 billion for mass transit. Importantly, this amount was approximately what was expected to be generated by the Highway Trust Fund, effectively ending the diversion of its revenue for deficit reduction. In addition, each state was guaranteed at least 90.5 percent of the revenue their highway users paid into the Highway Trust—an important issue for governors from so-called "donor" states, mostly outside of the Northeast, that provide more revenue to the Highway Trust Fund than they receive.[44]

Representative Shuster also opposed diversion of Airport and Airway Trust Fund revenue. He had a key role in the enactment of the Wendell H. Ford Aviation Investment and Reform Act for the 21st Century (AIR-21), signed into law by President Clinton on April 5, 2000. AIR-21 increased the Federal Aviation Administration's authorization level significantly, from $9.9 billion in FY 2000 to $12.6 billion in FY 2001, $13.3 billion in FY 2002, and $14 billion in FY 2003. These funding authorization levels exceeded the revenue generated by the Airport and Airway Trust Fund, effectively ending the diversion of its funds for other purposes. AIR-21 also included a provision making it "out-of-order" in the House or Senate to consider legislation that failed to use all trust fund receipts and interest annually. These funding guarantees were extended through FY2007 in the Vision 100—Century of Aviation Reauthorization

Act, signed into law by President George W. Bush (former Republican governor of Texas) on December 12, 2003.[45]

Scheduled to expire in 2003, TEA-21 took two years to be reauthorized. Here the consensus among governors over transportation policy broke down as those from donor states that paid more into federal coffers squabbled with donee states that received more federal funds. The deadlock was broken by increasing six-year funding from $218 billion (FY1998–2003) to $286.4 billion (FY2004–2009). The funding increase allowed congressional conferees to guarantee all states an eventual 92 percent rate of return, compared to ISTEA's 90.5 percent rate, while at the same time guaranteeing twenty-seven states that they will not receive less money than in the past. President Bush signed the six-year, $286.4 billion Safe, Accountable, Flexible, Efficient Transportation Equity Act—A Legacy for Users (SAFETEA) on August 10, 2005. It reauthorized federal surface transportation programs through the end of FY2009 and, importantly, provided governors additional flexibility to use innovative financing and tolls to generate revenue for highways.[46]

Governors have used SAFETEA's additional flexibility to utilize both innovative financing and tolls to generate revenue for highways. In 2005, tolls generated only about 5 percent of state highway revenue, but a nationwide survey of state transportation officials revealed that, in addition to the twenty-four states that already had toll roads, seven states were planning to toll for the first time, and sixteen of the twenty-four tolling states were planning to add new toll roads, either by tolling existing roads or building new toll roads. These new tolls are intended to finance additional highway capacity, maintain selected highways and bridges, and manage traffic congestion. Toll road advocates argue that tolls reduce road congestion by creating incentives for drivers to avoid driving alone, use public transportation, travel at less congested times, or travel on less congested routes, if available.[47] Others oppose tolls as a form of double taxation and, despite the introduction of special lanes utilizing electronic toll collection technology, as traffic bottlenecks. Some states are also considering leasing toll roads to private companies in exchange for cash up-front to build transportation infrastructure. For example, in 2006 Governor Mitch Daniels (R-Ind.) was instrumental in the leasing of the 157-mile Indiana Toll Road for seventy-five years to a consortium of Spanish and Australian companies for $3.8 billion.[48] Illinois (Chicago), Texas, and Virginia also have privately administered toll highways. In 2005, Governor Rick Perry (R-Tex.) proposed a fifty-year plan to build nearly 4,000 miles of privately administered toll roads along the portions of I-69 and I-35 that cross Texas. A consortium of private investors provided $7.2 billion for the Trans Texas Corridor's initial segment.[49] Oregon is experimenting with global positioning technology to determine the feasibility of imposing a mileage taxing system that is collected at gasoline stations to replace or supplement revenue from the gasoline tax.[50] Other states are experimenting with innovative "non-build" strategies to reduce traffic congestion, including congestion pricing, such as charging higher tolls during peak travel hours and imposing significantly higher parking fees in congested areas, to reduce peak-period vehicle trips and encourage ride sharing and mass transit use.

Conclusion

Since its inception, the National Governors Association has served as a forum for the exchange of ideas and best practices on a wide range of issues, including transportation policy. As the federal government's involvement in transportation policy increased, NGA became the primary means for governors to exert their collective influence on federal transportation policy. Because transportation policy is a distributive issue, partisan divisions on transportation policy have been muted. In the absence of partisan conflict, governors have found common ground in their shared desire to maximize federal transportation assistance while minimizing federal interference in the use of those funds. Historically, disagreements have generally been limited to the allocation of federal resources among states, such as the recent disagreements between governors from "donor" and "donee" states concerning the criteria employed to allocate Highway Trust Fund revenue among states.

Three common themes currently run through the governors' efforts to influence federal transportation policy. First, governors are united in their conviction that federal funding for building and maintaining highways, bridges, mass transit, railroads, and airports must be both predictable and sufficient to meet demand, especially for transportation projects that have interstate commerce implications. Second, governors insist that it is in the national interest to provide them maximum flexibility in the use of federal transportation funding because they are in a better position than federal officials to understand and address their state's unique and varying transportation needs. Third, given limited resources, governors are increasingly experimenting with innovative financing mechanisms to generate additional revenue for transportation infrastructure and, to a lesser extent, nonbuild strategies to reduce demand for additional transportation infrastructure.

Chapter 8
Gubernatorial Leadership and American K-12 Education Reform

MARIS A. VINOVSKIS

The history of state-level public policy in America is one of centralization and modernization. Yet, all policy areas did not proceed at the same pace. In some realms, like transportation, states took control early in the twentieth century. In other realms, such as education, localities continued to direct policy choices and resisted attempts at uniformity and centralization. In the late twentieth century, after the passage of the Elementary and Secondary Education Act of 1965, states took an even greater role in shaping education policy. An influx of federal financial support spurred states to professionalize and provide greater oversight over schools. However, just as localities opposed state centralization, states have resisted too much federal intervention in education policy. Today, where other areas of social policy have become largely federalized, states and local communities still pay most of the K-12 education costs and continue to try to maintain control.

This chapter investigates the slow process of centralization in education and asks how it is that states and governors emerged as leaders in education policy. Rather than following a uniform trajectory, this has been a process of fits and starts. Over the early twentieth century, state administration and funding of schools grew exponentially. Still, localities maintained control of their classrooms and governors rarely intervened in educational policy. In the second half of the twentieth century, federal intervention in education encouraged governors to pay more attention to the issue. *Brown v. Board of Education*, Sputnik, and the Great Society all made education an issue that governors could no longer ignore. By the late 1970s, governors embraced education as a critical policy responsibility. Southern governors, for example, adopted education as a tool for economic development. Through the National Governors Association, these governors helped return education to the national policy agenda. The result has been national attempts to apply more uniformity in student outcomes through programs such as Goals 2000 and No Child Left Behind. Even with these federal interventions, states and, in turn, governors continue to play an important role in education reforms.[1]

Localism in K-12 Education

For most of American history, K-12 education was a local responsibility. In the colonial era, most education occurred in the home. The few communities that had schools supported them with local funds. In the early nineteenth century, public common (elementary) schools and private academies gradually spread throughout the country—though the South continued to trail the nation. Some states, such as Massachusetts, created public high schools as early as 1821, but most children in the nation only received a common school education. Slaves and free blacks were denied equal educational opportunities despite their strong interest in learning to read and write. A few antebellum southern governors championed state school assistance, but New England and Midwest state school superintendents such as Henry Barnard, Horace Mann, and John Pierce were the most outspoken and successful common school advocates.[2]

Opportunities for formal education expanded after the Civil War. Facilities were created to provide education to African Americans in the South, although discrimination hampered progress. School reformers transformed education in urban areas, increasing the rates of high school attendance. These initiatives, however, remained largely local. In rural areas, many children continued to attend one-room schoolhouses. While the U.S. Constitution does not mention education as a federal responsibility, the antebellum national government had provided land for supporting public schools. A U.S. Department of Education was created in 1867 (reorganized shortly afterward as the Bureau of Education), but its function was mainly collecting and disseminating educational information and statistics.[3]

Most states had responsibility through their constitutions for ensuring the adequate education of their citizens; but usually they delegated that task to local communities or regional entities such as counties.[4] Thus, at the turn of the twentieth century, education remained primarily a local responsibility. States, however, began to expand their administrative role in education in the early years of the new century.[5] Some states such as Connecticut, Massachusetts, and Michigan had appointed education superintendents (or secretaries of the state board of education) early in the nineteenth century, but significant growth in state education bureaucracy occurred in the early 1900s. The number of state boards of education grew from twenty-nine in 1890 to forty-one in 1925. In 1890, many of the state education agencies were small operations staffed by only one or two professionals besides the superintendent. By 1925, the total number of state education staff members had increased by an astounding 300 percent.[6] Still the role of state education administrators was limited. Writing about the first half of the twentieth century, historians David Tyack and Elisabeth Hansot concluded that "in most places the state superintendent exercised little power. Educational reformers complained for over a hundred years that state executives were figureheads who collected statistics, disbursed funds, and relayed messages from the legislature and state board, with little opportunity for initiative or leadership."[7]

One area where state administrators played a larger role was in vocational education. The Smith-Hughes Act of 1917 provided federal funds to states on a matching dollar basis for vocational education teachers in order to encourage the study of agriculture, trade, and industry. With additional funds available for staff to administer the program, states dedicated much of their educational bureaucracy to administer vocational education. Even in the early twentieth century, federal initiative provided an incentive for expanding state education staffs and involvement.[8]

With so little state involvement in education, governors played a limited role in setting education policy. The work of governors such as Charles Brantley Aycock of North Carolina and Andrew Jackson Montage of Virginia to improve schools are notable exceptions in the period.[9] Over the 1920s and 1930s, however, state education agencies began to exert greater influence as they set higher minimum school performance standards, inspected local education activities, provided professional advice, and offered monetary rewards for local compliance with state directives. States pushed initiatives in areas such as teacher training and licensing, compulsory school attendance, health and safety issues, and reducing the number of rural school districts.[10]

While localities provided the majority of funds for schools, the share of state funding for education increased over these decades. Faced with budget shortfalls during the Great Depression, localities turned to the more solvent state governments to help fund their schools. Governors such as Indiana's Paul McNutt were noteworthy for working with state legislatures to increase education funding.[11] This national shift in the funding of education was significant. In 1900 local areas provided 82 percent of public school funding and states provided the rest; by 1939, the local share diminished to 68 percent, the state contribution rose to 30 percent, and the federal government added 2 percent.[12]

After World War II, education took on new importance for both state and federal governments. The baby boom after the war kept states and localities scrambling for decades to find enough classrooms, teachers, and funding to educate every child.[13] The 1946 National School Lunch program provided new federal assistance to primary and secondary schools. The 1954 Supreme Court decision in *Brown v. Board of Education* ending segregation in public education forced governors, especially those in the South, to confront issues of education on a statewide level.[14] The launch of Sputnik in 1957 highlighted the lagging achievements of American students. In response, the National Defense Education Act of 1958 funded foreign language, mathematics, and science instruction at all levels of education.[15] A demographic bubble, the Cold War, and federal initiatives had pushed the governors further into the realm of K-12 education; but it was in the 1960s that the state role in education would be transformed.

At the same time, the authority of governors over public policy expanded and the qualifications of governors increased. Most governors were not powerful state leaders in the nineteenth and early twentieth centuries. Gradually the governors' reach in the first half of the twentieth century increased as voters worried about the quality and competence of state legislatures as well as the proliferation of uncoordinated state agencies. By the mid-twentieth century the overall quality of governors improved and their responsibilities expanded. Changes in state constitutions increased the powers and staffs of governors and assigned them responsibility for coordinating the fragmented state agencies, including those dealing with education.[16]

Governors, the Federal Government, and Education in the 1960s

In his 1960 presidential campaign, John F. Kennedy pledged support for federal aid to elementary and secondary schools. Once elected, however, Kennedy faced the difficult task of finding a politically acceptable mechanism for distributing such aid. In 1961 federal officials met with a wide variety of groups to explore possible education alternatives. Included in their consultations were the nation's governors as embodied in the Governors' Conference (now known as the National Governors Association). Many governors supported federal aid to education as a way to alleviate the growing costs of education for the states. Yet, there was hardly consensus on this issue. Speaking at the 1961 Governors' Conference meeting in Honolulu, Governor Price Daniel of Texas criticized those willing to accept federal financial support for education. "They do not seem to realize," he explained, "that federal dollars come from the pockets of the same taxpayers as state and local tax dollars. Neither do they seem to realize that dependence on federal funds for operation of local schools will serve to lessen rather than strengthen local interest, improvements, efficiencies, and economies."[17] Still, the Governors' Conference approved a resolution asking for federal aid for K-12 school construction as well as loans for the construction and improvement of higher education facilities. A recommendation for federal aid for teacher salaries, however, was narrowly defeated.[18] Although President Kennedy made education one of his top five legislative priorities, Congress failed to enact a general K-12 education aid bill.[19]

When Lyndon B. Johnson assumed the presidency following the assassination of President Kennedy on November 22, 1963, he enthusiastically accepted Kennedy's domestic priorities, paying particular attention to improving education and eradicating poverty. Johnson and the Democratic Congress passed the Economic Opportunity Act of 1964.[20] With encouragement from several Republican legislators, Sargent Shriver, director of the new Office of Economic Opportunity, launched a massive summer Head Start program in 1965 to prepare disadvantaged children for entry into the elementary grades.[21]

In 1965, President Johnson and the now more Democratic 89th Congress passed the Elementary and Secondary Education Act (ESEA). In order to finesse the political problems associated with a general education aid bill, ESEA was designed as a categorical program targeted to helping disadvantaged K-12 students (though the eligibility requirements were so broadly defined that an estimated 95 percent of school districts qualified for federal assistance). Initially ESEA consisted of only five titles and included a dozen programs; by the 1978 reauthorization it had expanded to thirteen titles and more than one hundred individual programs. The major section was Title I, which assisted disadvantaged students and received nearly a billion dollars the first year (accounting for more than 80 percent of all ESEA monies).[22]

Before the bill had been sent to Congress, there was debate within the Johnson administration whether state education agencies were competent enough to oversee Title I implementation. Francis Keppel, U.S. Commissioner of Education, succeeded in making states responsible for redistributing the Title I funds to local school districts as well as monitoring their implementation. To strengthen state education agencies, Title V of ESEA and other federal programs provided monies that allowed these entities to double the size of their professional staffs.[23] In 2004, for example, of the 1,600 employees in the California Education Department, three-fourths were supported by federal monies.[24] Title I also provided wide autonomy for states in the implementation of ESEA. Since the law did not specifically indicate how the education of disadvantaged children might be improved, state education agencies now were expected to draft their own plans and evaluate the programs.[25]

Federal and State Education Initiatives in the 1970s and Early 1980s

The ESEA proved a jumping-off point for further federal intervention in K–12 education. Yet, in spite of these actions by the national government, states maintained considerable autonomy in this area. The period from 1965 through the early 1980s witnessed a decline of localism in public education. Writing in 2004, analyst Michael Kirst succinctly described this transformation. "Despite Washington's greatly enlarged role," he explained, "perhaps the most striking change in U.S. education governance in the last forty years has been the growth of centralized state control and the ascendance of governors over school policy in most states. Organizations of local administrators, teachers, and school board members dominated state policy agendas no longer."[26] As governors became more involved in education policymaking within their states in the late 1970s and early 1980s they added their voices to the national debate over education reform. The federal ESEA of 1965, then, led to decades of joint federal-state cooperation aimed at improving America's schools.[27]

From the late 1960s through the 1970s, the White House, Congress, and the courts facilitated other major federal initiatives to improve K-12 education at the state and local levels. During the Senate 1968 ESEA reauthorization, for example, a small bilingual education program was included as Title VII (generating considerable controversy in the years to come). The 1972 reauthorization of the Higher Education Act also added a seemingly minor amendment (Title IX) that barred any gender discrimination in education programs receiving federal funds (including equal athletic opportunities). In 1974 Congress reauthorized the Vocational Education Act, including a section banning discrimination against the disabled (leading to the influential but controversial 1975 special education law). At the same time, earlier programs such as ESEA and Head Start were reauthorized to provide substantial federal education assistance to states and local communities.[28] Ironically, these federal programs were more successful in facilitating state involvement in education than they were in fulfilling their primary goal of adequately helping disadvantaged children. Local and national evaluations of the Great Society education programs indicated that these initiatives by themselves did not substantially improve student learning.[29]

Education policy over these decades was affected by shifting notions of federalism. Over the 1970s, President Richard M. Nixon initiated a significant attempt to reformulate the relationship between the federal government and the states. Nixon's New Federalism sought to rationalize intergovernmental responsibilities by improving federal-state coordination, consolidating federal aid to states through comprehensive block grants, sharing general federal revenues with the states, and reallocating national and state responsibilities in areas such as welfare and education. Rather than trying to eliminate government involvement, Nixon tried to improve its management, distribution, and effectiveness. Nixon's initiatives strengthened state involvement in many areas and expanded state administrative and regulatory capabilities. At the same time that federal involvement in state and local education expanded, state assistance and oversight of local schooling also increased.[30]

Presidents Gerald R. Ford and Jimmy Carter continued many of the federal-state policies initiated during the Nixon administration, but neither made intergovernmental reforms a top priority. The election of Ronald Reagan in 1980, however, led to new attempts to substantially minimize federal domestic programs. Reagan wanted to reduce not only federal involvement, but also curtail state and local domestic activities. While the Reagan administration failed to achive one of its initial goals—abolishing the recently created U.S. Department of Education—it did manage to reduce federal education funding and eliminate the federal revenue sharing program. As a result, state programs in general suffered, and state education agencies, in particular, were adversely affected.[31]

In the midst of these shifts in federal-state relations, governors, especially those from the South, sought to overcome their states' economic difficulties by improving schools in order to enhance economic productivity and attract business investments. Given the rampant inflation of the 1970s and the decline in real family income, faith in education as a path to economic growth and worker productivity emerged as an impetus for reforms. Over the decade of the 1970s, for example, thirty-two states instituted minimum competency testing. This included eighteen states that required high school students to pass tests before graduating. Starting in the late 1970s and early 1980s, a new generation of governors such as Lamar Alexander (R-Tenn.), Bill Clinton (D-Ark.), Bob Graham (D-Fla.), James Hunt (D-N.C.), Thomas Kean (R-N.J.), Richard Riley (D-S.C.), and William Winter (D-Miss.) led the fight within their states to further reform education; later many of these reform governors played key roles in improving schools through the federal government.[32]

In spite of Reagan's desire to diminish federal involvement in education, his administration succeeded in providing a new focus on education reform in the 1980s. Education Secretary Terrel Bell, a GOP moderate, created the National Commission on Excellence in Education in August 1981 to assess American education. The eighteen-member panel worked harmoniously together and issued its seminal 1983 report, A Nation at Risk, which portrayed the state of American education as dire and warned of serious consequences for U.S. economic competitiveness abroad. The report pointed out the declines in student academic achievement and recommended strengthening state and local education by setting higher graduation standards, establishing challenging academic goals, improving teacher preparation, and holding officials accountable for making necessary improvements.[33] The report looked to states and local communities for reforming schools. School reformers and organizations such as the National Governors' Association (NGA) frequently cited A Nation at Risk in appealing for public support.[34] But states varied considerably in how many of the report's recommendations they adopted.[35]

The 1989 Charlottesville Education Summit

Following the publication of A Nation at Risk, governors redoubled their efforts to improve state and local education.[36] Disappointing student achievement scores led NGA at its August 1985 meeting to focus on school improvement. A year later NGA issued its widely publicized report, Time for Results: The Governors' 1991 Report on Education (the report, issued in 1986, recommended what states needed do over the next five years). Tennessee Governor Lamar Alexander, NGA chair, called for "some old-fashioned horse-trading. We'll regulate less, if schools and school districts will produce better results."[37] NGA acknowledged that school reforms would take at least five years and require substantially more money. Although the governors endorsed annual reporting, they opposed using standardized student test scores which would have allowed for state comparisons.[38]

In fact, finding appropriate measures for assessing educational progress remained a point of contention. The National Assessment of Educational Progress (NAEP), developed since 1969, provided one respected set of tests. Opposition to state comparisons, however, initially led to a prohibition against reporting those scores at the state level (instead only national and regional results were released). Another option provided by the Reagan administration in 1984 was the controversial "wall chart," which ranked states using ACT and SAT scores—even though these tests assessed only college-bound students.[39] In an effort to resolve differences on testing, Governor Alexander and H. Thomas James (former president of the Spencer Foundation) headed a NAEP study group which persuaded Congress to allow limited reporting of state-level NAEP scores on a trial basis. Still, it was not until the 1990s that the use of state-level NAEP scores was greatly expanded.[40]

During the 1988 presidential campaign, George H.W. Bush sought to portray himself as a moderate without directly challenging the Reagan administration's policies. To this end, Bush embraced the issue of education. Although Bush previously had not shown much interest in education reforms, he told campaign audiences that he planned to be the "education president." Following the election, President Bush moved to fulfill his campaign promises. Congress had reauthorized ESEA in 1988 with only a single dissenting vote in both the House and Senate. Still, concerned about the stalled first wave of education reforms following the publication of *A Nation at Risk*, the Bush administration proposed the Educational Excellence Act of 1989 to supplement Chapter 1 (the renamed Title I of ESEA). Most Democrats and even some Republicans, however, argued that it was better to funnel any additional federal monies through the seemingly successful ESEA Chapter 1 program rather than enact still another unproven education initiative.[41]

As the Education Excellence Act was meeting resistance in Congress, NGA pressed President Bush to cooperate with the nation's governors in education reform. The Bush administration, working closely with Governors Bill Clinton (D-Ark.) and Carroll Campbell (R-S.C.), chair and co-chair of NGA's education initiative, agreed to the historic September 1989 Charlottesville Education Summit. This summit would provide the opportunity for the president and the nation's governors to come to a consensus on the direction of education reform.[42]

At the Charlottesville Education Summit, President Bush and NGA ironed out some differences and issued a joint communiqué calling for setting national education goals, greater flexibility and more accountability in the use of federal assistance, state-by-state education restructuring, and issuing annual progress reports. They concluded their communiqué by pledging that "as elected chief executives, we expect to be held accountable for progress in meeting the new national goals, and we expect to hold others accountable as well." Finally, they forcefully asserted that "the time for rhetoric is past; the time for performance is now."[43]

Following further consultation between the White House and NGA, President Bush announced in his 1990 State of the Union message the six national education goals:

1. By the year 2000, all children in America will start school ready to learn.
2. By the year 2000, we will increase the percentage of students graduating from high school to at least 90 percent.

3. By the year 2000, American students will leave grades four, eight, and twelve having demonstrated competency over challenging subject matter, including English, mathematics, science, history, and geography.
4. By the year 2000, U.S. students will be first in the world in science and mathematics achievement.
5. By the year 2000, every adult American will be literate and possess the knowledge and skills necessary to compete in a global economy and exercise the rights and responsibilities of citizenship.
6. By the year 2000, every school in America will be free of drugs and violence and offer a disciplined environment conducive to learning.[44]

NGA praised the announcement of the national education goals as "a major step for education reform."[45] But the organization was disappointed that it did not have an opportunity to negotiate the final wording of those goals prior to their announcement. When the nation's governors met on February 25 in Washington, D.C., they accepted, almost verbatim, the President's six national education goals; but NGA added twenty-one specific objectives among them. These objectives dealt more with "enabling" or "opportunity-to-learn" indicators than with the student and adult education outcomes announced by President Bush.[46]

The White House accepted NGA's minor changes in the wording of the national education goals, as well as the more detailed objectives, but the public paid more attention to the six national goals, largely ignoring the specific objectives under each of the goals.[47] In addition, the White House and NGA agreed in mid-1990 to create a fourteen-member, bipartisan National Education Goals Panel to monitor the progress in reaching those goals.[48] The governors and the president agreed on the goals of education reform across the country; if these goals would or even could be met, however, remained an open question.

America 2000 and Goals 2000

Following the announcement of the six national education goals and the failure to pass the Educational Excellence Act, President Bush in early 1991 appointed former Tennessee Governor Lamar Alexander as Secretary of Education. Alexander developed a new legislative package of education reforms called the America 2000 Excellence in Education Act. America 2000, loosely reflecting the six national education goals, included initiatives such as seed money for "break-the-mold" New American Schools, merit funds to reward successful schools, more flexibility and accountability in education reforms, Chapter 2 monies for state-level school reforms, and parental choice about whether to send their children to private or public schools using federal compensatory education monies.

The Democratic Congress did not enact America 2000, especially objecting to the proposed school choice provisions. Yet the Bush White House managed to implement some of its proposed projects anyway. States were encouraged, for example, to become America 2000 participants (forty-four of them as well as many local communities did so). The Bush administration also emphasized standards-based education reforms and funded several projects to help develop rigorous national standards in core academic subjects such as mathematics, geography, science, English, and history. Concerned that congressional defeat of America 2000 might be used to rally public support for re-electing President Bush in 1992, Democrats in Congress introduced their own bills which incorporated the national education goals, called for substantially more federal education assistance, and mandated systemic state education reforms.[49] States such as California had already introduced some standard-based reforms. But analysts Marshall "Mike" Smith and Jennifer O'Day called for instituting systemic reforms whereby states would create rigorous academic content standards, align them with the appropriate curricula, and then develop challenging student assessments.[50]

The election of Arkansas Governor Bill Clinton to the presidency in 1992 portended continued national action on education reform. In Arkansas, Clinton had made improving education one of his top priorities; at the same time he had provided leadership within NGA on school reform. Similar to President Bush, candidate Clinton promised he would be an effective "education president."[51] Following the election, Clinton appointed former South Carolina Governor Richard Riley as his secretary of education and promoted K-12 school reforms throughout his administration. Skeptical of ESEA's effectiveness, Clinton refused to reauthorize that program as quickly as some House members wanted. Instead, the Clinton administration assembled components from America 2000 as well as earlier Democratic congressional education proposals to draft their Goals 2000 legislation. After considerable debate, especially because of GOP opposition to the proposed opportunity-to-learn standards, Congress finally passed Goals 2000 in March 1994. The centerpiece of Goals 2000 was systemic—or standards-based—reform (though often there was confusion among policymakers on exactly what the term "systemic reform" meant). The original six national education goals (and now two additional ones) were incorporated in Goals 2000 as well as the bipartisan National Education Goals Panel.[52]

About six months later, the Elementary and Secondary Education Act was reauthorized as the Improving America's School Act (IASA); that legislation also included the systemic framework as well as other key Goals 2000 provisions (and Chapter 1 was renamed Title I). While Goals 2000 provided assistance for all students and schools, IASA was more narrowly targeted to help disadvantaged students (though increasingly Title I monies were used to improve entire schools rather than just the at-risk children attending those institutions).[53]

Goals 2000 and IASA, like parts of the proposed America 2000 initiative, considerably enhanced the role of states in education reform and recommitted the nation to reaching the eight national education goals by the year 2000.[54] Governors now played a more active role in state and national education reforms due to the increasing gubernatorial influence in state education as well as their contributions to the National Education Goals Panel and NGA.[55]

Many educators and political leaders looked forward to closer federal and state coordination as well as more government involvement in school reforms—especially with Clinton in the White House and a Democratic Congress. The unexpected GOP capture of both the House and Senate in the 1994 midterm elections, however, weakened federal influence. The new 104th Republican Congress sought to eliminate the U.S. Department of Education, repeal Goals 2000, and reduce federal involvement in state and local schooling. While the Republicans failed to enact many of these changes, they succeeded initially in cutting federal education funding and lessening the impact of federal directives.[56]

Recognizing the electoral importance of the education issue, however, both Democrats and Republicans began competing to provide more federal monies for education reforms. Interestingly, both parties' approaches maintained the enhanced role of states in education policymaking. The GOP Congress sought to provide states with more flexibility in implementing education reforms; and the Clinton administration chose not to penalize states failing to meet their deadlines for creating math and reading content standards or developing rigorous student assessments. Amidst the ongoing battles over Goals 2000 and IASA, state involvement in education continued to increase. During the 1990s, total public elementary and secondary school revenues (in constant dollars) increased by 36 percent, and per student spending rose 16 percent. More than half of that increase came from state sources, with another third from local contributions. The federal government added 10 percent of the increase so that the federal share of public K-12 education costs edged upward from 6.2 percent in 1990–91 to 7.3 percent in 2000–2001.[57] Still, states and local communities were footing the bill for most education reform initiatives.

Since Goals 2000 was so intertwined with other federal programs, it is difficult to separate out its impact on state and local education precisely.[58] Not surprisingly, the question of whether the education reforms of the 1990s had much impact on student achievement scores nationally, or at the state level, continues to be debated, often along partisan lines. The Clinton administration and many Washington-based education groups emphasized the improvements made under Goals 2000 and IASA and urged the nation to "stay the course." The Republicans and their allies, on the other hand, pointed to the limited, if any, improvements in student achievement scores and urged the need for new education reforms. The congressionally mandated Independent Review Panel found a mixed picture with NAEP math scores increasing while reading scores had stabilized or only slightly increased. Overall the panel stated that "while this is encouraging, it is certainly no cause for celebration."[59]

Most states agreed to comply with the law in order to receive Goals 2000 and IASA funding, but they often applied the new mandates to their existing education systems slowly. A few states, such as Kentucky, North Carolina, and Texas, were more aggressive and successful in implementing the new programs. Many states made at least some progress in improving schools and raising student achievement; but student assessment scores in other states remained the same, and a few even saw declines.[60]

After the 1989 Charlottesville Education Summit, President George H. W. Bush and the nation's governors pledged to reach the national education goals by the year 2000. In addition, they announced that policymakers would be held accountable for reaching these goals. When Congress enacted the goals in 1994, that promise was reaffirmed and the National Education Goals Panel monitored the progress toward them. So what happened when the year 2000 arrived?

Of course, no one would expect that all eight of the national education goals would be achieved. After all, these goals were very ambitious and it would have been hard for anyone a decade earlier to predict exactly what might be achieved. However, none of the national education goals were reached by the year 2000—a very disappointing and largely unpublicized outcome.[61]

No Child Left Behind and the States

The election of 2000 brought another governor to the White House, George W. Bush of Texas. Bush had run as a "compassionate conservative" and emphasized his education reforms as governor. He stressed early reading instruction and called for a restructured Title I program that would help all children learn.[62] Once in office, President Bush made education a top domestic priority. Less than two weeks after his inauguration, Bush announced his No Child Left Behind initiative. Protracted negotiations over the bill forced Bush to make several compromises, including abandoning traditional GOP issues such as private school vouchers, and to accept an even higher federal education budget than he had originally envisioned.[63]

The No Child Left Behind Act (NCLB) of 2002 was similar in many ways to Goals 2000 and IASA. Rather than just calculating each school's overall student achievement score, however, the legislation also called for measuring the performance of several student subgroups (drawing upon earlier state efforts). Instead of postponing sanctioned evaluations, NCLB required annual evaluations and promptly penalized local districts and specific schools for failing to reach their intermediate objectives. The NCLB provisions included:

1. States receiving Title I money must develop "coherent and rigorous" academic standards, and all students must attain academic "proficiency" with regard to those standards in reading and math within twelve years.
2. Students must be tested statewide in reading and math every year from grades three through eight, and once again in high school (science testing was to be added a few years later).
3. Test results were to be reported in the aggregate, but also broken down by categories such as race and economic status in order to identify schools where high overall averages might hide pockets of failing students.
4. Schools must make "adequate yearly progress" toward the twelve-year deadline of universal proficiency.
5. The legislation imposed a series of corrective actions on schools and local school districts which failed to make adequate yearly progress for two or more consecutive years.
6. All teachers and paraprofessionals hired by Title I must be "highly qualified." By the end of the 2005–06 school year, every public school teacher must be "highly qualified."[64]

Compared to the governors' reactions to previous federal initiatives, the response to NCLB was mixed. Of course, many states and governors welcomed NCLB's emphasis on improving education standards and emphasis on helping all children reach those goals. But there were also complaints about the legislation's inflexibility and insufficient funding. Governor Jon Huntsman and the Utah legislature, for example, enacted a law in May 2005 requiring local educators to give higher priority to state objectives than NCLB whenever the goals of the two programs conflicted.[65] Texas directly challenged NCLB by stating that many of their school districts and schools were making adequate yearly progress even though they did not meet the more strict definitions according to federal law.[66]

Some states and organizations sued the federal government over NCLB even though earlier suits suggested that the courts might not be an easy avenue for challenging that law.[67] Connecticut, objecting to the NCLB's mandate for annual testing of students in grades 3–8, filed suit in U.S. District Court in Hartford challenging the legislation as an unfunded mandate. The U.S. Department of Education, joined by the Connecticut NAACP, defended NCLB. Judge Mark R. Kravitz dismissed three of the four Connecticut claims but continued the state's claim that the U.S. Department of Education had acted "arbitrarily and capriciously" in dealing with the provisions for nonnative English speakers and special education students.[68] And the National Education Association (NEA), along with ten of its affiliates, filed a suit in U.S. District Court also claiming that NCLB was an illegally underfunded mandate. Chief Judge Bernard A. Friedman ruled in November 2005 that Congress could require states, as a condition of accepting federal support for education, to comply with NCLB. Education Secretary Margaret Spellings welcomed that decision, but the NEA appealed it to the federal appeals court in Cincinnati.[69]

After Spellings replaced Rod Paige as secretary of education in November 2004, she allowed for more flexibility in how some of the specific regulations were enforced. While the federal government continued to insist that all students in states and local schools demonstrate academic proficiency by the end of the school year 2013–14, in the short run they provided dispensations in areas such as special education, the highly qualified teacher requirement, increases in the minimum student subgroup size for measuring progress, and dealing with the Hurricane Katrina refugees.[70] The U.S. Department of Education also allowed several states to experiment using a growth model to measure school progress.[71] Not every state official, however, was persuaded that the Bush administration had met the concerns over NCLB implementation. The Council of Chief State School Officers, for example, complained that "as the 2005–06 school year wound down . . . it became increasingly clear that the department was moving away from its earlier pronouncement of greater flexibility for states in the law's implementation."[72]

During his 2004 reelection campaign, President Bush called for mandating annual reading and mathematics tests in grades 9–11 and promised up to $1.5 billion for improving high schools in the FY2006 budget. The NEA rejected Bush's proposal as an unnecessary NCLB expansion, but Susan Traiman, director of education and workforce policy for the Business Roundtable, praised it.[73] At the same time, NGA, with the financial assistance of six foundations, announced a $42 million high school improvement initiative to raise graduation and college-readiness rates. As Virginia Governor Mark Warner, NGA chair, stated in 2005, "we are united in our conviction that high schools must be targeted for comprehensive reform and sustained change."[74] Despite President Bush's efforts on behalf of his high school proposal, however, neither the Democrats nor Republicans in Congress made the administration's initiative one of their educational priorities.[75]

As with Goals 2000 and IASA, considerable debate continues over the effectiveness of No Child Left Behind. The Bush administration cites the July 2005 long-term Trend NAEP scores as evidence of improvements in mathematics and reading over the past three decades. But the regular 2005 Main NAEP fourth- and eighth-grade mathematics and readings scores, released three months later, showed mixed results and indicated a recent slowdown in the rate of student improvement.[76]

On the fourth anniversary of the signing of No Child Left Behind, *Education Week* analyzed education trends in a special January 2006 issue, "Quality Counts." As part of that study, the weekly commissioned Educational Testing Service to analyze changes in state performance of fourth and eighth graders on NAEP reading and mathematics over time. The report's summary painted a mixed picture:

The conclusions are at once heartening and sobering. They're heartening because over the span from 1992 to 2005, student achievement has gotten better, particularly in mathematics and particularly for those students who started furthest behind. Meanwhile, an increasing number of states have embraced a standards-based-education framework, with some of the earliest and most ardent adopters of standards-based accountability systems making some of the most progress in raising achievement, as highlighted by the case studies on Delaware, Massachusetts, New York, North Carolina, and Texas in this report. . . .

At the same time, it would be hard to ignore the fact that progress has not come nearly far or fast enough. That's particularly true in reading, where average scores nationally have barely budged since 1992. It's also true that, despite the solid gains of poor, African-American, and Hispanic students during this period, the achievement gaps between those students and their more affluent and white peers remain disturbingly deep—at least 20 points in both grades and subjects, or the equivalent of two grade levels or more.

After widening a bit during the mid-1990s, those gaps have begun to close again. But in many cases, the gaps now mirror what they were in the early '90s, and progress in closing them has been less dramatic since 2003.[77]

While elementary and middle school students recently had made modest academic progress in reading and mathematics, high school students had not improved much. Moreover, overall student progress would not be sufficient to reach proficiency by the end of 2013–14 if NAEP standards were employed instead of the generally lower state standards.

On January 8, 2007, the fifth anniversary of the signing of No Child Left Behind, President Bush invited the 110th Congress to join him in reauthorizing NCLB.[78] Following the president's State of the Union address two weeks later, the Bush administration indicated that the reauthorized NCLB should expand to include improving middle and high school education as well as preparing graduates for college and careers. Among the other new provisions, states should create standards and assessments for two years of high school mathematics and English, standardize states' graduation data, and earmark specific monies to prevent students from dropping out of school. Student achievement in science would be added to the school evaluations of adequate yearly progress. States should also include NAEP scores as part of reporting their own test results; and the proposed Teacher Incentive Fund would reward teachers and principals on the basis of their improving student achievement scores.[79]

Several organizations such as the bipartisan Commission on No Child Left Behind offered specific suggestions for the reauthorization.[80] In March 2006 the National Governors Association issued a seven-page, detailed policy statement on education reforms. It noted that while the federal government could play an important supporting role, "education is primarily a state responsibility" and that "governors must maintain the authority to oversee the operation of education in their states at all levels." While supporting the basic tenets of No Child Left Behind, NGA urged Congress during the upcoming reauthorization to "reinforce and support sound education practices, roll back restrictions on states' ability to align and integrate delivery systems for students, assist and recognize the needs of our nation's teachers, and ultimately, support state efforts to raise student achievement."[81] NGA believed that, in spite of federal incursions, state government remains the major force in shaping educational policy. From the perspective of governors, the federal government should provide the support and the tools to help them deliver on the promise of a quality education for all. It should not, however, tie the hands of governors or direct all states down a single path of education reform.

Conclusion

In colonial and nineteenth-century America, education was mainly locally controlled and funded, often, at least initially, without clear distinctions between public and private involvement. By the 1930s, however, states increased their funding for local education, but still, in most cases, required local school districts to meet only minimal requirements. While the state role in education slowly grew in the middle of the twentieth century, the federal government did not play a large role in elementary and secondary education during these years. With the 1965 passage of ESEA and other programs, the federal government provided monies for elementary and secondary education as well as increased the responsibility and ability of state education agencies to assist local schools. State contributions to local education continued to increase so that by 2000 they equaled or exceeded local contributions in most states.

Starting in the 1970s, governors, especially those from the South, became more involved in education matters as they sought to improve the economic development of their states. Through NGA, governors also played an extensive role in fostering and implementing national education reforms such as national education goals, America 2000, Goals 2000, and No Child Left Behind. Former governors, particularly Presidents Bill Clinton and George W. Bush, played major roles in promoting national education reforms; and GOP and Democratic administrations recruited other former governors such as Lamar Alexander and Richard Riley to serve as their secretaries of education.

Historians have neglected the increasingly important role of states and governors in promoting and enacting education reforms. Scholars of nineteenth-century education have properly acknowledged the contributions of school reformers like Horace Mann and Henry Barnard; but historians of twentieth-century education usually focus their studies on urban schools or the increasing involvement of the federal government after the 1960s without adequate recognition to the growing importance of states or governors. Some education analysts, however, are now paying more attention to the increased state involvement in K-12 education. There are some useful case studies of the education involvement of governors in a few states, but we still need more in-depth, comparative studies of governors as well as of the role of NGA in K-12 schooling today.

States and their leaders play a much more extensive role in education than fifty or a hundred years ago. Not surprisingly, many issues await further investigation, such as determining the financial, administrative, and policy setting relationships between the states and local school districts. How should K-12 education be funded in the future? How might the responsibility for state participation in education be apportioned among state education agencies, state school superintendents, and governors? In light of increasing federal and state education involvement, what flexibility and decision-making should be exercised by local schools and superintendents? Should government monies be provided to parents who want to send their children to nonpublic schools?

During the past quarter-century, the American public became more aware and concerned about the quality of public education. Large-scale federal and state education initiatives (such as the national education goals, America 2000, Goals 2000, and No Child Left Behind) often set ambitious objectives and pledged that decision-makers will be held accountable for reaching them. Yet none of the eight national education goals were reached in the year 2000. Many states also failed either to implement the Goals 2000 requirements on time or to improve substantially student achievement, and many critics remain skeptical that No Child Left Behind will succeed in having all children proficient in math and reading by 2013–14.

Almost everyone acknowledges the importance of schooling and agrees that we must educate all of our citizens. But there is less of a consensus on the most effective ways of improving education and who should be responsible for them. Although many individuals and organizations believe that they already know what needs to be done, we still lack the scientific research knowledge necessary to provide policymakers with reliable and practical guidance for implementing those changes in different settings. As we face the diverse and competing challenges of the twenty-first century, it is essential that our educational needs are not slighted. Despite sustaining the current reforms for an unprecedented twenty-five years, there is no guarantee that future leaders or the public will continue investing more in education at the same time that the demands from an aging population and global insecurity grow. The nation's governors and all of us will need to work together in order to develop better ways of fostering high quality education for everyone as well as to find the necessary resources.

Chapter 9

From Charity Care to Medicaid

Governors, States, and the Transformation of American Health Care

COLLEEN M. GROGAN AND VERNON K. SMITH

Throughout the twentieth century, state governments in the United States have taken responsibility for health care policymaking. States regulate hospitals and outpatient clinics, they determine licensure for the plethora of health care providers, and they plan and direct the building and development of our health care infrastructure. While the federal government affects the financial health of hospitals (and other health facilities) and influences medical education when it writes Medicare policy for the aged, even these areas are primarily under state government control. Of all the health care policy issues states confront, however, it is the Medicaid program that dominates states' attention in the health policy domain.

That a health care program for the poor—a program that states have long complained about—dominates their attention may seem surprising. But, if we investigate more deeply, we see that despite an original intent that the program be contained for only the "truly needy," Medicaid has never been just a program for poor people. Indeed, over time states have acted to cover more and more nonpoor persons. As enrollment expanded and costs skyrocketed, governors developed a love-hate relationship with the program—embracing the ability to offer needed health coverage for poor and vulnerable populations in their state, while genuinely concerned with program costs and how fast they grow.

Governors depend heavily on Medicaid to provide much needed health care coverage to millions of American families. However, along with this dependence comes the fiscal burden of high Medicaid costs. Total Medicaid expenditures (including the state and federal share) have increased to $313 billion in 2005, including $179 billion in federal funds and $134 billion in state funds.[1] In recent decades, Medicaid spending has increased at an annual average rate of about 8 percent, while state budgets have increased at an average annual rate of just over 6 percent, making Medicaid a large and ever-increasing share of state budgets.[2] Indeed, in 2004, Medicaid became the largest single item in state budgets—in terms of total state spending, exceeding K-12 education, higher education, or any other category of total state spending.[3] In part because of their limited ability to fund rapid rates of growth of Medicaid expenditures, states have either pushed for Medicare expansions—which are of course financed and run by the federal government—or favored private sector solutions for expanding health care to the uninsured and underinsured. Yet, while preferring non-Medicaid expansions, states have ended up with a large and expanding Medicaid program on their hands.

The primary purpose of this chapter is to explain how this predicament came about. We argue that the main explanation has three parts: first, Medicaid covers populations—in both mandated and optional eligibility groups—that have very expensive health care needs, and no other public or private policy options exist to serve them; second, lack of national health care and the availability of coverage options through Medicaid means the groups not adequately covered are constantly knocking on state governments' door; and, third, the availability of federal Medicaid matching funds provided a strong financial incentive for states to rely on Medicaid to cover a variety of needy groups.

This chapter aims to explain the development of state-level health policy over the twentieth century. We show how key historical events led to this Medicaid build-up and how certain interpretations of the program influenced future policy decisions. From the outset we want to be clear that this discussion will not evaluate state-level policy and critique its value and effectiveness. Instead, we seek to explain why state-level policy developed as it did. In the first part of the chapter we show how in the early twentieth century, long before Medicaid was enacted, states took responsibility for the provision of health care for the poor. Even in this early period, states were pressured to help the nonpoor. Health care was expensive (relative to lower- and middle-class earnings at the time); therefore, when working families were sick and needed care, they often relied on the public sector to help them. Medicaid grew out of years of various state responses to this demand for health care from both the poor and nonpoor. In the second part of the chapter we illustrate how states have grappled with administering and financing this large Medicaid program, by considering three policy issues that have created persistent political ambiguities and tensions over time: long-term care for the elderly and disabled; health insurance for the uninsured; and classic cooperative federalism issues regarding how the states and the federal government should appropriately run and finance Medicaid. We conclude by considering what lessons might be drawn from a historical understanding of states' experiences with Medicaid.

State Health Care Policies Before Medicaid

CHARITY CARE FOR A FEW

The primary institution used to provide charity care in the early twentieth century was the dispensary—a publicly funded clinic that dispensed drugs and medical services to the needy poor. The use of the dispensaries began in the nineteenth century and continued up until 1920. The quality of care provided in these clinics was fairly well regarded early in the twentieth century because dispensaries served as a major training ground for apprenticing physicians.[4] Because physicians depended on dispensaries to conduct medical education, there was substantial growth in the number of these clinics. Due to the relatively high cost of medical care, sick working families often turned to dispensaries for their care.[5] In the early 1900s, 40 percent of low-income workers took advantage of free care in dispensaries in New York City.[6] Other cities also reported dependence of workers on free care. Many letters from physicians at the time, for example, document a great concern about the inappropriate use by working families of free care provided in dispensaries.[7] The debate over where to draw the line for who should receive publicly supported health care had begun.

The emergence of hospitals as the new favored location for practicing medical education in the 1920s led to an end in the use of dispensaries. Still, debates about middle-class abuse of publicly funded care and efforts to limit public supported care to only the "truly needy" persisted in the new hospital setting.[8] Most hospitals prior to the 1920s were heavily stigmatized as places where sick indigents would go to die. In an effort to move away from this image of death, the new modern hospital system was envisioned to be the primary place for care for all Americans to cure injuries and serious illnesses.[9] Yet, in their effort to include everyone, there was a simultaneous effort to develop clear distinctions between private-paying patients and public, charity care patients. Most hospitals created separate wards for charity care patients.[10] Yet, even then a sizable proportion of middle-class patients fell somewhere in between private pay and charity care. Similar to the controversy over dispensaries, debates ensued about the proper use of charity care services within the hospital. Memos from hospital trustees, administrators, and public officials document concerns about keeping public wards relatively small and reveal strategies to provide superior services to private-pay patients as incentives to pay for one's care. These strategies reflect a clear and ongoing concern about "appropriate" use of the public facilities and funds, and attempts to segregate out working persons from "dependents."

Two main historical developments explain the persistence of the question of who is deserving in health policy debates in the states. First, all major proposals for national health reform prior to 1945 assumed the continued use of the preexisting public health care system for the poor. In other words, even those who envisioned reforming health care in a comprehensive way supported the existence of a segregated system of charity care. While the larger reform measures failed, the suggested funding for charity care was often enacted (as demonstrated below) and therefore this segregated public system continued to develop over time. Incorporating the poor or nearly poor into health care reform proposals for the mainstream remained outside the discourse of reformers. Second, due to various pieces of federal labor legislation and tax incentives, private employer-based health insurance for "middle-class" working Americans developed over time.[11] As a result, because the poor received health care from a state-operated segregated public system, uninsured working individuals and families that did not fit neatly into either category persistently knocked on state government's door.

This pattern of designing a separate system of care for the poor within broader health care reform proposals started in the Progressive Era. At that time, a group of academic reformers formed the American Association of Labor Legislation (AALL) and in 1914 began a nationwide campaign with its model legislation for compulsory health insurance.[12] It was distributed throughout the nation and formed the basis for discussion of health insurance for the rest of the decade. The bill was designed for adoption by individual states—not the country as a whole—and only for full-time workers. They also argued that a separate system of care for indigents was necessary. Although the AALL's proposal never passed, it was significant in setting a pattern (still with us today) of intentionally excluding many needy groups from coverage: workers earning less than $1,200 annually, agricultural and domestic workers, and the middle class and the unemployed. The AALL's rationale was that those with higher incomes could presumably pay for doctors, whereas the very poor were allowed treatment in the public system already developed—dispensaries and physician charity—which could be expanded.[13] These exclusions and the rationale behind them persisted in all major health insurance proposals until the mid-1940s.

With no success in passing compulsory health insurance, by the 1920s reformers like the Committee on the Cost of Medical Care were calling for voluntary insurance plans for the middle class. Still, these reformers proposed using federal grants-in-aid to states to support public health programs, including medical care for the indigent.[14] From the very moment that the extension of voluntary insurance programs was proposed, reformers envisioned a separate, segregated health care system for the poor.

This central idea of government grants-in-aid to support health care for the poor was carried forward under Sheppard-Towner Act passed in 1921, which created the first federally funded intergovernmental program for maternal and child health in the United States. Sheppard-Towner had an immediate impact on state activity. The Children's Bureau allotted $5,000 to each state to be used by local health departments for maternal and child health services, and made available another $5,000 on a matching basis. In the first year alone, forty states took advantage of the matching funds. While many suggest the funding was negligible given the amount of need, it is important to recognize the foundational effects of these funds: "the act stimulated state funding, greatly increased the number of public health nurses, and provided a stimulus to health education."[15]

This stimulus for state health care spending was catapulted forward again during the New Deal. Among the eleven titles passed under the Social Security Act of 1935, two—Title V grants for maternal and child health and Title VI for public health work—had an enormous impact on the provision of health care services in the American states.[16] These grants-in-aid to states for public health services were not limited to population-wide *prevention* programs; in fact, a sizable portion of the funds was spent on health care *treatment* to the poor and nonpoor. In 1936, for example, over $500 million was paid out of these intergovernmental funds for all kinds of health services: public provision of hospital beds, school clinics for immunizations, and community clinics. From 1923 to 1935, the beds in hospitals supported through grants-in-aid increased 57 percent, whereas those in private hospitals increased only 17 percent.[17]

After the New Deal, national health care reform remained off the political agenda until President Truman fought for compulsory national health insurance in 1947. Compared to previous legislation on national health care reform, Truman's bill was viewed as fairly radical, in part, because it was the first time universal coverage—including care for the indigent—was promoted.[18] As an alternative to Truman's bill, some in Congress proposed more federal grants-in-aid to the states to enable each state to provide medical care for the indigent. The expectation under this bill was that individuals and families who were not indigent would secure medical care through private health insurance plans, and states would then fill in any gaps.[19] Since private health insurance plans, and specifically employer-based health insurance coverage, were growing quite rapidly at that time, most state policymakers thought indigent care would need to be provided to a relatively small group. As a result, states and most federal policymakers favored this approach. Based on this assumption of a small indigent population, Congress added, with little fanfare, a provision to the Social Security Amendments of 1950 called "Medical Vendor Payments."[20]

The Medical Vendor program allowed states to use federal matching funds to pay medical providers directly for services rendered to public assistance recipients.[21] The implementation of this program, however, reflected states' earlier experience with charity care. Despite the official policy of providing residual Medical Vendor Payments only to public assistance recipients, there was almost immediate pressure to expand the program. States needed help in providing for medical needs of those uninsured persons not receiving public assistance. In addition, the age of the U.S. population had increased dramatically over this time period leading to greater demand for nursing home services.[22] Responding to these demands, states pushed for more financial support from the federal government. Although Medical Vendor Payments were not financially significant over the first few years following the program's passage in 1950, the provision was revised and expanded in 1953, 1956, 1958, and 1960 such that cumulatively it had a substantial financial impact.[23] The enactment of vendor payments, along with these increment expansions, increased federal grants to states for payments to hospitals, doctors, and other providers of medical care from $52 million in fiscal year 1949–50 to $312 million in 1954–55, to $493 million in 1959–60.[24] While payments to hospitals consumed the largest share of vendor payments, it is noteworthy that nursing home care was already the second largest item—$108 million—in 1960.[25]

This early history shows first how grant-in-aid programs to the states, starting most significantly with the New Deal, solidified the notion that the poor would mainly receive their care in public institutions and that the states would remain the main administrator of charity medical care in the United States. Second, despite the government's official policy of segregating care for the poor and limiting care to the truly needy so as to promote private sector care, uninsured Americans, especially those who became sick and needed services, pushed to expand the boundaries of public care. Thus, we see the beginnings of a growing health care program for the poor in the American states even before Medicaid was passed.

COMPREHENSIVE CARE FOR THE "NEEDY"

After Truman's failure, proponents of the compulsory national health insurance approach decided to restrict their goals to expanding hospital benefits for elderly persons through Social Security.[26] With mounting public pressure to do something for the aged, Congress, in 1960, passed legislation proposed by Representative Wilbur Mills and Senator Robert Kerr entitled the Medical Assistance Act but more commonly known as the Kerr-Mills Act. Kerr-Mills contained two crucial provisions that would profoundly influence how states would later provide health care under Medicaid: comprehensive benefits and the concept of medical indigency. As an alternative to universal coverage for the elderly with a restricted benefit package, Kerr-Mills provided a means-tested program with comprehensive benefits (covering hospital, physician, and nursing home services).[27] Supporters argued that this approach would be more effective because it offered the truly needy more security. Moreover, although Kerr-Mills was a targeted program, it was designed to be distinct from welfare. Eligibility for benefits under Kerr-Mills was restricted to the "medically indigent." These were older persons who needed assistance when they became sick because they had large medical expenses relative to their current income. Proponents emphasized that the "medically indigent should not be equated with the totally indigent."[28] The latter term refers in this case to those who receive cash assistance. The moral argument behind this expansion reasoned that the sick elderly should not have to become completely impoverished. Indeed, the category of "medical indigency" was based in the idea that sickness should not cause impoverishment. Both policy concepts—comprehensive benefits and medical indigency—were eventually enacted under the Medicaid program in 1965.

With the introduction of Kerr-Mills (MAA), public payments for nursing homes increased almost tenfold from 1960 to 1965 consuming about one-third of total program expenditures.[29] By the end of 1965, all fifty states had programs of medical vendor payments and forty-seven had specific Kerr-Mills programs for the aged. Again, despite states' desire to confine their medical assistance programs to the truly needy, these programs expanded rapidly because of high demand, the incentive provided by the federal match, and the lack of other programs to meet these expensive health care needs.

In light of the widespread implementation of Medical Vendor Payments and Kerr-Mills, the adoption of Medicaid, which essentially combined these two provisions into one program, was not extraordinary. Yet, at the same time, most state and federal policymakers were surprised by the adoption of Medicaid in combination with Medicare because the two programs offered fundamentally competing notions of social provision.[30] The concept of medical indigency was strategically included under Kerr-Mills, and subsequently under "Eldercare" (Medicaid) bills, as an alternative to universalism.[31] As a result, the concept in light of universal Medicare often confused state policymakers. On the one hand, Medicaid was viewed as a restricted welfare program for the poor. On the other hand, the medical indigency concept provided a path to the comprehensive benefits of Medicaid, even for members of the middle class.

Despite these expansionary provisions, the federal government's estimates of Medicaid's future budgetary costs did not assume that the program would lead to a dramatic expansion of health care coverage.[32] Even assuming that all fifty states would implement the new program, the federal government projected Medicaid expenditures to be no more than $238 million per year above what was then being spent on medical-welfare programs. As it turned out, this expenditure level was reached after only six states had implemented their Medicaid programs. By 1967, thirty-seven states were implementing Medicaid programs, and spending was rising by 57 percent per annum.[33]

The reason for this rapid expansion lay with states setting generous eligibility standards for Medicaid. The debate over who should be eligible in New York provided an early and particularly dramatic demonstration. In March 1966, Governor Nelson Rockefeller sent to the legislature a bill to enable the Medicaid program, urging quick action on the measure to ensure federal reimbursement for the program for the entire year. Democrats added more generous provisions as amendments to the bill, and the compromise bill set the income ceiling level for a family of four at $6,000. When signing the bill, Rockefeller announced that it was "the most significant social legislation in three decades." In terms of the costs for the program, Rockefeller proved quite prescient.[34]

By setting such a high eligibility threshold, however, New York had potentially created a program well beyond the expectations of providing residual health care for the poor. As a point of comparison, by July 1991—twenty-five years later—thirteen states with medically needy programs set income eligibility levels below New York's 1966 standard of $6,000 in current dollars.[35]

Similar to the Kerr-Mills debates in 1959, New York state policymakers argued that a liberal definition of the medically needy population was required in order to distinguish the Medicaid program as a whole from welfare. Under the New York program, 70 percent of the state's Medicaid spending would go to medically needy claimants who did not receive cash assistance. New York was hardly alone in wishing to distinguish Medicaid from welfare. Eighteen other states also devoted more than half of their Medicaid budgets to persons not on welfare. In Wisconsin, for example, 74 percent of total Medicaid payments were for medically needy recipients in 1967.[36] Furthermore, in a very early Medicaid maximization effort, Rockefeller explained that a high level of eligibility would provide the maximum support for the program out of federal dollars with little additional costs for the state or for localities.[37]

Many policymakers disagreed with New York's expansionary use of the Medicaid program. In their view, Medicaid should be contained for a relatively small number of "truly" needy Americans, and costs should be controlled to reflect this restriction. In reaction to states pushing for a more expansive program, the federal government clamped down hard on New York's attempted liberalization. In 1967, only a year after the New York expansion began, Congress passed legislation lowering the medically needy eligibility level to 133⅓ percent of a state's AFDC means-tested level.[38] Recognizing the great costs the state would incur based on this eligibility change, Rockefeller urged President Lyndon Johnson not to sign the bill. Once the bill became law, however, Rockefeller called on the state legislature to "revamp" the recently created Medicaid program.[39] New York's generous $6,000 eligibility level for a family of four was thereby reduced to $3,900. As a result of this federal intervention, about 600,000 potentially eligible persons were denied medical benefits in 1967. The number of potential Medicaid recipients was reduced by 750,000 in 1968 and 900,000 persons in 1969.[40]

In halting New York's attempted liberalization in 1967, federal policymakers made a conscious decision to define Medicaid as a restricted welfare program, off-limits to the employed. "The House is moving toward a program where you provide medical care to those who can't pay, and expect people to pay it if they are working and can earn income," stated Senator Russell Long in floor debate.[41]

Despite this significant retrenchment in 1967, Medicaid expenditures continued to increase, in part because Medicaid policy still incorporated the "comprehensive benefits for the needy" approach. This approach allows for "traditionally" nonpoor people with expensive medical care needs to spend down their savings and eventually become eligible for Medicaid. In other words, the two expansionary seeds imbedded in Medicaid's beginnings—medical indigency and comprehensive benefits—were allowed to blossom over time and these flowers (or weeds, depending on your view) created the following persistent questions for state government: How to provide long-term care to the elderly and disabled? How to provide health insurance for the working uninsured? How can the federal government provide needed help and yet not stifle policy preferences or policy innovation?

States' Persistent Medicaid Policy Tensions

In 1964, proponents of national health insurance strategically accepted Medicare's limitations as a necessary compromise—as an incremental step on the way to universal coverage. Many others, however, viewed the passage of Medicare and Medicaid as largely "fixing" the problem of the uninsured. According to this latter view, each group in the population now had a program to meet their needs: Medicare for the elderly and disabled; employer-based health insurance for workers; and Medicaid for the "needy." The common understanding of Medicaid as a program intended only for poor people, emerged from this early period. Yet, this system left out many working adults and their children who did not have access to employer-based health insurance, and could not afford private insurance.[42] Medicaid, slowly, over time, became the program to fill the gaps of this imperfect system.

In the next section, we first document how states have been forced to use Medicaid to fill the long-term care gaps for the elderly and disabled in the U.S.; second, how states also rely on Medicaid to fill in the uninsured gap in the U.S. health care system; and third, how these policies create challenging issues for cooperative federalism.

Long-term Care for the Elderly and Disabled

While Medicaid's architects incorporated vendor payments and Kerr-Mills, which both covered nursing home benefits for indigent disabled and elderly, they did not expect Medicaid to become America's de facto long-term care (LTC) program. But the concepts of medical indigence and comprehensive benefits embedded in Medicaid's enabling legislation were sufficiently elastic that Medicaid naturally filled the gaping LTC hole. Medicare does not cover the costs of long-term custodial nursing home care, and relatively few Americans have been able or willing to purchase private LTC insurance during their working years. Yet nursing home costs are astronomical: in 2005, the national average for a private room was approximately $70,000 per year.[43] A relatively high proportion of elderly over age eighty-five rely on nursing home care: 17% of medical expenditures for the elderly over age eighty-five go toward nursing home stays, and Medicaid covers more than half of these expenses.[44]

Even as early as 1975, Medicaid was paying the bills of more than half of all nursing home residents. While many seniors in nursing homes are not eligible for Medicaid at the time of their admission, the average cost of nursing home care quickly depletes the resources of all but the affluent seniors. Between 27 and 45 percent of elderly nursing home residents become eligible for Medicaid after spending down their resources.[45] Given that Medicaid is the only program to cover these costs when elderly and disabled deplete their resources, it is perhaps not surprising that Medicaid expenditures are high for these groups: $55 billion for the aged and $102 billion for the disabled in 2003. Particularly shocking to state governments is how persistently the costs of LTC have increased over time: even adjusting for inflation (using 2003 dollars) the costs have increased 149 percent for the aged and an astounding 522 percent for the disabled since 1975.[46]

Given these cost figures, it is not surprising that LTC Medicaid costs have been an overriding concern in all the states as they grapple with how to responsibly design and administer their Medicaid programs. On top of these cost concerns, however, are additional tensions related to the sheer complexity of providing long-term care services and the moral dilemmas regarding who is deserving of such services.

Quality Concerns About Nursing Home Care

Shortly after Medicaid was enacted, it became clear that the program inherited a LTC delivery system with serious quality problems. A few exposés gave significant press to the topic. For example, a Ralph Nader report titled *Old Age: The Last Segregation* was published in 1971, revealing a stark portrait of inhumane nursing home care. Three years later, Mary Adelaide Mendelsohn published *Tender Loving Greed: How the Incredibly Lucrative Nursing Home Industry Is Exploiting America's Old People and Defrauding Us All.*[47] Both books documented how nursing homes were making substantial profits while providing substandard care to their residents, and scolded federal and state government's financial support of these institutions for the aged.

These manuscripts, and several other newspaper articles, eventually prompted hearings and the establishment of nursing home commissions across the American states, and led the federal government to hold congressional hearings through 1976 and 1977. Major new federal regulations were passed including certification guidelines, staffing requirements, and rules about dispensing medications and the use of restraints.[48] While very few nursing homes met these standards of care in the late 1970s, these regulatory standards, which state governments had to enforce, added up to significant change over time. By the 1990s, nursing homes were by no means devoid of quality problems but represented an extremely medicalized and regulatory environment now considered appropriate for the frailest elderly.

While new technology and these regulatory standards certainly contributed to the increasing costs of institutional care, state governments remain frustrated because quality concerns still persist. In 1995, for example, there was yet another set of federal congressional hearings on the quality of care provided in nursing homes.

Community-Based Alternatives

Primarily in response to the high cost of nursing home care, but also in part in response to growing concerns about caregiver burden and poor quality of care in nursing homes, state governors have been promoting alternatives to institutionalization since the early 1970s.[49] Federal law under the Omnibus Reconciliation Act of 1981 provided states with the opportunity to develop home and community-based services under special Medicaid waivers. At the federal level, all federal administrations since 1981 have encouraged states to experiment with these types of care, and governors responded enthusiastically. Home health care use has increased dramatically since the 1970s and, not surprisingly, expenditures followed suit: payments increased 250 percent from 1975 to 2003.

To the great disappointment of governors and state budget officials, this increase in home care use did not result in significant Medicaid savings in payments to institutionalized care. The hope was that home and community-based care options would allow elderly with chronic illnesses to live in the community indefinitely and avoid institutionalization altogether. Home and community-based care was often touted as providing better quality in a setting preferred by patients and at a significantly lower cost. Yet, studies have since found that this hope of lower cost was not always achieved. For persons with substantial disabilities, community-based home care can actually be more expensive than care provided by a nursing home. Such care does not necessarily prevent nursing home placement, as many thought it would. Community-based care seems to be used as a care method for earlier stages of illness, whereas nursing home placement is still used in the last stage.[50] Still, states remain committed to the use of home and community-based care. The share of Medicaid LTC spending in home and community-based settings almost tripled from 14 percent in 1991 to 41 percent in 2006.[51]

Middle-Class Reliance on Medicaid Long-Term Care

While much uncertainty exists around how to reform the delivery and payment of Medicaid's long-term care services, there is bipartisan agreement among the governors that middle-class elderly should not be allowed to rely on Medicaid for nursing home care. According to U.S. Secretary of Health and Human Services Michael Leavitt, former governor of Utah, "many older Americans take advantage of Medicaid loopholes to become eligible for Medicaid by giving away assets to their children. There is a whole industry that actually helps people shift costs to the taxpayer. We must close these loopholes and focus Medicaid's resources on helping those who really need it."[52]

216   Colleen M. Grogan and Vernon K. Smith

One way to discourage middle-class people from shedding assets to qualify for Medicaid is to retroactively recoup nursing home expenses incurred by Medicaid recipients from their estates (principally the proceeds of home sales) after death.[53] For many decades states had the option of tapping the estates of the deceased, but, in 1993, Congress actually mandated that every state have an estate recovery program. While a few states implement such programs with vigor, most states do not; the idea of taking money from families who just lost a loved one is not very well received. The Deficit Reduction Act of 2005 again called for states to conduct more stringent estate recovery programs. Again, states have pushed back against attempts to implement the policy. In 2006, Georgia Governor Sonny Perdue announced that the state would soften its Medicaid rules on recovering the cost of nursing home patients' care after they die, saying the rule "wasn't fair for those families."[54]

The provision of LTC under state Medicaid programs has persistently created tricky policymaking dilemmas for governors. On one hand, the reliance of the elderly on nursing home coverage encourages politicians to offer mainstream families ever greater protections and economic security. On the other hand, elected officials are deeply troubled by the use of Medicaid as a vehicle for protecting the assets of relatively well-off people.[55] The issue of home care and innovations has similar dilemmas. For example, many governors oppose providing payment vouchers to caregivers, because many of the caregivers are family members and there is a strong belief that caregiving should be a familial obligation and not subsidized by the state. In contrast, if subsidizing familial care would ultimately help keep the elderly and disabled in their homes, this seems like a reasonable state investment. In sum, despite ever-rising LTC costs, there is a persistent tension over whether to expand or restrict various aspects of Medicaid's long-term care role.

HEALTH INSURANCE FOR THE UNINSURED

Similar to long-term care, in the 1970s no one expected Medicaid to provide coverage for the nonpoor uninsured. However, with the help of federal financial incentives, and some federal requirements, this is exactly what states have done. While the federal government's mandated Medicaid eligibility for poor families with children remained strictly attached to cash assistance welfare throughout the 1970s, it gradually weakened this link in the 1980s by enacting incremental Medicaid expansions for children or pregnant women and infants in every year between 1984 and 1990.[56]

In the early 1980s, national attention was drawn to the fact that the rate of infant mortality in the United States was unacceptably high. The U.S. rate was higher than about twenty other industrialized countries.[57] In 1984 a group of southern governors created a task force on infant mortality. Southern governors were particularly concerned because infant mortality was extraordinarily high in their states—15 per 1,000 in Mississippi and South Carolina, for example.[58] Reducing infant mortality made good moral sense, but it also made good economic sense at the time.[59] South Carolina Governor Richard Riley, who headed the task force, concluded after a year of study that "prenatal and infant care can save $2 to $10 for every dollar invested."[60] While the task force recommended some state-only actions, prominent on its list was more funding from the federal government to expand Medicaid and Women, Infants, and Children (WIC) food supplements.

The Congressional response in 1986 was to create the National Commission to Prevent Infant Mortality. The fifteen-member commission was chaired by U.S. Senator (and later Florida governor) Lawton Chiles and included other members of Congress, the Secretary of Health and Human Services, two governors (Governor Riley of South Carolina and Governor Jim Thompson of Illinois), and experts in the field. Notably, membership included North Carolina Medicaid director Barbara Matula, then chair of the Medicaid directors association. It was the first time a Medicaid director had been included on such an august body, and it proved to be significant.

As the commission was completing its deliberations, the governors and Matula agreed on a set of recommendations and offered them to the commission. Among the most significant were proposals to expand Medicaid eligibility for pregnant women and infants and to simplify Medicaid eligibility procedures and requirements, including a previously untested concept of "presumptive eligibility" for pregnant women. Versions of these recommendations were enacted in 1986, 1988, and in 1990. This was a period when the governors used their Medicaid programs to reduce infant mortality and improve well child care.

Initially, states favored these federal expansions because the federal financial match was available if states chose to expand coverage (they had no obligation to do so). The 1986 legislation, for example, allowed matching funds for covering pregnant women and infants up to 100 percent of poverty level income and for children up to age five to improve the provision of well-child care in the states. Not surprisingly, since the idea emerged from the governors, states responded favorably to these optional inducements. For example, by 1988, two-thirds of all the states had expanded coverage to the optional maximum.[61]

In 1988, however, the federal government shifted from a policy of optional coverage to mandated coverage to be phased in for all children under nineteen up to 100 percent of poverty, and pregnant women, infants, and children under six up to 133 percent of poverty. Required to fully phase in these provisions by 2003, states expanded Medicaid coverage to approximately 5 million children and half a million pregnant women by that year.[62] While many governors welcomed the additional coverage for needy groups, almost all balked at the idea of federal mandates to do so. State officials expressed concern with both the mandated growth in state spending and the loss of autonomy in deciding their own program policies that comes with federal mandates.

Despite a significant increase in Medicaid coverage over the 1980s, the number of uninsured Americans continued to climb to 37 million by 1990 due largely to a reduction in employer-sponsored coverage.[63] Although many state governors and legislators wanted to help the uninsured gain coverage, they typically perceived the state's role as primarily supporting the employer-based system and using Medicaid to fill in the gaps. Reflecting this preference, states used Medicaid to expand coverage to the "deserving" poor in the late 1980s and 1990s, and simultaneously turned to private sector reforms for the working uninsured.

Of course, governors across the political spectrum have supported federal tax subsidy or incentive proposals to increase individuals' ability to purchase private health insurance. State governments' own private sector strategies, however, tend to fall into two main categories. First, states have mandated that employers offer health insurance to their employees while offering the uninsured access to a public or publicly subsidized insurance plan. Second, states have attempted to reform private health insurance policies to make its purchase more affordable for the uninsured.

Employer mandates and expansions requiring new state funding almost by definition effectively provide health coverage to the uninsured, or at least a subset of the uninsured deemed eligible. However, for successful implementation the mandates require state governments to raise revenues or impose the equivalent of a tax. For example, although an employer mandate does not technically require new state spending, it is typically viewed by the business community as a tax because employers are required to invest in an employee benefit that they may not otherwise purchase. When considering direct subsidies to the uninsured, whether in the form of an employer mandate, a voucher for health insurance, or direct access to a state plan, state governments must face the fundamental question—where will the funding come from?

Not surprisingly, what states quickly found was that health insurance legislation requiring new funding was extremely difficult to pass. While all fifty states had established an access commission, or a task force, or called for a health insurance study by 1993, only six states (Hawaii, Minnesota, Florida, Massachusetts, Oregon, and Washington) were actually able to enact statewide health care reform legislation. While the initial legislation in these six states called for significant expansions in coverage for the uninsured, several of these states were never able to implement their programs. In fact, at the end of this period of health care experimentation in the mid-1990s none of these states was able to guarantee statewide coverage.

For example, in 1993 Hawaii still had an uninsured rate ranging from about 4 to 7 percent, despite having an employer mandate policy since 1974.[64] Because the 1974 mandate required employers to offer health insurance only to employees working more than twenty hours a week, the uninsured Hawaiians were largely part-time workers. Therefore, in 1991, Hawaii passed the State Health Insurance Program and extended coverage for this group. However, because the program provided only the most basic coverage and still left a number of individuals uninsured, it was criticized for failing to adequately provide for the "gap" population. As a result, the state refocused its efforts on the Medicaid program where it could leverage federal funds. To implements such a program, however, the state had to overcome a hurdle created by the Employee Retirement Income Security Act of 1974 (ERISA). This federal law primarily applies to pensions and health plans offered by private businesses; yet, it also prevents states from requiring benefits from businesses that are self-insured without federal waiver. Without such a waiver, employer mandates are difficult for states to implement effectively because they do not apply to businesses that self-insure and in many states over half of the businesses self-insure.[65] In 1993, Hawaii sought and obtained a Medicaid waiver to implement its Health Quest program which allowed the state to expand access by leveraging federal funds. Even with an ERISA exemption, however, Hawaii was unable to solve the access problem on its own.

In three states, governors played a leadership role in reforming health care.[66] In Florida, Democratic Governor Lawton Chiles fought for the creation of a managed care system to both control costs and expand coverage. The plan, passed in 1993, created eleven community health purchasing alliances to allow employers, especially small business, to receive the best care for the cheapest price for their workers. In a compromise, however, Chiles agreed to exclude Medicaid recipients from these networks, placing them in a separate pool.[67] Support for health care reform in Florida only went so far. In 1994, in the midst of his reelection campaign, Chiles proposed providing subsidized coverage for uninsured people up to two and a half times the federal poverty level. This time his proposal was defeated. Securing new funding for the uninsured is where most states run into road blocks.

In Massachusetts, Governor Michael Dukakis, in the midst of a campaign for the Democratic nomination for president in 1988, pushed for health care reform in the state. Dukakis wanted to make Massachusetts the second state after Hawaii to implement employer mandated health coverage and to move toward universal coverage.[68] While the Health Security Act was passed in 1988, its implementation illustrated the difficulty states faced trying to finance coverage expansions on their own. While the state proceeded with incremental reforms expanding access, it continually pushed back its intention to achieve universal coverage. Even after the 1994 elections when Democrats held a solid majority in both Houses, the House voted unanimously (143–0) in December 1994 to delay implementation for another year, and the Senate followed suit shortly thereafter.[69] In August 1996, the legislature passed additional insurance coverage for children and the elderly, but repealed the employer mandate.[70]

Similarly, Washington passed a managed competition/employer mandate plan in 1993, and set the implementation date for 1999. However, because there was significant opposition to the employer mandate and the plan lacked a consistent and viable financing scheme, the act was never on stable ground. Indeed, after the November 1994 elections the composition of the Washington legislature changed, and most of the major provisions in the 1993 law, including the employer mandate, were repealed.

Oregon was also lauded as a leading innovator in health care reform in the early 1990s because of its efforts in designing a benefit plan that prioritized benefits for Medicaid recipients. They intended to use the savings from setting priorities to expand coverage. Yet, while its priority ranking of medical benefits received much national attention at the time, its other main financing mechanism—an employer mandate—was the central source of contention at home. After Oregon received the federal Medicaid waiver, the state was very reluctant to move ahead with all of its legislated reforms. In 1993, Senator Bob Shoemaker, a leader in Oregon's legislative efforts, voiced skepticism that was common in most states: "There continues to be resistance to the employer mandate. . . . I have to confess that (the plan) is in jeopardy."[71] In fact, in 1995, Oregon passed legislation stating that the employer mandate was contingent upon the state receiving an ERISA exemption by January 1996. Because the state did not receive the exemption, the employer mandate was eliminated.

Vermont was another state that was viewed as particularly ripe for health reform.[72] But after a two-year struggle to pass either a single-payer or regulated all-payer reform, Vermont was unable to pass anything. Again, financing was the key: the Senate Finance Committee voted down the employer mandate provision, and the House was unable to decide on a premium-based or tax-based financing mechanism to pay for expanding access.[73] Even though Governor Howard Dean, an advocate of reform, was reelected in 1994, Democratic Senator Cheryl Rivers voiced skepticism about the prospects for reform: "[the governor] doesn't have a reform plan; he has a plan to extend Medicaid coverage. . . . I think that a bill will pass this legislature, and it will be called health care reform. But it will mean the preservation of the status quo."[74]

In sum, chronic inaction at the federal level forced many states to grapple with the issue of care for people who were covered by neither private health insurance nor Medicaid. Yet, at the same time, a substantial portion of state budgets was already devoted to Medicaid coverage. The legislative expansions of the 1980s were leading to what many described as explosive cost increases in the early 1990s—state Medicaid spending increased 34 percent in 1992 and 13 percent in 1993.[75]

Regulatory reforms of private health insurance were initiated by numerous governors in the early 1990s. By 1994, forty-four states had enacted some type of health insurance reform law. The reason for their attraction was simple: such policies attempt to ease the affordability problem that small businesses have in purchasing health insurance by reforming insurance laws, rather than by appropriating any new funding for the working uninsured. The problem these laws attempt to address is the amount of variation in rates (or premiums) that insurance companies charge, and the fact that many small groups and individuals are priced out of the market.

The most popular policy (enacted by thirty-five states) to alleviate this problem is called a "rating band." This policy allows insurers to set different rates for different demographic groups but limits the difference between the lowest and highest premium rates. Premium rates are still allowed to vary according to medical risk factors and previous health care use, and in many of the states that enacted these reforms, premiums were allowed to vary quite substantially.[76]

A much more radical step is "pure" community rating because it requires insurers to charge everyone the same premium within a geographic market.[77] Whether health care coverage increased was related to the extent to which premiums under existing policies are allowed to increase to the "new" community rate. For example, individual coverage actually declined 12 percent in just one year after New York implemented its community rating law under which premiums for renewal and new policies were immediately adjusted upward to the community rate.[78] The individual coverage rate declined because those persons who already had individual coverage experienced an increase in their premium and therefore decided not to renew their policy.[79] Based on this experience, New York's Supervising Actuary in the Insurance Department opined that "community rating was never intended to be the be-all or end-all answer" to the problems of health insurance access and affordability.[80]

Other small group insurance reforms that were widely adopted but also ineffective in lowering the number of uninsured persons include: "guaranteed renewal" (adopted by forty-one states by 1993), which restricts insurers from canceling a group's coverage due to insurance claims or changes in health status, and "portability" (passed in forty states by 1993), which allows a person to move between plans (as a result of change in employment) without fulfilling a new waiting period before being covered for preexisting conditions. These reforms primarily helped the currently insured to keep their insurance.[81]

Yet another insurance reform—the "benefit mandate waiver" (also called the "bare bones" policy)—was very popular (enacted in thirty-seven states) and was meant to increase access for the working uninsured based on the assumption that small businesses would purchase insurance policies with limited benefits if the premium rates were significantly reduced. However, McLaughlin and Zellers's 1994 survey of 2,200 small businesses in seven cities suggests that this assumption was faulty. They found that, costs notwithstanding, "the majority of employers (61 percent) that do not offer health insurance to their employees were simply not interested in doing so."[82]

Medicaid Managed Care Reform

Medicaid enrollments kept expanding, national health reform failed yet again, and private health insurance coverage had not increased. Most governors by 1994 readily acknowledged Medicaid's crucial role in providing health coverage for millions of Americans.[83] Yet there was broad agreement—among Republicans and Democrats alike—that Medicaid suffered from serious structural flaws. Medicaid still failed to cover many needy persons, and the health care it offered was too often of low quality and provided inefficiently. Numerous studies documented that Medicaid recipients were much less likely than Americans with private health insurance to have a relationship with a primary care doctor or to receive needed preventive care, and much more likely to receive their care in hospital emergency room settings or public clinics with long waiting lines.[84] Despite the targeted efforts to increase prenatal care and well-child coverage in the 1980s, a large proportion of women on Medicaid received no, or only minimal, prenatal care.[85] Many children enrolled in Medicaid were failing to receive needed immuniza-tions.[86]

The federal government encouraged the idea of Medicaid managed care to deal with these flaws. In the 1980s, it funded managed care dem-onstration projects in the states,[87] and in 1993 President Bill Clinton ordered the federal government to make it easier for states to use Medi-caid funds to introduce new health care programs for low-income fami-lies.[88] By January 1995, forty-nine states (not Alaska) had implemented a Medicaid managed care program. Nationally, through capitated, risk-based health maintenance organizations, health insuring organizations and through state-operated "primary care case management" systems, total enrollment in Medicaid managed care nearly doubled in 1994 and increased 51 percent again in 1995.[89] It was a bipartisan effort where Democrats were just as eager to implement managed care reforms as were Republicans. Use of the most widespread form of Medicaid man-aged care—capitated, risk-based HMOs—promised to simultaneously reduce costs, achieve budget predictability, improve access by providing a clear medical home, and raise the quality of delivered services by requiring a managed care company to monitor services provided to enrollees. If efficiencies were realized, managed care might make funds available that could even be used to expand coverage to the uninsured.[90]

While some states realized cost savings through a reduction in inpa-tient use and improvements in quality of care through an increase in childhood immunizations, most states during the 1990s were not able to realize substantial cost savings to finance significant expansions in cover-age to the uninsured.[91] Under budget-neutral Medicaid waivers, states found it difficult to sustain expansions. Tennessee, for example, expanded coverage under its managed care program, TennCare, and then rolled back coverage when savings failed to materialize and costs exploded.[92] Nonetheless, states still favor managed care over the previ-ous fee-for-service system. In 2006, 65 percent of the total Medicaid pop-ulation in the United States was enrolled in some form of managed care. Forty out of the fifty states have over half of their Medicaid population enrolled in a managed care arrangement of one kind or another.[93]

The State Children's Health Insurance Program

Several states were leaders in child health coverage in the early 1990s. Responding to increasing interest in assuring health coverage for chil-dren, governors took the lead. Thirteen states had created child health programs outside of Medicaid by 1996. For example, in 1990, the Florida Healthy Kids Corporation was established to provide affordable health insurance for all Florida children between the ages of five and nineteen, uninsured (i.e. not enrolled in Medicaid or private insurance), and enrolled in school up through the twelfth grade. Children on the free or reduced-cost school lunch program had access to subsidized insurance, while others paid the entire cost of insurance. Healthy Kids served counties with half the state's uninsured children. Pennsylvania also created its own Children's Health Insurance Program, designed to cover uninsured children in families with incomes above Medicaid eligibility thresholds.

In 1992, California established CaliforniaKids, a limited health insurance product that focused on preventive care. The program began in Los Angeles and expanded to twenty-four counties. It covered uninsured children ages two to eighteen not eligible for any other health program, with family income below 200 percent of the poverty level. Colorado also established a Children's Health Plan in 1992 relying on a community-based health care program for low-income children up to 185 percent of the poverty level not eligible for Medicaid. The program initially targeted rural counties but was later expanded statewide.

All these state actions provided the template for subsequent federal action when Congress adopted the State Children's Health Insurance Program (SCHIP) in 1997 with the support of the National Governors Association (NGA). Under the SCHIP law, with an enhanced federal matching rate, states have the *option* to extend coverage to uninsured children three ways: through Medicaid; through the creation of an entirely new, separate program (with a "benchmark" benefit package); or through a combination of both. State policymakers responded enthusiastically to the SCHIP option to expand coverage for children. A key feature of the SCHIP legislation was the requirement that states conduct outreach to find and enroll low-income uninsured children. States found that of all children that applied for SCHIP, half or more were in fact found eligible for and enrolled into Medicaid. Since 1998, there has been a steady increase in enrollment in Medicaid and SCHIP. In the early years of SCHIP implementation, from 1998 and 2001, Medicaid and SCHIP enrollment grew by an average of 30 percent across the states. Enrollment declined in only three states over this time period.[94] By 2005, forty-one states had elected to cover children at or above 200 percent of the poverty line under Medicaid or SCHIP.[95] When states devoted resources to changing Medicaid's public image and ease of entry (through public relations campaigns highlighting the program's expanded scope and through administrative reforms and simplifications of the enrollment process), they were able to increase enrollment among working, uninsured Americans by significant amounts.[96] Through Medicaid and SCHIP combined, 28 million poor and low-income children were covered in 2005.[97]

As many of the legislative architects of SCHIP hoped, Medicaid coverage increased significantly among children in families who do not receive welfare payments. By 2000, "forty percent of all low-income children were enrolled in Medicaid and SCHIP . . . and two-thirds of these children live in families with one or two full-time workers."[98] Along with the de-linking of Medicaid from welfare as part of the federal welfare reform in 1996, this is the most significant programmatic shift away from welfare medicine since the Medicaid program was enacted in 1965. The SCHIP authorization expired in September 2007. As of this writing it is unclear in what form the program will be reauthorized. The central tension in the SCHIP debate focuses on competing notions of SCHIP's intended target population—stark disagreements over whether the program has inappropriately reached into covering "able" families—raising central questions about the appropriate level of generosity.

COOPERATIVE FEDERALISM?

As the above two sections illustrate, many governors have been significant leaders in creating innovative programs for LTC and expanding coverage to uninsured groups. Perhaps because states are usually not able to achieve innovations until they have secured a federal waiver—which sometimes can be a fairly onerous process—governors often believe that federal requirements are impediments to effective program design and administration. This has been a longstanding source of tension between state and federal governments.

Over the past decade, as states extended Medicaid coverage above the federal poverty level for children, families, and other adults, states have increasingly advocated for more flexibility to structure a Medicaid benefit to more closely resemble employer sponsored health insurance. State flexibility was a key objective of a major Medicaid reform effort by six governors in 1996. The six governors included NGA chair, Governor Tommy Thompson of Wisconsin, and NGA vice chair, Governor Bob Miller of Nevada, two Republican governors (Michael Leavitt of Utah and John Engler of Michigan), and two Democratic governors (Roy Romer of Colorado and Lawton Chiles of Florida). The governors spent almost one hundred hours in face-to-face meetings, including consultations with the federal political leadership on Capitol Hill and in the White House. The goal was to craft a proposal that could be adopted by the full NGA membership.

The plan crafted by the team of governors was adopted unanimously by NGA in February 1996. It was regarded as a remarkable event to have achieved bipartisan agreement among the governors on such a far-reaching plan to restructure Medicaid, reflecting both the governors' commitment to the program itself and the depth of concern for the future fiscal implications for states and their ability to finance it. With the support of the governors, the plan served as the template for the Medi- caid Restructuring Act of 1996, introduced by Representative Thomas Bliley, Jr., chair of the House Committee on Commerce, and Senator Wil- liam Roth, chair of the Senate Committee on Finance. As advocated by the governors, the proposed legislation would have provided additional flexibility and latitude for states to design their programs, including greater ability to define eligibility, benefits, reimbursement, service deliv- ery, rights of appeal, financing, and administration.

A huge stumbling block, however, was that this bill also called for a shift in financing from Medicaid's matching formula to a block grant, and in addition, would have stripped Medicaid of its entitlement status. Due to this change, despite the unanimous NGA vote, many governors also ended up speaking out against the bill. While states abhor federal restrictions and mandates, many often are surprisingly wary of federal block grants when they are actually put on the table. They are wary for the obvious reason that they are never sure the set funding amount will be adequate at a future date when the economy may worsen and Medi- caid rolls and costs inevitably increase. However, they are also wary for a less obvious reason: federal law provides to states an open-ended entitle- ment to federal Medicaid matching funds on all state expenditures that qualify under Medicaid criteria. Governors have been able to use the open-ended entitlement nature of Medicaid much to their fiscal advan- tage.

The main way the open-ended entitlement benefits states financially is through the various Medicaid maximization schemes that states began to pursue fervently in the 1990s. Medicaid maximization simply means that states seek to obtain all the federal funds to which they are entitled. One way to do this is to shift expenditures for programs and services that were paid for under state-only dollars to Medicaid to take advantage of the federal Medicaid matching rate. Such arrangements must meet all Medicaid requirements and be approved by the federal government in the Medicaid state plan. State funding for mental health care services is the most common example. States have always had full responsibility for the provision of mental health care services. Although the federal gov- ernment clearly limits which mental health diagnoses can be defined as a disability for Medicaid eligibility, states realized that many low-income clients who were eligible for Medicaid were receiving mental health ser- vices under state-only funding. After shifting these services over to Medi- caid (sometimes only after changing provider qualification, service definition, or documentation requirements to meet Medicaid standards), such expenditures qualified for federal Medicaid matching funds and states were able to realize significant savings of state dollars. Many developmentally delayed children can similarly be covered under Medicaid. Medicaid maximization is the positive side of states' love-hate relationship with Medicaid.

Nonetheless, the ideas around increasing flexibility from the 1996 NGA proposal remained alive. Governors continued to push for reforms that would provide them authority to restructure their programs. One by one, many of these ideas were adopted at later times.[99] The Balanced Budget Act of 1997, for example, repealed the Boren Amendment, which since 1980 had defined Medicaid reimbursement for hospitals and nursing homes. Repeal of this provision was one of the key tenets of NGA's proposal in 1996.

The Deficit Reduction Act (DRA) of 2005 also included provisions long advocated by governors for flexibility in structuring Medicaid benefits and allowing larger and enforceable beneficiary copayments. In part, this flexibility was intended to allow and encourage other states to adopt a plan similar to the one pioneered by Utah Governor Michael Leavitt (later Secretary of Health and Human Services.) While governor, he had obtained a Section 1115 Medicaid waiver to create a special, limited-benefit program for low-income, uninsured adults without children.[100]

Three states—Kentucky, West Virginia, and Idaho—responded quickly to this increased flexibility under DRA. A common theme among all three states was targeting benefits for specific population groups with the purpose of promoting personal responsibility. For example, Kentucky Governor Ernie Fletcher, together with his secretary of health, Mark Birdwhistle, created four benefit packages with varying service limits and cost-sharing requirements: "Global Choices" (the "default" package for those not falling into another package); "Family Choices" (for children, including SCHIP); "Optimum Choices" (for persons with mental retardation/developmentally disabled needing long-term care services); and "Comprehensive Choices" (for elderly and disabled in need of long-term care services). Kentucky's plan also included "Get Healthy" incentives for beneficiaries to encourage responsible health behavior. The rewards could be used for services otherwise not covered such as dental, vision, or nutritional or smoking cessation counseling. Under this plan, Kentucky was the first state to make Medicaid copayments enforceable, as allowed under the DRA.

Similarly, West Virginia Governor Joe Manchin developed a plan with his Medicaid director, Nancy Atkins, to provide an "enhanced" benefit for eligible low-income families, who sign and conform to a "Medicaid Member Agreement." A scaled-back benefit was also available for those who failed to sign the agreement or do not fulfill their obligations under the agreement. West Virginia also plans to pilot "Healthy Reward Accounts" that will allow beneficiaries to earn credits for healthy behaviors that can be used to cover medical and pharmaceutical copays.

Besides securing substantial freedoms to structure beneficiary-specific benefit packages, governors also recently won a significant increase in federal funding. In the early 2000s, governors across the country were battling the worst fiscal conditions since World War II. Across the states, budget shortfalls were mounting: $50 billion in 2003 and $80 billion in 2004. The problems were so widespread among the states they could no longer be considered just regional issues or to be wholly caused by local factors. As a result, NGA lobbied Congress for fiscal relief.[101]

The Congressional debate over a state fiscal relief package lasted nearly two years before final approval. NGA first started lobbying Congress for help with the Medicaid program in the fall of 2001 as state revenues fell flat and the program's cost spiraled upward. As the states' fiscal situation continued to deteriorate over 2002 and early 2003, governors increased their efforts to spur congressional action. The combined efforts of NGA and a bipartisan group of Senators—including Olympia Snowe (R-Maine), Gordon Smith (R-Ore.), Ben Nelson (D-Neb.), and John Rockefeller (D-W.V.)—were instrumental in overcoming significant opposition in both Congress and the White House to any form of aid to the states, especially in the form of expanding the federal commitment to Medicaid.[102]

The fiscal relief bill both enhanced, on a temporary basis, the federal Medicaid matching percentage and provided funding through separate block grants. This method of fiscal relief is unprecedented and significant for two reasons. First, it shows that the federal government is willing to adjust the federal matching assistance percentage due to cyclical downturns in the economy. Second, it introduces a new concept of supplementing Medicaid budget shortfalls with separate grants to allow more flexibility for each state to respond to their particular needs.

Conclusion: Lessons Learned

Understanding how states' health care policy for the poor evolved over time leading to the creation of Medicaid is crucial for grasping how a program that was intended to be restricted charity care for the poor became an expensive comprehensive program for many nonpoor people. The two expansionary seeds imbedded in Medicaid's beginnings—medical indigency and comprehensive benefits—have pushed this program in ways no one envisioned.

But it is really the larger health care system in the United States that has always left a sizable group of uninsured Americans knocking on states' doors, elderly and disabled Americans with no other program to cover their needs; and a federal matching rate that provides significant incentives (and now responds to economic downturns) that has repeatedly pushed states toward Medicaid—even when governors really did not want to go in that direction.

Many governors argue that long-term care, at least for the elderly, should be shifted to the federal government. They have consistently argued that long-term care for the elderly is appropriately a federal responsibility because the federal government runs the Medicare program. Some point to the Medicare Prescription Drug bill, which shifted Medicaid prescription drug costs for the elderly to the Medicare program, as hope that the federal government will continue to expand coverage to include all the services needed by the elderly. Yet members of Congress are already complaining about the enormous costs of the Medicare prescription bill, and it is just a drop in the bucket compared to what long-term care costs would be. The cost factor makes the hope for a federal takeover of LTC seem particularly futile at least for the near future. Moreover, it is important to realize that the significant increase in long-term care costs comes from the disabled population—many children of lower- and middle-income families—which no one has argued is appropriately a federal responsibility. But, most important, Medicaid has expanded too much for even a big change like that to fundamentally change the program.

Governors are clearly very keen to continue thinking creatively about how to expand coverage for the uninsured. Interestingly, after initial interest following the passage of the Deficit Reduction Act in 2005, few other states have chosen to use the flexibility options governors advocated for many years. Instead, the focus of Medicaid reform for many policymakers has shifted toward more comprehensive health reform, such as that in Massachusetts, Vermont, and California.

While governors still favor policies that encourage employers to offer health insurance to their employees or encourage workers to purchase private insurance, states are moving in a slightly different direction from the health reforms tried in the early 1990s by leveraging Medicaid to help bring about private sector reforms. In April 2006, for example, Massachusetts Governor Mitt Romney signed into law legislation that would provide nearly universal health care coverage to state residents. A central component of the bill is a so-called individual mandate that requires every adult person in the state to purchase health insurance. To assure that individuals can reasonably fulfill their mandate to purchase, the state uses a number of government subsidies to ensure affordability. The main subsidy source is the state's Medicaid program through which it is able to heavily leverage federal funds to expand coverage to the unin-

sured. The state uses its Medicaid managed care program to assure that
individuals can purchase insurance through state contracted insurance
plans. And, Massachusetts hopes to use its leverage as a volume pur-
chaser to obtain a competitive price. In turn, building on notions of
Medicaid managed care, the state also hopes that plans will efficiently
manage the care provided to Medicaid and non-Medicaid enrollees,
thereby controlling costs.[103]

California Governor Arnold Schwarzenegger offered a plan in January
2007 that would extend health insurance to all Californians, including
over 6.5 million uninsured and all illegal immigrants. Similar to proposals in the early 1990s, it would be financed with assessments on physicians and hospitals, and an employer mandate so that employers not
offering insurance would be subject to an annual assessment.

Lessons from the 1990s suggest that unless the states figure out how to
bridge expansions to Medicaid reforms, the private employer-mandate
proposal might be doomed. The advantage of building on Medicaid
managed care contracting with private plans—as long as there is clear
monitoring—is that states can begin to set up a "health plan infrastructure" whereby small business employers and uninsured individuals can
more affordably purchase insurance from these state-contracted health
plans.

Note, however, that with these reforms, states are coming to the conclusion that statewide coverage cannot be achieved without some type
of compulsion—an individual mandate or an employer mandate. The
key to whether a compulsory requirement is feasible depends on the
state being able to create a health plan infrastructure that allows the purchase of health insurance to be affordable—no easy task.

Finally, while relatively wealthy states like California and Massachusetts may be able to afford health reform plans offering statewide coverage beyond the federal financial assistance levels received through
Medicaid, it is especially challenging for poorer states—even when they
have the political will—to do that. Indeed, to reach universal coverage—
not necessarily equal coverage for all, but access to some level of health
coverage for everyone—most states will need to leverage federal dollars,
and to do that states will need to figure out how best to use Medicaid.

Afterword: A Legacy of State-Building

ETHAN G. SRIBNICK

This volume provides a starting point for evaluating the role of American governors in shaping public policy. The chapters above document the central role governors played in confronting many of the major challenges faced by the American republic. Together, however, these essays demonstrate more than just the role of governors in directing policy over the twentieth century; they also highlight the role of governors in developing the very institutions of American government. While historians and political scientists continue to debate the nature of American state-building the essays in this volume highlight the importance of states and, particularly, governors in this process.

Over the past hundred years, this process of state-building unfolded in various ways. Sometimes governors and state governments created new institutions that were later adopted by the federal government. Ron Haskins has explained how Progressive Era mothers' pensions were later incorporated into the federal Social Security Act and how, in the 1990s, state social policy experiments became the basis for national welfare reform. In other cases governors have innovated in the spaces left open by federal inaction. Governors such as Christine Todd Whitman of New Jersey, Sarah Phillips has noted, led the nation in the attempt to curb greenhouse gases. As Colleen M. Grogan and Vernon K. Smith have reported, governors such as Michael Dukakis of Massachusetts have, at various times, taken command of the effort to expand health insurance coverage.

In many instances American government has been formed by a convoluted combination of state and federal power. Ajay Mehrotra and David Shreve have recounted the century-long struggle of governors to find effective methods of revenue collection in light of the federal system of taxation. Jason Sokol has uncovered instances in which governors turned to the federal courts to provide political cover in the painful process of racial integration. The chapters by Jon C. Teaford and Brooke Masters demonstrate how governors, by instituting policies to enhance the economic stature of their states, enhanced the national economy. At times, state-building has occurred through explicit cooperation between state and federal government. As both Robert Jay Dilger and Maris A. Vinovskis have explained, governors have been central players in working with the federal government to develop systems of transportation and education across the nation. In all these ways, governors have bequeathed a legacy of innovation.

This legacy continues; governors remain active participants in shaping and reforming the American polity to meet the needs of both today and the future. More than ever, governors now work to make their states thrive, not only in a national context, but also in an international one. In a time of increasing globalization, governors stand on the front lines of efforts by their states and the entire nation to maintain a vital role in the world. With the threat of terrorism made abundantly clear by the events of September 11, 2001, governors now prepare for the possibility of their states becoming a battleground in an international struggle. If history provides any indication, governors will guide the responses to these public policy challenges. Through leadership within their states, through cooperation with other governors, and through partnership with the federal government, governors will continue to shape the American nation.

Timeline of Governors and States in the Twentieth Century

1900   Hawaii acquires territorial status.

Hurricane devastates Galveston, Tex.

1901   Former New York governor/current vice president Theodore Roosevelt becomes president upon assassination of William McKinley.

Connecticut becomes first state to pass an automobile law, setting speed limit at twelve miles per hour.

1905   U.S. Forest Service created. Gifford Pinchot, later governor of Pennsylvania, is first director.

Colorado has three governors in one day due to a political squabble.

California becomes model in separating state and local revenue sources, leaving property taxes within the purview of local governments.

Former Idaho Governor Frank Steunenberg killed by bomb. Famed union organizer "Big Bill" Haywood of the Western Federation of Miners is among accused perpetrators.

1906   Earthquake and related fires destroy much of San Francisco.

People of New Mexico and Arizona vote on joint statehood. New Mexico votes in favor and Arizona against.

1907   Roosevelt administration establishes the Inland Waterways Commission. This commission recommends holding a conference of governors to discuss conservation.

New York and Wisconsin become first states to establish public utility commissions.

Oklahoma becomes a state.

1908   Washington, D.C., May 13–15. Governors meet for the first time at request of President Roosevelt to discuss conservation.

Oregon's Corrupt Practices Act (regulating campaign expenditures and practices) adopted.

1910   NGA meetings: Washington, D.C., May 13–15, and Frankfort and Louisville, Ky., Nov. 29–Dec. 1. Governors begin meeting independently. They discuss women's suffrage and state automobile laws.

Governor Charles Evans Hughes of New York appointed to U.S. Supreme Court.

1911   NGA meeting: Spring Lake, N.J. Governors take their first official action as a group, appointing three governors to represent the organization in pending Supreme Court case. Governors discuss gubernatorial powers.

Illinois becomes first state to provide mothers' pensions statewide.

California and Wisconsin establish boards to prepare state budgets.

Wisconsin becomes first state to adopt workers' compensation program.

Kansas becomes first state to pass a "blue sky" law (regulating sale of securities).

Wisconsin adopts income tax law that becomes a model for other states, using nonpolitical state officials in collection and relying on individual taxpayer self-reporting.

1912   NGA meeting: Richmond, Va. Governors adopt Articles of Organization for Governors' Conference. Organization's purposes are to exchange views on subjects of importance to states, promote greater uniformity in state legislation, and attain greater efficiency in state administration. Governors discuss divorce laws.

Arizona and New Mexico join the Union. After admission, Arizona restores provision for recall of judges by popular vote—the basis for its statehood being vetoed by President Taft in 1911.

Alaska acquires territorial status.

Massachusetts legislature enacts first minimum wage law for women and children.

1913   NGA meeting: Colorado Springs, Colo. Governors discuss state initiatives and referendums, campaign finance, and candidates' use of private money and contributions.

Former New Jersey Governor Woodrow Wilson inaugurated president. Former Indiana Governor Thomas Marshall inaugurated vice president.

Sixteenth and Seventeenth Amendments to Constitution (federal income tax and direct election of U.S. senators) ratified.

Minnesota rate cases—U.S. Supreme Court rules that Interstate Commerce Commission has authority to regulate intrastate rail rates discriminating against interstate commerce.

Illinois implements first comprehensive administrative reorganization program.

Ford introduces moving assembly line process, reducing automobile prices.

1914   NGA meeting: Madison, Wis. Western governors express concern over federal control of lands and its potential threat to tax revenue.

Federal Trade Commission Act (prevents unfair competition in interstate trade) passed.

Smith-Lever Act (provides grants for agricultural extension programs) passed.

American Association of Labor Legislation begins national campaign for compulsory health insurance.

Moses Alexander of Idaho elected first Jewish governor.

1915   NGA meeting: Boston, Mass. Governors discuss capital punishment.

Nevada legislation simplifies divorce process.

First official Western Governors' Conference takes place.

Alaska adopts old-age pension law—first among states and territories.

Great Migration begins. Ku Klux Klan revived with the release of the movie *Birth of a Nation*.

1916   NGA meeting: Washington, D.C. Governors discuss relatively new concept of an "executive budget" and problem of legislative appropriations exceeding revenue. War Department official thanks governors of Arizona, New Mexico, and Texas for providing troops to assist in fighting Mexican guerrilla forces.

Federal Road Act passed.

U.S. Supreme Court justice and former New York Governor Charles Evans Hughes is Republican nominee for president, loses to incumbent Wilson.

1917   Smith-Hughes Act provides federal funds to states for vocational education teachers.

Residents of Puerto Rico become U.S. citizens.

U.S. enters World War I. Only year since the adoption of bylaws that governors do not meet.

1918   NGA meeting: Annapolis, Md. The secretary of war addresses governors. Governors discuss whether demobilization and reconversion following the war will lead to labor unrest.

Mississippi becomes last existing state to enact a compulsory education law.

1919   NGA meeting: Salt Lake City, Utah. Governors discuss high cost of living and recent conference of the seven governors most affected by nationwide coal strike.

Eighteenth Amendment to Constitution (prohibition) ratified.

Oregon becomes first state to levy a gasoline tax.

1920   NGA meeting: Harrisburg, Pa. Governors discuss affordable housing shortage, farmers' financial crisis, and fears that population shift from rural to urban will lead to starvation in cities.

U.S. Census reports urban residents now outnumber rural residents.

Nineteenth Amendment to Constitution (women's suffrage) ratified.

1921   NGA meeting: Charleston, S.C. Governors discuss recommendations of the Committee on Inter-State Compacts.

Former Governor Calvin Coolidge of Massachusetts becomes vice president.

North Dakota first state in which a governor (Lynn Frazier) is recalled.

Federal Aid Highway Act (ensures that federal aid is expended on major roads) passed.

Sheppard-Towner Act (provides funding to states for maternal and child health care) is passed.

1922   NGA meeting: White Sulphur Springs, W.Va. Governors hear an address on the uniformity of marriage and divorce laws and discuss Ku Klux Klan.

Seven states—Arizona, California, Colorado, Nevada, New Mexico, Utah, and Wyoming—sign an interstate compact governing the allocation of water from the Colorado River.

Georgia Governor Thomas Hardwick appoints first female member of U.S. Senate—Rebecca Felton—following her husband's death.

1923   NGA meeting: West Baden, Ind. Governors discuss uniformity of state laws and the plight of farmers.

Upon Harding's death, Calvin Coolidge inaugurated president.

Oklahoma Governor J. C. Walton declares martial law because of widespread violence perpetrated by the Ku Klux Klan.

1924   NGA meeting: Jacksonville, Fla. Executive Committee enlarged from three to five members. Governors discuss state use of prison labor.

American Indians accorded U.S. citizenship.

1925   NGA meeting: Poland Springs, Maine. Director of federal Budget Bureau urges states to follow federal suit and reduce spending. Governors discuss federal aid and their concerns that accepting matching grants gives too much control to the federal government.

Nellie Tayloe Ross (Wyoming) and Ma Ferguson (Texas) become the first women governors.

Great Tri-State Tornado—Missouri, Illinois, and Indiana—kills nearly 700 people.

1926   NGA meeting: Cheyenne, Wyo. Governors adopt resolution urging Congress to pass legislation aiding agriculture in attaining equal footing with other industries in the world market.

States adopt plan for first interstate highway system, the U.S. Routes.

1927   NGA meeting: Mackinac Island, Mich. Governors discuss federal government's encroachment on state authority with Water Power Act of 1920 and National Defense Act of 1926, and recent flooding of the Mississippi River.

1928   NGA meeting: New Orleans, La. Governors discuss severance tax and wisdom of governmental intervention with the failing economy.

1929   NGA meeting: New London, Conn. Governors discuss crime and gun control, and aviation.

Stock market crash triggers Great Depression.

1930   NGA meeting: Salt Lake City, Utah. Governors hold first "governors-only session." New York Governor Franklin Roosevelt speaks in favor of unemployment insurance.

Former New York Governor Charles Evan Hughes becomes chief justice of U.S. Supreme Court.

1931   NGA meeting: French Lick, Ind. Governors reject recommendation to establish a research arm for the association. They discuss what power states should have over local expenditures.

1932   NGA meeting: Richmond, Va. President Hoover addresses governors regarding nation's economic problems.

Al Capone imprisoned for tax evasion. Dwight Green, future governor of Illinois, served as a prosecutor in the trial.

Emergency Relief and Construction Act (makes funds available to states for relief efforts) passed.

Wisconsin becomes first state to enact an unemployment insurance plan.

Mississippi becomes first state to adopt a general sales tax.

Federal government adopts its first gasoline tax.

1933   NGA meeting: Sacramento and San Francisco, Calif. Former Governor George Dern of Utah, now secretary of war, speaks to governors about the National Industrial Recovery Act. Governors adopt resolution supporting federal efforts to fight organized crime.

New York Governor Franklin D. Roosevelt inaugurated president.

Twentieth and Twenty-first Amendments to Constitution (presidential terms of succession and repealing prohibition) ratified.

Roosevelt's New Deal begins: Federal Deposit Insurance Corporation; Civilian Conservation Corps; Public Works Administration; and the Tennessee Valley Authority.

Federal Emergency Relief Act passed (disburses $500 million in assistance to states).

Dust storms sweep the Midwest.

1934 NGA meeting: Mackinac Island, Mich. Attendance low due to transportation interruptions associated with nationwide labor strikes. Governors discuss gangsterism and state response to repeal of prohibition. Federal officials speak to governors regarding relief programs.

Hayden-Cartwright Act penalizes states that divert state gasoline tax revenue to non-highway purposes.

Unicameral legislature adopted in Nebraska.

Southern Governors' Association founded.

Dust storms sweep the Plains states.

1935 NGA meeting: Biloxi, Miss. Governors discuss federal plans to use relief funds for road construction. They are briefed on federal legislation providing old-age assistance and aid for dependent children.

Social Security Act passed.

Rural Electrification Administration established.

Interstate Crime Conference held to discuss state and federal cooperation in combating crime and developing interstate parole compacts.

U.S. Senator Huey Long—former governor of Louisiana—assassinated.

1936 NGA meeting: St. Louis, Mo. Governors discuss Social Security Act and new requirements for state unemployment programs. Puerto Rico approved for membership in the association.

Former Kansas Governor Harry Woodring becomes secretary of war.

1937 NGA meeting: Atlantic City, N.J. Governors discuss pending legislation that would for the first time provide federal education aid to the states. They call for a conference on conflicting taxation between levels of government. After meeting, governors travel to Washington to meet with Roosevelt.

New England Governors' Conference founded.

Missouri establishes first-of-its-kind conservation commission.

1938   NGA meeting: Oklahoma City, Okla. Great New England Hurricane results in low attendance. Governors discuss how state laws and regulations (e.g., trucking rules and taxes) create interstate trade barriers.

New York becomes first state to pass law requiring a medical test as a prerequisite for marriage license.

Construction begins on the nation's first superhighway, the Pennsylvania Turnpike.

1939   NGA meeting: Albany and New York, N.Y. Governors discuss history of federal involvement in state public health matters and the extent to which state budgets are burdened by provisions of the Social Security Act.

Former Michigan Governor Frank Murphy becomes U.S. attorney general.

1940   NGA meeting: Duluth, Minn. Governors discuss state-federal relations in administration of public relief programs. Adopt resolution expressing consensus that all necessary steps should be taken to provide for the defense of the United States and pledging each state's resources.

1941   NGA meeting: Boston and Cambridge, Mass. Fiorello LaGuardia, director of civilian defense, addresses governors regarding role of states in event of enemy attack. Resolution urges that matters of civilian defense go through states, not localities.

States agree to "loan" employment service to federal government for war production emergency.

James Byrnes, later governor of South Carolina, appointed to U.S. Supreme Court.

Governor Eugene Talmadge fires University of Georgia education dean for promoting racial equality, leading to revocation of university's accreditation.

Attack on Pearl Harbor leads to U.S. entry into World War II.

1942   NGA meeting: Asheville, N.C. Governors discuss federal emergency wartime authority and returning of state authority after the war. Adopt resolution objecting to federal interference with respect to inherent taxation powers of state and local governments.

Roosevelt authorizes internment of Japanese Americans.

Gasoline rationing initiated in seventeen eastern states and expands to all states by year's end.

1943   NGA meeting: Columbus, Ohio. General George Marshall addresses governors regarding strategy for military victory.

Executive Committee enlarged to nine members to ensure quorum.

Roosevelt freezes wages and prices in effort to curb inflation.

1944   NGA meeting: Hershey, Pa. Governors meet at Gettysburg battlefield. One northern and one southern governor speak. Federal officials urge support of legislation facilitating the conversion of wartime to peacetime industry for sake of maintaining stable employment levels. Resolution requests returning control of employment services to states.

White House conference on rural education assesses prospects for federal educational assistance to states.

1945   NGA meeting: Mackinac Island, Mich. Governors discuss United Nations Charter, returning veterans, postwar industrial recovery, aviation, and prepaid health care coverage.

New York passes first state anti-discrimination law, establishes State Division of Human Rights.

Roosevelt dies and Vice President Harry Truman becomes president.

World War II ends.

1946   NGA meeting: Oklahoma City, Okla. Generals Dwight Eisenhower and Omar Bradley address governors. Governors discuss veterans and lagging educational system.

Federal Airport Act passed (provides federal aid for airport development).

Federal government officially returns Employment Service system to states.

1947   NGA meeting: Salt Lake City, Utah. Governors discuss the responsibility of states and the organization of state government, housing for veterans, agricultural subsidies, water resources, and tourism.

Conference of members of Congress and governors discusses coordination of national and state taxation.

President Truman advocates compulsory national health insurance.

1948   NGA meeting: Portsmouth, N.H. Edward R. Murrow speaks on end of U.S. isolationism and espouses position that U.S. influence around the world will come not from spending but from setting a positive example.

Ohio River Valley Water Sanitation Compact (Illinois, Indiana, Kentucky, New York, Ohio, Pennsylvania, Virginia, and West Virginia) established.

Former Massachusetts Governor Maurice Tobin appointed secretary of labor.

Fourteen southern governors establish Board of Control for Regional Education.

1949   NGA meeting: Colorado Springs, Colo. Subjects of discussion include social security, welfare, highways, education, and intergovernmental relations.

Following Ku Klux Klan raids, Governor James Folsom of Alabama signs legislation forbidding the wearing of masks.

Soviets detonate their first atomic bomb.

1950   NGA meeting: White Sulphur Springs, W.Va. Governors discuss water resources.

Federal Civil Defense Act and Disaster Relief Act (first federal emergency response programs)

Social Security Act amended to provide Medical Vendor Program allowing states to use federal matching funds to pay medical providers directly for services to public assistance recipients.

America enters Korean conflict.

1951   NGA meeting: Gatlinburg, Tenn. Governors addressed by federal officials regarding Korean conflict and defense readiness. Administrator of Civil Defense argues modern warfare will be won or lost on the home front, requiring preparations.

Twenty-second Amendment to U.S. Constitution (limits presidency to two terms) ratified.

1952   NGA meeting: Houston, Tex. Resolution asks for revenue from federal gasoline tax and freedom to build highways and bridges without federal interference.

Governors' Interstate Indian Conference held, attended by governors of sixteen states with large Native American populations.

Oregon Governor James McKay appointed secretary of interior.

Puerto Rico becomes a commonwealth.

Illinois Governor Adlai Stevenson is Democratic candidate for president, loses to Eisenhower.

1953   NGA meeting: Seattle, Wash. Governors discuss baby boom and its anticipated effect on education system.

Korean War armistice signed.

Governor Earl Warren of California appointed chief justice of the U.S. Supreme Court.

1954   NGA meeting: Lake George, N.Y. Vice President Nixon asks for governors' support of Eisenhower's plan for new interstate highway program. Committee formed to examine proposal.

Governors hold national conference on mental health.

Brown v. Board of Education outlaws racial segregation in public education.

1955   NGA meeting: Chicago, Ill. Governors discuss recent defeat of federal highway aid legislation and financing methods, juvenile delinquency, and mental illness.

Air Pollution Control Act passed.

First White House Conference on Education held.

1956   NGA meeting: Atlantic City, N.J. Governors discuss White House Conference on Education.

Federal Aid Highway Act passed.

Great Lakes Commission represents eight states on environmental and economic issues.

1957   NGA meeting: Williamsburg, Va. Governors request appointment of a committee to study problem of air pollution. Eisenhower warns that failure of states to assume traditional state responsibilities is likely to result in further federal incursion.

Eisenhower sends federal troops to enforce integration of Central High School in Little Rock, Arkansas, after resistance by Governor Orval Faubus.

Soviet Union launches Sputnik.

1958   NGA meeting: Bal Harbour, Fla. Dag Hammarskjold, secretary-general of United Nations, addresses governors about Cold War and peaceful uses of atomic energy. Governors adopt resolutions urging federal funding for construction of fallout shelters.

Association's 50th Anniversary.

National Defense Education Act passed.

1959   NGA meeting: San Juan, P.R. Executive Committee members report on their trip to Soviet Union. Office of Chairman established, to alternate annually between two parties. Standing Committee on Roads and Highway Safety established. Governors addressed on likely effects of nuclear fallout.

Alaska and Hawaii become states.

Former Massachusetts Governor Christian Herter appointed secretary of state.

Permanent Advisory Commission on Intergovernmental Relations established.

1960   NGA meeting: Glacier National Park, Mont. Governors discuss pending legislation to provide medical care for the elderly and Soviet superiority in the arms race and education.

Kerr-Mills Act passed (provides funding to states to aid medical coverage of elderly).

Congress passes the first general aid-to-education bill.

1961   NGA meeting: Honolulu, Hawaii. Federal officials ask governors to support federal education assistance to states. Resolution urges Congress to enact program providing federal grants-in-aid to assist construction of classroom facilities, loans for the construction and improvement of facilities for higher education, and funds to expand adult education programs.

Former North Carolina Governor Luther Hodges appointed secretary of commerce.

Delaware River Basin Compact includes Delaware, New Jersey, New York, and Pennsylvania.

1962 NGA meeting: Hershey, Pa. Heated debate over civil rights. Resolution defeated to endorse program of medical care for the aged. Resolution adopted urging constitutional amendment for voluntary participation in prayer in public schools.

Baker v. Carr establishes that the issue of reapportionment is justiciable, enabling courts to intervene in cases of legislative reapportionment.

Governor Ross Barnett tries to block African American James Meredith's admission to University of Mississippi. Found guilty of contempt.

Midwestern Governors Association founded.

1963 NGA meeting: Miami Beach, Fla. Vice President Lyndon Johnson relates that civil rights is top priority for Kennedy administration.

University of Alabama desegregated after Governor George Wallace is confronted by federally deployed National Guard troops.

President John F. Kennedy assassinated.

Republican Governors Association founded.

1964 NGA meeting: Cleveland, Ohio. Governors discuss civil rights, Cold War education, extending civil defense to natural disasters, support for medical assistance to elderly, Economic Opportunity Act of 1964, and pending legislation to involve the federal government in child support enforcement.

President Johnson declares War on Poverty.

Twenty-fourth Amendment to U.S. Constitution (prohibiting poll tax) ratified.

Reynolds v. Sims establishes that both houses of a state legislature must be apportioned on the basis of population.

Civil Rights Act passed.

Wilderness Act and Land and Water Conservation Fund Bill passed.

1965 NGA meeting: Minneapolis, Minn. Via video message, Johnson asks governors to support his goals in Vietnam and sends plane to bring governors to White House. Resolution to study problem of water pollution. Name of organization changed to National Governors' Conference.

First U.S. combat troops arrive in Vietnam.

Massachusetts becomes first state to pass "Racial Imbalance" legislation, leading to busing protests.

New York Governor Nelson Rockefeller launches Pure Waters Program.

Congress creates Medicaid.

Elementary and Secondary Education Act passed and Project Head Start initiated.

Voting Rights Act passed.

1966 NGA annual meeting: Los Angeles, Calif. Governors resolve to hold conference on juvenile delinquency and urge states to establish commissions on crime and delinquency. First "interim meeting" held, leading to regular winter meetings. Office of Federal-State Relations established. Resolution reaffirms support for president's Vietnam policies.

Kentucky becomes first southern state to enact comprehensive civil rights legislation.

Medicare begins.

1967 Governors hold their annual meeting in part aboard the *S.S. Independence* en route to the Virgin Islands. Governors discuss principles of tax sharing and consolidating more than 200 existing federal grants. Resolution affirms law enforcement to be responsibility of state and local governments.

Twenty-fifth Amendment to U.S. Constitution (terms for succession to presidency) ratified.

National Bellas-Hess, Inc. v. Illinois Department of Revenue rules that states cannot levy sales tax on mail-order products purchased from out-of-state companies.

Loving v. Virginia declares interracial marriage laws unconstitutional, affecting sixteen states.

Illinois Governor Otto Kerner named head of National Advisory Commission on Civil Disorders.

1968 NGA annual meeting: Cincinnati, Ohio. Governors discuss poverty and urban America. Astronaut Neil Armstrong talks about upcoming launch of first Apollo space mission and how every state contributed resources. Committee on Transportation established, chaired by Governor Ronald Reagan. Resolutions urge federal shift from categorical to block grants and support revenue sharing. Association holds first official winter meeting and first seminar for new governors.

Martin Luther King, Jr., and Robert Kennedy assassinated.

1969   NGA annual meeting: Colorado Springs, Colo. President Nixon
       speaks on revenue sharing, welfare, and universal health insur-
       ance program. Governors express support for shift from fed-
       eral-state program of assistance to the aged, blind, disabled,
       and dependent children to a federally financed, state-adminis-
       tered program. At winter meeting, Vice President Agnew
       announces establishment of Office of Intergovernmental Rela-
       tions.
       Maryland Governor Spiro Agnew becomes vice president.
       Michigan Governor George Romney appointed secretary of hous-
       ing and urban development.
       Massachusetts Governor John Volpe appointed secretary of trans-
       portation.
       In *Shapiro v. Thompson*, rules that residency requirements for wel-
       fare eligibility violate fundamental right to travel.
       President Nixon proposes Family Assistance Plan.
       Alexander v. Holmes County mandates immediate school integra-
       tion in fourteen states.
1970   NGA annual meeting: Lake of the Ozarks, Mo. Director of the
       Office of Management and Budget discusses proposal for Envi-
       ronmental Protection Agency. Governors endorse continua-
       tion of Highway Trust Fund and for establishment of Airport/
       Airways Development and Urban Mass Transportation Trust
       Funds. Resolution declares third week in April "Earth Week."
       At winter meeting, President Nixon addresses governors
       regarding his welfare reform plan (Family Assistance Plan).
       Four students killed at Kent State University by Ohio National
       Guardsmen. Former Pennsylvania Governor William Scranton
       heads Commission on Campus Unrest in the wake of these
       deaths and those of two students at Jackson State University in
       Mississippi.
       Federal Airport Act passed (reflects NGA endorsement of Airport
       and Airway Trust Fund).
       California passes nation's first no-fault divorce law.
       Despite strong anti-busing sentiment in Virginia, Governor Lin-
       wood Holton enrolls daughters in predominantly African
       American schools in Richmond.
       Clean Air Act passed.
1971   NGA annual meeting: San Juan, P.R. Agnew reports positive
       response to administration's wage-price freeze sparked by ris-
       ing inflation. Governors discuss national health insurance, no-
       fault auto insurance, and, after Attica prison riot, prisons. At

winter meeting, President Nixon briefs governors on revenue sharing program.

Melvin Evans elected first black governor of Virgin Islands.

Swann v. Charlotte-Mecklenburg County says busing appropriate remedy for racial segregation in schools.

Twenty-sixth Amendment to U.S. Constitution (voting age eighteen) ratified.

1972   NGA annual meeting: Houston, Tex. Governors discuss rising crime rates, drug abuse, and court rulings against the use of property taxes as the primary source of school financing. Astronaut Alan Shepard presents states with flags carried to moon on Apollo 14 mission. Representatives of the National Welfare Rights Organization disrupt winter meeting discussion of welfare reform.

Alabama Governor George Wallace shot while campaigning for presidency in Maryland.

Watergate scandal begins.

Furman v. Georgia suspends state capital punishment laws.

General Revenue Sharing begins.

1973   NGA annual meeting: Lake Tahoe, Nev. Governors discuss energy crisis and revenue sharing proposals pending in Congress. Resolution supports federal assumption of welfare payments for aged, blind, and disabled. At winter meeting, governors discuss federal initiatives in domestic policy and details of revenue sharing.

Roe v. Wade decision issued.

U.S. soldiers leave Vietnam.

Vice President Agnew resigns and pleads no contest to income tax evasion charges.

OPEC begins oil embargo against United States and other Western nations.

To conserve fuel and heighten safety, federal government orders states to reduce interstates' speed limit to fifty-five miles per hour.

1974   NGA annual meeting: Seattle, Wash. Governors discuss government reform in aftermath of Watergate scandal. At winter meeting, governors discuss the energy crisis. Responsibilities are assigned to an executive director. Center for Policy Research and Analysis established.

Emergency Highway Energy Conservation Act prohibits approval of federal highway projects in states with speed limits over fifty-five miles per hour.

Rather than face impeachment, President Nixon resigns. Gerald

Ford becomes president and former New York Governor Nelson Rockefeller is confirmed as vice president.

Community Development Block Grant program authorized.

James Longley of Maine becomes first popularly elected Independent governor.

1975 NGA annual meeting: New Orleans, La. Governors discuss state-local relations, oil research and development, and gas taxes. At winter meeting, governors discuss the nation's energy needs. Association disaffiliates from Council of State Governments.

Ella Grasso of Connecticut takes office as the first female governor elected in own right.

Individuals with Disabilities Education Act (IDEA) passed.

1976 NGA annual meeting: Hershey, Pa. Governors endorse welfare reform, to include elimination of work disincentives. At winter meeting, revenue sharing is discussed.

Gregg v. Georgia leads to resumption of the use of capital punishment suspended in 1972.

Federal Resource Conservation and Recovery Act passed.

Coalition of Northeastern Governors founded.

1977 NGA annual meeting: Detroit, Mich. Governors discuss President Carter's proposals for welfare reform. At winter meeting, governors discuss energy shortage and need for overhaul of Medicaid administration. Name changed to National Governors' Association (NGA).

Former Georgia Governor Jimmy Carter inaugurated president.

Former Idaho Governor Cecil Andrus becomes secretary of interior.

North Dakota becomes first state to finish assigned mileage in Federal Controlled Access Highway System.

Clean Water Act passed.

1978 NGA annual meeting: Boston, Mass. Governors debate whether to continue supporting the goal of a balanced federal budget. At winter meeting, governors discuss Supreme Court's pending decision on affirmative action in education. Association membership approved for Northern Mariana Islands.

California's Proposition 13, a tax limit initiative, ushers in new era of direct democracy.

President Jimmy Carter declares a federal emergency at Love Canal (buried chemical waste creating serious health hazard).

UC-Davis v. Bakke establishes affirmative action in education constitutional under specific conditions.

Western Governors' Policy Office founded.

Camp David Accords signed.

1979   NGA annual meeting: Louisville, Ky. Carter cancels scheduled
        speech to preside over energy crisis summit. Governors discuss
        Carter's strategy for dealing with rising oil prices. Resolutions
        support deregulation of domestic oil prices and extending rev-
        enue sharing. At winter meeting, governors discuss recent
        establishment of Committee on International Trade and For-
        eign Relations.
        Federal Emergency Management Agency created (in response to
        NGA request).
        Partial core meltdown occurs at the nuclear generating plant at
        Three Mile Island in Pennsylvania.
        Carter holds ten-day energy summit at Camp David to discuss
        plan to reduce dependence on foreign oil. Governors partici-
        pate.
        Neil Goldschmidt, later governor of Oregon, appointed secretary
        of transportation.
        Sagebrush Rebellion: legislatures of five western states call for
        state control of lands managed by the federal Bureau of Land
        Management.
        Iranian militants storm U.S. Embassy in Tehran, seizing ninety
        hostages.
1980   NGA annual meeting: Denver, Colo. Governors launch multiyear
        discussion and strategy for restoring balance to the federal sys-
        tem. During winter meeting, conference held with representa-
        tives of federal government, state governments, private sector,
        and academia to discuss national hazardous waste manage-
        ment program.
        Boatlift from Port of Mariel brings 125,000 Cuban refugees.
        U.S. Department of Education established.
        Former Maine Governor Edmund Muskie appointed secretary of
        state.
        Mount St. Helens erupts in Washington, killing sixty-one people.
        Superfund and Low-Level Radioactive Waste Policy Act passed.
        Revenue-sharing program ends.
1981   NGA annual meeting: Atlantic City, N.J. Vice President George
        H. W. Bush assures governors of congressional support for
        President Reagan's budget and tax recommendations and also
        for regulatory relief. At winter meeting, governors are addressed
        regarding president's economic recovery program.
        Former California Governor Ronald Reagan inaugurated presi-
        dent.
        Former South Carolina Governor James Edwards becomes secre-
        tary of energy.

Assassination attempt injures Reagan and his press secretary, James Brady.

AIDS first detected.

IBM introduces personal computer.

Omnibus Budget Reconciliation Act passed (tightens welfare eligibility).

Sandra Day O'Connor appointed as first woman Supreme Court justice.

Social Services Block Grant created.

1982 NGA annual meeting: Afton, Okla. At winter meeting, a compromise federalism policy statement is approved unanimously by governors. At both meetings, proposal for support of a constitutional amendment to balance the federal budget defeated.

1983 NGA annual meeting: Portland, Maine. Governors begin long-term discussions of education reform. At winter meeting, governors call on Congress to adopt a budget resolution for fiscal 1984 that would reduce federal deficit to about 2 percent of GNP by 1988. Position of Vice Chairman/Chairman-elect established.

National Commission on Excellence in Education issues report *A Nation at Risk.*

Democratic Governors Association founded.

Two terrorist attacks in Lebanon—U.S. Embassy and Marine base—kill more than 150 people.

1984 NGA annual meeting: Nashville, Tenn. Governors discuss employment issues. At winter meeting, they talk about health care. They adopt a proposal targeted at raising federal revenue by 5 percent over two years, reducing defense and entitlement program spending, and giving the president line-item veto authority.

Congress passes legislation to cut federal highway funds to states that do not raise the legal drinking age to twenty-one.

Western Governors' Association formed through merger of Western Governors' Conference and Western Governors' Policy Office.

1985 NGA annual meeting: Boise, Idaho. Governors discuss the trade deficit. Recommend that the federal government should define standards for solid waste disposal and leave enforcement to state and local authorities. At winter meeting, Alan Greenspan addresses governors regarding economic conditions.

Former Indiana Governor Otis Ray Bowen becomes secretary of health and human services.

1986   NGA annual meeting: Hilton Head, S.C. Governors hear reports of seven task forces created the previous year to study school leadership and management, teaching, school choice, readiness, school facilities, technology, and whether college students are learning. At winter meeting, U.S. Supreme Court Chief Justice Warren Burger emphasizes the role of the states in nation's establishment and system of government. NGA issues *Time for Results: The Governors' 1991 Report on Education.*
Nebraska: Kay Orr defeats Helen Boosalis in the first gubernatorial race between two women.

1987   NGA annual meeting: Traverse City, Mich. Bill Clinton serves as chair. Governors discuss Barriers Project, composed of five NGA task forces on welfare dependency, school dropouts, teen pregnancy, adult illiteracy, and alcohol and drug abuse. At winter meeting, governors adopt policy position seeking welfare reform.
Federal-Aid Highway Act allows states to increase speed limits to sixty-five miles per hour on rural interstate highways without incurring federal highway project penalties.
Dow Jones Industrial Average drops 22.6 percent, on Black Monday (October 19).
Iran-Contra scandal develops.

1988   NGA annual meeting: Cincinnati, Ohio. Governors discuss aspects of federalism (unfunded and underfunded mandates, preemption of traditional state authority, and Supreme Court decisions removing Tenth Amendment protections). At winter meeting, federalism experts make presentations on the history and current status of state-federal relations. Former Governor Busbee of Georgia proposes a constitutional convention to sort out local, state, and federal responsibilities.
Evan Mecham of Arizona becomes first governor in more than fifty years to be impeached.
Former Pennsylvania Governor Richard Thornburgh becomes U.S. attorney general.
Family Support Act expands Aid to Families with Dependent Children (AFDC) and creates Jobs Opportunities and Basic Skills Training Program (JOBS).
Indian Gaming Regulatory Act passed.
Massachusetts Governor Michael Dukakis defeated in presidential election by George H. W. Bush.
Disaster Relief and Emergency Assistance Act (Stafford Act) passed.

1989   NGA annual meeting: Chicago, Ill., President Bush speaks about welfare reform via the Family Support Act of 1988. At winter meeting, governors discuss health care, education, and foreign relations. Henry Kissinger tells governors not to place trust in a single Soviet leader like Mikhail Gorbachev. Governors call for stronger auto emission control measures.

First National Summit on Education held in Charlottesville, Virginia.

1990   NGA annual meeting: Mobile, Ala. At both the annual and winter meetings, governors discuss global climate change and goals from 1989 National Education Summit.

Reunification of Germany and breakup of Soviet Union occur.

California new car emissions and clean fuel requirements become a model for other states.

Joan Finney of Kansas becomes first woman to defeat an incumbent governor.

1991   NGA annual meeting: Seattle, Wash. Governors discuss achieving affordable and comprehensive national health care system within next decade. At winter meeting, governors addressed concerning high cost of health care and President Bush's block grant proposal.

Douglas Wilder of Virginia takes office as the first elected African American governor.

Operation Desert Storm forces Iraqi withdrawal from Kuwait.

Former Tennessee Governor Lamar Alexander appointed secretary of education.

Minnesota becomes first state to enact a Charter School law.

Intermodal Surface Transportation Efficiency Act (ISTEA) passed.

1992   NGA annual meeting: Princeton, N.J. Annual and winter meetings focus on need for improvement in educational system.

Twenty-seventh Amendment to U.S. Constitution (compensation restrictions for congressmen) ratified.

Quill v. North Dakota establishes that with a company's insufficient presence in a state, its mail-order products can not be subject to state's sales tax.

Federal Facilities Compliance Act compels federal government to comply with federal, state, and local solid and hazardous waste regulations.

1993   NGA annual meeting: Tulsa, Okla. President Clinton addresses governors about his proposal for health care reform. Governors adopt a "permanent policy" on federalism, calling for a new partnership based on federal forbearance and the avoidance of federal preemption of traditional state roles, and for

program flexibility for states in administering federal initiatives. At winter meeting, Clinton addresses governors concerning welfare reform.

Arkansas Governor Bill Clinton inaugurated president.

Former South Carolina Governor Richard Riley becomes secretary of education.

Former Arizona Governor Bruce Babbitt appointed secretary of
interior.

Branch Davidians standoff takes place in Waco, Texas.

Mississippi River flooding occurs in Illinois, Iowa, Kansas, Minnesota, Missouri, Nebraska, North Dakota, South Dakota, and
Wisconsin.

North Carolina's Smart Start program establishes a national
model.

1994   NGA annual meeting: Boston, Mass. Steven Spielberg, director of
Schindler's List, speaks about using film as a tool to teach toler-
ance. At winter meeting, governors discuss Goals 2000 Educate
America Act pending in Congress as well as Medicaid.

North American Free Trade Agreement (NAFTA).

School-to-Work Opportunities Act passed.

Republican Party wins control of U.S. House of Representatives
for first time in forty years.

1995   NGA annual meeting: Burlington, Vt. Governors focus on importance of early childhood development. At winter meeting, governors also discuss childhood development and legislation
pending in Congress for relief from unfunded federal mandates.

Unfunded Mandates Reform Act passed.

Bombing of Alfred P. Murrah Federal Building in Oklahoma City
kills 168 people.

Congress lifts speed limits as a condition of receiving approval for
federal highway projects.

1996   NGA annual meeting held in Fajardo, P.R. Governors discuss welfare reform, the changing role of the media in elections, and
interstate sharing of ideas on a wide variety of issues. At winter
meeting, governors reach bipartisan agreement on federal welfare reform that influences federal legislation giving states primary responsibility for welfare to work. Center for Policy
Research renamed as Center for Best Practices.

Personal Responsibility and Work Opportunity Act passed
(returns control of most welfare to the states).

Advisory Commission on Intergovernmental Relations dis-
banded.

1997   NGA annual meeting: Las Vegas, Nev. Bill Gates speaks on impor-
        tance of technology to American education. Governors discuss
        early childhood development at both annual and winter meet-
        ings.
        Gary Locke of Washington becomes first Asian American gover-
        nor in forty-eight continental states.
        State Children's Health Insurance Program (S-CHIP) begins
        (coverage for low-income children).

1998   NGA annual meeting: Milwaukee, Wis. At winter and annual
        meetings, governors discuss effect on states of policies regard-
        ing taxation of electronic commerce.
        Transportation Equity Act for the 21st Century (TEA-21) passed.
        Workforce Investment Act passed.
        Bill Richardson, later governor of New Mexico, appointed secre-
        tary of energy.
        Internet Tax Freedom Act passed.
        Forty-six states, two commonwealths, three territories, and D.C.
        sign agreement with tobacco industry for reimbursement over
        twenty-five years of $206 billion in health care costs linked to
        tobacco usage.
        President Bill Clinton impeached for perjury and obstruction of
        justice.

1999   NGA annual meeting: St. Louis, Mo: President Clinton updates
        governors on progress with welfare reform. Governors discuss
        environmental management. At winter meeting, they discuss
        educational and technological improvements to make states
        more competitive. Governors outline challenges for states in
        developing a national domestic terrorism strategy and clarify-
        ing the role of National Guard.
        President Clinton acquitted by U.S. Senate.
        Education Flexibility Partnership Act (Ed-Flex) passed.
        Shootings occur at Columbine High School in Littleton, Colo-
        rado.

2000   NGA annual meeting: State College, Pa. At annual and winter
        meetings, governors discuss competitiveness in the new global
        economy.
        Governor George Ryan of Illinois declares moratorium on death
        penalty.
        Streamlined Sales Tax Project is established to seek uniformity
        among states of definitions for exempt and nonexempt items.
        Aviation investment and Reform Act for the Twenty-first Century
        passed.
        Vermont becomes first state to legalize same-sex unions.

2001   NGA annual meeting: Providence, R.I. Theodore Roosevelt IV, great-grandson of Teddy Roosevelt, addresses governors on conservation. At winter meeting, governors hear reports on the federal budget surplus and need to rebuild traditional communities. Governors urge Congress to reform Medicaid.

Texas Governor George W. Bush inaugurated president.

Former Missouri Governor John Ashcroft becomes U.S. attorney general.

New Jersey Governor Christine Todd Whitman appointed head of Environmental Protection Agency (EPA).

Governor Tommy Thompson of Wisconsin appointed secretary of health and human services.

Terrorist attacks occur on September 11 at World Trade Center and Pentagon.

2002   NGA annual meeting: Boise, Idaho: Governors discuss state leadership in new global economy. At winter meeting, governors discuss state and regional economic competitiveness.

No Child Left Behind Act passed.

2003   NGA annual meeting: Indianapolis, Ind. Governors discuss school accountability and student performance as well as role of National Guard in homeland security. At winter meeting, governors continue discussions of childhood development. Name of organization simplified to National Governors Association.

Pennsylvania Governor Tom Ridge becomes the first secretary of homeland security.

U.S. invades Iraq.

Georgia adopts a new flag, eliminating depiction of Confederate battle flag in design.

Federal government provides fiscal relief to the states for Medicaid.

2004   NGA annual meeting: Seattle, Wash. Governors call for enhanced prevention of juvenile delinquency. At winter meeting, governors discuss the subject of aging with dignity and health care for older Americans.

Congress passes Goals 2000 (enhances role of states in education reform).

Internet Tax Nondiscrimination Act passed.

EPA informs thirty-one states that new pollution controls must be developed to meet federal standards.

Improving America's School Act passed (targets needs of disadvantaged students).

2005   NGA annual meeting: Des Moines, Iowa. For the first time, states reach a common definition for their high school graduation rate. At winter meeting, governors hold National Education Summit on High Schools.

Nebraska Governor Mike Johanns appointed secretary of agriculture.

Former Utah Governor Mike Leavitt appointed secretary of health and human services.

Safe, Accountable, Flexible, Efficient Transportation Equity Act (SAFETEA) passed.

Hurricane Katrina devastates New Orleans and much of the Gulf Coast.

Federal Deficit Reduction Act passed (provides more flexibility for governors in Medicaid administration).

2006   NGA annual meeting held in Charleston, S.C. In aftermath of Katrina, governors call for greater coordination between the federal government and state governments in economic recovery from disasters. Janet Napolitano (Arizona) becomes first woman to chair NGA. At winter meeting, governors discuss health and wellness.

Idaho Governor Dirk Kempthorne appointed secretary of interior.

2007   NGA annual meeting: Traverse City, Mich. At annual and winter meetings, governors urge increased federal funding for State Children's Health Insurance Program (S-CHIP) and discuss improving the nation's economic competitiveness through innovation.

Massacre on campus of Virginia Tech occurs.

Collapse of Minneapolis interstate highway bridge triggers Federal Highway Administration to instruct states to inspect similarly designed bridges.

2008   NGA celebrates its centennial in Philadelphia.

Sources

Baughman, Judith S., Victor Bondi, Richard Layman, Tandy McConnell, and Vincent Tompkins, eds. *American Decades*, 9 vols. Detroit: Gale Research, 1996.

Carter, Susan et al. *Historical Statistics of the United States.* New York: Cambridge University Press, 2006.

SHG Resources, www.shgresources.com/resources/facts.

State Government (monthly publication of American Legislators' Association/ Council of State Governments)

Teaford, Jon. *The Rise of the States: Evolution of American State Government.* Baltimore: Johns Hopkins University Press, 2002.

"Timeline of Twentieth Century," http://history1900s.about.com/library/weekly/aa110900a.htm

"Year by year, 1900–2007," www.infoplease.com/yearbyyear.html.

Thanks to the following individuals for their assistance: Bob Cullen, American Association of State Highway and Transportation Officials; Harley Duncan, Federation of Tax Administrators; Liz Purdy, Southern Governors' Association; Chris McKinnon, Western Governors' Association; and Bert Waisanen, National Conference of State Legislatures.

Notes

Introduction. Directing Democracy

The author would like to thank Saladin Ambar, Lou Galambos, Chi Lam, James Lawson, Ethan Sribnick, and Barry Van Lare.

1. Laboratory directors in the late twentieth century soon found that their own scientific expertise, or even their considerable administrative talent, was not up to the challenges of "big science." Projects like the Hubble Space Telescope called for coalition-building that not only brought together warring factions of the scientific community, but also built alliances with NASA officials, Congress, and even sympathetic journalists. Robert W. Smith, "The Biggest Kind of Big Science: Astronomers and the Space Telescope," in Peter Galison and Bruce Hevly, eds., *Big Science: The Growth of Large-Scale Research* (Palo Alto, Calif.: Stanford University Press, 1992), 184–211; Larry Sabato, *Goodbye to Good-time Charlie: The American Governorship Transformed*, 2nd ed. (Washington, D.C.: Congressional Quarterly Press, 1983), 2.

2. Jon C. Teaford, *The Rise of the States: Evolution of American State Government* (Baltimore: Johns Hopkins University Press, 2002), 10; Lee A. Iacocca, *Iacocca: An Autobiography* (New York: Bantam Books, 1984), 192.

3. For an excellent study of the way women used the vote to take advantage of interest group politics, see Lorraine Gates Schuyler, *The Weight of Their Votes: Southern Women and Political Leverage in the 1920s* (Chapel Hill: University of North Carolina Press, 2006).

4. Morton Keller, "State Power Needn't Be Resurrected Because It Never Died," *Governing* 2, no. 1 (October 1988): 56. On the "proministrative" state, see Balogh, *Chain Reaction: Expert Debate and Public Participation, in American Commercial Nuclear Power, 1945–1975* (New York: Cambridge University Press, 1991).

5. Edward S. Corwin, "The Passing of Dual Federalism," in Alpheus T. Mason and Gerald Garvey, *American Constitutional History: Essays by Edward S. Corwin* (New York: Harper and Row, 1964), 145–164, cited in Martha Derthick, *Keeping the Compound Republic* (Washington, D.C.: Brookings Institution Press, 2001), 45.

6. Robert H. Wiebe, *The Search for Order: 1877–1920* (New York: Hill and Wang, 1967); Eldon J. Eisenach, *The Lost Promise of Progressivism* (Lawrence: University Press of Kansas, 1994); Elisabeth S. Clemens, *The People's Lobby: Organizational Innovation and the Rise of Interest Group Politics in the United States, 1890–1925* (Chicago: University of Chicago Press, 1997).

7. Teaford, *Rise of the States*, 6.

8. Richard L. McCormick, "The Discovery that Business Corrupts Politics: A Reappraisal of the Origins of Progressivism," *American Historical Review* 86, no. 2 (April 1981): 260, 266, 267; Hughes quoted in McCormick, "Discovery," 267.

9. McCormick, "Discovery," 273, 271, 268; George Gilliam, "Making Virginia

Progressive: Courts and Parties, Railroads and Regulators" (Ph.D. dissertation draft, University of Virginia, 2007, in author's possession.)

10. Wilson quoted in Sabato, *Goodbye*, 6.

11. Masters essay, this volume, 151–152; Daniel Holt, "Policing the Margins: The Legitimacy of American Securities Markets and the Origins of Federal Securities Regulation, 1890–1937" (Ph.D. dissertation chapter, University of Virginia, 2007, in author's possession), 2; Masters essay, 151. Regarding Cannon, see Masters essay, 152.

12. Phillips essay, this volume, 26, 32.

13. Phillips essay, 32–33; Mehrotra and Shreve essay, this volume, 59–60, 62–63.

14. Sokol essay, this volume, 125; Bruce J. Schulman, *The Seventies: The Great Shift in American Culture, Society, and Politics* (New York: Free Press, 2001), 211, 209.

15. Haskins essay, this volume, 85–93. As Haskins points out, the National Governors Association had already played an important role in reforming AFDC through an influential study of welfare reform in the late 1980s. (Haskins essay, 87–88).

16. Haskins essay, 89–90.

17. Vinovskis essay, this volume, 191.

18. Grogan and Smith essay, this volume, 220.

19. Schuyler, *Weight of Their Votes*, 2.

20. James T. Patterson, *Grand Expectations: The United States, 1945–1974* (New York: Oxford University Press, 1996), 29, 585; Stephen Thernstrom and Abigail Thernstrom, *America in Black and White: One Nation, Indivisible* (New York: Simon & Schuster, 1997), 157.

21. *Reynolds v. Sims*, 377 U.S. 533 (1964), available at the Oyez Project, http://www.oyez.org/cases/1960–1969/1963/1963_23/; Sabato, *Goodbye*, 78–79.

22. David P. Thelen, *Robert M. La Follette and the Insurgent Spirit* (Boston: Little, Brown, 1976), 47.

23. Masters, essay, 153–154; Holt, "Policing the Margins," 14.

24. Phillips essay, 32; Mehrotra and Shreve essay, 55.

25. Teaford, *Rise of the States*, 70; Georgia governor quoted in Keller, "State Power," 56; Charles Evans Hughes quoted in Teaford, *Rise of the States*, 71; Teaford, *Rise of the States*, 61–65.

26. Pinchot demonstrated that expertise was a relative matter. In the American context, his training, which was laughable by European standards, turned out to be "good enough for government." Brian H. Balogh, "Scientific Forestry and the Roots of the Modern American State: Gifford Pinchot's Path to Progressive Reform," *Environmental History* 7, no. 2 (April 2002): 199–225; Phillips essay, 30; Samuel P. Hays, *Conservation and the Gospel of Efficiency: The Progressive Conservation Movement, 1890–1920* (Cambridge: Harvard University Press, 1959).

27. Dilger essay, this volume, 172–173.

28. Brian H. Balogh, "Securing Support: The Emergence of the Social Security Board as a Political Actor, 1935–1939," in Donald T. Critchlow and Ellis W. Hawley, eds., *Federal Social Policy: The Historical Dimension* (University Park: Pennsylvania State University Press, 1988), 55–78; Martha Derthick, *The Influence of Federal Grants: Public Assistance in Massachusetts* (Cambridge: Harvard University Press, 1970). On the long history of concern about corruption in social provision, see Theda Skocpol, *Protecting Soldiers and Mothers: The Political Origins of Social Policy in the United States* (Cambridge: Harvard University Press, 1992). For the impact of federal oversight on state-provided old age assistance, see Jerry R.

Cates, *Insuring Inequality: Administrative Leadership in Social Security, 1935–54* (Ann Arbor: University of Michigan Press, 1983).

29. Teaford, *Rise of the States*, 202–204; George A. Bell quoted in Teaford, *Rise of the States*, 204; Teaford, *Rise of the States*, 202–205; Senator Capper, in John Mark Hansen, *Gaining Access: Congress and the Farm Lobby, 1919–1981* (Chicago: University of Chicago Press, 1991), 32.

30. Vinovskis essay, 189; Michele Deitch, "Hard Times: Governors and the Transformation of the American Penal State" manuscript, May 2007, in author's possession, 4.

31. Samuel H. Beer, "The Modernization of American Federalism," *Publius* 3, no. 2 (Autumn 1973): 49–95.

32. Mark Kornbluh, *Why America Stopped Voting: The Decline of Participatory Democracy and the Emergence of Modern American Politics* (New York: New York University Press, 2000); Michael E. McGerr, *The Decline of Popular Politics: The American North, 1865–1928* (New York: Oxford University Press, 1986), 7; Paul Kleppner, *The Cross of Culture: A Social Analysis of Midwestern Politics, 1850–1900*, 2nd ed. (New York: Free Press, 1970), is one example of this approach.

33. Brian H. Balogh, "Reorganizing the Organizational Synthesis: Federal-Professional Relations in Modern America," *Studies in American Political Development* 5, no. 1 (Spring 1991): 119–172; Brian H. Balogh, " 'Mirrors of Desires': Interest Groups, Elections and the Targeted Style in Twentieth Century America," in Meg Jacobs, William Novak, and Julian Zelizer, eds., *The Democratic Experiment* (Princeton, N.J.: Princeton University Press, 2003), 222–249.

34. McGerr, *Decline of Popular Politics*, 205.

35. Thelen, *La Follette*, 29–30; Sabato, *Goodbye*, 145.

36. Masters essay, 153–154; *Bankers* magazine cited in Holt, "Policing the Margins,"15; Holt, "Policing the Margins," 15–16.

37. Phillips essay, 27.

38. Phillips essay, 38–39.

39. Paul Milazzo, *Unlikely Environmentalists: Congress and Clean Water, 1945–1972* (Lawrence: University Press of Kansas, 2006), 18–37; Phillips essay, 39–40.

40. Brian H. Balogh, *A Government out of Sight: The Mystery of Nineteenth Century National Authority* (New York: Cambridge University Press, 2008); on migration, see James R. Grossman, *Land of Hope: Chicago, Black Southerners, and the Great Migration* (Chicago: University of Chicago Press, 1989), Richard Franklin Bensel, *The Political Economy of American Industrialization, 1877–1900* (New York: Cambridge University Press, 2000).

41. Mary L. Dudziak, *Cold War Civil Rights: Race and the Image of American Democracy* (Princeton: Princeton University Press, 2000).

42. Matthew D. Lassiter, *The Silent Majority: Suburban Politics in the Sunbelt South* (Princeton, N.J.: Princeton University Press, 2006).

43. Sokol essay, 126–127; Martha Derthick, "Crossing Thresholds: Federalism in the 1960s," in Balogh, ed., *Integrating the Sixties: The Origins, Structures, and Legitimacy of Public Policy in a Turbulent Decade* (University Park: Pennsylvania State University Press, 1996), 64–80; Sokol essay, 128–129.

44. Sokol essay, 130–132.

45. Sokol essay, 135–137; *Boston Globe* cited in Sokol essay, 140.

46. Masters essay, 157–159.

47. Teaford essay, 113–115.

48. Teaford essay, 114–115, 121–122.

49. Teaford essay, 116–117; Vinovskis essay, 194–195, 197–198.

50. Louis Galambos, "Myth and Reality in the Study of America's Consumer Culture," paper presented to the Johns Hopkins University Seminar, 1996, 10–11.

51. Meg Jacobs, *Pocketbook Politics: Economic Citizenship in Twentieth-Century America* (Princeton, N.J,: Princeton University Press, 2005). One of the ways that governors and local officials responded to sensitivity about the *way* in which service was delivered was to privatize a range of services. For an excellent discussion of this issue, see Bruce Schulman, "The Privatization of Everyday Life: Public Policy, Public Services and Public Space in the 1970s and 1980s," paper presented to the Twentieth Century Workshop, Department of History, University of Virginia, November 16, 2001.

52. Jack Citrin, "Do People Want Something for Nothing: Public Opinion on Taxes and Government Spending," *National Tax Journal* 32 (1979): 113, 117–118, 115; Timothy Conlan, "Federal, State, or Local? Trends in the Public's Judgment," *Public Perspective* 4, no. 2 (January–February 1993): 3–5; "Americans Lose Trust and Confidence in All Government but Local Government Remains Most Trusted," *Illinois Municipal Review* (September 1992): 11–13.

53. Dilger essay, this volume, 173–174.

54. Teaford, *Rise of the States*, 7; Dilger essay, 174–175; Teaford, *Rise of the States*, 7.

55. Haskins essay, 76.

56. Michael B. Katz, *The Undeserving Poor: From the War on Poverty to the War on Welfare* (New York: Pantheon, 1989); Michael B. Katz, *In the Shadow of the Poorhouse: A Social History of Welfare in America* (New York: Basic Books, 1986); Jill S. Quadagno, *The Color of Welfare: How Racism Undermined the War on Poverty* (New York: Oxford University Press, 1994); Edwin Amenta, *Bold Relief: Institutional Politics and the Origins of Modern American Social Policy* (Princeton, N.J.: Princeton University Press, 1998).

57. Haskins essay, 82.

58. Grogan and Smith essay, this volume, 223–225.

59. Grogan and Smith essay, 229–230.

60. Ballard C. Campbell, *The Growth of American Government* (Bloomington: Indiana University Press, 1995), 34.

61. Campbell, *Growth of American Government*, ch. 2; Phillips essay, 40–41.

62. Dilger essay, 169–170, 178–180; Sabato, *Goodbye*, 173; Teaford, *Rise of the States*, 205.

Chapter 1. Resourceful Leaders

I thank Jeff Decker and Sarah Vogel for their research assistance.

1. The work of Samuel P. Hays remains indispensable; see *Conservation and the Gospel of Efficiency: The Progressive Conservation Movement, 1890–1920* (Cambridge: Harvard University Press, 1959); *Beauty, Health, and Permanence: Environmental Politics in the United States, 1955–1985* (Cambridge: Cambridge University Press, 1987); and *A History of Environmental Politics Since 1945* (Pittsburgh: University of Pittsburgh Press, 2000). Adam Rome clarifies the postwar transition with *The Bulldozer in the Countryside: Suburban Sprawl and the Rise of American Environmentalism* (Cambridge: Cambridge University Press, 2001).

2. See Alan Brinkley, *The End of Reform: New Deal Liberalism in Recession and War* (New York: Vintage Books, 1995); Robert Collins, *More: The Politics of Economic Growth in Postwar America* (Oxford: Oxford University Press, 2000); Meg Jacobs, *Pocketbook Politics: Economic Citizenship in Twentieth-Century America*

(Princeton, N.J.: Princeton University Press, 2005); and Alan Wolfe, *America's Impasse: The Rise and Fall of the Politics of Growth* (Boston: South End Press, 1981).

3. Paul C. Milazzo, *Unlikely Environmentalists: Congress and Clean Water, 1945–1972* (Lawrence: University Press of Kansas, 2006).

4. The professionalization of state executives is analyzed in Larry Sabato, *Goodbye to Good-Time Charlie: The American Governor Transformed, 1950–1975* (Lexington, Mass.: D. C. Heath, 1978). Budgetary and economic constraints are described in Jerry F. Medler, "Governors and Environmental Policy," *Policy Studies Journal* 17, 4 (1989), and Paul E. Peterson, *The Price of Federalism* (Washington, D.C.: Brookings Institution, 1995).

5. *Proceedings of a Conference of Governors in the White House, Washington, D.C., May 13–15, 1908* (Washington, D.C.: Government Printing Office, 1909), ix–x.

6. Char Miller, *Gifford Pinchot and the Making of Modern Environmentalism* (Washington, D.C.: Island Press, 2001), 162–69; Brian Balogh, "Scientific Forestry and the Roots of the Modern American State: Gifford Pinchot's Path to Progressive Reform," *Environmental History* 7, no. 2 (2002).

7. Gifford Pinchot, *The Fight for Conservation* (Garden City, N.Y.: Harcourt, Brace, 1910).

8. Bruce J. Schulman, "Governing Nature, Nurturing Government: Resource Management and the Development of the American State, 1900–1912," *Journal of Policy History* 17, no. 4 (2005).

9. *Proceedings*, 1908, 6.

10. Ibid., 104.

11. Ibid., 101. On the Adirondacks' crucial role in American conservation history, see Frank Graham, Jr., *The Adirondack Park: A Political History* (Syracuse, N.Y.: Syracuse University Press, 1978), and Philip G. Terrie, *Contested Terrain: A New History of Nature and People in the Adirondacks* (Syracuse, N.Y.: Adirondack Museum/Syracuse University Press, 1997).

12. *Proceedings*, 1908, 119–121, emphasis added.

13. Ibid., 162–163.

14. Ibid., 169.

15. Ibid., 130. The definitive study of the early reclamation program is Donald J. Pisani, *Water and American Government: The Reclamation Bureau, National Water Policy, and the West, 1902–1935* (Berkeley: University of California Press, 2002). For an introduction to the politics of the western range, see Karen R. Merrill, *Public Lands and Political Meaning: Ranchers, the Government, and the Property Between Them* (Berkeley: University of California Press, 2002).

16. *Proceedings, 1908*, 194.

17. Glenn E. Brooks, *When Governors Convene: The Governor's Conference and National Politics* (Baltimore: John Hopkins University Press, 1961); Donald H. Haider, *When Governments Come to Washington* (New York: Free Press, 1974); "NGA Winter Term History," NGA file in possession of author.

18. Hays, *Conservation and the Gospel of Efficiency*, 132. Also see two online collections of the Library of Congress: "State-Level Conservation Initiatives Following the Governors' Conference of 1908" (http://memory.loc.gov/ammem/amrvhtml/consbib9.html, accessed July 3, 2007), and "State-Level Fish and Game Conservation Measures, c. 1850–1920" (http://memory.loc.gov/ammem/amrvhtml/consbib5.html, accessed July 3, 2007).

19. Dave Dempsey, *Ruin and Recovery: Michigan's Rise as a Conservation Leader* (Ann Arbor: University of Michigan Press, 2001), 62.

20. Sarah T. Phillips, *This Land, This Nation: Conservation, Rural America, and the New Deal* (Cambridge: Cambridge University Press, 2007).

21. David E. Nye, *Electrifying America: Social Meanings of a New Technology* (Cambridge: MIT Press, 1990), 287, 297, 304.

22. Phillips, *This Land, This Nation,* 25–27.

23. Ibid., 71.

24. Ibid.

25. Ibid.; Donald J. Pisani, "Federal Water Policy and the Rural West," in R. Douglas Hurt, ed., *The Rural West Since World War II* (Lawrence: University Press of Kansas, 1998).

26. Pisani, "Federal Water Policy." "River-pushers" comes from Donald Worster, *Rivers of Empire: Water, Aridity, and the Growth of the American West* (Oxford: Oxford University Press, 1985).

27. Norris Hundley, Jr., *The Great Thirst: Californians and Water: A History* (Berkeley: University of California Press, 2001).

28. Ethan Rarick, *California Rising: The Life and Times of Pat Brown* (Berkeley: University of California Press, 2005), 210–211.

29. Rarick, *California Rising;* Hundley, *Great Thirst.*

30. Rarick, *California Rising,* 349.

31. Hundley, *Great Thirst;* John C. Bollens and G. Robert Williams, *Jerry Brown: In a Plain Brown Wrapper* (Pacific Palisades, Calif.: Palisades Publishers, 1978).

32. Richard N. L. Andrews, *Managing the Environment, Managing Ourselves: A History of American Environmental Policy* (New Haven: Yale University Press, 1999); Hal K. Rothman, *The Greening of a Nation? Environmentalism in the United States Since 1945* (Fort Worth: Harcourt Brace, 1998); Rome, *The Bulldozer in the Countryside;* Hays, *Beauty, Health, and Permanence.*

33. Pete Daniel, *Toxic Drift: Pesticides and Health in the Post-World War II South* (Baton Rouge: Louisiana State University Press/ Smithsonian Museum of American History, 2005).

34. Rachel Carson, *Silent Spring* (Boston: Houghton Mifflin, 1962), 188.

35. Adam Rome, " 'Give Earth a Chance': The Environmental Movement and the Sixties," *Journal of American History* 90, no. 2 (September 2003); Robert Gottlieb, *Forcing the Spring: the Transformation of the American Environmental Movement* (Washington, D.C.: Island Press, 1993); Warren Belasco, *Appetite for Change: How the Counterculture Took on the Food Industry* (Ithaca, N.Y.: Cornell University Press, 1993).

36. Collins, *More.*

37. Rome, "Give Earth a Chance"; Schlesinger quoted in Rome, 528.

38. Martin Melosi, "Lyndon Johnson and Environmental Policy," in Robert Divine, ed., *The Johnson Years: Vietnam, the Environment, and Science* (Lawrence: University Press of Kansas, 1987).

39. Thomas R. Huffman, *Protectors of the Land and Water: Environmentalism in Wisconsin, 1961–1968* (Chapel Hill: University of North Carolina Press, 1994); Bill Christofferson, *The Man From Clear Lake: Earth Day Founder Senator Gaylord Nelson* (Madison: University of Wisconsin Press, 2004).

40. Andrews, *Managing the Environment;* Milazzo, *Unlikely Environmentalists.*

41. Sabato, *Goodbye to Good-Time Charlie.*

42. Dempsey, *Ruin and Recovery.*

43. Peter Siskind, "Shades of Black and Green: The Making of Racial and Environmental Liberalism in Nelson Rockefeller's New York," *Journal of Urban History* (forthcoming).

44. Ibid. Also see Robert H. Connery and Gerald Benjamin, *Rockefeller of New York: Executive Power in the Statehouse* (Ithaca: Cornell University Press, 1979).

45. Andrews, *Managing the Environment.*

46. Ibid..

47. Martha Derthick, "Crossing Thresholds: Federalism in the 1960s," in Brian Balogh, ed., *Integrating the Sixties: The Origins, Structures, and Legitimacy of Public Policy in a Turbulent Decade* (University Park: Pennsylvania State University Press, 1996).

48. Daniel C. Kramer, *The Days of Wine and Roses Are Over: Governor Hugh Carey and New York State* (Lanham, Md.: University Press of America, 1997).

49. Kramer, *Days of Wine and Roses,* 211.

50. Dave Dempsey, *William G. Milliken: Michigan's Passionate Moderate* (Ann Arbor: University of Michigan Press, 2006), 86, 103. Also see Dempsey, *Ruin and Recovery.*

51. Russell W. Peterson, *Rebel with a Conscience* (Newark: University of Delaware Press, 1999), 127–128, 131, 141, italics in original.

52. Brent Walth, *Fire at Eden's Gate: Tom McCall and the Oregon Story* (Portland: Oregon Historical Society Press, 1994); William G. Robbins, *Landscapes of Conflict: The Oregon Story, 1940–2000* (Seattle: University of Washington Press, 2004).

53. Walth, *Fire at Eden's Gate,* 5.

54. Charles E. Little, *The New Oregon Trail: An Account of the Development and Passage of State Land-Use Legislation in Oregon* (Washington, D.C.: Conservation Foundation, 1974), 35.

55. The literature on the modern conservative movement is vast. For a solid overview, see Michael Schaller and George Rising, *The Republican Ascendancy: American Politics, 1968–2001* (Arlington Heights, Ill.: Harlan Davidson, 2002).

56. R. McGreggor Cawley, *Federal Land, Western Anger: The Sagebrush Rebellion and Environmental Politics* (Lawrence: University Press of Kansas, 1993).

57. Dan Balz, "In Conservative Arizona, Democrat Tries to Mark Out Liberal Path," *Washington Post,* February 21, 1981.

58. David Osborne, "The Poker Player," *Washington Monthly,* February 1988; Bruce Babbitt, *Cities in the Wilderness: A New Vision of Land Use in America* (Washington, D.C.: Island Press, 2005); Peter Iverson, "Cultural Politics of Water in Arizona," in Richard Lowitt, ed., *Politics in the Postwar American West* (Norman: University of Oklahoma Press, 1995).

59. S. V. Dáte, *Quiet Passion: A Biography of Senator Bob Graham* (New York: Penguin, 2004); "Governor Bob Graham," in Robert D. Behn, ed., *Governors on Governing* (Washington, D.C.: National Governors' Association, 1991), 57.

60. Michael E. Kraft, "U.S. Environmental Policy and Politics: From the 1960s to the 1990s," in Otis L. Graham, Jr., ed., *Environmental Politics and Policy, 1960s–1990s* (University Park: Pennsylvania State University Press, 2000); Barry G. Rabe, *Fragmentation and Integration in State Environmental Management* (Washington, D.C.: Conservation Foundation, 1986); DeWitt John, *Civic Environmentalism: Alternatives to Regulation in States and Communities* (Washington, D.C.: Congressional Quarterly Press, 1994), 9–10.

61. Kraft, "U.S. Environmental Policy"; Evan J. Ringquist, *Environmental Protection at the State Level: Politics and Progress in Controlling Pollution* (Armonk, N.Y.: M. E. Sharpe, 1993); Barry G. Rabe, "Power to the States: The Promise and Pitfalls of Decentralization," in Norman J. Vig and Michael E. Kraft, eds., *Environmental Policy in the 1990s: Reform or Reaction?* (Washington, D.C.: Congressional Quarterly Press, 1997); "Summary of FFCA Requirements," NGA memo in possession of author.

62. Barry G. Rabe, *Statehouse and Greenhouse: The Emerging Politics of American Climate Change Policy* (Washington, D.C.: Brookings Institution, 2004), xi.

63. Rabe, *Statehouse and Greenhouse*, 3.

64. Christine Todd Whitman, *It's My Party Too: The Battle for the Heart of the GOP and the Future of America* (New York: Penguin, 2005), 163, 165.

65. In 2003, Pataki asked New Yorkers to adopt California's stringent carbon-reduction program, and he bequeathed to the state a richly expanded system of parks, open space, and river-based recreational areas. See also George Pataki with Daniel Paisner, *Pataki: An Autobiography* (New York: Viking, 1998).

66. Karen Breslau, "The Green Giant," *Newsweek*, April 16, 2007.

67. Rabe, *Statehouse and Greenhouse*.

Chapter 2. "To Lay and Collect"

An earlier version of this chapter was presented at the Boston University School of Law's Junior Tax Scholars Conference. The authors thank the participants at that venue for their comments. For their suggestions, comments, and encouragement, the authors would also like to thank Gerald Baliles, Neil Buchanan, Adam Chodorow, Allison Christians, Dan Ernst, Victor Fleischer, David Gamage, Morton Keller, Leandra Leaderman, Isaac Martin, Miranda Perry Fleischer, Bill Popkin, Ethan Sribnick, Joe Thorndike, Dennis Ventry, and the anonymous reviewer. Thanks also to Ryan Guillory for invaluable research assistance.

1. On the importance of sectionalism for twentieth-century American political development, see generally, Richard Franklin Bensel, *Sectionalism and American Political Development, 1880–1980* (Madison: University of Wisconsin Press, 1984). For more on how U.S. regional differences shaped the early development of American tax policy, see Robin Einhorn, *American Slavery/American Taxation* (Chicago: University of Chicago Press, 2006); on the importance of early inequality for the comparative historical development of taxation in North America, see Kenneth L. Sokoloff and Eric M. Zolt, "Inequality and Taxation: Evidence from the Americas on How Inequality May Influence Tax Institutions," *Tax Law Review* 59 (2006): 167.

2. For an introduction to the vast tax literature on fiscal federalism, see generally, Richard M. Bird, "Fiscal Federalism," in *The Encyclopedia of Taxation and Tax Policy*, ed. Joseph J. Cordes et al. (Washington, D.C.: Urban Institute Press, 1999), 127–129. Historians have long recognized the importance of federalism to American economic and political development, see generally Harry N. Scheiber, "Federalism and the American Economic Order, 1789–1910," *Law and Society Review* 10, no. 1 (Autumn 1975); for a recent theoretical and comparative perspective see Jonathan A. Rodden, *Hamilton's Paradox: The Promise and Perils of Fiscal Federalism* (New York: Cambridge University Press, 2006).

3. This chapter builds upon and is deeply indebted to the recent scholarship that has focused on the development of state governments. See generally Larry Sabato, *Goodbye to Good-time Charlie: The American Governorship Transformed*, 2nd ed. (Washington, D.C.: Congressional Quarterly Press, 1983); Morton Keller, *Regulating a New Economy: Public Policy and Economic Change in America, 1900–1933* (Cambridge, Mass.: Harvard University Press, 1990); Jon Teaford, *The Rise of the States: Evolution of American State Government* (Baltimore: Johns Hopkins University Press, 2002).

4. Lizabeth Cohen, *A Consumers' Republic: The Politics of Mass Consumption in Postwar America* (New York: Knopf, 2003); William Leach, *Land of Desire: Merchants, Power, and the Rise of a New American Culture* (New York: Pantheon Books,

1993); Richard Wrightman Fox and T. J. Jackson Lears, *The Culture of Consumption: Critical Essays in American History, 1880–1980* (New York: Pantheon Books, 1983).

5. The classical historical studies of this period remain Robert H. Weibe, *Search for Order, 1877–1920* (New York: Hill & Wang, 1967); Samuel P. Hays, *The Response to Industrialism, 1885–1914* (Chicago: University of Chicago Press, 1957); Louis Galambos, "The Emerging Organizational Synthesis in Modern American History," *Business History Review* 44 (1970): 279–290.

6. Wallis, "American Government Financing"; David P. Thelen, *The New Citizenship: Origins of Progressivism in Wisconsin, 1885–1900* (Columbia: University of Missouri Press, 1972), 203–210. Keller, *Regulating a New Economy*, 210–215.

7. Herbert Croly, *The Promise of American Life* (New York: Macmillan, 1909), 318.

8. For more on the history of the property tax and its defects, see generally, Clifton K. Yearley, *The Money Machines: The Breakdown and Reform of Government and Party Finance in the North, 1860–1920* (Albany, N.Y.: State University of New York Press, 1970); Glenn Fisher, *The Worst Tax? A History of the Property Tax in America* (Lawrence: University Press of Kansas, 1996); Einhorn, *American Taxation/American Slavery*.

9. Yearley, *The Money Machines*, 38–39; Alfred D. Chandler, Jr., *The Visible Hand: The Managerial Revolution in American Business* (Cambridge, Mass.: Belknap Press, 1977); William G. Roy, *Socializing Capital: The Rise of the Large Industrial Corporation in America* (Princeton, N.J.: Princeton University Press, 1997).

10. Emmet O'Neal, "Report of Committee on Rural Credits," in *Proceedings of the Seventh Meeting of the Governors of the States of the Union* (Madison, Wis., 1914), 36–37.

11. W. Elliot Brownlee, *Progressivism and Economic Growth: The Wisconsin Income Tax, 1911–1929* (Port Washington, N.Y.: Kennikat Press, 1975); R. Rudy Higgens Evanson, *The Price of Progress: Public Services, Taxation, and the American Corporate State, 1877 to 1929* (Baltimore: Johns Hopkins University Press, 2003).

12. K. M. Williamson, "The Present Status of Low-Rate Taxation of Intangible Property," in *Proceedings of the Eighteenth Annual Conference on Taxation Under the Auspices of the National Tax Association* (New York, 1926), 90–128.

13. Wade J. Newhouse, *Constitutional Uniformity and Equality in State Constitutions* (Ann Arbor: University of Michigan Press, 1959); John I. Dinan, *The American State Constitutional Tradition* (Lawrence: University Press of Kansas); Teaford, *Rise of the States*, 47–49; Gladys C. Blakey, *A History of Taxation in Minnesota* (Minneapolis, 1934).

14. *Report of Commission on Taxation in California, 1906* (Sacramento, 1906); David R. Doerr, *California's Tax Machine: A History of Taxing and Spending in the Golden State*, ed. Ronald Roach (Sacramento, 2000); Lawson Purdy, "Outline of a Model System of State and Local Taxation," *National Tax Association Proceedings* 1 (1908): 54.

15. Doerr, *California's Tax Machine*; Teaford, *Rise of the States*, 52–54.

16. Henry George, *Progress and Poverty: An Inquiry into the Cause of Industrial Depressions, and of Increase of Want with Increase of Wealth, The Remedy* (1879); Arthur N. Young, *The Single Tax Movement in the United States* (Princeton, 1916); Louis Freeland Post, *What Is the Single-Tax?* (New York, 1926), 132. See also, John L. Thomas, *Alternative America: Henry George, Edward Bellamy, Henry Demarest Lloyd and the Adversary Tradition* (Cambridge, Mass.: Belknap Press, 1983); Jeffrey Sklansky, *The Soul's Economy: Market Society and Self-hood in American Thought, 1820–1920* (Chapel Hill: University of North Carolina Press, 2002), ch. 4.

17. On the history of the Wisconsin income tax, see generally Brownlee, *Progressivism and Economic Growth*; John D. Buenker, *The History of Wisconsin*, vol. 4, *The Progressive Era, 1893–1914* (Madison: State Historical Society of Wisconsin, 1998); Ajay K. Mehrotra, "Forging Fiscal Reform: Constitutional Change, Public Policy, and the Creation of Administrative Capacity in Wisconsin, 1880–1920," *Journal of Policy History* (forthcoming).

18. Ajay K. Mehrotra, "Envisioning the Modern American Fiscal State: Progressive-Era Economists and the Intellectual Foundations of the U.S. Income Tax," *UCLA Law Review*, 52, no. 6 (August 2005). See also, Nancy Cohen, *The Reconstruction of American Liberalism, 1865–1914* (Chapel Hill: University of North Carolina Press, 2002); Daniel T. Rodgers, *Atlantic Crossings: Social Politics in a Progressive Age* (Cambridge, Mass.: Harvard University Press, 1998); James T. Kloppenberg, *Uncertain Victory: Social Democracy and Progressivism in European and American Thought, 1870–1920* (New York: Oxford University Press, 1986).

19. Richard T. Ely, *Taxation in American States and Cities* (1888), 288–289.

20. David P. Thelen, *Robert M. LaFollette and the Insurgent Spirit* (Boston: Little, Brown, 1976), 29; Brownlee, *Progressivism and Economic Growth*; Buenker, *The History of Wisconsin*.

21. "Governor Calls Income Tax Just," *Milwaukee Sentinel*, July 14, 1911.

22. United States Advisory Commission on Intergovernmental Relations (ACIR), *Significant Features of Fiscal Federalism, Volume 1: Budget Processes and Tax Systems*, June 1994. *A History of Mississippi, Volume II*, ed. Richard A. McLemore (Hattiesburg: University and College Press of Mississippi, 1973), 58. Edwin R. A. Seligman, *Essays in Taxation* (1895), 72. See also, Seligman, *The Income Tax* (1912); Higgens-Evenson, *Price of Progress*, 85.

23. *Proceedings of the Fifth Meeting of the Governors of the States of the Union 1912* (Lakewood, N.J.: Lakewood Press, 1912), 96; John Buenker, *The Income Tax and the Progressive Era* (New York: Garland, 1985).

24. Jonathan Williams, "Paying at the Pump: Gasoline Taxes in America," Tax Foundation Background Paper No. 56.

25. Keller, *Regulating a New Economy*, 218–220; Brunori, *State Tax Policy*, 60–61.

26. Ronald L. Heinemann, *Harry Byrd of Virginia* (Charlottesville: University Press of Virginia, 1996), 58–60, 60–64.

27. Though the distribution was decidedly more progressive when they were first introduced in the 1920s than it became in later decades, the gasoline excise tax, as Walter Heller noted in 1973, was "moderately regressive—about the same as the beer tax, but considerably less so than the cigarette and local telephone taxes." Walter W. Heller, "A New Role for the Gasoline Tax?" *Wall Street Journal*, June 8, 1973.

28. Heinemann, *Harry Byrd of Virginia*.

29. Teaford, *Rise of the States*, 55.

30. Joseph J. Thorndike, "The Depression and Reform: FDR's Search for Tax Revision in N.Y.," *Tax Notes* 101, no. 1129 (December 1, 2003); Keller, *Regulating a New Economy*, 219–220; ACIR, *Significant Features of Fiscal Federalism, Volume 1, Budget Processes and Tax Systems*, Table 13, p. 34.

31. "Roosevelt Appeals to People to Back His Taxation Plan," *New York Times*, March 8, 1929, 1; Joseph J. Thorndike, "Franklin Roosevelt, Agriculture, and New York Property Taxation," *Tax Notes*, 101, no. 911 (November 17, 2003); Thorndike, "The Depression and Reform."

32. "Governor Demands Reform of Tax Laws," *New York Times*, March 6, 1930, 5.

33. "Roosevelt Opposes General Sales Tax," *New York Times*, December 15, 1931, 8.

34. "Governor's Message on State's Financial Problem," *New York Times*, January 13, 1932, 20.

35. Robert H. Jackson, *That Man: An Insider's Portrait of Franklin D. Roosevelt*, ed. John Q. Barrett (New York: Oxford University Press, 2003), 128.

36. "Governor's Message on State's Financial Problem." *New York Times*, January 13, 1932, 20.

37. *New York Times*, January 13, 1932, 1.

38. Thorndike, "The Depression and Reform," 14.

39. Alvin H. Hansen, *State and Local Finance in the National Economy* (New York: Norton, 1944), 264. Hansen also noted, in 1941, that the income tax collections of just four states, New York, Massachusetts, Wisconsin, and California, accounted for 72 percent of all state income tax collections. Ibid.

40. See *Proceedings of the Governors' Conference 1930* (Washington, D.C.: Governors' Conference, 1930); and Robert W. Wells, Jr., "A Political Biography of George Henry Dern," master's thesis, Brigham Young University, 1971.

41. Thomas G. Alexander, "From War to Depression," in Richard D. Poll, general editor, *Utah's History* (Provo: Brigham Young University Press, 1978), 463–480.

42. John Henry Evans, *The Story of Utah: The Beehive State* (New York: Macmillan, 1933), 326–327.

43. *Proceedings of the Governors' Conference 1931* (Washington, D.C.: Governors' Conference, 1931).

44. William Winter, "Governor Mike Conner and the Sales Tax, 1932," *Journal of Mississippi History* 41 (August 1979); Richard A. McLemore, ed., *A History of Mississippi*, 2 vols. (Hattiesburg, 1973), 2:102; Teaford, *Rise of the States*, 136.

45. "Historical Review of State and Local Government Finances," in *State and Local Government Special Studies* 25 (June 1948): 20.

46. Robert M. Haig, "Backward States in Tax Legislation: Florida-Illinois-Michigan-Ohio," *Taxbits* 3 (November 1935): 3–4; Teaford, *Rise of the States*, 137.

47. Quoted in T. Harry Williams, *Huey Long* (New York: Knopf, 1970), 308.

48. *Proceedings of the Governors' Conference 1928* (Tallahassee, Fla.: Governor's Conference, 1928), 37–40.

49. Ronald E. Weber, "Historical Development of the Louisiana State Tax Structure," in James A. Richardson, *Louisiana's Fiscal Alternatives: Finding Permanent Solutions to Recurring Budget Crises* (Baton Rouge: Louisiana State University Press, 1988), 44–48. After state voters rejected a constitutional amendment in 1940 that would have increased the state income tax, Governor Jones reinstituted the repealed sales tax.

50. By 1939, income taxes provided only 6 percent of all Louisiana revenue, making it the sixth most prominent source of state revenue. Weber, "Historical Development," 48. The 1921 Louisiana constitutional revisions limited the state income tax to a 3 percent equal and uniform rate.

51. Creel quoted in Kevin Starr, *California: A History* (New York: Modern Library, 2005), 211.

52. See Jackson K. Putnam, "The Progressive Legacy in California," in William E. Deverell and Tom Sitton, eds., *California Progressivism Revisited* (Berkeley: University of California Press, 1994), 250–255.

53. Putnam, "The Progressive Legacy in California," 254–255.

54. Ibid., 104.

55. *Proceedings of the Governors' Conference 1940* (Chicago: Governors' Conference, 1940), 65.

56. Ibid., 65–66, 166–167.

57. Ibid., 67–70.

58. *Proceedings of the Governors' Conference 1941* (Chicago: Governors' Conference, 1941), 157–160.

59. Jordan A. Schwarz, "John Nance Garner and the Sales Tax Rebellion of 1932," *Journal of Southern History* 30 (May 1964): 173; Teaford, *Rise of the States*, 138; For a brief history of national attempts at general sales tax, see Steven A. Bank, "The Progressive Consumption Tax Revisited," *Michigan Law Review* 101 (May 2003): 2238.

60. *Proceedings of the Governors' Conference 1942* (Chicago, Governors' Conference, 1942), 179.

61. Hansen, *State and Local Finance in the National Economy*, 263.

62. *Historical Statistics of the United States: Earliest Times to the Present*, ed. Susan B. Carter et al. (New York: Cambridge University Press, 2006), Table Ea132–159; W. Elliot Brownlee, *Federal Taxation in America: A Short History* (New York, Cambridge University Press, 2004), 96. For more on how the federal government was able to inculcate a mass taxpaying culture, see Carolyn C. Jones, "Mass-Based Income Taxation: Creating a Taxpaying Culture, 1940–1952," in W. Elliot Brownlee, ed., *Funding the Modern American State* (New York: Cambridge University Press, 1996), 107–147.

63. *Proceedings of the Governors' Conference 1945* (Chicago: Governors' Conference, 1945), 27–28.

64. *Proceedings of the Governors' Conference 1947* (Chicago: Governors' Conference, 1947), 50–96.

65. *Proceedings of the Governors' Conference 1949* (Chicago: Governors' Conference, 1949), 114.

66. *Proceedings of the Governors' Conference 1960* (Chicago: Governors' Conference, 1960), 79, 90, 91.

67. Ibid., 100.

68. *Proceedings of the Governors' Conference 1949*(Chicago: Governors' Conference, 1949), 121; *Proceedings of the Governors' Conference 1956* (Chicago: Governors' Conference, 1956), 6.

69. Sabato, *Goodbye to Good-Time Charlie*, 108–109.

70. From West Virginia in 1961 to New Jersey in 1976, eleven states adopted new income taxes; from Texas in 1961 to Vermont in 1969, ten states adopted new sales taxes. ACIR, *Significant Features of Fiscal Federalism*, 34.

71. National Governors' Conference, *State of the States, 1974* (Washington, D.C.: National Governors' Conference, 1974, 12.

72. Sabato, *Goodbye to Good-Time Charlie*, 109; Teaford, *Rise of the States*, 218–219.

73. Richard J. Hughes, "A Moral Recommitment for New Jersey: Special Message to the Legislature," Office of the Governor, Trenton, April 25, 1968. Quoted in Sabato, *Goodbye to Good-Time Charlie*, 108.

74. *Proceedings of National Governors' Conference 1965* (Chicago: Governors' Conference, 1965), 52, 54.

75. Dommel, *The Politics of Revenue Sharing*, 72–73; Walter W. Heller, *Revenue Sharing and the City* (Baltimore: Johns Hopkins University Press, 1968); Sabato, *Goodbye to Good-Time Charlie*, 174–176.

76. Will Myers and John Shannon, "Revenue Sharing for States: An Endan-

gered Species," *Intergovernmental Perspectives* 5 (Summer 1979): 12; Richard A. Snelling, "American Federalism in the Eighties," *State Government* 53 (Autumn 1980): 169.

77. Isaac W. Martin, *In Defense of Privilege: How the Property Tax Revolt Transformed American Politics* (Palo Alto, Calif.: Stanford University Press, forthcoming), ch. 4; U.S. Advisory Commission on Intergovernmental Relations, *Public Opinion and Taxes* (Washington, D.C.: ACIR, 1972); Proceedings of the National Governors Association Annual Meeting, 1972, 1973.

78. Bruce J. Schulman, *The Seventies: The Great Shift in American Culture Politics and Society* (New York: Free Press, 2001), 205–206.

79. Lisa McGirr, *Suburban Warriors: The Origins of the New American Right* (Princeton: Princeton University Press, 2002); Robert O. Self, *American Babylon: Race and the Struggle for Postwar Oakland* (Princeton: Princeton University Press, 2003), 16–26. The tax revolts of this period were not limited to anti-statist protests from the suburbs. Urban working-class homeowners were equally outraged by rising property taxes and they often looked to the government for social protection from rising housing prices. See, Martin, *In Defense of Privilege*, ch. 3.

80. Article 13A, California Constitution; Robert Kuttner, *Revolt of the Haves: Tax Rebellions and Hard Times* (New York: Simon and Schuster, 1980), 81–82; David O. Sears and Jack Citrin, *Tax Revolt: Something for Nothing in California* (Cambridge, Mass.: Harvard University Press, 1982), 26–31.

81. Martin, *In Defense of Privilege*, ch. 5. See also Steven D. Gold, "Circuit Breakers and Other Relief Measures," in C. Lowell Harris, *The Property Tax and Local Finance* (New York: Academy of Political Science, 1983), 148–157; and Arlo Woolery, "Alternative Methods of Taxing Property," in ibid., 180–188.

82. ACIR, *Significant Features of Fiscal Federalism* (1995), 130–137.

83. Kuttner, *Revolt of the Haves*; Martin, *In Defense of Privilege*; Self, *American Babylon*.

84. "Proceedings of the National Governors' Conference Annual Meeting 1984," unpublished.

85. Nicholas Johnson et al., *State Income Tax Burdens on Low-Income Families in 2000: Assessing the Burden and Opportunities for Relief* (Washington, D.C.: Center on Budget and Policy Priorities, 2001), 9; Iris J. Lav, Elizabeth McNichol, and Robert Zahradnik, *Faulty Foundations: State Structural Budget Problems and How to Fix Them* (Washington, D.C.: Center on Budget and Policy Priorities, 2005), 42–44.

86. Quoted in Jeffrey Gettleman, "A Tax Increase? 1.2 Billion? Alabamians It Seems, Say No," *New York Times*, September 6, 2003.

87. Susan Pace Hamill, "An Argument for Tax Reform Based on Judeo-Christian Ethics," *Alabama Law Review*, 54, no. 1 (Fall 2002); Dale Russakof, "Alabamans Tied in Knots by Tax Vote: Riley Stuns GOP by Stumping for Hike," *Washington Post*, August 17, 2003.

88. The deduction for federal taxes paid had been introduced by Alabama constitutional amendment number 225, passed in 1965. See Susan Pace Hamill, "Constitutional Reform in Alabama: A Necessary Step Toward Achieving a Fair and Efficient Tax Structure," Working Paper to Assist the Committee on Taxation and Debt of the Alabama Citizens Commission for Constitutional Reform, October 15, 2002, 3.

89. Russakoff, "Alabama Tied in Knots by Vote."

90. David Halbfinger, "Alabama Voters Crush Tax Plan Sought by Governor," *New York Times*, September 10, 2003.

91. Kavan Peterson, "States Open Wallets, Tackle Big Agendas," *Stateline.org*, April 28, 2006. Accessed May 15, 2006.

92. Pamela Prah, "Food Sales Tax on State's Chopping Block," *Stateline.org*, January 29, 2007. Accessed March 27, 2007.

93. See David Brunori, ed., *The Future of State Taxation* (Washington, D.C.: Urban Institute, 1998), especially chapters 2 and 3. See also Donald Bruce and William F. Fox, "State and Local Sales Tax Revenue Losses from E-Commerce: Estimates as of July 2004," *State Tax Notes*, August 2004. The amount of goods and services subject to state sales taxes has fallen from a national median of 51.3 percent in 1990 to 43.3 percent in 2003. See Lav, McNichol, and Zahradnik, *Faulty Foundations*, 11.

94. See "States Release First Set of Proposals for New Sales Tax System; Announce Public Hearing," Streamlined Sales Tax Project, press release, September 21, 2000.

95. Lav, McNichol, and Zahradnik, *Faulty Foundations*, 9–10.

96. Ibid., 18–20.

Chapter 3. Governors and the Development of American Social Policy

1. Under the term social programs I am including the insurance programs (Old Age and Survivors, Disability, Unemployment Compensation, and Medicare) as well as the means-tested programs including those that provide cash, medical benefits, food, housing, certain education programs, and jobs and training.

2. Nicholas Eberstadt, "Why Poverty Doesn't Rate," American Enterprise Institute, September 2006; Robert Rector, "How Poor Are America's Poor? Examining the 'Plague' of Poverty in America," Heritage Foundation, August 27, 2007.

3. Eugene Debs enjoyed some brief success, especially in the elections of 1916 and 1920, as the socialist party candidate for president. However, he never again equaled his 1920 vote total; see Charles A. Beard and Mary R. Beard, *A Basic History of the United States* (New York: Doubleday, Doran, 1944), 390–391.

4. A series of major riots in U.S. cities in the mid-1960s were primarily a reaction to the assassinations of Martin Luther King, Jr., and Robert F. Kennedy and perhaps a reaction to discrimination and white racism. But they were not directed toward any clear political objective. See National Advisory Commission on Civil Disorders, *Report of the National Advisory Commission on Civil Disorders* (Washington, D.C.: U.S. Government Printing Office, 1968).

5. Franklin D. Roosevelt, "Presidential Statement upon Signing the Social Security Act, August 13, 1945," *The Public Papers and Addresses of Franklin D. Roosevelt* (New York: Random House, 1938), 324–326.

6. Theda Skocpol, *Protecting Soldiers and Mothers: The Political Origins of Social Policy in the United States* (Cambridge: Harvard University Press, 1992), 9; Linda Gordon, *Pitied But Not Entitled: Single Mothers and the History of Welfare* (Cambridge: Harvard University Press, 1994).

7. Skocpol, *Protecting Soldiers and Mothers*, 9; Gordon, *Pitied But Not Entitled*.

8. Price Fishback and Shawn Everett Kantor, *A Prelude to the Welfare State: The Origins of Workers' Compensation* (Chicago: University of Chicago Press, 2000).

9. Skocpol, *Protecting Soldiers and Mothers*, chapter 7.

10. Ibid., 513.

11. Ibid., 446–447.

12. Winifred Bell, *Aid to Dependent Children* (New York: Columbia University Press, 1965).

13. Marvin Olasky, *The Tragedy of American Compassion* (Wheaton, Ill.: Crossway, 1992).

14. For a somewhat similar overview, see James T. Patterson, *America's Struggle Against Poverty, 1900–1985* (Cambridge, Mass.: Harvard University Press, 1981), chapter 4; Walter I. Trattner, *From Poor Law to Welfare State: A History of Social Welfare in America*, 6th ed. (New York: Free Press, 1999), especially chapter 13.

15. Vincent Burke and Vee Burke, *Nixon's Good Deed: Welfare Reform* (New York: Columbia University Press, 1974).

16. House of Representatives, Committee on Ways and Means, *2004 Green Book* (Washington, D.C.: U.S. Government Printing Office, 2004), sec. 4.

17. Most economists agree that taxes paid by employers into unemployment trust funds would have been paid to employees as earnings if the taxes to support the trust fund had not been required by law.

18. House Committee on Ways and Means, *2004 Green Book*, sec. 1.

19. Unemployed workers drawing Unemployment Compensation payments are required to be available for work, but as long as the unemployed meet this requirement (which is only loosely enforced), they are viewed by the public as receiving benefits they deserve, not least because their employers have paid what amount to premiums for the coverage.

20. The federal government requires states to establish an Unemployment Compensation program and to operate the program, including decisions about taxation and benefit levels, at the state level. However, the state programs must meet a host of federal requirements and all the money is kept in trust funds at the federal level. States must also meet rules about the operation of the trust funds. Federal control of the system is so great that many states send more money to the federal government to pay for program administration than they receive back from the federal government to administer their own Unemployment Compensation program. In other words, the federal government, in effect, transfers administrative funds from richer states to poorer states. This approach may be good policy, but it illustrates yet again that the federal government is able to dominate social policymaking.

21. Edwin Witte kept a diary of his experiences in helping write the Social Security Act; this diary has been a major source of information about behind-the-scenes details of how the act was written. See Sylvester J. Schieber and John B. Shoven, *The Real Deal: The History and Future of Social Security* (New Haven, Conn.: Yale University Press, 1999), 32.

22. Michael L. Gillette, *Launching the War on Poverty: An Oral History* (New York: Twayne, 1996).

23. Scott Stossel, *Sarge: The Life and Times of Sargent Shriver* (Washington, D.C.: Smithsonian Institution Press, 2004).

24. VISTA is now part of Americorps, a federal agency that runs several programs that attempt to involve young Americans in nonprofit service organizations such as schools, public health facilities, and churches to perform socially useful tasks.

25. Edward Zigler and Susan Muenchow, *Head Start: The Inside Story of America's Most Successful Educational Experiment* (New York: Basic Books, 1994).

26. Stossel, *Sarge*.

27. Daniel Patrick Moynihan, *Maximum Feasible Misunderstanding: Community*

Action in the War on Poverty (New York: Free Press, 1970); Adam Walinsky, "Maximum Feasible Misunderstanding," *New York Times Book Review,* February 2, 1969.

28. The Medicaid program was also enacted during President Johnson's War on Poverty in 1965. Medicaid pays for health care for the poor and for nursing home care for the destitute elderly. It has become the nation's most expensive and most rapidly growing poverty program. House Committee on Ways and Means, *2004 Green Book,* sec. 15, pp. 26–83.

29. For details on the history of the Food Stamp program, see Jean Yarvis Jones, *Chronology and Brief Description of Federal Food Assistance Legislation, 1935–1983* (Washington, D.C.: Congressional Research Service, 1984).

30. This section is based primarily on Ron Haskins, *Work over Welfare: The Inside Story of the 1996 Welfare Reform Law* (Washington, D.C.: Brookings Institution Press, 2006).

31. By 1975, Wisconsin had the second highest benefits among the continental states; see Lawrence M. Mead, *Government Matters: Welfare Reform in Wisconsin* (Princeton, N.J.: Princeton University Press, 2004), 21. Jason DeParle, in his superb book *American Dream: Three Women, Ten Kids, and a Nation's Drive to End Welfare* (New York: Vintage, 2004), tells the story of three mothers who moved from Chicago to Milwaukee to take advantage of Wisconsin's relatively high welfare benefits and low housing costs. Research on the magnitude of the magnet issue for Wisconsin, however, was ambiguous; see Mead, *Government Matters,* chapter 2.

32. Governor Tommy Thompson and William Bennett, "The Good News About Welfare Reform: Wisconsin's Success Story" (Washington, D.C.: Heritage Foundation, 1997), 6; Mead, *Government Matters,* 28.

33. Governor Tommy Thompson, Testimony for the Senate Committee on Finance, "Restructuring Welfare and Medicaid, the Governors' Proposal," 104th Congress, 2nd Sess., February 22, 1996.

34. Ed Schilling, Testimony for the House Committee on Ways and Means, Subcommittee on Human Resources, "Welfare Overhaul," 104th Congress, 2nd Sess. May 23, 1996.

35. Isabel Wilkerson, "Wisconsin Makes Truancy Costly by Tying Welfare to Attendance," *New York Times,* December 11, 1989, A1; Edward Walsh, "Wisconsin's Plan: Work Not Welfare," *Washington Post,* December 11, 1993, A8.

36. William J. Clinton, "Remarks to the National Governors Association, February 2, 1993," *The Public Papers and Addresses of William J. Clinton* (Washington, D.C.: U.S. Government Printing Office, 1994), 29.

37. Kant Pantel and Mark E. Rushefsky, *Politics, Power, and Policy Making: The Case of Health Care Reform in the 1990s* (Armonk, N.Y.: M. E. Sharpe, 1998).

38. I was a staffer with the House Ways and Means Committee during this period and attended many of the sessions with Engler and his staff. As almost always happens in legislative situations involving negotiations over mundane issues, staff conducted much of the negotiations. Although E. Clay Shaw, Jr., who was chairman of the welfare subcommittee of Ways and Means and the main author of all the House welfare reform bills, talked directly with Carper, the Democratic governor of Delaware and co-lead on welfare reform for NGA, nearly all the negotiations with governors in drafting their new welfare reform proposal was handled by Engler and his staff. It was not always possible to tell whether the positions Engler took were truly those of NGA or his own. Several of the block grants he pushed hard to draft and move through Congress the previous year—the child nutrition, Medicaid, and child protection block grants

come to mind—turned out to have strong opposition from some Democratic governors and even stronger opposition from Democrats in Congress and, in the case of both the child nutrition and Medicaid block grants, from President Clinton as well.

39. Jason DeParle, "Clinton Considers Taxing Aid to Poor to Pay for Reform," *New York Times*, February 13, 1994, A1.

40. Haskins, *Work over Welfare*, chapter 6.

41. Governor Tom Carper, Testimony for the U.S. House of Representatives, Committee on Ways and Means, "Governors' Welfare Proposals," 104th Congress, 2nd Sess., February 20, 1996.

42. Robert Pear, "Republican Squabble Delays Welfare Debate," *New York Times*, April 28, 1995, A19.

43. Robert Pear, "On Social Policy, Governors Quietly Split the Difference," *New York Times*, February 8, 1996, A1; Helen Dewar and John E. Yang, "Fearful of 'Do-Nothing' Label, Hill Republicans Plan Legislative Revival," *Washington Post*, February 9, 1996, A6.

44. Major Garrett, *The Enduring Revolution: How the Contract with America Continues to Shape the Nation* (New York: Crown Forum, 2005).

45. Many members of the House referred to the Republicans as Nazis and called the Republican welfare reform bill mean, low-down, nasty, evil, cruel, and several other colorful things. For their part, Republicans compared welfare recipients to wolves and alligators that should not be fed by human hand lest they become dependent; see Haskins, *Work over Welfare*, especially 150, 182, 184, 188, 191.

46. The block grant of the old Aid to Families with Dependent Children program (and the work program associated with it), for example, was funded at $16.5 billion for 1997. That amount has not changed in a decade, the first time in the history of the program (now called Temporary Assistance for Needy Families) that funding did not increase nearly every year.

47. In the case of AFDC, the basis of entitlement is Section 402(a)(10), but it was not until the courts interpreted this section as providing an entitlement during the 1960s that AFDC achieved entitlement status. See Hugh Heclo, "The Politics of Welfare Reform," in *The New World of Welfare*, ed. Ron Haskins and Rebecca Blank (Washington, D.C.: Brookings Institution Press, 2001), 169–200; and R. Shep Melnick, *Between the Lines: Interpreting Welfare Rights* (Washington, D.C.: Brookings Institution Press, 1994), chapter 5.

48. Pietro S. Nivola, Jennifer L. Noyes and Isabel V. Sawhill, "Waive of the Future? Federalism and the Next Stage of Welfare Reform," Brookings Institution, March 2004.

49. Haskins, *Work over Welfare*, 177.

50. Kenneth S. Baer, *Reinventing Democrats* (Lawrence: University Press of Kansas, 2000).

51. As Howard Rolston, formerly a senior administrator with the Department of Health and Human Services and now with the research firm Abt Associates, has pointed out to me, the concept of entitlement is somewhat less clear cut than implied here. Consider the difference between the entitlement to Social Security benefits and the entitlement to AFDC benefits before the 1996 reform law. In the former case, anyone who meets the qualifications must receive the benefits from the day of eligibility. There is almost no question about who qualifies and the method of determining eligibility is definitive and applies equally to everyone in the nation. By contrast, even before the 1996 reforms, states could

determine eligibility and there was therefore great variability in who was quali-fied for the AFDC benefit. Under the new "nonentitlement" regime of TANF, states can make applicants meet various requirements before they receive the benefit, such as search for work for thirty days. States can also end the cash bene-fit of those who don't cooperate with work requirements, something that was much harder to do under AFDC. In essence, while states appear to give TANF to all applicants who meet the requirements (there are no waiting lists as there are in other welfare programs such as housing), states impose a lot more requirements, especially having to do with promoting work, than they used toand getting the benefit is often contingent on meeting the requirements.

52. Surprisingly, as an official position of the National Governors Association, governors were willing to accept a minimum national benefit that permitted some regional variation in the Aid to Families with Dependent Children pro-gram if the federal government would assume responsibility for other welfare programs.

53. This overview of the development of American social policy is by no means complete. There are many additional social programs, mostly means-tested, that were enacted between passage of the Social Security Act in 1935 and the 1996 welfare reform law. The nation's housing programs have been estab-lished by a long series of legislative initiatives and amendments, beginning even before 1935, that have resulted in more than twenty federal housing programs costing more than $35 billion in 2005. In addition, a very expensive prescription drug benefit was added to Medicare in 2002 that, like most other Social Security Act programs, is entirely federal and was both developed and implemented with-out significant input from the states. In addition to these programs, the Child Support Enforcement program (Title IV-D of the Social Security Act) and the Earned Income Tax Credit were created in 1975, and the current form of the major foster care and adoption programs (Titles IV-B and IV-E of the Social Security Act) was enacted in 1980. In each case except the EITC (which was started as a federal program and has since been adopted by many states), consid-erable authority was moved from the local and state to the federal level, continu-ing the trend started with the Social Security Act in 1935.

54. Congressional Research Service, "Cash and Noncash Benefits for Persons with Limited Income," March 27, 2006.

55. Morton Grodzins, "The Federal System," in *Goals for Americans: The Report of the President's Commission on National Goals* (New York: Columbia University Press, 1960), 265. I thank Richard Nathan for pointing me to the Grodzins paper, as well as the Derthick paper referenced below.

56. Richard P. Nathan, *Updating Theories of American Federalism* (New York: Rockefeller Institute of Government, February 2006).

57. Alice M. Rivlin and Joseph R. Antos, *Restoring Fiscal Sanity 2007: The Health Spending Challenge* (Washington, D.C.: Brookings Institution Press, 2007).

58. Congressional Research Service, "Cash and Noncash Benefits for Persons with Limited Income," March 27, 2006.

59. From time to time, Congress has given special waiver authority for specific programs, usually by amending the statute that governs that particular program. Waivers granted by Congress for the child protection programs in Titles IV-B and IV-E of the Social Security Act provide an excellent example. See *2004 Green Book*, Sec. 11, pp. 66–72.

60. House Committee on Ways and Means, *2004 Green Book*; Sec. 8, pp. 434–435; Haskins, *Work Over Welfare*.

61. Daniel Friedlander and Gary Burtless, *Five Years After: The Long-Term Effects of Welfare-to-Work Programs* (New York: Russell Sage, 1995); Anu Rangarajan and others, *Postemployment Services to Promote Job Retention Among Welfare Recipients* (Washington, D.C.: Mathematica Policy Research, February, 1996); Alan Werner and Robert Kornfield, "The Evaluation of 'To Strengthen Michigan Families': Third Annual Report," Abt Associates, May 1995.

62. Since approximately the 1960s, large-scale social experiments based on random-assignment designs have enabled social scientists to identify programs that produce significant impacts on participants and those that do not. Some of the studies also permit the calculation of program costs and program benefits (in dollar terms), perhaps the best type of information to inform policymaking. This knowledge, although not always welcome by programs' sponsors, can and has influenced policy. See Larry L. Orr, *Social Experiments: Evaluating Public Programs with Experimental Methods* (Thousand Oaks, Calif.: Sage, 1999); Peter H. Rossi, Howard Freeman and Mark W. Lipsey, *Evaluation: A Systematic Approach*, 6th ed. (Thousand Oaks, Calif.: Sage, 1999).

63. For SSI benefits see www.ssa.gov/oact/cola/ssi.html (accessed August 30, 2007); for state supplements, see House Committee on Ways and Means, *2004 Green Book*, sec. 3, pp. 21–25.

64. U.S. Census Bureau, *Statistical Abstract of the United States: 2007* (Washington, D.C.: U.S. Department of Commerce, 2007), 455.

65. One reason the federal government has greater fiscal capacity than the states is that for several decades the federal fiscal has run large deficits while nearly every state has legal or constitutional provisions that require balanced budgets. See Ronald K. Shell, "State Balanced Budget Requirements: Provisions and Practice," National Conference of State Legislatures, www.ncsl.org/programs/fiscal/balbuda.htm (accessed on August 30, 2007).

66. Nick Kotz, *Judgment Days: Lyndon Baines Johnson, Martin Luther King Jr., and the Laws that Changed America* (New York: Mariner, 2006).

67. Martha Derthick, "The American Constitution and the Administrative State," *Public Administration Review*, 47, no. 1 (January–February 1987): 66–74.

Chapter 4. Governors and Economic Development

1. Albert Lepawsky, *State Planning and Economic Development in the South* (Washington, D.C.: National Planning Association, 1949), 8.

2. D. L. Corbitt, ed., *Public Papers and Letters of Cameron Morrison, Governor of North Carolina, 1921–1925* (Raleigh, N.C.: Edward and Broughton Company, 1927), 46–47.

3. Lepawsky, *State Planning*, 8.

4. Ralph J. Rogers, "The Effort to Industrialize," in Richard A. McLemore, ed., *A History of Mississippi*, 2 vols. (Hattiesburg: University and College Press of Mississippi, 1973) 2: 241.

5. Ernest J. Hopkins, *Mississippi's BAWI Plan: An Experiment in Industrial Subsidization* (Atlanta: Federal Reserve Bank of Atlanta, 1944), 8.

6. *New York Times*, September 27, 1936, E11.

7. Hopkins, *Mississippi's BAWI Plan*, 61.

8. Oliver Emmerich, "Collapse and Recovery," in McLemore, *History of Mississippi*, 2: 117.

9. H. C. Nixon, "The Southern Governors' Conference as a Pressure Group," *Journal of Politics* 6 (August 1944): 338.

10. *New York Times*, April 12 , 1938, 34.

11. Robert A. Lively, "The South and Freight Rates: Political Settlement of an Economic Argument," *Journal of Southern History* 14 (August 1948): 364.

12. *New York Times*, December 10, 1939, 98.

13. Lively, "South and Freight Rates," 375.

14. Ellis Gibbs Arnall, *The Shore Dimly Seen* (Philadelphia: J. B. Lippincott Company, 1946), 23, 166–167.

15. *New York Times*, September 19, 1943, 50.

16. *New York Times*, October 24, 1937, 11.

17. *New York Times*, January 15, 1938, 21.

18. *New York Times*, July 15, 1938, 25.

19. Archibald Cox, "Federalism in the Law of Labor Relations," *Harvard Law Review* 67 (June 1954): 1303; F. Ray Marshall, *Labor in the South* (Cambridge, Mass.: Harvard University Press, 1967), 320.

20. "Excerpts from Governors' Messages—1949," *State Government* 22 (March 1949): 64, 92.

21. Marvin E. DeBoer, *Dreams of Power and the Power of Dreams* (Fayetteville: University of Arkansas Press, 1988), 998.

22. James C. Cobb, *The Selling of the South: The Southern Crusade for Industrial Development, 1936–1990*, 2nd ed. (Urbana: University of Illinois Press, 1993), 78.

23. Ibid., 75.

24. Virginius Dabney, "Albertis S. Harrison, Jr.: Transition Governor," in Edward Younger and James Tice Moore, eds., *The Governors of Virginia, 1860–1978* (Charlottesville: University Press of Virginia, 1982), 366; Cobb, *Selling of the South*, 134.

25. Leslie W. Dunbar, "The Changing Mind of the South: The Exposed Nerve," *Journal of Politics* 26 (February 1964): 20.

26. Luther H. Hodges, *Businessman in the Statehouse: Six Years as Governor of North Carolina* (Chapel Hill: University of North Carolina Press, 1962), 29–30.

27. Ibid., 40.

28. *New York Times*, July 4, 1957, 32.

29. Hodges, *Businessman in the Statehouse*, 59–60.

30. *New York Times*, October 15, 1957, 45.

31. Hodges, *Businessman in the Statehouse*, 60.

32. Ibid., 62–63.

33. Ibid., 74–75.

34. Ibid., 203, 223.

35. *New York Times*, January 4, 1952, 26.

36. *New York Times*, February 5, 1954, 29.

37. Cobb, *Selling of the South*, 76; *New York Times*, August 26, 1955, 8.

38. Cobb, *Selling of the South*, 138, 146.

39. Elton K. McQuery, "For Western Industrial Expansion," *State Government* 22 (January 1949): 9.

40. *New York Times*, December 18, 1951, 63; July 17, 1956, 9.

41. *New York Times*, March 19, 1950, SM5.

42. David Koistenen, "Public Policies for Countering Deindustrialization in Postwar Massachusetts," *Journal of Policy History* 18 (2006): 337, 341–342.

43. *New York Times*, March 12, 1976, 55.

44. *New York Times*, April 29, 1976, 72.

45. James A. Rhodes, "How Ohio Landed Honda: Hard Work, 'Providence,'" Ward's Auto World, April 1, 1990, http://www.encyclopedia.com/doc/1G1 -8952401.html (accessed May 25, 2007).

46. David Osborne, *Laboratories of Democracy* (Boston: Harvard Business School Press, 1988), 21–32, 175–210.

47. Thad L. Beyle, "Issues Facing the States and Governors, 1982," *State Government* 56 (1983): 65–66.

48. Osborne, *Laboratories of Democracy*, 153.

49. Ibid., 48.

50. Paul Luebke, *Tar Heel Politics: Myths and Realities* (Chapel Hill: University of North Carolina Press, 1990), 77.

51. Timothy J. Bartik, "Tennessee," in R. Scott Fosler, ed., *The New Economic Role of American States* (New York: Oxford University Press, 1988), 174–176, 188.

52. *New York Times*, February 18, 1985, A18.

53. Bartik, "Tennessee," 191.

54. National Governors Association, "Enhancing Competitiveness: A Review of Recent State Economic Development Initiatives—2005," 12, www.nga.org/files/pdf/0604enhancecompib.pdf (accessed February 25, 2007).

55. Jeffrey Finkle, "State Economic Development Strategies: Job Growth and Retention in a Recovering Economy," *The Book of the States* 37 (2005): 566.

56. *Innovation America: The 2007 State New Economy Index: Benchmarking Economic Transformation in the States* (Washington, D.C.: National Governors Association Center for Best Practices, 2007), i.

57. *Innovation America* (Washington, D.C.: National Governors Association, 2006), www.nga.org/Files/pdf/06napolitanobrochure.pdf (accessed May 27, 2007).

58. National Governors Association, "The Role of the Arts in Economic Development," 1, www.nga.org/Files/pdf/062501artsdev.pdf (accessed May 26, 2007).

59. "Governor Patrick Announces Massachusetts' New Life Sciences Initiative," Official Website of the Governor of Massachusetts—Press Release, May 8, 2007, www.mass.gov.

Chapter 5. Uneasy Executives

The author would like to thank Ethan Sribnick, David Shreve, the National Governors Association, the Woodrow Wilson Presidential Library, Derek Chang, Jeff Cowie, Nina Louise Morrison, Aaron Sachs, Michael Smith, Michael Trotti, and Rob Vanderlan.

1. The National Governors Association graciously provided the author with these statistics.

2. This debate has occurred mostly among political scientists. See note 66 for more details.

3. Examples of classic portraits of southern governors include Dan Carter, *The Politics of Rage: George Wallace, the Origins of the New Conservatism, and the Transformation of American Politics* (New York: Simon and Schuster, 1995); Robert Sherrill, *Gothic Politics in the Deep South: Stars of the New Confederacy* (New York: Grossman, 1968); Roy Reed, *Faubus: The Life and Times of an American Prodigal* (Fayetteville: University of Arkansas Press, 1997).

4. On "strategic accommodation," see Joseph Crespino, *In Search of Another*

Country: Mississippi and the Conservative Counterrevolution (Princeton: Princeton University Press, 2007).

5. Many of the books on northeastern governors in the 1960s and 1970s— Martha Wagner Weinberg, *Managing the State* (Cambridge, Mass.: MIT Press, 1977), on Francis Sargent, and Robert Howe Connery, *Rockefeller of New York: Executive Power in the Statehouse* (Ithaca, N.Y.: Cornell University Press, 1979), for example—all but ignore school desegregation and other issues of black civil rights. In contrast, books on southern governors seem consumed with issues of race.

6. A body of scholarship invests the term "muddling through" with a technical meaning—as one concrete style of policy-making, as opposed to the "rational policymaker model." I do not use the term in this distinct sense. Perhaps the impulse to "muddle through" racial conflicts was quite a rational one for many governors. See Weinberg, *Managing the State*, 7.

7. This chapter will not touch on affirmative action. See Thomas Sugrue, "Affirmative Action from Below: Civil Rights, the Building Trades, and the Politics of Racial Equality in the North, 1945–1969," *Journal of American History* 91 (June 2004); Timothy Minchin, *The Color of Work: The Struggle for Civil Rights in the Southern Paper Industry, 1945–1980* (Chapel Hill: University of North Carolina Press, 1991); Timothy Minchin, *Hiring the Black Worker: The Racial Integration of the Southern Textile Industry, 1960–1980* (Chapel Hill: University of North Carolina Press, 1999). Gary Orfield argues that busing was too highly charged an issue for elected leaders to tackle, and that busing policies therefore fell to the court. "Given the unwillingness of elected officials at any level of government to devise their own policies to end segregation in American cities, the Court's solutions were usually the only solutions there were." Gary Orfield, *Must We Bus? Segregated Schools and National Policy* (Washington, D.C.: Brookings Institution, 1978), 11.

8. Robert Pratt, *The Color of Their Skin: Education and Race in Richmond, Virginia, 1954–89* (Charlottesville: University Press of Virginia, 1992), 6–9; James Ely, "J. Lindsay Almond, Jr.: The Politics of School Desegregation," in Edward Younger, ed., *The Governors of Virginia, 1860–1978* (Charlottesville: University Press of Virginia, 1982), 35.

9. Ely, "J. Lindsay Almond, Jr.," 354, 357; Helen Fuller, "The Defiant Ones in Virginia," *New Republic* (January 12, 1959). See Pratt, *The Color of Their Skin*, on the idea of "passive resistance." On the movement for open schools, see Matthew Lassiter and Andrew Lewis, eds., *The Moderates' Dilemma: Massive Resistance to School Desegregation in Virginia* (Charlottesville: University Press of Virginia, 1998), and Matthew Lassiter, *The Silent Majority: Suburban Politics in the Sunbelt South* (Princeton: Princeton University Press, 2005); see also Bob Smith, *They Closed Their Schools: Prince Edward County, Virginia, 1951–1964* (Chapel Hill: University of North Carolina Press, 1965).

10. Earl Black, *Southern Governors and Civil Rights: Racial Segregation as a Campaign Issue in the Second Reconstruction* (Cambridge, Mass.: Harvard University Press, 1976), 115.

11. See Edward Brooke, *Bridging the Divide: My Life* (New Brunswick, N.J.: Rutgers University Press, 2007), for his thoughts about the color-blindness of Massachusetts's electorate.

12. Martha Biondi complicates distinctions between de facto and de jure forms of segregation. See Biondi, *To Stand and Fight* (Cambridge, Mass.: Harvard University Press, 2003).

13. Kathleen Kilgore, *John Volpe: The Life of an Immigrant's Son* (Dublin, N.H.: Yankee Books, 1987), 136; Alan Lupo, *Liberty's Chosen Home: The Politics of Violence in Boston* (Boston: Little, Brown, 1977), 135–150.

14. J. Michael Ross and William Berg, *"I Respectfully Disagree with the Judge's Order": The Boston School Desegregation Controversy* (Washington, D.C.: University Press of America, 1981), 48–49.

15. Massachusetts Advisory Committee on Racial Imbalance and Education, *Because It Is Right Educationally*, parts 1 and 2 (1965–1975), Ten-Year Report, 3.

16. Frank Levy, *Northern Schools and Civil Rights: The Racial Imbalance Act of Massachusetts* (Chicago: Markham, 1971), 4, 49. Levy argues that this law was in effect passed by the Yankee legislature, over and against the opposition of Irish Boston. He sees it as analogous to the federal government passing civil rights legislation despite the pleas of a recalcitrant white South.

17. Ross and Berg, *"I Respectfully Disagree with the Judge's Order,"* 53.

18. Ross and Berg, *"I Respectfully Disagree with the Judge's Order,"* 57.

19. The initial report named Boston, Springfield, Medford, and Cambridge. The latter two cities soon developed proposals to comply.

20. For Holton's campaign ads, see: http://www.sorenseninstitute.org; Lassiter, *The Silent Majority*, 263–64; Jack Bass and Walter DeVries, *The Transformation of Southern Politics: Social Change and Political Consequence Since 1945* (New York: Basic Books, 1976), 358; J. Harvie Wilkinson III, "Linwood Holton: An Idealist's Demise," in Younger, ed., *The Governors of Virginia*, 397.

21. The South had elected racially moderate governors before. North Carolina's Terry Sanford, for one, presided over limited school desegregation during the early 1960s. But Holton (and other New South governors, particularly Askew) made racial moderation a central part of their platforms.

22. Jack Bass, Interview with Linwood Holton, September 25, 1973. Southern Oral History Program, Southern Historical Collection, University of North Carolina, Chapel Hill; Wilkinson, "Linwood Holton," 397; *Washington Post*, January 2, 1974.

23. Lassiter, *The Silent Majority*, 280–285.

24. Pratt, *The Color of Their Skin*, 48.

25. *Washington Post*, July 26, 1970.

26. *Washington Post*, August 4, 1970.

27. Many leaders shaped their busing positions around small distinctions. They opposed busing when its intent was to achieve a percentage-based "racial balance." Yet they supported busing if it possessed the more straightforward goal of ending segregation.

28. *New York Times*, January 22, February 9, April 12, 1970; August 8, September 12, 1971; *Washington Post*, September 23, 1970.

29. Lassiter, *The Silent Majority*, 287.

30. Pratt, *The Color of Their Skin*, 49–53.

31. *New York Times*, September 1, 1970; Pratt, *The Color of Their Skin*, 60.

32. *Washington Post*, April 21, 1971.

33. *Washington Post*, August 19, 1971.

34. *Washington Post*, August 20, August 26, 1971, February 12, 1972.

35. *Washington Post*, February 12, 1972.

36. *Washington Post*, March 31, 1972.

37. Francis Sargent, *The Sargent Years: Selected Public Papers of Francis W. Sargent, Governor.* ed. Jack Flannery (Boston, 1976), 60; Weinberg's *Managing the State* remains the most thorough look at Sargent's tenure as governor.

38. Sargent, *The Sargent Years*, 108, 110, 152; *Bay State Banner*, July 13, 1972; Sargent offered to give the city until June 8, and proposed extra funding for Springfield's METCO program. Sargent vowed he would not sign such a bill if it passed. "The bill strikes at the heart of the racial imbalance law, by depriving the Board of Education of its only effective method of enforcing that law." The Senate quickly passed the bill.

39. Sargent, *The Sargent Years*, 204–205; See Lupo, *Liberty's Chosen Home*, for a debunking of the progressive myth.

40. Sargent, *The Sargent Years*, 207, 259; Ronald Formisano, *Boston Against Busing: Race, Class, and Ethnicity in the 1960s and 1970s* (Chapel Hill: University of North Carolina Press, 1991), 53, 60; Ross and Berg, *"I Respectfully Disagree with the Judge's Order,"* 100, 89.

41. Formisano, *Boston Against Busing*, 112, 63; Ross and Berg, *"I Respectfully Disagree with the Judge's Order,"* 123, 127.

42. Sargent, *The Sargent Years*, 260.

43. Sargent, *The Sargent Years*, 261.

44. Sargent, *The Sargent Years*, 261.

45. As historian Ronald Formisano wrote, "Only . . . Sargent's vetoes prevented repeal or passage of crippling amendments." Formisano, *Boston Against Busing*, 53.

46. Ross and Berg, *"I Respectfully Disagree with the Judge's Order,"* 136; Sargent, *The Sargent Years*, 262.

47. Ross and Berg, *"I Respectfully Disagree with the Judge's Order,"* 136.

48. As journalist Alan Lupo wrote, the "state of Massachusetts—the predominantly Catholic legislature and the liberalish Yankee Republican Governor Francis Sargent—took the clout out of the Racial Imbalance Act . . . by removing the state Board of Education's power to redistrict and order busing." Lupo, *Liberty's Chosen Home*, 154.

49. *Bay State Banner*, June 13, 1974.

50. J. Anthony Lukas's *Common Ground: A Turbulent Decade in the Lives of Three Families* (New York: Alfred A. Knopf, 1985), and Formisano's *Boston Against Busing* remain the best books on the crisis.

51. Orfield, *Must We Bus?* 4.

52. Formisano, *Boston Against Busing*, 90.

53. *New York Times*, March 1, 1970; March 25, 1972, May 3, 1972.

54. *New York Times*, March 23, March 25, April 27, May 15, 1972.

55. Lupo, *Liberty's Chosen Home*, 210, 11.

56. Ross and Berg, *"I Respectfully Disagree with the Judge's Order,"* 261.

57. Richard Gaines and Michael Segal, *Dukakis and the Reform Impulse* (Boston: Quinlan, 1987), 94; *Boston Globe*, June 12, 1988.

58. Gaines and Segal, *Dukakis and the Reform Impulse*, 98.

59. *Boston Globe*, May 19, 1988.

60. *Boston Globe*, March 18, 2007.

61. *Boston Globe*, May 19, 1988.

62. *New York Times*, December 16, 1974.

63. Orfield, *Must We Bus?* 273.

64. Among the many books that deal with the Willie Horton episode, Dan Carter's *From George Wallace to Newt Gingrich: Race in the Conservative Counterrevolution* (Baton Rouge: Louisiana State University Press, 1996), contains a sharp distillation.

65. *New York Times*, September 25, 1989.

66. Laurence Moreland, Robert Steed, and Tod Baker, *The 1988 Presidential Election in the South: Continuity Amidst Change in Southern Party Politics* (New York: Praeger, 1991), 242.

67. Margaret Edds, *Claiming the Dream: The Victorious Campaign of Douglas Wilder of Virginia* (Chapel Hill, N.C.: Algonquin, 1990), 26; Jack Bass, Interview with Douglas Wilder (March 15, 1974), Southern Oral History Program, Southern Historical Collection, University of North Carolina, Chapel Hill.

68. J. L. Jeffries, *Virginia's Native Son: The Election and Administration of Governor L. Douglas Wilder* (West Lafayette, Ind.: Purdue University Press, 2000); Raphael Sonenshein, "Can Black Candidates Win Statewide Elections?" *Political Science Quarterly*, 105, no. 2 (Summer 1990); Ruth Ann Strickland and Marcia Lynn Whicker, "Comparing the Wilder and Gantt Campaigns: A Model for Black Candidate Success in Statewide Elections," *PS: Political Science and Politics*, 25, no. 2 (June 1992); Robert C. Smith, "Recent Elections and Black Politics: The Maturation or Death of Black Politics?" *PS: Political Science and Politics*, 23, no. 2 (June 1990).

69. Edds, *Claiming the Dream*, 3.

70. *New York Times*, November 3, November 8, 1989.

71. *New York Times*, November 13, 1989; *Washington Post*, October 5, 1989.

72. Edds, *Claiming the Dream*, 129.

73. *Washington Post*, November 8, 1989; *New York Times*, November 13, 1989; Jonathan Yardley, "Virginia's Election: No Small Victory," *Washington Post*, November 20, 1989.

74. National Public Radio, October 13, 2006.

75. *Boston Globe*, November 8, 2006; *USA Today*, November 1, 2006.

76. *Boston Globe*, May 11, 2007.

77. *Boston Globe*, May 11, 2007.

78. Lukas, *Common Ground*, 326; Charles P. Pierce, "The Optimist," *Boston Globe Magazine*, December 31, 2006.

79. Pierce, "The Optimist," *Boston Globe Magazine*, December 31, 2006.

80. "Rosa Parks Took Her Stand for Civil Rights – By Sitting Down," *Christian Science Monitor*, November 29, 1985. On the ambiguous legacy of the civil rights movement, see Lerone Bennett, Jr., "Have We Overcome?" in Dorothy Abbott, ed., *Mississippi Writers: Reflections of Childhood and Youth*, volume 2: Nonfiction (Jackson: University Press of Mississippi, 1986), 3–12. Also see William Chafe, *Civilities and Civil Rights: Greensboro, North Carolina, and the Black Struggle for Freedom* (New York: Oxford University Press, 1980), vii–viii; David Goldfield, *Black, White, and Southern: Race Relations and Southern Culture, 1940 to the Present* (Baton Rouge: Louisiana University Press, 1990); Waldo Martin, ed., *Brown v. Board of Education: A Brief History with Documents* (Boston: Bedford/St. Martin's, 1998), 223, 234; Harvard Sitkoff, *The Struggle for Black Equality, 1954–1992* (New York: Hill and Wang, 1993), 210, 221, 233; Robert Norrell, *Reaping the Whirlwind: The Civil Rights Movement in Tuskegee* (New York: Alfred A. Knopf, 1985), 208, 210; For differing perspectives, see also David Hollinger, *Postethnic America: Beyond Multiculturalism* (New York: Basic Books, 1995); and George Lipsitz, *The Possessive Investment in Whiteness: How White People Profit from Identity Politics* (Philadelphia: Temple University Press, 1998).

81. *New York Times*, June 30, 2007.

Chapter 6. Balancing Economic Development with Investor Protection

The author would like to thank former governors Mike Castle and Pete du Pont for help in reconstructing events in Delaware, David Shreve for his substantial assistance on the Kansas section, and the *Financial Times* for supporting her outside endeavors.

1. Bill Janklow, interview Sioux Falls, S.D., August 24, 2004, in "Secret History of the Credit Card," *Frontline*, PBS.

2. John Gapper, "Capitalist Punishment," *FT Weekend Magazine*, January 29, 2005, 16.

3. S. J. Woolf, "Two Candidates for the Governorship: Roosevelt and Ottinger Discuss the Tasks of Public Office," *New York Times*, October 7, 1928, XX4.

4. Thomas A. McNeal, "Report of the Annual Meeting: The Governors of Kansas," *Kansas Historical Quarterly*, February 1936, 77.

5. Quoted in Craig Miner, *Kansas: The History of the Sunflower State, 1854–2000* (Lawrence: University Press of Kansas, 2002), 230.

6. Quoted in ibid., 112. Like Stubbs, Bristow's career waxed and waned with the fate of Bull Moose Republicanism. See also A. Bower Sageser, "The Postal Career of Joseph L. Bristow," *Kansas Historical Quarterly*, Spring 1968, 1–9.

7. See Robert Sherman La Forte, *Leaders of Reform: Progressive Republicans in Kansas, 1900–1916* (Lawrence: University Press of Kansas, 1974), 44.

8. Quoted in ibid., 6.

9. Quoted in Francis W. Schruben, "The Kansas Refinery Law of 1905," *Kansas Historical Quarterly*, Autumn 1968, 312.

10. Quoted in William Frank Zornow, *Kansas: A History of the Jayhawk State* (Norman: University of Oklahoma Press, 1957), 217.

11. "Message of Governor W. R. Stubbs to the Kansas Legislature, January 12, 1909," Kansas Governors' Messages, Kansas State Library; available from http://www.kslib.info/ref/message/stubbs/1909.html, accessed August 11, 2006.

12. Ibid.

13. Charles Hill, "Progressive Legislation in Kansas," *Collections of the Kansas State Historical Society, 1911–1912* (Topeka: Kansas State Printing Office, 1912), 76–77. See also Will Payne, "How Kansas Drove Out a Set of Thieves," *Saturday Evening Post*, December 2, 1911.

14. Hill, "Progressive Legislation in Kansas," 77.

15. Jonathan R. Macey and Geoffrey P. Miller, "Origin of the Blue Sky Laws," *Texas Law Review*, 70, no. 2 (December 1991), 351.

16. Ibid., 362, 369.

17. Paul G. Mahoney, "The Origins of the Blue Sky Laws: A Test of Competing Hypotheses," *Journal of Law and Economics*, 46 (April 2003), 229.

18. Molly Ivins, "It's Rarely Politics As Usual to the South Dakota Governor," *New York Times*, August 30, 1980, 1.

19. T. R. Reid, "With Much at Stake, Both Parties Turn to S.D.; Close, Unpredictable House and Senate Races Draw National Attention, Lots of Money," *Washington Post*, October 22, 2002, A04. Bill Richards, "Prairie Promoter: Gov. Janklow Exhibits Strange Personal Style, But He Means Business—Luring Jobs to South Dakota Endears Him to Voters; An Invitation to Bankers—In Bunny Suit or Burnoose," *Wall Street Journal*, March 12, 1984.

20. James R. Dickenson, "Divisive South Dakota GOP Primary Set Gov. Janklow Shapes Up as Serious Challenger To First-Term Sen. Abdnor," *Washington Post*, February 23, 1986, A07.

21. Michael Janofsky, "Congressman's Driving History Clouds Future," *New York Times*, August 21, 2003, 14.

22. AP, "Jail Time for Ex-Rep Janklow," *New York Times*, January 23, 2004, 12.

23. Richards, "Prairie Promoter."

24. Janklow, *Frontline* interview.

25. Janklow, *Frontline* interview.

26. Douglas Hajek, "South Dakota Takes Center Stage," Northwestern Financial Review, September 15–30, 2004. http://findarticles.com/p/articles/mi_qa3799/is_200409/ai_n9415461.

27. Walter Wriston, interview, "Secret History of the Credit Card," *Frontline*, April 28, 2004.

28. Wriston, *Frontline* interview.

29. *Marquette National Bank v. First of Omaha Service Corp.,* 439 U.S. 299 (1978).

30. Robin Stein, "The Ascendancy of the Credit Card Industry," in "The Secret History of the Credit Card," *Frontline*, PBS.org (online, no page numbers).

31. Janklow, *Frontline* interview.

32. Wriston, *Frontline* interview.

33. "South Dakota Invites Citibank's Credit-Card Unit into State," *Wall Street Journal,* March 13, 1980.

34. Janklow, *Frontline* interview.

35. Robert A Bennett, "Banks May Shift Units Out of State," *New York Times,* June 11. 1980, D1.

36. "Highlights South Dakota: The Birth of a Banking Center," *New York Times,* June 29, 1980, 17.

37. Richards, "Prairie Promoter."

38. Janklow, *Frontline* interview.

39. Janklow, *Frontline* interview.

40. Thomas M. Reardon, "T. M. Reardon's first-hand account of Citibank's move to South Dakota," Northwestern Financial Review, September 15–30, 2004, http://findarticles.com/p/articles/mi_qa3799/is_200409/ai_n9415537.

41. Hajek, "South Dakota Takes Center Stage."

42. Federal Reserve Board, "Consumer Credit," press release, April 6, 2007.

43. Federal Reserve Board, "Household Debt Service and Financial Obligations Ratio," press release, March 13, 2007.

44. Eileen Alt Powell, Associated Press, "Americans Labor Under Crushing Load of Debt, Bankruptcies Hit Record Level; Savings Rate Continues to Drop," *Houston Chronicle,* January 12, 2004, 5.

45. Janklow, *Frontline* interview

46. Gapper, "Capitalist Punishment."

47. L. J. Davis, "Delaware Inc.," *New York Times Magazine,* June 5, 1988.

48. Laurie P. Cohen, "Lipton Tells Clients That Delaware May Not Be a Place to Incorporate," *Wall Street Journal,* November 11, 1988, C1.

49. Larry Nagengast, *Pierre S. du Pont IV, Governor of Delaware 1977–85* (Dover: Delaware Heritage Press, 2007), 88.

50. Davis, "Delaware Inc."

51. Paul Barrett, "Delaware Moves Closer to Adopting an Anti-Takeover Law," *Wall Street Journal,* December 9, 1987.

52. Nagengast, *Pierre S. du Pont IV,* 90.

53. Ibid., 5.

54. Pierre S. "Pete" du Pont IV, telephone interview with author, April 30, 2007.

55. Nagengast, *Pierre S. du Pont IV,* 59.

56. Du Pont interview.

57. Du Pont interview.

58. William T. Quillen and Michael Hanrahan, "A Short History of the Delaware Court of Chancery 1792–1992," Widener University School of Law, 1993.

59. Du Pont interview.

60. Du Pont interview.

61. Quillen and Hanrahan, "A Short History."

62. Michael Castle, telephone interview with author, July 5, 2007.

63. Michael Hanrahan, telephone interview with author, April 12, 2007.

64. Davis, "Delaware Inc."

65. E. Norman Veasey, "Business Forum: Delaware's Takeover Law: A Statute Was Needed to Stop Abuses," New York Times, February 7, 1988, 3.

66. Barrett, "Delaware moves closer."

67. Hanrahan interview.

68. Cohen, "Lipton Tells Clients."

69. Castle interview.

70. Castle interview.

Chapter 7. Moving the Nation

This chapter represents the conclusions and views of the author and should not be considered to represent the views of the Congressional Research Service or of the U.S. Library of Congress.

1. U.S. Office of Management and Budget, The Budget for Fiscal Year 2008, Historical Tables (Washington, D.C.: U.S. Government Printing Office, 2007), 66; and U.S. Bureau of the Census, State and Local Government Finances, 2003–2004 (Washington, D.C.: U.S. Government Printing Office, 2006), Table 1. Current expenditures extrapolated from 2004 expenditures.

2. American Association of State Highway Officials (AASHO), The First Fifty Years, 1914–1964 (Washington, D.C.: AASHO, 1965), 35; and Bruce W. McCalley, "Model T Ford Sales, 1908–1919," Model T Ford Club of America, http://www.mtfca.com/encyclo/fdsales.htm. Accessed February 25, 2007.

3. Proceedings of a Conference of Governors in the White House, May 13–15, 1908 (Washington, D.C.: U.S. Government Printing Office, 1909), 104.

4. John B. Rae, The Road and Car in American Life (Cambridge, Mass.: MIT Press, 1971), 33–39.

5. Joint Committee on Federal Aid in the Construction of Post Roads, Federal Aid to Good Roads, 63rd Congress, 3rd sess., November 25, 1914 (Washington, D.C.: U.S. Government Printing Office, 1915), 119–120.

6. Ibid., 159.

7. Richard F. Weingroff, "For The Common Good: The 85th Anniversary of a Historic Partnership," Public Roads 64, no. 5 (March–April 2001), http://www.fhwa.dot.gov/infrastructure/rw01a.htm; and Bruce E. Seely, Building the American Highway System: Engineers as Policy Makers (Philadelphia: Temple University Press, 1987), 40–45.

8. U.S. Advisory Commission on Intergovernmental Relations (ACIR), Categorical Grants: Their Role and Design (Washington, D.C.: ACIR, 1978), 16, 17; and Seely, Building the American Highway System, 36–51.

9. Herman Mertins, Jr., National Transportation Policy in Transition (Lexington, Mass.: Lexington Books, 1972), 14, 15.

10. U.S. Department of Transportation, "Unease in the Golden Age: Thomas

H. MacDonald" (Washington, D.C.: U.S. Department of Transportation, 2007), http://www.fhwa.dot.gov/infrastructure/hwyhist04b.cfm#s07.

11. Rae, *The Road and Car in American Life*, 36–39; and Seely, *Building the American Highway System*, 72–80.

12. U.S. Bureau of the Census, *Historical Statisticsl of the United States: Colonial Times to 1970*, Part 2 (Washington, D.C.: U.S. Government Printing Office, 1975), 712–714. Spending figures reflect capital outlays for roads and bridges and maintenance minus intergovernmental transfers.

13. Ibid., 712; Mark H. Rose, *Interstate: Express Highway Politics, 1939–1989*, revised edition (Knoxville: University of Tennessee Press, 1990), 4; Seely, *Building the American Highway System*, 73, 210.

14. Mark Rose, Bruce E. Seely. and Paul F. Barrett, *The Best Transportation System in the World* (Columbus: Ohio University Press, 2006), 30, 31, 46.

15. Senator Carl Hayden, "The History of Federal-Aid Highway Legislation," *The History and Accomplishment of Twenty-Five Years of Federal Aid for Highways: An Examination of Policies from State and National Viewpoints* (Washington, D.C.: American Association of State Highway Officials, 1914), 14; Rae, *The Road and Car in American Life*, 74–76; and Richard F. Weingroff, "From 1916 to 1939: The Federal-State Partnership at Work," *Public Roads*, 60, no. 1 (Summer 1996).

16. Seely, *Building the American Highway System*, 94.

17. U.S. Bureau of the Census, *Historical Statistical of the United States: Colonial Times to 1970*, 710–714.

18. *Proceedings of the Governors' Conference, 1948* (Chicago: Governors' Conference, 1948), 172.

19. Rose, *Interstate*, 4.

20. *Proceedings of the Governors' Conference, 1946* (Chicago: Governors' Conference, 1946), 52, 128; and Glenn E. Brooks, *When Governors Convene: The Governors' Conference and National Politics* (Baltimore: Johns Hopkins Press, 1961), 63.

21. *Proceedings of the Governors' Conference, 1945* (Chicago: Governors' Conference, 1945), 244; *Proceedings of the Governors' Conference, 1946* (Chicago: Governors' Conference, 1946), 199; *Proceedings of the Governors' Conference, 1947* (Chicago: Governors' Conference, 1947) 279, 280; and *Proceedings of the Governors' Conference, 1948* (Chicago: Governors' Conference, 1948), 144.

22. Brooks, *When Governors Convene*, 78; *Proceedings of the Governors' Conference, 1952* (Chicago: Governors' Conference, 1952), 195; and *Proceedings of the Governors' Conference, 1953* (Chicago: Governors' Conference, 1953), 205.

23. U.S. Department of Transportation, "Highway History: President Eisenhower Takes Charge" (Washington, D.C.: U.S. Department of Transportation, 2007) , http://www.fhwa.dot.gov/infrastructure/hwyhist07a.cfm#sup220.

24. Brooks, *When Governors Convene*, 79.

25. *Proceedings of the Governor's Conference, 1954* (Chicago: Governors' Conference, 1954), 90.

26. Brooks, *When Governors Convene*, 77–81; Seely, *Building the American Highway System*, 214, 215; and AASHO, *The First Fifty Years, 1914–1964*, 58, 59. Other members of the governors highway committee were: Frank J. Lausche (D-Ohio), John Lodge (R-Conn.), Paul L. Patterson (R-Ore.), John Howard Pyle (R-Ariz.), Allan Shivers (D-Tex.), and Lawrence W. Wetherby (D-Ky.). Governor Robert Kennon (D-La.), as Chairman of the Governors' Conference, served as an ex officio member.

27. "Postwar Highway Program." in *Congress and the Nation, 1945–1964* (Washington, D.C.: Congressional Quarterly Service, 1965), 524; Walter J.

Kohler, "Statement Before the House Committee on Public Works," in National Highway Program, Hearings before the House Committee on Public Works, 84th Congress, 1st sess. (Washington, D.C.: U.S. Government Printing Office, May 4, 1955), 366; and James A. Dunn, Jr., *Driving Forces: The Automobile, Its Enemies, and the Politics of Mobility* (Washington, D.C.: Brookings Institution Press, 1998), 34, 35.

28. "Postwar Highway Program," in *Congress and the Nation, 1945–1964*, 524; and U.S. Department of Transportation, "Highway History: President Eisenhower Takes Charge: The Clay Plan," http://www.fhwa.dot.gov/infrastructure/hwyhist07e.cfm#s10.

29. *Proceedings of the Governors' Conference, 1960* (Chicago: Governors' Conference, 1960), 179, 180.

30. Robert Jay Dilger, *National Intergovernmental Programs* (Englewood Cliffs, N.J.: Prentice-Hall, 1989), 129–131.

31. *Proceedings of the National Governors' Conference, 1967* (Chicago: National Governors' Conference, 1967), 144.

32. *Proceedings of the National Governors' Conference, 1969* (Chicago: National Governors' Conference, 1969), 201.

33. Ibid., 199–204; *Proceedings of the National Governors' Conference, 1970* (Chicago: National Governors' Conference, 1970), 185.

34. Jeremy J. Warford, *Public Policy Toward General Aviation* (Washington, D.C.: Brookings Institution, 1971), 58–67; U.S. Department of Transportation, *Administrator's Fact Book, April 2000* (Washington, D.C.: U.S. Department of Transportation, April 2000), 37; and U.S. Department of Transportation, *Administrator's Fact Book, December 2006* (Washington, D.C.: U.S. Department of Transportation, December 2006), 33.

35. Robert Jay Dilger, *National Intergovernmental Programs*, 129–131.

36. Rose, *Interstate: Express Highway Politics*, 111.

37. National Governors' Association (NGA), *Policy Positions, 1980–81* (Washington, D.C.: NGA, 1980), 159; NGA, *Policy Positions, 1981–82* (Washington, D.C.: NGA, 1981), 160; NGA, *Policy Positions, 1982–83* (Washington, D.C.: NGA, 1982), 162; NGA, *Policy Positions, 1983–84* (Washington, D.C.: NGA, 1983), 193; NGA, *Policy Positions, 1984–85* (Washington, D.C.: NGA, 1984), 230; NGA, *Policy Positions, 1985–86* (Washington, D.C.: NGA, 1986), 253, 255; NGA, *Policy Positions, 1986–87* (Washington, D.C.: NGA, 1986), 275, 276; NGA, *Policy Positions, 1987–88* (Washington, D.C.: NGA, 1988), 199, 200; NGA, *Policy Positions, 1988–89* (Washington, D.C.: NGA, 1988), 223; and NGA, *Policy Positions, 1989–90* (Washington, D.C.: NGA, 1989), 255, 259.

38. NGA, *Policy Positions, 1980–81*, 158; NGA, *Policy Positions, 1981–82*, 160; NGA, *Policy Positions, 1982–83*, 159, 162; NGA, *Policy Positions, 1983–84*, 193; NGA, *Policy Positions, 1984–85*, 227; NGA, *Policy Positions, 1985–86*, 251; NGA, *Policy Positions, 1986–87*, 271; and NGA, *Policy Positions, 1987–88*, 196.

39. NGA, *Policy Positions, 1985–86*, 255; NGA, *Policy Positions, 1986–87*, 275; and NGA, *Policy Positions, 1987–88*, 199, 200; NGA, *Policy Positions, 1988–89*, 223; NGA, *Policy Positions, 1989–90*, 259; and NGA, *Policy Positions, 1990–91* (Washington, D.C.: NGA, 1990), 271.

40. Carol S. Weissert and Sanford F. Schram, "The State of American Federalism, 1995–1996," *Publius: The Journal of Federalism*, 26, no. 3 (Summer 1996): 25.

41. NGA, *Policy Positions, 1993–94* (Washington, D.C.: NGA, 1993), 252, 253; NGA, *Policy Positions, 1994–95* (Washington, D.C.: NGA, 1994), 39; NGA, *Policy Positions, 1995–96* (Washington, D.C.: NGA, 1995), 39, 40; NGA, *Policy Positions,*

1996–97 (Washington, D.C.: NGA, 1996), 54, 55; and NGA, *Policy Positions, 1997–98* (Washington, D.C.: NGA, 1997), 46.

42. Dunn, *Driving Forces*, 40–41.

43. U.S. House of Representatives, Committee on Transportation and Infrastructure, *Streamlining and Improving Efficiency of Transportation and Infrastructure Programs*, 104th Congress, 1st sess. (Washington, D.C.: U.S. Government Printing Office, 2005), http://commdocs.house.gov/committees/Trans/hpw104-1.000/hpw104-1_0f.htm.

44. Dilger, *American Transportation Policy*, 65, 137.

45. Ibid., 137, 138; and Vision 100—Century of Aviation Reauthorization Act, Public Law 176, 108th Congress, 1st sess., December 12, 2003.

46. Safe, Accountable, Flexible, Efficient Transportation Equity Act: A Legacy for Users, Public Law 59, 109th Congress, 1st sess., August 10, 2005.

47. Government Accountability Office, *2006 Highway Finance: States' Expanding Use of Tolling Illustrates Diverse Challenges and Strategies* U.S. GAO-06-554 (Washington, D.C.: U.S. Government Printing Office, June 2006), 3–5, 7.

48. Jim Provance, "Indiana Governor Pleased by Turnpike-Lease Results: Similar Deal Might Work for Ohio, Daniels Says," *Ohio News*, August 22, 2006, http://toledoblade.com/apps/pbcs.dll/article?AID=/20060822/NEWS24/608220391/-1/NEWS.

49. Office of the Governor of Texas, "Gov. Perry Announces Development Agreement for Trans Texas Corridor," March 11, 2005, press release, Austin, http://www.governor.state.tx.us/divisions/press/pressreleases/PressRelease.200 5–03–11.1043/view.

50. Eric Pryne, "Oregon to Test Mileage Tax as Replacement for Gas Tax," *Seattle Times*, July 5, 2004, http://seattletimes.nwsource.com/html/localnews/2001972174_mileagetax05m.html.

Chapter 8. Gubernatorial Leadership and American K-12 Education Reform

The chapter was prepared while I was a fellow at the Eisenberg Institute for Historical Studies at the University of Michigan. I am grateful to Dane Linn, Jeffrey Mirel, Ethan Sribnick, Tracy Steffes, and Eric Vettel for providing helpful suggestions on earlier drafts of this essay.

1. States continue to play an important, though somewhat diminishing, role in financing public higher education, but this chapter will not address that topic. State and federal governance systems for K-12 schools and higher education are substantially separated from each other; analyzing higher education would require considerable additional investigation and space for discussion. Some policymakers now, however, are recommending integrating administratively these two education systems in the future by focusing on P-16+ schooling (early childhood education through college and beyond) rather than dealing with elementary and secondary schools or postsecondary education institutions separately. For example, the National Governors Association recently proposed the Innovation America initiative, which called for a strong federal-state partnership to develop skilled individuals by focusing on P-16+ education to improve math, science, and foreign language proficiency. National Governors Association and Council on Competitiveness, "Innovation America: A Partnership" (February 24, 2007), http://www.nga.org.

2. Janet D. Cornelius, *When I Can Read My Title Clear: Literacy, Slavery, and Reli-*

gion in the Antebellum South (Columbia: University of South Carolina Press, 1991); Carl F. Kaestle, *Pillars of the Republic: Common Schools and American Society, 1780–1860* (New York: Hill and Wang, 1983); Carl F. Kaestle and Maris A. Vinovskis, *Education and Social Change in Nineteenth-Century Massachusetts* (Cambridge: Cambridge University Press, 1980); Gerald F. Moran and Maris A. Vinovskis, "Literacy, Common Schools, and High Schools in Colonial and Antebellum America," in William Reese and John Rury, eds., *Rethinking the History of American Education: Essays on the Post-Revisionist Era and Beyond* (New York: Palgrave Macmillan, 2007); William Reese, *The Origins of the American High School* (New Haven: Yale University Press, 1995).

3. Kaestle, *Pillars of the Republic*; Ward M. McAfee, *Religion, Race, and Reconstruction: The Public School in the Politics of the 1870s* (Albany: State University of New York Press, 1998); J. Mills Thornton, "Fiscal Policy and the Failure of Radical Reconstruction in the Lower South," in J. Morgan Kousser and James M. McPherson, eds., *Region, Race, and Reconstruction: Essays in Honor of C. Vann Woodward* (New York: Oxford University Press, 1982), 349–394; David Tyack, Thomas James, and Aaron Benavot, *Law and the Shaping of Public Education, 1785–1954* (Madison: University of Wisconsin Press, 1987).

4. John M. Matzen, *State Constitutional Provisions for Education: Fundamental Attitude of the American People Regarding Education as Revealed by State Constitutional Provisions, 1776–1929* (New York: Teachers College, Columbia University, 1931); Tyack et al., *Law and the Shaping of Public Education.*

5. Surprisingly little attention has been paid to the increasingly important contributions of state education agencies and governors, though a few scholars are analyzing their participation since the 1960s. David Tyack and Thomas James, "State Government and American Public Education: Exploring the 'Primeval Forrest'," *History of Education Quarterly* (Spring 1986): 39–69. Tracy Steffes has just completed a study of education and the states from 1890 to 1933. Tracy L. Steffes, "A New Education for a Modern Age: National Reform, State-building, and the Transformation of American Schooling, 1890–1933," Ph.D. diss., University of Chicago, 2007. For a brief overview of the role of states in education the post-World War II period, see Frederick M. Wirt and Michael W. Kirst, *The Political Dynamics of American Education*, 3rd ed. (Richmond, Calif.: McCutchan, 2005).

6. Henry E. Schrammel, *The Organization of State Departments of Education* (Columbus: Ohio State University Press, 1926).

7. David Tyack and Elisabeth Hansot, *Managers of Virtue: Public School Leadership in America, 1820–1980* (New York: Basic Books, 1982), 190. For the most recent and in-depth discussion of this issue, see Steffes, "A New Education for a Modern Age."

8. Larry Cuban, "Enduring Resiliency: Enacting and Implementing Federal Vocational Education Legislation," in Harvey Kantor and David B. Tyack, eds., *Work, Youth, and Schooling: Historical Perspectives on Vocationalism in American Education* (Stanford, Calif.: Stanford University Press, 1982), 45–78. I am indebted to Tracy Steffes for bring the importance of Smith-Hughes Act for state-level education staffing to my attention.

9. Ellwood P. Cubberley, *Public Education in the United States: A Study and Interpretation of American Educational History*, rev. ed. (Boston: Houghton Mifflin, 1934), 663–687.

10. Fred F. Beach and Andrew H. Gibbs, *Personnel of State Departments of Education* (Washington, D.C.: Federal Security Agency, Office of Education, 1952); Donald L. Layton, "Historical Development and Current Status of State Depart-

ments of Education," in Robert F. Campbell, Gerald E. Sroufe, and Donald H. Layton, eds., *Strengthening State Departments of Education* (Chicago: University of Chicago, 1967), 5–17; Tracy L. Steffes, "Solving the 'Rural School Problem': New State Aid, Standards, and Supervision of Local Schools, 1900–1933," *History of Education Quarterly* (forthcoming).

11. I. George Blake, *Paul V. M. McNutt: Portrait of a Hoosier Statesman* (Indianapolis: Central Publishing, 1966); David Tyack, Robert Lowe, and Elisabeth Hansot, *Public Schools in Hard Times: The Great Depression and Recent Years* (Cambridge, Mass.: Harvard University Press, 1984).

12. Susan B. Carter, Scott Sigmund Gartner, Michael Haines, Alan Olmstead, Richard Sutch, and Gavin Wright, *Historical Statistics of the United States: Earliest Times to the Present*, millennial ed. (New York: Cambridge University Press, 2006), vol. 2, tables Bc906–908; T. D. Snyder, A. G. Tan, and C. M. Hoffman, *Digest of Education Statistics, 2003* (NCES2005–025) (Washington, D.C., 2004), table 156. As overall state expenditures grew during the twentieth century, a significant portion of those monies went to education (including higher education). In 1902 states spent 13 percent of their direct expenditures on education; by 1940 the proportion declined slightly to 11 percent. In 1965, the percentage of state direct expenditures for education rose to 20 percent; by 2000, education received 22 percent of state direct expenditures. Carter et al., *Historical Statistics of the United States*, vol. 5, tables Ea401, Ea403–406.

13. Diane Ravitch, *The Troubled Crusade: American Education, 1945–1980* (New York: Basic Books, 1983).

14. James T. Patterson, *Brown v. Board of Education: A Civil Rights Milestone and its Troubled Legacy* (New York: Oxford University Press, 2005).

15. Frank J. Munger and Richard F. Fenno, Jr., *National Politics and Federal Aid to Education* (Syracuse, N.Y.: Syracuse University Press, 1962); Sidney W. Tiedt, *The Role of the Federal Government in Education* (New York: Oxford University Press, 1966).

16. Larry Sabato, *Goodbye to Good-Time Charlie* (Lexington, Mass.: Lexington Books, 1978); Alan Tarr, *Understanding State Constitutions* (Princeton: Princeton University Press, 1998); Jon C. Teaford, *The Rise of the States: Evolution of American State Government* (Baltimore: Johns Hopkins Uninversity Press, 2002).

17. National Governors' Association, "Meeting Summary: 1961 NGA Annual Meeting," retrieved from http://www.nga.org.

18. Leo Egan, "Governors Urge U.S. School Help," *New York Times* (June 29, 1961)

19. Graham, *The Uncertain Triumph;* Lawrence John McAndrews, *Broken Ground: John F. Kennedy and the Politics of Education* (New York: Garland, 1991).

20. Graham, *The Uncertain Triumph.*

21. Maris A. Vinovskis, *The Birth of Head Start: Preschool Education Policies in the Kennedy and Johnson Administrations* (Chicago: University of Chicago Press, 2005).

22. Eugene Eidenberg and Roy D. Morey, *An Act of Congress: The Legislative Process and the Making of Education Policy* (New York: Norton, 1969).

23. Jerome T. Murphy, *State Education Agencies and Discretionary Funds* (Toronto, 1974); Kenneth E. Smith, "The Impact of Title V on State Departments of Education," in Robert F. Campbell, Gerald E. Sroufe, and Donald H. Layton, eds., *Strengthening State Departments of Education* (Chicago: University of Chicago, 1967), 61–75.

24. Wirt and Kirst, *The Political Dynamics of American Education*, 225.

25. Stephen K. Bailey and Edith K. Mosher, *ESEA: The Office of Education*

Administers a Law (Syracuse, N.Y.: Syracuse University Press, 1968); Julie Jeffrey, *Education for Children of the Poor: A Study of the Origins and Implementation of the Elementary and Secondary Education Act of 1965* (Columbus: Ohio State University Press, 1978).

26. Michael W. Kirst, "Turning Points: A History of American Governance," in Noel Epstein, ed., *Who's in Charge Here? The Tangled Web of School Governance and Policy* (Washington, D.C.: Brookings Institution Press, 2004), 28.

27. For an important and innovative analysis of the recent relationship between federal and state education policymaking, see Paul Manna, *School's In: Federalism and the National Education Agenda* (Washington, D.C.: Georgetown University Press, 2006).

28. Christopher T. Cross, *Political Education: National Policy Comes of Age* (New York: Teachers College Press, 2004); Patrick J. McGuinn, *No Child Left Behind and the Transformation of Federal Education Policy, 1965–2005* (Lawrence: University Press of Kansas, 2006).

29. Maris A. Vinovskis, "Do Federal Compensatory Education Programs Really Work? A Brief Historical Analysis of Title I and Head Start," *American Journal of Education* (May 1999): 187–209.

30. Timothy Conlan, *From New Federalism to Devolution: Twenty-Five Years of Intergovernmental Reform* (Washington, D.C.: Brookings Institution Press, 1998).

31. Conlan, *From New Federalism to Devolution*.

32. Charles Flynn Allen, "Governor William Jefferson Clinton: A Biography with a Special Focus on his Educational Contributions," Ph.D. diss., University of Mississippi, 1991; Jennie Carter, "How Three Governors Involved the Public in Passing Their Education Reform Programs," Ed.D. diss., Vanderbilt University, 1992; Alvin S. Felzenberg, *Governor Tom Kean: From the New Jersey Statehouse to the 9–11 Commission* (New Brunswick, N.J.: Rutgers University Press, 2006); Wayne Grimsley, *James B. Hunt: A North Carolina Progressive* (Jefferson, N.C.: McFarland, 2003); Gordon E. Harvey, *A Question of Justice: New South Governors and Education, 1968–1976* (Tuscaloosa: University of Alabama Press, 2002); Thomas Toch, *In the Name of Excellence: the Struggle to Reform the Nation's Schools, Why It's Failing, and What Should Be Done* (New York: Oxford University Press, 1991).

33. National Commission on Excellence in Education, *A Nation at Risk: The Imperative of Educational Reform* (Washington, D.C.: U.S. Government Printing Office, 1983).

34. David T. Gordon, ed., *A Nation Reformed? American Education Twenty Years after a Nation at Risk* (Cambridge, Mass.: Harvard Education Press, 2003).

35. Wirt and Kirst, *The Political Dynamics of American Education*, 232–234.

36. Even as gubernatorial involvement in state education increased, there was considerable variation among the states in how governors interacted with other state officials and agencies in this realm in the 1980s. Although governors generally participated more in education governance at the state level, they were by no means the only, or sometimes even the most influential, individuals. Robert D. Behn, ed., *Governors on Governing* (Lanham, Md.: University Press of America, 1991); Catherine Marshall, Douglas Mitchell, and Frederick Wirt, *Culture and Education Policy in the American States* (New York: Falmer Press, 1989).

37. National Governors' Association, *Time for Results: The Governors' 1991 Report on Education* (Washington, D.C.: National Governors' Association, 1986), 3.

38. National Governors' Association, *Time for Results*, 3–7.

39. Alan L. Ginsburg, Jay Noell, and Valena White Plisko, "Lessons from the Wall Chart," *Educational Evaluation and Policy Analysis* (Spring 1988): 1–12.

40. Lyle V. Jones and Ingram Olkin, eds., *The Nation's Report Card: Evolution and Perspectives* (Bloomington, Ind.: Phi Delta Kappa Educational Foundation in cooperation with the American Educational Research Association, 2004); Maris A. Vinovskis, *Overseeing the Nation's Report Card: The Creation and Evolution of the National Assessment Governing Board* (Washington, D.C.: National Assessment Governing Board, 1998).

41. McGuinn, *No Child Left Behind*; Maris A. Vinovskis, *From a Nation at Risk to No Child Left Behind: National Education Goals and Federal Education Policies from Ronald Reagan to George W. Bush* (New York: Teachers College Press, forthcoming).

42. Maris A. Vinovskis, *The Road to Charlottesville: The 1989 Education Summit* (Washington, D.C.: National Education Goals Panel, 1999).

43. "A Jefferson Compact," *New York Times* (October 1, 1989).

44. Office of the White House Press Secretary, "National Education Goals" (January 31, 1990).

45. Julie A. Miller, "Bush's Education Goals Not Final, Governors Say," *Education Week* (November 7, 1990).

46. National Governors' Association, "National Education Goals, 25 February" (Washington, D.C., 1990).

47. David Schumacher, "Bush, Governors Adopt Goals, Seek Strategies to Meet Them," *Education Daily* (February 27, 1990): 1–2.

48. Vinovskis, *From a Nation at Risk to No Child Left Behind*.

49. John F. Jennings, *Why National Standards and Tests? Politics and the Quest for Better Schools* (Thousand Oaks, Calif.: Sage Publications, 1998).

50. Jennifer A. O'Day and Marshall S. Smith, "Systemic Reform and Education Opportunity," in Susan H. Fuhrman, ed., *Designing Coherent Education Policy* (San Francisco: Jossey-Bass, 1993), 250–312.

51. Allen, "Governor William Jefferson Clinton"; McGuinn, *No Child Left Behind*.

52. Elizabeth H. DeBray, *Politics, Ideology, and Education: Federal Policy During the Clinton and Bush Administrations* (New York: Teachers College Press, 2006); Jennings, *Why National Standards and Tests?*

53. Jennings, *Why National Standards and Tests?*

54. Jaekyung Lee, "State Activism in Education Reform: Applying the Rasch Model to Measure Trends and Examine Policy Coherence," *Educational Evaluation and Policy Analysis* (Spring 1997): 29–43; Betty Malen, "Tightening the Grip? The Impact of State Activism on Local School Systems," *Educational Policy* (May 2003): 195–216.

55. Manna, *School's In*; Vinovskis, *From a Nation at Risk to No Child Left Behind*.

56. DeBray, *Politics, Ideology, and Education*; Jennings, *Why National Standards and Tests?*; Vinovskis, *From a Nation at Risk to No Child Left Behind*.

57. The Title I proportion of federal education monies for public elementary and secondary education, however, dropped from nearly half in FY1992 to about one-third in FY2000 as federal assistance for specific programs such as class size reduction or special education increased (by FY2001 funding for Goals 2000 ended). Vinovskis, *From a Nation at Risk to No Child Left Behind*.

58. A U.S. Government Accounting Office report concluded that Goals 2000 provided flexible monies to states and local areas; the most common use of those funds was to institute state or district content and performance standards. Much of federal assistance for public K-12 schools still came from the Title I

program, with most of those monies supporting hiring additional teachers (or teacher aides) and providing some instructional assistance and program administration funding. U.S. General Accounting Office, *Goals 2000: Flexible Funding Supports State and Local Education Reform*, HEHS-99–10 (Washington, D.C., 1998).

59. Independent Review Panel, *Measured Progress: The Report of the Independent Review Panel on the Evaluation of Federal Education Legislation* (Washington, D.C., 1999), 6.

60. Stephen J. Carroll, Cathy Krop, Jeremy Arkes, Peter A. Morrison, and Ann Flanagan, *California's K-12 Public Schools: How Are They Doing?* (Santa Monica: Rand Corporation, 2005); Margaret E. Goertz, "Standards-based Accountability: Horse Trade or Horse Whip?" in Susan H. Fuhrman, ed., *From the Capitol to the Classroom: Standards-based Reform in the States*, One Hundred Yearbook of the National Society for the Study of Education, Part II (Chicago, 2001), 39–59; David Grissmer and Ann Flanagan, "Searching for Indirect Evidence for the Effects of Statewide Reforms, in Diane Ravitch, ed., *Brookings Papers on Education Policy, 2001* (Washington, D.C.: Brookings Institution Press, 2001), 181–229; Andrew C. Porter and John L. Smithson, "Are Content Standards Being Implemented in the Classroom? A Methodology and Some Tentative Answers," in Susan H. Fuhrman, ed., *From the Capitol to the Classroom: Standards-based Reform in the States*, One Hundred Yearbook of the National Society for the Study of Education, Part II (Chicago, 2001), 60–80.

61. Vinovskis, *From a Nation at Risk to No Child Left Behind*.

62. Michael Nelson, ed., *The Elections of 2004* (Washington, D.C.: Congressional Quarterly Press, 2005).

63. DeBray, Politics, *Ideology, and Education*; McGuinn, *No Child Left Behind*.

64. Kristen Tosh Cowan, *The New Title I: The Changing Landscape of Accountability*, March 2005 ed. (Washington, D.C.: Thompson Publishing, 2005); Manna, *School's In*.

65. Joetta L. Sack, "Utah Passes Bill to Trump 'No Child' Law," *Education Week* (April 27, 2005): 22, 25.

66. David J. Hoff, "Texas Stands Behind Own Testing Rule," *Education Week* (March 9, 2005): 1, 23.

67. Benjamin Superfine, "Legal Hurdles and Arguments: Using the Courts to Affect the Implementation of No Child Left Behind," Ph.D. diss., University of Michigan, 2005.

68. Andrew Trotter, "Three of Four Claims in Conn.'s NCLB Suit Dismissed," *Education Week* (October 4, 2006): 16.

69. Andrew Trotter, "Suit Challenging NCLB Costs is Dismissed," *Education Week* (December 7, 2005): 28.

70. Michelle R. Davis, Alan Richard, and Erik W. Robelen, "Bush Proposes Evacuee Aid for Districts, School Vouchers," *Education Week* (September 21, 2005): 17; Catherine Gewertz, "Ed. Dept. Grants N.Y.C., Boston, Waivers on NCLB Tutoring," *Education Week* (November 16, 2005): 13; Lynn Olson, "New Rules on Special Ed. Scores Help Schools Meet NCLB Targets," *Education Week* (September 21, 2005): 25.

71. David J. Hoff, "Education Dept. Poised to Approve More States for Growth-Model Pilot," *Education Week* (November 8, 2006): 21.

72. David J. Hoff, "Chiefs: Ed. Dept. Getting Stingier on NCLB Flexibility," *Education Week* (December 13, 2005): 19.

73. Christina A. Samuels, "Bush Promotes Plan for High School Tests," *Education Week* (January 19, 2005): 21, 23.

74. Lynn Olson, "Summit Fuels Push to Improve High Schools," *Education Week* (March 9, 2005): 1.

75. Erik W. Robelen, "House Panel Turns Down Bush's High School Agenda," *Education Week* (June 15, 2005): 21, 23.

76. Vinovskis, *From a Nation at Risk to No Child Left Behind.*

77. Lynn Olson, "A Decade of Effort," *Education Week* (January 5, 2006): 9–10.

78. Office of the White House Press Secretary, "President Bush Marks Fifth Anniversary of No Child Left Behind" (January 8, 2007), http://www.white house.gov/news/releases.

79. U.S. Department of Education, *Building on Results: A Blueprint for Strengthening the No Child Left Behind Act* (Washington, D.C., 2007); Andrew Brownstein, "Bush Unveils NCLB Proposals," *Title I Monitor* (February 2007): 1–2, 7–8.

80. Travis Hicks, "Bipartisan Panel Pushes National Standards, Effective Teachers in New NCLB Blueprint," *Title I Monitor* (March 2007): 12–14.

81. National Governors Association, "Policy Position ECW-02: Education Reform" (March 1, 2006), http://www.nga.org.

Chapter 9. From Charity Care to Medicaid

The authors would like to thank Ethan Sribnick, as well as Raymond Scheppach and other anonymous reviewers at the National Governors Association, for very helpful information, criticism, and feedback, and NGA staff for their able assistance. David Shreve provided the initial enthusiasm (and invitation) to write this piece, and Eric Vettel, from the Woodrow Wilson Presidential Library, provided much needed research funds for this chapter. This work was also supported in part by a Robert Wood Johnson Foundation Investigator Award in Health Policy Research. The views expressed imply no endorsement by the Robert Wood Johnson Foundation.

1. Aaron Caitlin et al., "National Health Spending in 2005: The Slowdown Continues," *Health Affairs* 26, no. 1 (January–February 2007): 150.

2. National Association of State Budget Officers, *Fiscal Survey of States,* June 2006.

3. National Association of State Budget Officers, *State Expenditure Report,* December 2005.

4. Charles E. Rosenberg, "Social Class and Medical Care in Nineteenth-Century America: The Rise and Fall of the Dispensary," *Journal of the History of Medicine and Allied Sciences* 29 (1974): 32–54.

5. Ibid.; David Rosner, *A Once Charitable Enterprise: Hospitals and Health Care in Brooklyn and New York, 1885–1915* (Cambridge: Cambridge University Press, 1982); Gert H. Brieger, "The Use and Abuse of Medical Charities in Late-Nineteenth-Century America," *American Journal of Public Health* 67 (March 1977): 264–267.

6. Beatrix R. Hoffman, *The Wages of Sickness: The Politics of Health Insurance in Progressive America* (Chapel Hill: University of North Carolina Press, 2001), 20.

7. Rosenberg, "Social Class and Medical Care."

8. Ibid.; Rosner, *A Once Charitable Enterprise.*

9. Morris J. Vogel, "Transformation of the American Hospital, 1850–1920," in Susan Reverby and David Rosner, eds., *Health Care in America: Essays in Social History* (Philadelphia: Temple University Press, 1979), 112.

294 Notes to Pages 206–210

10. Rosner, *A Once Charitable Enterprise.*

11. Jacob S. Hacker, *The Divided Welfare State: The Battle over Public and Private Social Benefits in the United States* (New York: Cambridge University Press, 2002); Jennifer Klein, *For All These Rights: Business, Labor, and the Shaping of America's Public-Private Welfare State* (Princeton, N.J.: Princeton University Press, 2003).

12. Ronald L. Numbers, *Almost Persuaded: American Physicians and Compulsory Health Insurance, 1912–1920* (Baltimore: Johns Hopkins University Press, 1978); Beatrix Hoffman, "Health Care Reform and Social Movements in the United States," *American Journal of Public Health* 93, no. 1 (2003): 75–85.

13. Numbers, *Almost Persuaded*; Hoffman, "Health Care Reform and Social Movements in the United States," 29.

14. Hoffman, "Health Care Reform and Social Movements in the United States," 76. Bonnie Bullough and George Rosen, *Preventive Medicine in the United States, 1900–1990: Trends and Interpretations* (Canton, Mass.: Science History Publications/USA, 1992), 123.

15. John Duffy, *The Sanitarians: A History of American Public Health* (Urbana: University of Illinois Press, 1990), 248.

16. Rosemary Stevens, *American Medicine and the Public Interest* (New Haven: Yale University Press, 1971).

17. Edwin Witte, Public address to Association of Clinical Medicine, Eau Claire, Wisconsin. Wisconsin State Historical Society, Witte Papers, Box 321.

18. The first compulsory national health insurance bill was actually introduced in 1943. Although it became the now famous Wagner-Murray-Dingell Bill, at the time it never made it out of committee. Note compulsory taxation—in addition to universal coverage—was also quite controversial.

19. George W. Bachman and Lewis Meriam, *The Issue of Compulsory Health Insurance*, A Study Prepared at the request of Senator H. Alexander Smith, Chairman of the Subcommittee on Health of the Senate Committee on Labor and Public Welfare (Washington, D.C.: Brookings Institution, 1948).

20. Hacker, *The Divided Welfare State*; Klein, *For All These Rights.*

21. Robert B. Stevens and Rosemary Stevens, *Welfare Medicine in America: A Case Study of Medicaid* (New York: Free Press, 1974).

22. C. Haber, *Beyond Sixty-five: The Dilemma of Old Age in America's Past* (New York: Cambridge University Press, 1983); C. Haber and B. Gratton, *Old Age and the Search for Security: An American Social History* (Indianapolis: Indiana University Press, 1994).

23. J. F. Follmann, *Medical Care and Health Insurance: A Study in Social Progress* (Homewood, Ill.: Richard D. Irwin, 1963). Follmann was director of information and research for Health Insurance Association of America. Monte M. Poen, "The Truman Legacy: Retreat to Medicare," in Ronald Numbers, ed., *Compulsory Health Insurance: The Continuing American Debate* (Westport, Conn.: Greenwood Press, 1982), 97–114; Stevens and Stevens, *Medical Care and Health Insurance.*

24. Stevens cited the following as her source for these statistics: Dorothy P. Rice and Barbara S. Cooper, "National Health Expenditures, 1929–70," *Social Security Bulletin* 34 (January 1971): table 3.

25. Follmann, *Medical Care and Health Insurance.*

26. Theodore R. Marmor, *The Politics of Medicare* (New York: Aldine, 1973).

27. Ibid.

28. Sidney Fein, "The Kerr-Mills Act: Medical Care for the Indigent in Michigan, 1960–1965," *Journal of the History of Medicine and Allied Sciences* 53, no. 3 (1998): 285–316.

29. Bruce C. Vladeck, *Unloving Care: The Nursing Home Tragedy* (New York: Basic Books, 1980).

30. While unexpected, the adoption of both in hindsight makes sense given the incentives of key political actors at the time. For further explanation see C. M. Grogan and E. Patashnik, "Between Welfare Medicine and Mainstream Program: Medicaid at the Political Crossroads," *Journal of Health Politics, Policy and Law* 28, no. 5 (October 2003): 821–858.

31. The popular lore about Medicaid was that Wilbur Mills put it in the larger Medicare bill in the last hour and it was a mere "afterthought." For a slightly different version see C. M. Grogan, "Health Care for You and Me! (By-the-way, It's Called Medicaid)," in James Morone, Theodor Litman, and Leonard Robins, *Health Politics and Policy*, 4th ed. (New York: Delmar Thompson, 2007); C. M. Grogan, "A Marriage of Convenience: The History of Nursing Home Coverage and Medicaid," in Rosemary A. Stevens, Charles E. Rosenberg, and Lawton R. Burns, eds., *Putting the Past Back In: History and Health Policy in the United States* (New Brunswick, N.J.: Rutgers University Press, 2006).

32. Stevens and Stevens, *Medical Care and Health Insurance.*

33. Congressional Research Service, *Medicaid Source Book: Background Data and Analysis, A 1993 Update* (Washington, D.C.: U.S. Government Printing Office, 1993), 30.

34. Stevens and Stevens, *Medical Care and Health Insurance*, 84–86.

35. Congressional Research Service, *Medicaid Source Book.*

36. Stevens and Stevens, *Welfare Medicine in America*, table 15; Congressional Research Service, *Medicaid Source Book.*

37. Stevens and Stevens, *Medical Care and Health Insurance*, 92–93.

38. This bizarre fractional percent to determine eligibility is a testament to Medicaid's complexity.

39. Stevens and Stevens, *Medical Care and Health Insurance*, 162–163.

40. U.S. Senate Committee on Finance, *Social Security Amendments of 1967, Part 3*, 90th Cong., 1st sess., September 20–22 and 26, 1967, 1546. See also Stevens and Stevens, *Medical Care and Health Insurance*, 162–163.

41. U.S. Senate Committee on Finance, *Social Security Amendments of 1967, Part 3*, 1547.

42. Of course, it left out more than these two groups mentioned, but these were the groups whose health access limitations became the most concerning to policymakers.

43. Kaiser Public Opinion Spotlight, "Cost of Nursing Home Care," http://www.kff.org/spotlight/longterm/10.cfm.

44. National Institute on Aging. DHHS, "Growing Older in America," 2007. Data from Health and Retirement Study, 2002.

45. Data drawn from Kaiser Family Foundation website: www.kff.org/medicaid/7387.cfm.

46. Data drawn from Department of Health and Human Services, Center for Medicare and Medicaid website: http:www.cms.gov. Original source is Health Care Financing Review, statistical supplement, 2004.

47. Mary Adelaide Mendelson, *Tender Loving Greed: How The Incredibly Lucrative Nursing Home "Industry" Is Exploiting America's Old People And Defrauding Us All* (New York: Knopf, 1974); Claire Townsend, *The Nader Report. Old Age: The Last Segregation* (New York: Grossman, 1971).

48. Nancy L. Fox, *You, Your Parent, and the Nursing Home* (Buffalo, N.Y.: Prometheus Books, 1986).

49. F. G. Abdellah, "Long-term Care Policy Issues: Alternatives to Institu-

tional Care," *Annals of the American Academy of Political and Social Science*, 438 (July 1978): 28–39; V. L. Greene, M. E. Lovely, and J. I. Ondrich, "Do Community-Based, Long-Term Care Services Reduce Nursing Home Use? A Transition Probability Analysis," *Journal of Human Resources* 28, no. 2 (1993): 297–317.

50. Peter Kemper, R. Applebaum, and M. Harrigan. "Community Care Demonstrations: What Have We Learned?" *Health Care Financing Review* 8, no. 4 (Summer 1987): 87–100; Peter Kemper, "The Evaluation of the National Long Term Care Demonstration. 10. Overview of the Findings," *Health Services Research* 23, no. 1 (April 1988): 161–174. Contrary to these findings, Greene, Lovely, and Ondrich found that specific community-based services targeted to specific needs can prevent nursing home entry ("Do Community-Based, Long-Term Care Services Reduce Nursing Home Use?).

51. Vernon Smith, Kathleen Gifford, Eileen Ellis, Robin Rudowitz, Molly O'Malley, and Caryn Marks, "As Tough Times Wane, States Act to Improve Medicaid Coverage and Quality: Results from a 50-State Medicaid Budget Survey State Fiscal Years 2007 and 2008," Kaiser Commission on Medicaid and the Uninsured, October 2007, 12. Accessed at www.kff.org/Medicaid/7699.cfm.

52. Mike Leavitt, Secretary of Health and Human Services, Speech to World Health Care Congress, Washington D.C., February 1, 2005.

53. Jane Bryant Quinn, "New Law Lets Medicaid Tap Middle-Class Seniors' Estates," *Washington Post*, October 10, 1993, H3.

54. Andy Miller, "Perdue Softens Bite on Estates," *Atlanta Journal-Constitution*, August 18, 2006, Metro News, 1D.

55. Colleen Grogan and Erik Patashnik, "Universalism Within Targeting: Nursing Home Care, the Middle Class, and the Politics of the Medicaid Program," *Social Service Review* 77, no. 1 (2003): 51–71.

56. Colleen Grogan and Erik Patashnik, "Between Welfare Medicine and Mainstream Program: Medicaid at the Political Crossroads," *Journal of Health Politics, Policy and Law* 28, no. 5 (2003): 821–858; Sandra J. Tannenbaum, "Medicaid Eligibility Policy in the 1980s: Medical Utilitarianism and the 'Deserving' Poor," *Journal of Health Politics, Policy, and Law* 20, no. 4 (1995).

57. Spencer Rich, "Lawmakers Declare War on Infant Death Rate; Unusual Coalition Says It Wants to Expand Medicaid Without Increasing Welfare Rolls," *Washington Post*, April 18, 1986, A5.

58. Spencer Rich, "South Attempts to Lower Infant Death Rate; Governors' Task Force Recommends Increased Health Services, Benefits for Poor," *Washington Post*, November 19, 1985, A15.

59. Alice Sardell and Kay Johnson, "The Politics of EPSDT Policy in the 1990s: Policy Entrepreneurs, Political Streams, and Children's Health Benefits," *Milbank Quarterly* 76, no. 2 (1998): 175–205; Tannenbaum, "Medicaid Eligibility Policy in the 1980s."

60. Rich, "South Attempts to Lower Infant Death Rate."

61. Grogan and Patashnik, "Between Welfare Medicine and Mainstream Program."

62. Sara Rosenbaum, "Medicaid Expansions and Access to Health Care," in Diane Rowland, Judith Feder, and Alina Salganicoff, eds., *Medicaid Financing Crisis: Balancing Responsibilities, Priorities, and Dollars* (Washington, D.C.: AAAS Press, 1993), 45–82.

63. John Holahan and Sheila Zedlewski, "Expanding Medicaid to Cover Uninsured Americans," *Health Affairs* 10, no. 1 (1991): 45–61. The reduction is explained by a dramatic increase in the cost of employer-sponsored coverage

during this period. See Kaiser/HRET Survey of Employer-Sponsored Health Benefits, 2006.

64. GAO, *Health Care in Hawaii: Implications for National Reform* (Washington, D.C.: GAO/HEHS-94-68, February 1994).

65. Note, however, states can mandate an individual to buy health insurance.

66. Paul-Shaheen, "The States and Health Care Reform," 357.

67. Larry Rohter, "Florida Blazes Trail to a New Health-Care System,"

68. Paul-Shaheen, "The States and Health Care Reform," 335.

69. Intergovernmental Health Policy Project, *State Health Notes* 16 (January 9, 1995): 195.

70. Paul-Shaheen, "The States and Health Care Reform," 352.

71. Bureau of National Affairs, "Five State Officials Encourage Bipartisan, Boldness for Change," *Health Care Daily,* December 1, 1993.

72. H. M. Leichter, "Health Care Reform in Vermont: A Work in Progress," *Health Affairs* 12, no. 2 (Summer 1993): 71–81.

73. Intergovernmental Health Policy Project, *State Health Notes* 15 (June 13, 1994): 182.

74. Intergovernmental Health Policy Project, *State Health Notes* 15 (December 12, 1994): 194.

75. S. D. Gold, "State Fiscal Problems and Politics," in S. D. Gold, ed., *The Fiscal Crisis of the States: Lessons for the Future* (Washington D.C.: Georgetown University Press, 1995).

76. D. A. Parde and C. F. Popolo, "Health Care Reform in the States: A Special Report on State Health Care Reform Initiatives," Council for Affordable Health Insurance, August 1994.

77. An insurer must only have one family and one individual rate for each insurance package it offers.

78. Intergovernmental Health Policy Project (IHPP), *State Health Notes* 15 (November 28, 1994): 193.

79. Ibid.

80. Ibid.

81. Such reforms are perceived as economically important because they are viewed as alleviating the problem of "job lock"—the situation where workers are reluctant to switch jobs because they (or a family member) may not be covered for an existing health problem under a new insurance policy.

82. C. G. McLaughlin and W. K. Zellers, "Small Business and Health Care Reform: Understanding the Barriers to Employee Coverage and Implications for Workable Solutions," Survey by the University of Michigan School of Public Health, Regents of the University of Michigan (Ann Arbor: University of Michigan, 1994), 44.

83. Christopher Connell, "States Divided over Potential Medicaid Cuts," *Charleston Gazette*, September 26, 1995, 1A.

84. Stephen M. Davidson and Stephen A. Somers, eds., *Remaking Medicaid: Managed Care for the Public Good* (San Francisco: Jossey-Bass, 1998); Congressional Research Service, *Medicaid Source Book.*

85. Don Colburn, "Pregnant Women on Medicaid Get Less Care than Others," *Washington Post,* October 29, 1991, z5.

86. Gordon Slovut, "Many Kids Under 5 Lack Shots, HMO Says," *Minneapolis Star Tribune,* June 28, 1991, 3B.

87. Robert E. Hurley, Deborah A. Freund, and John E. Paul, *Managed Care in Medicaid: Lessons for Policy and Program Design* (Ann Arbor, Mich.: Health Administration Press, 1993).

88. Thomas L. Friedman, "President Allows States Flexibility on Medicaid Funds," *New York Times*, February 2, 1993, A1.

89. Jane Horvath and Neva Kaye, *Medicaid Managed Care: A Guide for States*, 2nd ed. (Portland, Me.: National Academy for State Health Policy, 1995); Colleen M. Grogan, "The Medicaid Managed Care Policy Consensus for Welfare Recipients: A Reflection of Traditional Welfare Concerns," *Journal of Health Politics, Policy and Law* 22, no. 3 (1997): 815–838.

90. Robert E. Hurley and Stephen A. Somers, "Medicaid and Managed Care: A Lasting Relationship?" *Health Affairs* 22, no. 1 (2003): 77–88.

91. Ibid.; Davidson and Somers, *Remaking Medicaid.*

92. G. Bonnyman, "TennCare—A Failure of Politics, Not Policy: A Conversation with Gordon Bonnyman. Interview by Robert E. Hurley," *Health Affairs (Project Hope)* 25, no. 3 (2006): 217–225.

93. Center for Medicaid and Medicare Services, Medicaid Managed Care Report, June 30, 2006.

94. Cindy Mann, David Rousseau, Rachel Garfield, and Molly O'Malley, *Reaching Uninsured Children Through Medicaid: If You Build It Right, They Will Come* (Washington, D.C.: Kaiser Commission on Medicaid and the Uninsured, 2002).

95. See Kaiser Family Foundation website: www.kff.org statedata.

96. Donna Cohen Ross and Laura Cox, *Enrolling Children and Families in Health Coverage: The Promise of Doing More* (Washington, D.C.: Kaiser Commission on Medicaid and the Uninsured, 2002).

97. Ibid.

98. Mann et al., *Reaching Uninsured Children Through Medicaid*, 1.

99. The debate in 1996 prepared the governors for debate on the SCHIP legislation in 1997, for example. The Balanced Budget Act of 1997, which established the State Children's Health Insurance program, included a state option for a separate, stand-alone SCHIP program. This provision can be traced directly to the advocacy of governors for the latitude to structure their Medicaid programs in the same way.

100. Ironically, the final DRA language prohibited such an application of the DRA flexibility provisions.

101. Matt Salo, "Fiscal Relief," NGA Working Paper in possession of author.

102. Ibid.

103. See Kaiser Family Foundation Web site, www.kff.org, April 2006.

Further Resources

For more information on governors, states, and the National Governors Association, see NGA's Web site at www.nga.org. In addition to current news on the organization's centers and initiatives, there is an extensive database of current and past governors, a comprehensive timeline, detailed summaries of the organization's annual meetings, and numerous resources in celebration of their 2008 centennial.

The Woodrow Wilson Presidential Library, which helped in this project by hosting postdoctoral fellows, has an expansive e-library on President Wilson and the Wilsonian era. To access this library and find out more information about visiting the presidential library and birthplace museum, see its Web site at www.woodrowwilson.org.

Contributors

Brian Balogh is associate professor of history at the University of Virginia and co-director of the Miller Center of Public Affairs American Political Development Program. He is completing a book entitled *A Government Out of Sight: The Mystery of National Authority in Nineteenth-Century America* and is author of *Chain Reaction: Expert Debate and Public Participation in American Commercial Nuclear Power, 1945–1975.* Balogh served as an adviser to New York City Council President Carol Bellamy and directed several income maintenance programs in the New York City Human Resources Administration during the Koch administration.

Robert Jay Dilger is assistant director and senior specialist in American national government at the Congressional Research Service of the U.S. Library of Congress. Previously, he served for fourteen years as the founding director of the Institute for Public Affairs and as a professor of political science at West Virginia University. He has also served as a research analyst for the National League of Cities, the U.S. Advisory Commission on Intergovernmental Relations, and the Brookings Institution. He is the author of eight books, including *West Virginia Politics and Government* (second edition, 2008), *Welfare Reform in West Virginia* (2004), *American Transportation Policy* (2003), and *Neighborhood Politics* (1992). He has written extensively on many aspects of American intergovernmental relations, welfare policy, and transportation policy.

Colleen M. Grogan is associate professor in the School of Social Service Administration at the University of Chicago. Her areas of research interest include health policy, health politics, and the American welfare state. Grogan's most recent work (with co-author Michael Gusmano) is *Healthy Voices/Unhealthy Silence: Advocating for Poor Peoples' Health* (2007).

Ron Haskins is a senior fellow in the Economic Studies Program and co-director of the Center on Children and Families at the Brookings Institution and senior consultant at the Annie E. Casey Foundation in Baltimore. He is the author of *Work over Welfare: The Inside Story of the 1996 Welfare Reform Law.* From February to December 2002 he was the senior advisor to the president for welfare policy at the White House. Prior to joining Brookings and Casey, he spent fourteen years on the staff of the House Ways and Means Human Resources Subcommittee. Haskins has also co-edited several books, including *Welfare Reform and Beyond: The Future of the Safety Net* (2002), *The New World of Welfare*, (2001), and *Policies for America's Public Schools: Teachers, Equity, and Indicators* (1988).

Brooke Masters is a Lex writer for the Financial Times where she covers corporate governance, regulation, and the pharmaceutical industry. She previously reported on the criminal justice system and a variety of other beats for the *Washington Post*. She is the author of *Spoiling for a Fight: The Rise of Eliot Spitzer* (2006).

Ajay K. Mehrotra teaches law and history at Indiana University—Bloomington. He has held grants and fellowships from the National Endowment for the Humanities, the William Nelson Cromwell Foundation, and the American Academy of Arts and Sciences. Mehrotra wrote his contribution to this volume while he was a Visiting Scholar at the American Academy. He is currently at work on a book about taxation and American state-building during the Progressive Era.

Sarah Phillips, assistant professor of history at Columbia University, specializes in twentieth-century American political history and environmental history. She is the author of *This Land, This Nation: Conservation, Rural America, and the New Deal* (2007), articles in *Environmental History* and *Agricultural History*, and anthology chapters on transatlantic agrarian history and the Franklin Roosevelt presidency.

David Shreve is an economic historian specializing in twentieth-century U.S. economic history. He was assistant professor at the Miller Center of Public Affairs at the University of Virginia. A former budget analyst for the Louisiana legislature, he is a member of the Virginia Organizing Project Tax Reform Advisory Committee. He is also the editor and assistant editor of five volumes of *The Presidential Recordings: John F. Kennedy* (2001), and *The Presidential Recordings: Lyndon B. Johnson* (2005, 2007) and the author of the forthcoming book, *American Promise: Kennedy, Johnson, Nixon, and the Forging of the Modern American Economy*.

Vernon K. Smith is an expert in state and federal health policy, with an emphasis on Medicaid and Medicare reforms. He is a principal at Health Management Associates where he assists state agencies in managed care, long-term care, and understanding the impact of economic trends and welfare reform on Medicaid enrollment. Previously he served as Medicaid director for the state of Michigan. He has authored numerous reports on Medicaid and SCHIP enrollment trends, the impact of welfare reform on Medicaid, the use of Medicaid as a source of financing in state health programs, and exemplary practices in Medicaid primary care case management programs.

Jason Sokol is visiting assistant professor of history and Mellon postdoctoral fellow at Cornell University. He is the author of *There Goes My Everything: White Southerners in the Age of Civil Rights* (2006). In addition, his writings have appeared in the *Nation*, the *American Prospect Online*, and other publications. He is beginning work on a book about politics and race in the Northeast after World War II.

Ethan G. Sribnick is a National Governors Association Post-Doctoral Fellow at the Woodrow Wilson Presidential Library. He is currently completing a book examining the history of child welfare policy in the United States from 1945 to 1980.

Jon C. Teaford is professor emeritus of history at Purdue University. He is the author of several books including *The Metropolitan Revolution: The Rise of Post-Urban America* (2006), *The Rise of the States: Evolution of American State Government* (2002), and *Post-Suburbia: Government and Politics in the Edge Cities* (1997).

Maris A. Vinovskis is the Bentley Professor of History, Research Professor at the Institute for Social Research, and Professor of Public Policy at the Gerald R. Ford School of Public Policy at the University of Michigan. He worked in the 1990s in the U.S. Department of Education on questions of educational research and policy, in both Republican and Democratic administrations. Vinovskis has published nine books, edited seven books, and written more than one hundred scholarly essays.

Index

Acknowledgments

The number of individuals responsible for creating this book is too voluminous to list. However, it is necessary to point out a few for thanks. David Shreve deserves particular thanks for his role in putting this volume together. Clayton McClure Brooks, Eric Vettel, and others at the Woodrow Wilson Presidential Library have played important roles in preparing this book. Many people at NGA have contributed time and energy to this venture. Jay Hyde, Jodi Omear, Nelle Sandridge, Ray Scheppach, Laura Shiflett, and Barry Van Lare require particular thanks. Brian Balogh, as always, went beyond what was required in providing his assistance.